IDENTI ... IN

THE POLITICS OF METHOD

Identities and Social Change in Britain since 1940

The Politics of Method

MIKE SAVAGE

OXFORD
UNIVERSITY PRESS

OXFORD
UNIVERSITY PRESS

Great Clarendon Street, Oxford OX2 6DP
United Kingdom

Oxford University Press is a department of the University of Oxford.
It furthers the University's objective of excellence in research, scholarship,
and education by publishing worldwide. Oxford is a registered trade mark of
Oxford University Press in the UK and in certain other countries

Published in the United States of America by Oxford University Press
198 Madison Avenue, New York, NY 10016, United States of America

British Library Cataloguing in Publication Data
Data available

Library of Congress Cataloging in Publication Data
Data available

ISBN 978-0-19-958766-7

Contents

2002: Preface and Acknowledgements

This book tells a story of sociocultural change in Britain during the 1950s and 1960s. It does so not by invoking familiar motifs about epochal change and social transformation, or about how the 'swinging sixties' led to a liberation from the traditional hidebound conformism of post-war austerity Britain. Rather, I examine how social science sampling methods – associated with letter writing, questionnaires, interviews, and surveys – mined down to reveal mundane, ordinary life, in miniature, and how such research was implicated in a broader process of building a modern, rational, post-imperial nation. This is therefore not a story of the emergence of popular culture welling up from below, so much as a study of the remaking of relations between intellectualism, skill, and technique, which repudiated the cultural elitism associated with gentlemen intellectuals and which embraced a more earthy technical orientation. I examine the remarkable new role for social scientific expertise in these years. I show how the deployment of new research techniques involved the remaking of politics and culture, notably as the arts and the humanities were increasingly demarcated away from the everyday. I show how new understandings of time, change, space, class, and gender were all refashioned as part of this intensification, through the deployment of myriad classifications, social aggregates, and abstracted territorial entities, in ways which endure into the twenty-first century. This book is therefore both a contribution to our historical understanding of social change in post-war Britain, but also a reflection about the nature of social sciences themselves, both how they have been in the past and – perhaps more importantly – how they should be in the present.

Because I have been a practising social scientist over the past three decades, this is also a personal account, which draws on my own experiences of social research. And I should start by explaining how this volume emerged from a rather different book which I imagined writing when I began research in 2002 funded by a Leverhulme Major Research Fellowship. My proposal had been to study in depth the archived material of a number of famous social scientific studies in the 1950s and 1960s. I saw this as plugging an important gap. Historians continued to rely for their prime source material on official documentary sources, media and literary representations, and occasionally oral histories and interviews, and rarely touched social scientific sources.[1] Social scientists, similarly, rarely conducted detailed historical research on their own qualitative sources, which were therefore left largely undisturbed in the archives. This gave me the germ of an idea. What would happen if these archived sources were themselves used as primary material for an historical sociology of post-war Britain? This idea fascinated me

---

[1] This situation has changed, in important ways, in the past decade, and I draw attention to this literature where appropriate in this book.

as a historian-turned-sociologist, someone who has conducted original histor- ical research on conventional documentary sources,[2] before turning to the staples of social science methods – the secondary analysis of surveys, the application of new surveys on original topics, and the use of in-depth interviews.[3] During the course of my research, I have benefited hugely from talking to numerous histo- rians of modern Britain. In particular, I would like to thank Patrick Joyce, Jon Lawrence, Shinobu Majima, Peter Mandler, Frank Mort, Mark Peel, John Pick- stone, Selina Todd, as well as the contributors to a special issue of *Contemporary British History* on the theme of 'Contesting Affluence' where some of the argu- ments of this book were first aired. I would also like to thank Nick Hubble for his literary expertise.

Initially, my interest was on what these social science sources revealed about the changing nature of popular identities in recent decades. Much has been written about the fragmentation of traditional collective identities, notably those associated with social class, and the rise of new kinds of 'identity politics' based on ethnicity, gender, sexuality, and lifestyle.[4] But the evidence adduced for such shifts are – to say the least – partial. We have some rather contradictory findings from questions asked on sample surveys since the 1960s, though these often only cover a few topics, notably social class. We might extrapolate from media or literary sources. No one has assembled a detailed historical record of what people themselves talk about over a sustained period of time. Surely, a full and proper reflection on the numerous archived sources deriving from social scientists in the 1950s and 1960s could allow a truly systematic account of the changing nature of popular identities over the post-war period, and in this process allow me the personal satisfaction of bringing together all my varied inquiries into class, gender, and inequality which have preoccupied me over the years.

This was a project which therefore spoke to my own complex intellectual biog- raphy, a means of personally coming to terms with my own voyage through recent British history. I am thankful to the Leverhulme Trust for their support of my simple idea, and for awarding me a Major Research Fellowship which provided the time and resources to conduct most of the fieldwork necessary for my study between 2002 and 2005. I must thank Louise Corti and Libby Bishop at the Qual- idata Archive at Essex, and Dorothy Sheridan at the Mass-Observation archive at Sussex for their enthusiasm for my project, and in being so hospitable. During my studies at Essex, I was fortunate to have the support of Paul Thompson, who also made available to me life history interviews he had conducted with several pioneering sociologists and anthropologists of the post-war period, and which

---

[2] Savage (1988).

[3] For examples of my secondary use of surveys, see Savage et al. (1992); for in-depth inter- views, see Halford, Savage, and Witz (1997) and Savage, Bagnall, and Longhurst (2005); and for interviews, focus groups, and conducting new survey research, see Bennett et al. (2009). I would like to thank my numerous collaborators for all their advice, reflections, and comments over the years.

[4] With respect to class, the issues are discussed in Savage (2000) to which this book can be seen as an empirical elaboration and extension.

also proved an invaluable resource. I was also very warmly encouraged by many of those social scientists whose sources I was examining. They were happy to share their own reflections on their research endeavours during the post-war years and comment on my own reflections, usually with great forbearance. Particular thanks are due here to Elizabeth Bott-Spillius, Rosemary Crompton, John Goldthorpe, Ray Pahl, Jennifer Platt, and Ronnie Frankenberg. I hope they will put up with my no-doubt idiosyncratic reading of their role and significance.

As I began work, I increasingly realized that using social science sources to conduct historical enquiry raised methodological and theoretical issues that I had not grasped at the outset, and which have come to be central to the concerns of this book. It became clear that using such sources is provocative to both social scientists and historians. Social scientists are usually methodologically concerned about collecting new data, using procedures which are deemed legitimate by their colleagues and which appeal to scientific standards concerning reliability and validity. It is for these reasons that John Goldthorpe has famously argued that social scientists should leave historical 'relics' to be studied by historians, whilst they seize the opportunity of doing new research where they are not constrained by the accident of what is left behind and can have complete control over their research design.[5] But as philosophers of time have emphasized, the present, with all its hopes, desires, fears, and worries, slips uncannily and ineluctably into the past. Social science data, just like everything else, is no sooner collected than it too becomes a 'relic'. What does it therefore mean to use these records – intended as interventions in the present and future – as historical source material? And how do we avoid teleological accounts of disciplinary histories and recover the messiness and indeterminacy of the research process itself. In wrestling with this issue and seeking to distance myself from my personal location within the institutional structures of British sociology, I had the good fortune to collaborate with Tom Osborne and Nikolas Rose in elaborating an alternative 'dirty' disciplinary history of sociology.[6] We pursued a means of understanding its history not through its great thinkers or its theoretical frameworks but through its routine empirical inquiries, and I hope the marks of this valuable collaboration are evident in this book.

If social scientists are uncomfortable with their own relics, historians often feel that they lack the expertise or legitimacy to engage critically with social science sources in the same way that they would scrutinize government records, the diaries of leading politicians, or the minute books of political parties or trade unions. It is not incidental that although British historians of distant historical epochs have been happy to critically dissect and analyse 'social science' sources, ranging from the Domesday Book, the Census, to the poverty inquiries of Booth

---

[5] Goldthorpe (1991) generated an intense debate about the prospects of 'grand historical sociology'. Readers will see that my book offers a contribution to this debate through seeking to reconfigure the relationship between history and sociology.

[6] In our joint editorship of the centenary issue of *Sociological Review* (56, 4), on 'Sociology and its inscription devices' which readers may want to consult alongside this book.

and Rowntree and the social investigations of Henry Mayhew, they become markedly more hesitant to do this in the period after 1945.[7] This is itself a telling indicator of the continued power of the rift between two cultures, of the arts and humanities on the one hand, and the sciences on the other, which was famously diagnosed by C. P. Snow in 1959.[8] It is precisely the ability to create enduring sources of data whose meaning can only be readily fathomed by fellow social scientists that is itself an important feature of modern ways of knowing. The social science apparatus has itself become an important feature in the intensification of the mundane practices of contemporary life. But, in order to understand the nature and the character of their role we need to go back in time, to conduct an historical, genealogical, and archaeological excavation of their expertise which challenges the separation between 'past-centred' (humanities) and 'future-centred' (science) modes of knowledge and which seeks to recover alternative, messier framings which do not seek to winnow out the past from the future in such stark ways. As this book shows, this is no easy task. The ability of the social sciences to cover their own traces is, indeed, one of their signal achievements.

In pursuing these interests, I also became fascinated by a recurring theme, evident in the field notes, interview transcripts, letters, notes, and drafts which confronted me. Individuals whose testimonies were being elicited by social scientists usually located themselves physically in some kind of geographical landscape. Who they thought they were usually bore some relationship to where they thought they were. Social scientists, by contrast, usually sought to render people's narratives as markers of disembodied social aggregates, especially of classes, nations, and genders. The generation of social categories, it appeared, involved wresting people from the landscape and arraying them in general and categorical terms. This process also involved construing notions of social change which were held to be 'objective' processes, somehow impacting on the world from some kind of lofty position. This preoccupation with measuring and adjudicating on change itself seemed to be associated with the endeavour of post-war social science apparatus to construct a modern, rational nation which was amenable to intervention and 'management', and which depended on defining a homogeneous nation, with clear geographical boundaries, made up of specific social groups. In reflecting on these issues, I became fascinated by the understanding of the competing visions of landscape and change developed within sociology and social anthropology during the 1950s and 1960s, and in this book I try to recover a more contextualized account, embedded in community studies, which was somehow disrupted by the development of more 'scientific' sociology during the 1960s. In working through these concerns, I benefited greatly from

---

[7] On the earlier period, see, for example, Szreter, *Fertility, Class and Gender*, Thompson and Yeo (1972), Hennock (1976), and more generally Bulmer, Bales, and Kish (1992). The recent work of Selina Todd and Peter Mandler on the post-1945 period is an interesting indication that this situation is changing. See further the special issue of *Contemporary British History* (2008) devoted to 'Affluence and Social Change'.

[8] Snow (1969). See the interesting discussion in Edgerton (2006, chapter 5).

working with Jeanette Edwards and Sharon Macdonald in editing a special issue of the *Sociological Review* devoted to the work of its long-time editor, Ronnie Frankenberg.[9] My related concern to understand the importance of the Welsh border with England has also been aided by the reflections of Huw Beynon and Gareth Rees.

This led me to another theme which has also become a major part of my book. Rather than the romantic nation embedded in literature, history, and 'culture', we can see during the post-war years, more scientific idioms of a nation, defined in terms of indicators and its 'average' or 'ordinary' properties, as revealed by the work of the social sciences themselves. Accounts of popular identity were formed in an intersection between experts and different groups of people themselves, as their views were elicited to establish their typicality and ordinariness. I thereby seek to unravel this complex web which linked popular identity, social science expertise, and the modern nation. Although my focus in this book only goes as far as 1970, the mobilization of this 'modern ordinary nation' remains hugely significant today, and unpicking this formation is a central part of my concerns. In tackling this theme, I necessarily explore how both time and space are organized within the social science apparatus, seeking to unravel the ways that change could be levered out of the physical landscape and defined abstractly.[10]

My ability to pursue the interdisciplinary discussions provoked by these reflections was greatly enhanced under the auspices of the ESRC Centre for Socio-Cultural Change (CRESC) of which I have been a Director since its inauguration in 2002. I would have been unable to formulate the ideas of this book without the provocation of the sociologists, anthropologists, historians, cultural and media studies researchers, and political economists who work within its ranks. Although it is no doubt invidious to single out individuals, I would like to thank Tony Bennett, Jeanette Edwards, Gillian Evans, Sarah Green, Penny Harvey, Hannah Knox, Patrick Joyce, Shinobu Majima, Andy Miles, Niamh Moore, Mick Moran, John Pickstone, Madeleine Reeves, Evelyn Ruppert, and Selina Todd, who have all valuably commented on various drafts. The fact that CRESC has been such a stimulating and enjoyable place from which to work is also due to involvement of its marvellous research student community and the brilliant administrative skills of Josine Opmeer. I am also grateful to the Leverhulme for letting me take the second year of my Major Research Fellowship on a half-time basis over two years so that I could run it alongside my Directorship of CRESC. I would like to thank the ESRC for their support for CRESC, one of their more speculative and

---

[9] I myself was the editor of the *Sociological Review* whilst I was conducting the archival work for this study, and readers will be able to see, especially in Chapter 6, how I see the history of this journal within the wider context of sociology.

[10] I have been indebted to the discussions in Massey (2005) and Deleuze and Guattari (1987). The idea of the social sciences as pursuing abstraction and 'locationless logic' is developed in Mitchell (2002) to which I am also indebted. I have also been influenced by Sarah Green's anthropological treatment of landscape in *Notes from the Balkans*.

blue skies investments. I hope this book is evidence that their generosity, as well as that of Leverhulme, has – at least in part – been repaid.

If the research for my book began with a simple idea, as I came to write it, I came to focus on an even simpler one. There is no more telling way of understanding historical change than by focusing on the methods and practices of social scientists themselves. I began with the somewhat naive idea that I would look at the archived data collected by social scientists and re-analyse it according to my own concerns. I would therefore bracket out as much as practicable the actual arguments made by the social scientists of the time. But as I went on, I came to think that there was much more than this. The encounters between social scientists and their subjects tell us a lot about what can, and cannot, be said in different times and places, by different kinds of agents. The processes by which knowledge – in the form of assumptions, tools, data, methods, and accounts – is generated is itself of great interest in understanding the nature of popular identities themselves. This, I want to emphasize, is not to endorse a strongly social constructionist perspective in which social science experts are held to have the power to 'make up' and construct the world in manners of their own choosing. The people that social scientists talk to are often recalcitrant and unruly, and cannot be tidied into neat boxes or categories. Hence, by using elicited narratives as a device for revealing unanticipated aspects of popular accounts, it is possible to explore the limits and absences of the social sciences themselves. Using this perspective, it turns out that my book is not just about history but is actually a deeply sociological reflection on why we use the methods we do, and in particular why the sample survey and the interview enjoy such exalted status, and how we might reflect on the potential of other ways of doing sociology. Without expecting it at the start of my project, I have therefore ended up becoming engaged in debates about the future of social science methods. I hope that my historical vantage point in these debates gives me a distinctive, if unusual, angle of approach to our understanding of current issues. I would especially like to thank Huw Beynon, Roger Burrows, Fiona Devine, John Law, Nik Rose, Tom Osborne, Nick Crossley, Angela Dale, Jennifer Mason, James Nazroo, Carol Smart, Alan Warde, Gindo Tampubolon, Johs Hjellbrekke, and Modesto Gayo-Cal for all their comments, advice, assistance, even when eyebrows were raised at some of my more provocative comments![11] I would like to thank Liz Stanley for her astute and astringent comments on the entire manuscript, and Dominic Byatt at OUP for his patience. Richie Nimmo has helped shape up the final version of this book with detailed comments and reflections.

This has been a long project, and along the way I have used this book's source material discussed in journal papers. All the chapters of this book are freshly written for this volume, but at times I have borrowed elements of the source material and argument from these papers. I would therefore like to thank Taylor

---

[11] See notably the reactions to Savage and Burrows (2007), which made me aware to the sensitivities involved in defending the social science apparatus. See also our further commentary in 'Some further reflections on the coming crisis…'

and Francis for allowing me to draw on material I published in the *International Journal of Social Research Methodology* for Chapter 1[12] and in *Contemporary British History* for Chapters 2 and 3.[13] I would like to thank Wiley-Blackwell for letting me use material from *Sociological Review* in Chapter 7,[14] Sage for letting me draw on a paper in *Sociology* for Chapter 9,[15] and *Sociological Research Online* for letting me use material published in Chapter 9 and the Conclusion.[16]

Finally, for reasons that will become apparent as the book unfolds, in seeking to recover a landscaped conception of social change, I want to position myself. There is a very real sense in which by standing outside the metropolitan framing, this book could only have been written from my experience of living and working in the North of England over the past three decades. During this time, I have moved between York, Lancaster, Stoke-on-Trent, and Manchester (with a short break in Brighton and Guildford). Perhaps appropriately, I now commute regularly across the Pennines from my home in York. Having been brought up in suburban London (though with maternal family roots in Teesside), moving to York as an eighteen-year old revealed to me the magical and strange world of the English north which I have never been able to entirely shrug off. Rendering Northern English identities, in all their complexity, is a fundamental part of this book, and I would like to thank all of those who have been, for at least some of the time, on the same routes. I would like to make a special mention of Helen Hills, Bardy Hills-Savage, Simon Duncan, Brian Longhurst, and Andy Miles.

July 2009

[12] Savage (2008*b*).   [13] Savage (2008*d*).   [14] Savage (2008*c*).
[15] Savage (2005*b*).   [16] Savage (2007).

List of Figures

List of Tables

Abbreviations

BJS	*British Journal of Sociology*
BSA	British Sociological Association
CEMA	Council for the Encouragement of Music and the Arts
CRESC	Centre for Socio-Cultural Change
GSS	Government Social Survey
ICS	Institute of Community Studies
LSE	London School of Economics
OPCS	Office of Population, Census and Surveys
OU	Open University
RSS	Royal Statistical Society
SPSS	Statistical Package for the Social Sciences
TLS	*Times Literary Supplement*
UCL	University College London

1962: Introduction

In 1962, two budding Cambridge sociologists, John Goldthorpe and David Lockwood, led a team of young and enthusiastic interviewers to the prosperous town of Luton in the English Midlands.[1] They wanted to know whether manual workers in the new mass production industries, with their relatively high wages, were developing the kind of attitudes and lifestyles which meant that they were becoming 'middle class'.[2] An intensive programme of interviews began with 229 men, firstly in their workplaces, and then at home, where their wives were also expected to be present. On the face of it, there was nothing very special about these men. They were not the source of any obvious social problems, nor was there any 'moral panic' about their behaviour (other than a slight unease that their superior purchasing power might attract them to consumer 'fripperies'[3]). Instead, these workers had been chosen to explore a specifically sociological question, ultimately derived from Marx's view of their revolutionary potential: what was the state of the working class in an affluent age? Were they still a group apart or had they been incorporated into mainstream society?[4]

When the programme of household interviews began, there was a flurry of excitement on the streets of Luton. This was a time when it seemed to be an honour to be interviewed – in Glossop, near Manchester in the mid-1950s, less than 2 per cent of those approached by researchers refused to be interviewed.[5] In Luton, the sociologists were welcomed in most households, whose members might have felt it a badge of honour to be specially chosen for interview. On one occasion, the interviewer noted that the wife was

'heavily made up (very unusual in my experience), white cardigan and skirt with crystal beads over a concertina fabric blue blouse. Treated the interview as an occasion. Special cleaning the day before, veto on neighbour's children in the house

---

[1] In order to avoid cluttering the text with descriptions of the various projects whose sources I use here, readers are referred to the appendix which includes details on each of their aims, as well as details of publications which arose from them, including the debates they generated. Map 1 indicates the location of these studies.

[2] The authors' initial sceptical remarks which formed the foundation for their enquiry are to be found in 'The Affluent Worker', 1963.

[3] On which, see famously, Hoggart (1957) and, more recently, Black (2003).

[4] For a fuller account of the 'affluence' debate, see Devine (1992).

[5] See Birch (1959, 192). Nine out of 641 refused.

Map 1 Location of fieldwork sites for the studies consulted for this book

during the day. Had wondered if I had been on TV with Bamber Gascoigne. Ham for sandwiches.[6]

This concern to impress the interviewer was sometimes taken precisely as evidence of the 'middle-class' aspirations of these assembly line workers.

> Both disgustingly aspiring, especially wife – it absolutely oozed out right from the moment when I walked in to a specially prepared tea ('high' of course, with Tupperware 'cruets').[7]

> I got the impression that having me in the house was a great event to suck to its full sweetness, not for my scintillating wit, etc, but because of my connection with the ivory tower. They were delighted that I had to call for a second session a week later and I was lionised royally again.[8]

But it was not just the interviewees who wanted to be the centre of attention. The researchers themselves had a clear sense of their own importance, and sometimes expected to be treated with the appropriate grace and respect.

> The TV set was turned on when they finally came in and remained on all evening, with the sound full blast despite a series of progressively louder hints from me. The wife was the main culprit here, though they were both incriminated in this piece of rudeness. She's of Italian extraction and maybe this has left her with a sort of cultural residue which manifests itself as passion for conducting conversations on which as many people as possible are shouting at one another. Anyway I had to contend with such formidable opponents as Ena Sharples, Robin Day, Dimbleby and even, god bless us, Victor Sylvester. The wife more or less made it plain that if either TV or interview had to be terminated she was in no doubt as to the order in which this would take place.

The conventions governing relations between the researcher and the researched were unclear. The very idea of social scientists from a top university actually coming to a working-class town and finding it interesting to get the views of workers presented challenges to both sides. How were the parties to treat each other – as potential friends, salesmen, consumers, intellectuals, professionals, or as subjects? The notes indicate the lack of clarity in the relationship. On one occasion, the interviewee's wife 'prepared cooked meal for my wife and I (as it was a Saturday I took my wife along with me for a "day out")'.[9] It was not always clear who should be grateful to whom. Sometimes the interviewer was thanked for an 'interesting evening'.[10] Full meals were whisked up for hungry interviewers, some of whom seemed positively peeved if tea, sandwiches, and cake were not supplied. Whiskies were handed out, and interviewers were driven back home,[11] after they had been shown off to inquisitive neighbours. Remarkable hospitality could be extended and at times scholarly orientations gave way to admiration and affection for the interviewees.

> I stayed the night and they put me up on the bed settee. I had bacon and egg for breakfast with the two boys....A couple of above average intelligence, wanting a

---

[6] SN 4871, Luton Interview 92. [7] SN 4871, Luton Interview 138.
[8] SN 4871, Luton Interview 143. [9] SN 4871, Luton Interview 117.
[10] SN 4871, Luton Interviews 82, 84. [11] SN 4871, Luton Interview 74.

better than average home and living, and still very nice people. PS the wife cadged my James Bond off me.[12]

It was not always like this. Just a year later, on the terraced streets of the Yorkshire town of Huddersfield, Brian Jackson was having an altogether harder time of it. A local working-class boy, who had succeeded in getting to Cambridge, and was enjoying a meteoric career as an educational sociologist with the ear of government, Jackson returned to his hometown to write about the meaning of community to young couples. In a few cases, he also got the red carpet treatment: on one occasion 'they asked me about myself, and were very much in awe of my Cambridge experience. Eager to hear what it was really like'.[13] But Jackson also faced the problem that – unlike affluent Luton – there seemed to be no culture of inviting strangers into one's house. He was often forced to conduct rather stilted interviews on the doorstep. Jackson records his travails openly, including the time when during a doorstep interview his respondent tells his neighbour that 'he's coming along to see you in a minute or two', which provoked an instant response 'in alarm and hostility "oh no, he's seen me, he'd better not, I've seen him once, I don't want to see him again"'.[14]

This was a particular problem since Jackson wanted to interview both husbands and wives, both of whom could not stand on the doorstep together. This lack of clarity about the expected gender conventions in the interview process came out here in the problems he faced in interviewing women, most of whom were not used to strange men knocking on their doors in order to ask questions.

> She wouldn't let me in, came to the door with a needle in her hand, seemed a bit apprehensive, said she was busy, obviously she was merely sewing. A large cow like girl, very pregnant and heavy with it. Might have been pretty a few months ago...but the situation was too difficult to keep a conversation going there on the doorstep in the driving wind.[15]

Jackson's interest in Mrs Jones's physical appearance is revealing. He had not learnt to distinguish appearances from the conversation – a point I return to in a later chapter. What is also interesting is how Jackson dealt with these rebuffs by treating himself as a romantic, misunderstood, character, boldly going out on winter nights in search of reluctant popular 'voices'.

> it was a dark and blowy night, with some rain in the air. The young man opened the door. But when I mentioned Clubs, he said he wasn't that interested. I thought at first that he wasn't interested in the Interview, but it turned out that he was just answering my question about Clubs. Obviously he expected the thing to be fairly short and he didn't invite me in. His wife was inside watching television. In spite of all this, he stood shivering on the doorstep and even came out later to show me his scooter which was for sale....I said that I'd call round and see his wife sometime when he was out, and he didn't say no.[16]

[12] SN 4871, Luton Interview 81.   [13] SN 4870 Box C5, Mr. and Mrs. Davis.
[14] SN 4870 Box C5, Mr. Garside.   [15] SN 4870 Box C5, Mrs. Jones.
[16] SN 4870, Box C5.

The terms of the interview are not clear to either side. Mr Garside is not unfriendly, but thinks an interview can be done on the doorstep. Jackson feels he has to ask his permission to interview his wife.

There are numerous other examples of the protean nature of the relations between the researcher and the researched at this time. It was common to enrol students, especially adult education, to conduct research. The youthful geographer-turned-sociologist Ray Pahl thus recruited a group of housewives, on an extra-mural class, to develop and conduct a survey questionnaire to examine the mother's role in the suburb. One woman found this so challenging that she dropped out, citing 'personal and domestic circumstances'.[17] Another woman, in a four-page reflection on the interview schedule they were drawing up, commented that her husband

> has just read through what I've written so far...and also feels I'm using you as my private psychiatrist. You'll just have to take my word for it that I'm not. It has just stemmed from the way the questionnaire was going – and not the other way round – and I realise that because I've just been writing this down without any sorting out I've got the two points of (a) equality and (b) sexuality muddled up a bit. I do feel they are connected, of course, but if I'd just thought about it a bit more before writing, I could have classified it with respect to the questionnaire.[18]

The same openness cropped up when Ray Pahl enrolled a group of corporate executives who he had taught at management education classes at Cambridge to be his research subjects. He was interested in what the phenomenon of 'spiralism' – the geographical mobility of managers as they were promoted through different locations in large companies, entailed for the social life of modern Britain. These managers were not only respondents, though they did patiently fill in his questionnaires. They were his correspondents, even drinking partners and friends. One of them wondered if Pahl would write him a job reference.[19] He also enrolled their wives into the project, leading to further batches of questionnaires, interviews, and personal disclosures. One woman confided – using the best sociological concepts of the time – the reasons why her marriage had broken up.[20] His wife, Jan Pahl, became involved too, co-authoring *Managers and Their Wives* with him.

We see from these examples that just fifty years ago, the protocols involved in interviewing 'ordinary' people in the name of sociological research were therefore uncertain. One response today would be to reflect on the sexism, snobbery, and condescension in these kinds of encounters and reflect on how far professional standards have improved. Today, surely, we would be more adept in distinguishing

---

[17] SN 4863, Letter 21–6–64.   [18] SN4863, File 15/2.   [19] SN 4863, File 15/5.
[20] In my own case, for instance, 'it is only recently that I have felt relatively free of subcultural demands on the female role which have been fed into me from my parents and the small town lower middles I meet when return home to Lancashire....I always had the feeling of being somewhat of a fish out of water in Lancashire (lack of intellectual companionship etc), a fact which probably attracted me so strongly to Malcom in the first place but once I entered University a whole new life opened up, and, dare I say it, I think now that had I gone to a "mixed" college rather than Bedford, I doubt Malcom and I would ever have married' (SN 4865, Interview 65/20).

social research from therapy. We would not be so vague about whether we were interviewing individuals or couples. Professionalization, reflections on best practice, ethical guidelines, the feminist critique of interviewing methods, and better research methods training mean that today we might pat ourselves on the back and reflect on 'how far we have come'. Phew! However, this is not the line I want to pursue in this book. To accept this framing would be to adopt the kind of 'internalist' reading of the social sciences that sociologists would be loath to bestow on the natural sciences.[21] I want to take the professionalization of sociology itself as an object of interest, as an important process in its own right which brings with it unanticipated consequences. Although Huddersfield and Hertfordshire in the early 1960s may appear a world away from current preoccupations, we are still living with the research apparatus which we see being trialled there.

What we might detect is the routinization of social research itself and its mundane embedding into everyday life. Comparing the aforementioned accounts with my own experiences of interviewing from the mid-1980s is instructive.[22] By this time, there was no sense of novelty in the interview encounter or a feeling of entering uncharted territory. It was still common to be offered tea, coffee, and biscuits, yet the relationship now took on a more choreographed and formal kind with both parties knowing roughly what was expected of them.[23] Respondents usually had a clear idea about what was involved in providing accounts for strangers, even if this went against the grain of daily life. I remember a young girl in Slough in the mid-1980s returning from school to find her father patiently answering my questions who asked in horrified tones: 'But Dad: why is the TV turned off?' She was told 'I am just answering this man's questions, it won't take long'. Interviewees rarely treated it as a badge of honour to be interviewed, and researchers were well aware that they could not expect their subjects to treat them with any particular esteem. The amount of time to be set aside for the interview was normally negotiated in advance, and many people would grow restive if interviews dragged on. In projects such as the Affluent Worker project, or Richard Brown's study of Tyneside shipbuilders,[24] interviews could continue for three, four, or even more hours, sometimes even ending in the early hours of the morning.[25]

---

[21] The principle of 'symmetry', whereby all kinds of account are seen as valid as any other, is one which was famously developed by David Bloor and other members of the Edinburgh School in their influential work in the sociology of science during the 1960s.

[22] I conducted about sixty structured interviews in Slough, Derby, and Burnley in 1986–7 as part of a project on housing and social stratification (see Saunders 1990), thirty semi-structured workplace interviews in 1993, mainly in Birmingham, as part of a study of career patterns and equal opportunities (see Halford, Savage, and Witz 1997), fifty household interviews in 1999 in Manchester exploring people's attitudes to place and attachment (see Savage, Bagnall, and Longhurst 2005), and a handful of interviews in 2003–4 exploring cultural taste and participation in the United Kingdom (see Bennett et al. 2009).

[23] Though not entirely. A common source of embarrassment for interviewees was whether they should offer tea or coffee at the start, or the end, of the interview.

[24] SN 5514.

[25] The interviewer notes rarely record that the respondents were harried by the amount of time taken to complete the interview, though there were exceptions. On one occasion 'Husband had a hot

This routinization is important, but there is another reason for resisting the professional, teleological narrative. We need to recognize how novel, and indeed how radical, the interviewers of the 1960s were compared to what came before. For, if the research conventions of the 1960s are different from those today, they are even more distinct from those which prevailed before the Second World War. During this earlier period, social research was routinely ingrained in the daily work of social workers, clergy, doctors, school inspectors, and the police. The episodic inquiries of investigative journalists and 'social observers', as well as the more sustained and systematic field research projects, for instance, those of the poverty inquiries, had a long, weighty history.[26] This earlier research tradition was innately concerned with differentiating and classifying populations. Its focus was to elicit, pathologize, and sometimes exoticize the morally deviant and disreputable, separating them out from the respectable and legitimate. It was those who presented problems who were the focus of interest. What we see happening in England, in the years between 1945 and 1970, is a new kind of social relationship through which the academic social sciences, and notably sociology, established themselves by sampling an ordinary, everyday social world, one no longer cast in overtly moral terms, but rather as exemplifying what Susan Igo, in her study of the social impact of American social science during the 1930s, calls the 'averaged' population.

My emphasis on sampling registers the way that this new empirical research emphasized that one could write about the whole on the basis of accounts from a few of its parts. This insertion into the social tissue was part of the proliferation of social research, the importance of which remains to be recognized. Sociologists have, in recent decades, announced innumerable kinds of epochal change which we are currently said to be undergoing, from postmodernization through to globalization and the network society.[27] With few exceptions, they do not place themselves at the centre of such changes, preferring to act as commentators on events – the contemporary equivalents of soothsayers. More empirically minded social scientists then evaluate such claims, normally by abstracting 'findings' from their research process, so that they can be laid out and dissected in the form of textual accounts, survey responses, and the like. This all involves a considerable research apparatus, one which does not sit above the social world but which is itself embedded in contemporary life. There is a curious blindness as to the footprint of the social sciences themselves.

Reflection shows that this is not incidental: modern social science methods themselves, with their ethical concern to protect anonymity, to champion confidentiality, to avoid making value judgements on their samples, and to seek

---

tip for the 2.30 somewhere which was brought to him by one of his friends mid-morning—he wanted to get away and cash in on this—but in fact I kept him too long' (Interview 71).

[26] See amongst many others, Poovey (1998), Abrams (1968), Marsh (1982), and Bulmer, Bales, and Kish (1992).

[27] An exhaustive list of references would take up a whole chapter. A representative range of recent texts would include Beck (1992), Giddens (1991), and Castells (1996). For a further discussion of this current of work, see Savage (2009*b*).

systematic methods which allow rigorous comparison, prove remarkably effective in hiding their own traces. Rather like the skilled surgeon whose stitch scars after even a difficult operation are designed not to be visible on the patient's body, so the 'best practice' of the contemporary social scientist is to smooth away the traces of their own interventions. This is for good and understandable reasons: there should be no place for snobbery, racism or sexism, homophobia, and so on. Yet it also makes it more challenging to unpick the historical role and significance of the social sciences themselves whose imprint is thereby covered up.

Let me give an example. The year is 1951. An exciting new research project is under way. Anthropologists, psychologists, and social psychologists based at the Tavistock Institute of Human Relations in London, worried about rising divorce rate in the stressful post-war gloom of 'Austerity Britain' have launched a new project to look in detail at the relationships between husbands and wives so that they might better understand why certain relationships are more robust than others. They do so by focusing not on couples whose marital relations had broken down, to find out the reasons why they cannot live up to the legitimate standards of the day, but by choosing to research a small number of 'ordinary' couples. By 'ordinary' they did not mean that the households were typical, a representative sample of the population. They recognized that with only twenty households, it was not possible to generalize. Rather, by deliberately seeking couples who appeared to be getting on with each other, they wanted to understand how normal, routine family life actually took place. They embarked on an unusually intensive inquiry, interviewing the couple up to twenty times to gain a comprehensive account of their personal and marital relationships and their family histories. The couples were also expected to undergo psychological testing. And, when Elizabeth Bott published the resulting book of the project, *Family and Social Network* in 1957, it was to become a foundational work in the development of modern sociology.[28]

In the course of the fieldwork we see, just as with slightly later studies I have cited earlier, how protean the relationships between the researcher and the researched really were. The two main interviewers, social psychologist Jim Robb and social anthropologist Elizabeth Bott, were also young and in the process of forming families of their own. Their psychological training gave them a means of talking about the complex interpersonal force field which built up between them and their respondents in terms of emotional 'transference', and they pondered their own role as therapists for their interviewees.[29] Jim Robb tried to build up rapport with the household members by treating them as potential friends. However, he realized that this approach failed when he found that he could not talk about the death of his own baby to comfort a couple whose baby had also just died.[30] In a letter to his colleague Elizabeth Bott, he ruminated:

[28] This study is considered in detail in Savage (2008c).

[29] The importance of the psychological formation of this project is an issue which I explore fully in Savage (2008c). More generally, see the essential work of Rose (1999a) and his collected work with Peter Miller which focuses on the research programme of the Tavistock Institute.

[30] SN 4852, File 19.

You may also remember my usual difficulty with working class families that I was always acutely conscious of and uncomfortable about the difference between my standards and theirs in terms of housing....I always felt that they must regard me as a bit of a fraud in that, on the one hand I was at least as conscious of being as hard up as they were, and on the other hand paid four or five times as much rent and occupied what they would have regarded as almost palatial quarters.[31]

The practical conduct of the research itself generated distance between the parties, making the researchers themselves aware of their own specific roles which generated boundaries which ultimately differentiated them from those they researched. The same issue confronted Bott, though in a different way. Having written her first academic paper, on the ways in which her interviewees thought about social class,[32] she thought it only right that she should show it to her respondents to include them in evaluating the research. Yet it is clear from her subsequent notes from a meeting with one family that this was to be an uncomfortable experience for everyone. A copy of her paper lay visible at the side of the room, but it was never mentioned explicitly. It seemed that the young couple felt they had been made into research guinea pigs, rather than genuine partners in mutual inquiry. After stilted conversation, 'Mrs C' finally broached the topic of the paper. She said that 'the chief difficulty (with the paper) was that there wasn't a single clear problem that people could grasp'. Bott sought to close this awkward gap between herself and the interviewees by identifying with their reaction, humorously observing that the researchers themselves had often thought the same thing! Bott explained again the context for the research by emphasizing that they were not trying to differentiate 'problem' from normal families, but were trying instead to understand the values and identities of normal families in their own terms. The young couple then responded:

Mrs C said she'd been very upset by reading about herself like that – she sounded so, she couldn't find the right word but settled on vindictive....She realised that the upsetting thing, really, is realising that there are things about oneself that one isn't aware of....Mr C said that with respect to the point that one's personal experience was important in forming one's ideas about class, he 'could see how that worked out'. He sees this in personal terms, 'he said that his views on it had also been influenced by not knowing who he really was'.

Articulating people's own sense of themselves as an explicit issue worthy of scholarly debate and reflection poses worries and anxieties for the respondents because it makes explicit that they are subject to processes of social classification over which they lose control. Respondents become aware that they themselves are being 'classified', and in ways which they might not themselves choose. The process of treating the researched in a non-stigmatizing way thus did not prove as straightforward as might have been hoped. Even though Bott and Robb were seeking to be non-judgemental, they could not but create new kinds of social relations through their own research practice which embodied differentiation.

---

[31] SN 4852, File 19.   [32] See Bott (1954).

We see an interesting shift here. Normative judgements were pushed away from direct evaluations of the moral standing and respectability of particular households, but were transplanted into reflections on how the research itself could best be done according to proper scientific norms and standards. Morality is displaced, or replaced, from the ends to the means. And so it is that defining the appropriate norms which should surround research is now a central feature of the teaching of research methods, a process which detaches issues of method from their socio-historical context in the name of providing 'best practice' tools and instruments for social research.

Let me tease out this point even further. The very distinction between researchers and researched itself cannot be presupposed. In the 1950s, the researchers, Bott and Robb, were in many respects rather similar to those they studied. They were part of a young, metropolitan, educated, left-wing formation committed to the value of social scientific research in what they saw as a rationally planned welfare state. And it also turns out that – although diverse in occupational terms, and in the precise way that they were enrolled into the project – in intellectual and political terms the twenty households were actually rather similar to them. Of the eighteen households of which detailed notes exist, seven were members of the Labour Party (three of them being very active in it), and one had been very active in the Communist Party. Several were active social researchers, including an economist. Another was the editor of a newspaper. Three others were involved in trade unions. A further (and different) five had overt interests in research. Two were enthusiastic members of Workers Education Association classes in psychology. Mrs Bruce was interested in 'medicine, economics, social history and social research of the survey variety'. Only three households do not appear to be affiliated to this kind of metropolitan, intellectual, research-oriented, 'leftish' constituency. These were manual workers who, although Labour supporters, had no formal affiliation to them.

I am not rehearsing these details to make the banal point that this was an 'unrepresentative group', or to criticize Bott and her colleagues for not seeking a more diverse range of households. What is more interesting is to recognize that the sample itself presented to the researchers because they were attracted by the very idea of being researched. As I go on to elaborate in Chapter 3, through their participation in the Tavistock research they were actively forming themselves as a distinctive group dedicated to the importance of technical and scientific activity. Yet, despite Bott's remarkable honesty in discussing how her sample was chosen and the limits to the inferences that can be drawn from their accounts, the fact that this group were predisposed to social research is entirely opaque from her published account. It is only by re-inspecting her field notes that we can divine this point.

My book's argument, then, is that one of the most interesting yet signally ignored changes of the second half of the twentieth century is the creeping rise of the social science apparatus. Chapters of this book pin down how we can see the footprint of the social researcher affecting mundane practices and attitudes: people's sense of identity and belonging and their attitudes towards place, locality, expertise, education, learning, science, and art. We see the emergence of a language of social group and relationship, and a concern with delineating change and modernity. I track down these shifts deploying the very evidence produced by social scientists, using archived social science sources as historical relics, which can now be read in ways different from those imagined by their founders. These very same sources reveal the recalcitrance, as well as the enthusiasm, of different kinds of subjects for being enrolled by these methods and hence reveal the unevenness with which the social science apparatus permeated social relations. By seeking to expose this social science footprint, by restoring the contextual features of the research itself and juxtaposing this with the abstracted 'data' and 'findings', my aim is not just to correct the historical record, but also to disrupt the terms of settlement which emerged between the social sciences, humanities, and natural sciences in the post-war years, and thereby provoke new, unsettling questions in our understanding of recent historical change. I argue that many of our enduring preconceptions of identity need to be understood in terms of the specific ways that they originated in the specific historical events of the 1950s and 1960s.

ORIENTATIONS

In the course of this book, I draw eclectically, and critically, on several bodies of theory. I do not wish to settle my accounts with these perspectives here as this distracts me from the main historical focus of this book. Nonetheless, it is reasonable for readers to expect me to lay out briefly my main sources of intellectual inspiration so that they can see 'where I am coming from'. At the outset, I was indebted to Walter Benjamin's concern to 'read history against the grain', to refuse teleological narratives, and to use the forgotten detritus of earlier periods to recover a sense of contingency and possibility in the present, as well as the past.[33] In fact, Benjamin's quest to see the possibility of redemption in the mundane and everyday has parallels with sociologists themselves, in their determination to reveal social relations in the imprint of ordinary life.[34] Like Benjamin too, my interest is in how 'there is no document of culture which is not at the same time a document of barbarism'.[35] I strive accordingly to unpack the power relationships embedded in the mundane interview schedule.

This orientation explains my ambivalence to undoubtedly the most impressive and wide-ranging body of literature to explore the political implications of the human sciences – that associated with Michel Foucault's work. Certainly, in keeping with Benjamin, Foucault's genealogy refuses to see the rise of new kinds of expertise in evolutionary or teleological terms, and allows us to recognize the power relations which are enacted through their institutional embedding in projects of governmentality. I thus argue for the importance of a distinctive break between what I term

[33] See Benjamin (2003).
[34] This link has been especially explored with respect to Mass-Observation, see Hubble (2006).
[35] See Benjamin (2003, 392).

'gentlemanly' social science (as a means of making its masculine and bourgeois aspects explicit) which prevailed in 1950, and an emergent professional and 'demoralized' social science which was ascendant by the mid-1960s. Furthermore, Foucault's preoccupation with 'knowledge and power' vitally directs our attention not to disputing the 'truth' of the post-war social sciences, but rather to teasing out what we might term the unacknowledged consequences of their truths.[36]

These debts acknowledged, I do not fully work within this framing. Despite Foucault's recognition of the relationship between discourse and institutional practices, there is a tendency to a discursive constructionism which can overemphasize the textual terms deployed in scientific literatures, and downplay the material practical encounters out of which such texts develop. Thus, I emphasize that we need to recognize the limits that knowledge involved, in Ian Hacking's memorable phrase, in 'making up' people.[37] People vary in the extent and the means by which they are enrolled. A highly pertinent case in point is the arguments developed by Nikolas Rose on the formative role of 'psy-sciences' in constructing notions of the self-governing and regulating self that become complicit in neo-liberal governmentality. Although my debts to Rose's seminal work are clear, I argue that he overstates the importance of the psy-sciences and understates the role of other social sciences, which have historically deployed a different, more 'social' conception of the self.[38] In keeping with Benjamin, I prefer a more messy reading of the historical record which does not overemphasize the overarching power of a unifying discourse or set of practices (for instance, those of neo-liberalism). My perspective is nearer to that developed by scholars such as Nicholas Dirks, Gyan Prakash, and Timothy Mitchell who seek to add ethnographic and historical context to Foucauldian concerns through their interest in the knowledge generated in the colonial encounters (in India and Egypt).[39] But I am also interested in how the late twentieth-century social sciences depart in important ways from the kinds of concerns exposed by Dirks and Mitchell, which were based on mapping, census registration, land surveying, and taxation records. Here, I am interested in how concerns to make whole populations knowable was disrupted by a social science concerned with anonymity, sampling, and selection, which come to dominate post-war concerns, and which broke in important ways with the mapping tradition which Dirks and Mitchell concentrate on.

It is for these reasons that I find attractive the emphasis on materiality within science and technology studies, and more especially actor–network theory (notably the arguments of Bruno Latour, Michel Callon, and John Law). Their emphasis on the agency of technical devices is highly pertinent to my concerns here, and offers a powerful alternative to conventional histories of the social sciences in terms of their disciplinary arrangements, theoretical currents, or

[36] It is not my aim here to argue that surveys or interviews are somehow 'wrong' and should be abandoned and replaced by other kinds of social science method. It is precisely because they are so often right that we need to better understand their operation and effectivity.

[37] See Hacking (2006).

[38] For a detailed discussion of my indebtedness to, but also differences with, Rose's work, see Savage (2008c).

[39] See Dirks (2003), Prakash (1990), and Mitchell (2002).

substantive findings. It recognizes the power of the mundane instruments which are actually deployed in research activity. Callon and MacKenzie's concern with agency as 'made up of human bodies but also of prostheses, tools, equipment, technical devices, algorithms, etc which together constitute agencement' is valuable here. Yet I have two caveats with this important body of work. Firstly, there continues to be a tendency within the social studies of science to adopt the sociological tradition of exposing the natural sciences in the name of a particular kind of critical ethnographic sociology which itself has its own procedures.[40] Part of the reason for this is that many of the key studies have been on the natural sciences, ranging from physics laboratories[41] to biological interventions.[42] There is less work within this tradition of exploring how the social sciences are to be understood in these terms. Law's important account of *After Method* is unusual in its explicit focus on the active role of social science methods, and his recent account of survey analysis has resonances with that developed here.[43] The work of Callon who has shown how markets are constructed through the *agencement* of economic reasoning and MacKenzie's detailed study of how the Black–Scholes model proved essential to the formation of modern economic trading offer valuable exemplars.[44] They both show how the discipline of economics creates the very kind of market order that it then claims to dissect. Yet this focus on economics is also problematic, since I argue here that much post-war British social science took its cue from a critique of economics, and that the undoubted legitimacy and effectiveness of economics in certain domains was premised on distancing itself from conceptions of the social which also had considerable provenance.

My second concern about actor–network theory is that in the hands of Latour in particular, associational sociology is pitched as a critique of an interest in social groups and classes.[45] My argument here is that we enrich the study of social stratification and inequality through attention to inscription devices and procedures, and that it is indeed vital to see how social groups are both mobilized by, and themselves deploy, various kinds of device. My story thus once again conjures up Walter Benjamin, an emphasis that there were predictable losers from the emergence of the social science apparatus – those lacking resources and capital.

It is because I wish to link my concern with devices and materiality to issues of social closure and inequality that I have found it useful to draw on the social anthropology of expertise and knowledge. Of particular relevance here is Marilyn Strathern's exploration of literalization.[46] The English, she argues, seek to describe, yet the process of making these descriptions, of rendering transparent, actually

---

[40] It is, of course, a key argument of STS since the pioneering work of Bloor and the early Edinburgh School that there should be 'symmetry' between the kinds of accounts given by sociologists, and those which they themselves deploy. Nonetheless, symmetry is more easily invoked rhetorically than in practice: there are not many natural scientists who are allowed to comment on social science in the same way as social scientists comment on natural science.

[41] See Latour and Woolgar (1979–86) and Law (1994).

[42] See Latour(1988).   [43] See Law (2004).

[44] See Callon (1998) and MacKenzie (2008).   [45] See notably, Latour (2005).

[46] Strathern (1990, 138): 'the one and same procedure – making the basis of one's current values explicit – both constitutes the nature of present reality as it is perceived and leads to its displacement'.

changes them. The act of exposing and 'making visible' is doomed to failure in its own terms, as it relies on occluding and obscuring other features. This argument has been traced into concerns with accounting and audit which parallel many of the arguments I make here. I am particularly drawn to the argument of Timothy Mitchell concerning the role of knowledge in abstracting from landscape, creating what Mitchell calls 'locationless logic'.[47] Here I have been further influenced by Sarah Green's concern to render the landscape, in all its forms and inscriptions, as an active social agent, an argument I lay out in Chapter 1 and return to frequently throughout the book. In linking these concerns to British obsessions with class and gender, I have also found the writing of historians such as Carolyn Steedman important in linking the landscape to questions of social identity.[48]

In encapsulating all these different concerns, I have found it useful to see the main intellectual framework of this book as linked to 'field analysis'.[49] There is a deliberate, provocative, historical reference point here. It was an early version of this field analysis which held considerable provenance during the immediate post-war years, which was then dispelled in the name of 'scientific' social science. In seeking to rehabilitate field analysis, I focus on two key features: firstly, a commitment to situated case studies, and secondly a form of relational analysis which maps out the stakes linked to specific tensions and divisions and which emphasizes the contestation over positions and competition over resources.[50] Both these features involve a concern with spatiality, in both fixed geometric and intensive forms, which provides an important point of contact with the varied theoretical approaches I have discussed earlier.[51]

Michael Burawoy tells an interesting story about what he calls the 'global ethnography' tradition, which overlaps with my invocation of field analysis. He associates this firstly with the interwar Chicago School, and then – mediated by African ethnography – with the Manchester School social anthropology led by Gluckman during the 1950s and 1960s with its use of the 'extended case method'. He then sees it as feeding into the thinking of the French sociologist of culture and power, Pierre Bourdieu (of whom more later, especially in Chapter 2), and into the 'ethnography unbound' school associated with Burawoy himself at Berkeley.[52] I have an even more catholic definition which would include the modern Chicago ecological tradition associated with Andrew Abbott, the social network tradition associated with Harrison White and his colleagues, and research on life history associated with Daniel Bertaux and Paul Thompson.[53]

---

[47] See Mitchell (2002) and Green (2005).   [48] See Steedman (1986).
[49] For a longer discussion, see Savage (2010).   [50] See generally, Martin (2003).
[51] For instance, on Benjamin's urban thinking, see Gilloch (1997); for Foucault's concern with the 'spatialization of reason', see Flynn (2003); and for actor–network theory's interest in spatiality, see Mol and Law (1994).
[52] The most provocative discussion here is indeed Burawoy et al. (2000). See also Savage (2010).
[53] See notably Abbott (1998, 2001) and White (2000). In American sociology, this grouping has close overlaps with researchers in 'comparative and historical sociology'. On life history, see Bertaux and Thompson (1997).

These writers are different in numerous respects and would probably be surprised to be grouped together here. Yet they all share an interest in the processes by which competition generates identities, and through this process invokes conflict, dissension, and solidarity. All these writers begin from a critique of the kind of 'variable centred' social science which came to predominate in the post-war period. From Bourdieu, we can recognize how the social sciences were implicated in the deployment of new kinds of cultural capital and forms of domination.[54] From Abbott, we can understand the politics by which claims to intellectual jurisdiction are developed, and consider how this is a process of contestation which involves agents battling for niches in a competitive environment.[55] From White, and his associates such as Ann Mische, we gain the fundamental insight that identity emerges from contingency.[56] In the work of all these writers, there is an unusual openness to what the social sciences can learn from the natural sciences: mathematics in the case of Bourdieu, biology in the case of Abbott, and mathematics and physics in the case of White. There is an unrelenting interest in the politics, as well as the science, of method.

A particular point of interest in field theory is with spatiality. There is an undoubted ambivalence here as to whether space is treated metaphorically – in which social relations are treated as if they were physically located – or whether it is deemed important to 'really' locate social life within fixed spatial relations. Part of this concerns the desire to make local studies speak to global concerns.[57] Bourdieu's field theory, which at various points veers between making clear distinctions between social and physical space, and at other times seems to evoke a kind of spatial determinism, is a striking case in point.[58] In my view, these ambivalences are productive ones, which are not amenable to simple analytical resolution, but point to genuine tensions.[59] It is for similar reasons that field theory provides tools for avoiding the kind of familiar dualisms that litter social research books: quantitative versus qualitative, structural versus interpretative, and so on. One of my side arguments in this book is that the much debated merits of qualitative (in-depth interview, ethnographic) versus quantitative (survey) methods fail to recognize that they actually have a lot in common. They both seek to derive the whole from the parts using some kind of sampling procedure, and they can both be seen as originating in the post-war social science apparatus. I find field analysis the most useful means of recognizing how forms of expertise and methods are themselves agents within fields, and that there are contestations over their legitimacy.

[54] See notably, Bourdieu (1985). My relationship to Bourdieu's arguments is more fully elaborated in Chapter 2, and see more generally, Bennett et al. (2009).

[55] See Abbott (1988, 2001).

[56] See White (2000) and Mische and White (1999). For further discussion of this tradition of work, see Knox, Savage, and Harvey (2006).

[57] This is the issue which preoccupies Burawoy et al. (2000).

[58] I have discussed these issues in Savage (2010).

[59] Deleuze and Guattari's analysis (1987) of the complex relations between intensive and extensive, striated and smooth space in *A Thousand Plateaux* is germane to these discussions.

METHODOLOGY

Underpinning my study is the rescue of ethnographic aspects of documentary research. It is not enough to read the published texts of the social scientists and subject these to critical analysis. We need to use archival sources to reconstruct, as best we can, the research process itself so that we can get inside the research 'boiler room' to see how distinctive kinds of social objects and relationships are generated. In the course of this book I have therefore read archival sources connected to seven major social science projects, details of which are listed in the appendix. I recognize the challenges posed by this effort. When one conducts secondary analysis of survey research, one invariably gains access to some kind of codebook and a data file. Although there is rarely detailed contextual material about how the research was conducted or formulated, the researcher can gain ready access to abstracted sets of data collected at different points in time, allowing quantitative trends to be readily established. By contrast, records archived by qualitative researchers have no common standard governing their format. Typically, there is considerable information on the conduct of the study itself, such as correspondence with sponsors, colleagues, and respondents, alongside the actual 'data'. Various field notes, diaries, and papers are kept in differing states of organization. Where in-depth interviews have been conducted – even when these are systematically filed – they are not amenable to quick analysis in part because they are not machine-readable (although this situation may change as a result of initiatives towards the digitization of paper copy).[60] There is no easy way of producing 'aggregate' findings, in the way equivalent to that of the quantitative researcher who can, within seconds, run frequencies on their data. More seriously still, the samples chosen for study by qualitative research vary enormously, and rarely (if ever) approximate to the kind of representative sample that allows quantitative researchers to report national demographic trends.

The result is that most studies of social trends rely overwhelmingly on quantitative data. Consider the most authoritative volume on social trends in twentieth-century Britain, the edited collection of Halsey and Webb.[61] This contains nineteen chapters covering diverse aspects of demographic, economic, social, political, and cultural change over the twentieth century. Each of these chapters relies upon data from documentary and official data from different time periods, buttressed by sample surveys, as the bedrock of their analysis. Qualitative data is hardly used, even for those topics, such as the family, religious belief, crime, or health, where they might be thought to be essential. What we see here is a politics of knowledge akin to that discussed by Timothy Mitchell in his study of the production of social scientific knowledge in twentieth-century Egypt. Mitchell argues that the very act of constructing quantitative data is a central feature of abstracting, modernizing, processes which produce forms of 'locationless logic',

---

[60] Qualidata is currently digitizing some of its material and making it available for download, though this process is expensive and time consuming. In fact, it is uncertain how far digitization will proceed given possible ethical problems in reproducing testimony in reproducible format.

[61] Halsey and Webb (2000). The first edition of this influential book was published in 1971.

which are fundamental to the very project of forming, and governing, modern capitalist societies. The very idea that social trends can be determined from abstract indicators is an intrinsic part of this process, and the many absences which this data contains, about context, meaning, and narrative, themselves become concomitant invisibilities upon which abstract knowledge depends.

In order to provide alternative accounts of historical change, I therefore propose that we take advantage of the messiness of qualitative data. These can be read 'against the grain',[62] as relics revealing features of the research process itself. This means that we do not worry about how such qualitative data bears on the questions asked by the original researchers, but rather that we should construe the data as equivalent to that which historians use when confronted with disparate sources.[63] We should not therefore focus on how we might validate or disprove the arguments made by qualitative social scientists by going back to their data and showing whether they misinterpreted their own work. Apart from any other considerations, the kinds of field notes left behind by qualitative researchers simply are not (except in very rare circumstances) of the kind which would allow later researchers to dispute or confirm original interpretations. Nor is it possible to treat the data left behind as 'raw data', which can be used in ways not intended by the researchers themselves: the purposive nature of qualitative research would make such an enterprise highly problematic.

This emphasis on rereading the messy data left behind by social science sources poses serious questions.[64] There is a vast amount of archived work which could be used, and a lone scholar such as myself is only able to scratch the surface of the available material. Given that I wanted to look at a range of studies, I had little chance but to sample material, and for some of the larger studies, notably that of Mass-Observation, I could only sample relatively small amounts of any particular directive. As I have already indicated, and as I go on to explore in Chapters 7 and 8, the idea that sampling allows one to extract key social data is fundamental to the post-war social sciences, and leaves me inevitably addressing the same kinds of issues as those of my protagonists in this book. Pragmatically, I reveal in the appendix my sampling for each of the sources I examine. There is variation. In some cases (as for the Affluent Worker study), I have reread the entire sample. Elsewhere, and especially when consulting the voluminous Mass-Observation archive, my approach has been to adopt a version of the 'theoretical sampling' strategy adopted by Bertaux and Bertaux-Wiame, where one continues reading additional cases until one feels that no new repertoires are being presented.[65] In some cases, I have followed Jennifer Mason's invocation to use simple counts to give a sense of the patterning of responses.[66] Though this is not an argument I develop here, this approach is part of my broader interest in championing a descriptive sociology appropriate to laying out field dynamics, one which uses both quantitative and qualitative methods to elaborate the patterning of social life.[67]

---

[62] See Savage (2005*a*).   [63] See Moore (2007).
[64] There is now a considerable debate about the 'reuse' of qualitative data. A valuable overview is in Thompson and Corti (2004), as well as in Moore (2007). See also the discussion in Law (2004).
[65] Bertaux and Bertaux-Wiame (1981).   [66] Mason(1998).
[67] See Savage (2009*a*).

It follows from these methodological views that it is not appropriate to focus on each archived source in turn, and at some length, bringing out its specific character and qualities, and so fully doing justice to them. Although this strategy has its uses,[68] it limits the value of the analysis by focusing on the concerns of the original researcher, making it more difficult to attempt a radical re-rendering of the sources to allow a more fundamental analysis to be conducted. Rather as I have done in this chapter, I therefore draw eclectically across the studies I have examined to address particular analytical points. As well as allowing me to challenge teleological accounts, this means that the book is more cohesive and integrated than would otherwise have been the case.

Finally, I want to end on an ethical point. It would be easy to cherry-pick archived material to expose the prejudices or partialities of the original researchers. As readers already have seen from the first part of the chapter, it is important for my purposes to reveal details – perhaps uncomfortable ones – of the research encounter. I am precisely interested in what can, and what cannot, be brushed under the carpet in different times and places. I have thought long and hard about how to do this in ways which do not over-personalize this study. Where I cite collaborative projects, notably the Affluent Worker project, I do not identify specific interviewers. In sole projects, there is no choice but to do so. But I hope readers see that my aim is not to castigate particular individuals. For what it is worth, I want to put on record my admiration for all the researchers whose material I have used here. In extending the repertoires of social research and in seeking to treat those they researched as people with important stories to tell they have put us all in their debt.

THE CHAPTERS OF THIS BOOK

In the remainder of this introduction, I lay out a guide to explain the route I follow. Chapter 1 is an historical overture to the themes I explore in greater detail in later parts of the book. It takes a particular research question – people's attachment to their place of residence – and shows what findings are generated by different kinds of inquiry since the later 1930s. I deliberately start with the findings from my contemporary research, which use conventional survey and interview methods, and then move back in time, as a means of reversing 'time's arrow'. Chapter 1 is thus an overture where I introduce, even briefly, most of the studies that I use in the rest of the book, to give the reader a flavour of the kind of material I will be using, and to show how this can provide unexpected insights into understanding social and cultural change.

Substantively, in Chapter 1, I contrast the contemporary capacity of significant numbers of people to 'electively belong', to evoke an enchanted landscape, saturated with personal aesthetic and moral markers, with the more functional and

---

[68] Indeed, I have followed this strategy in some of the specific papers I have written during my project: Savage (2005*b*, 2007, 2008*c*). I have drawn on these papers in this book, though in every case have substantially reworked the papers.

pragmatic accounts articulated by respondents' in earlier periods. Taking issue with the findings from much urban sociology and anthropology from the 1960s to the 1990s, I argue that the kinds of divisions which have been emphasized between 'locals' and 'migrants' should not prevent us from recognizing during this period a largely shared practical orientation to place. Here, people were placed in a landscape from which they could not easily abstract social from physical characteristics. Although a few people in the mid-twentieth century exemplify certain features of 'elective belonging', I show how these individuals are aware of their own particularity, and by drawing attention to their own eccentricity they demonstrate the social marginality of their mode of orientation. This example shows how we can use archived qualitative data to explore historical change, by focusing on the styles and format of people's accounts. Finally, I return to my concern with the agency of the social researcher, showing how we can trace the existence of an aesthetic orientation to place as integrally linked to an interest in social research. Using detailed accounts from Elizabeth Bott's intensive interviews in the early 1950s, I show how the few people who had a conception of an enchanted landscape were the very same ones who elaborated an abstract language of social groups. We can thereby trace how the emergence of a social vocabulary was implicated in abstracting from the landscape. This theme, of how the relationship between the physical landscape and the social is both dependent upon and also helps to generate a new kind of academic social science, is one that I return to in later chapters.

Having provided my overture, Chapters 2 and 3 provide an historical grounding to the emergence of the post-war social sciences. They focus on the middle years of the twentieth century to argue for the emergence of a new social identity in the immediate post-war years. This was a cadre of the technically and intellectually engaged who were vested in scientific idioms (and social research in particular). I draw on directives from Mass-Observation between 1938 and 1949 to show subtle changes in the repertoires of the literate middle classes. Taking my cue from Bourdieu's arguments about the distinction between cultured intellectuals and pragmatic industrialists, I argue that we need to recognize a third and in my view increasingly important constituency, of technical experts who cannot easily be placed within Bourdieu's framing. I show how this identity appealed because it allowed elements from the traditional middle classes to avoid increasingly staid and snobbish claims to cultural superiority, since it enabled people to position themselves as technically valuable and with the kind of meritocratic skills that a modern nation required. I also bring out the gendered, misogynistic, aspects of this male, technical grouping. The rise of this constituency, I argue, has not been systematically studied, although it actually comes to play a vital role in post-war society, not least in providing a distinctive constituency for the social sciences.

Chapter 4 introduces the idea of the 'gentlemanly social sciences' which I show dominated not only in the first part of the twentieth century, but well into the 1950s. This was a concern with mapping populations and separating out groups according to their moral worth and respectability, depended fundamentally on visual inspection, and did not have a repertoire which permitted the interview or the questionnaire to have a major stake. I argue that until the early 1950s, it was gentlemanly social science which was expanding, a process which can be traced in the formation of the British Sociological Association (BSA) and the idea of sociology as a synthetic, non-empirical social science.

Chapter 5 looks at the moment of sociology, the way that in the early 1960s a more empirically focused form of specialist sociology emerged which challenged gentlemanly protocols and which embraced the new and the modern. I trace this story partly through the interesting example of *New Society*, launched in 1962 to major effect, and also through examining the changing role of sociology in the academic social sciences. I show how the social sciences hardly existed within the University system in the immediate aftermath of the Second World War, but how, in the following fifty years they came to expand both in absolute and relative terms, to the extent that they could be regarded as central agents by the early twenty-first century. Much of this growth, especially in the 1950s and 1960s, took the form of a social movement, in which social science became vested with unprecedented hopes and aspirations. This dramatic expansion largely went unacknowledged: in 1959, the famous writer and scientist C. P. Snow could continue to talk about the two cultures based on the arts and the sciences, seemingly unaware of the expansion of a social science apparatus which challenged this binary divide. I emphasize in particular how sociology depended on claiming expertise and jurisdiction over the 'new' and 'emergent', a process which largely involved displacing intellectuals located within the 'gentlemanly' humanities. I show how the idea of change itself played a vital role in justifying the new expansion of the social sciences, since it explained what the social sciences could do which the traditional humanities disciplines could not. In short, the social scientists were not innocent observers of change, but imported it as an essential feature of their self-identity.

Chapter 6 then turns to consider how a new breed of social scientists sought to define an ordinary, average, national society. In this process, it was influences from outside England which were to be vital in allowing established and assumed national characteristics to be understood in a new, apparently social light. Against teleological arguments which see the development of professional sociology as inevitable, I argue that until the early 1960s professional sociology could not find its own distinctive area of intellectual jurisdiction, nor the specific research tools which could allow it to justify a distinct role. It was social anthropology which proved more effective in developing a demoralized social science. This proved especially apparent with the remarkable emergence of a new tradition of community studies which was based on mobility over the Welsh borders, and which for the first time seriously questioned the assumed normality of English life. Compared to this pivotal moment which saw the emergence of a critical social science, I then show how relations between sociology and social anthropology fractured in the early 1960s over the issue of change, as sociology seized the banner of the new as a means of justifying its distinctive expertise, thus consigning anthropology a subordinate role.

Chapter 7 turns to the first of the key devices which became central to post-war social science: the interview. Rather than the kind of observational emphasis that had permeated previous research, the use of interviews to elicit ordinary narratives came to play an increasingly vital role in justifying the expertise of the sociologist. I show how research associated initially with the Tavistock Institute allowed a different kind of social science to take shape, one dedicated to the idea of eliciting the normal, through the deployment of distinctive research instruments. I trace how Elizabeth Bott helped to shape this new social science, and in the process displaced concerns with personality and morality which had been fundamental to earlier social science.

Chapter 8 turns to the remarkable proliferation of social survey research from the 1950s, showing how it created a distinctive politics of the abstracted individual articulated as member of a modern rational nation. Surveys came to be seen as a quintessential research arm of the modern state. Key political interventions of the post-war years were dependent on the survey. This was especially true with the introduction of comprehensive schooling which depended on the demonstration that working-class children were structurally disadvantaged in education. The introduction of new local government boundaries and the reform of the civil service were all dependent on the deployment of survey results as a means of challenging the culture of implicit knowledge. Whereas today it is the national random sample survey which predominates, in this period most surveys studied particular sub-populations of interest, and hence were implicated in the formation of social groups. I examine the issue of gender in particular detail, showing how this form of research was involved in the elimination of women as major subjects of social research, even though they had been highly visible in earlier periods.

The last chapter focuses on how the social science infrastructure explored the changing – yet also remarkably resilient – character of popular identities in the post-war period. Drawing on data from all the research projects I have examined, I argue against epochalist accounts, which see any simple changes in popular identities. I show the persistence of enduring themes in working-class values: an emphasis on practical skill, on being 'born and bred', on dwelling in place, yet I also show how these cultures have been marginalized through their changing relationship to technical forms. Whereas in 1945 skilled workers had a vital stake in technical work, by 2000 the values of technique had been monopolized by the educated technocratic middle classes. I also show how the middle classes avoided overt forms of cultural elitism and became more confident in their assertion of meritocratic and technocratic values.

Finally, in my conclusion, I return to pull together my arguments about the politics of method. Using the accounts of Mass-Observers from the 1990s, I show how routinely correspondents were able to draw on the idioms of social science, and how 'class talk' and an awareness of classification was largely routine. I finish by exploring the challenge of new modes of digital information to these repertoires. If post-war Britain was marked by the footprint of demoralized social science, the twenty-first century appears on the verge of a new kind of social science, one which is focused once more on the politics of whole populations as arrayed by digital process, and one in which the academic social sciences may face a major competitor to their jurisdiction over the social. In tracing out the nature of this challenge, I reflect on the need to recover the positive features of demoralized social science, so that we can retain its enduring strength in the social science yet to come.

Chapter 1

2005 to 1938: Lifting Social Groups Out of the Landscape

The theme of disenchantment and loss has been central to British thinking about social change over the twentieth century. Yet this has taken place in a century which saw, especially in its second half, the most dramatic improvement in living conditions ever seen in the nation. Yet this remarkable rise in income levels, in the quality of housing, and in the range and quality of material goods available and affordable has not fended off, indeed seems to have encouraged, a sense of malaise.[1] The sociologist Max Weber famously explored how the rise of instrumental reasoning associated with material advance facilitated the 'disenchantment of the world', a sense of the loss of mystery and wonder which were attached to precious values. This thinking chimes with other romantics lamenting versions of 'the loss of innocence'. In this chapter, I begin to trace the relations between technology, change, and identity, through a focus on the role of the social sciences in eliciting and shaping cultural idioms of change and attachment in the post-war period. By drawing on the narratives extracted by social scientists concerning people's feelings about their neighbourhood and home over a fifty-year period, we can begin to recognize how there is indeed striking change in people's feeling of belonging, yet in ways which are not easily assimilated to the theme of 'disenchantment'. Focusing especially on the form, rather than the content, of popular accounts we can detect the growing significance of the imagined landscape for those seeking to 'put down roots' and find a 'place of their own'. Whereas in the middle years of the twentieth century most people had a functional and pragmatic conception of place, this gives way to a rich world of evocative locality.

In making this argument, I have two subsidiary points. Firstly, people's ability to talk of an enchanted landscape is premised on a contingent relationship to place. It is mobility between different places which allows people to use abstract aesthetic, ethical, and pragmatic criteria to evaluate them. But this also involves the abstraction of social groups from the physical landscape. I will show how those who evoked an enchanted landscape were also able to define social groups in abstract terms. We see a process by which people and places are prised apart. This relates to my second concern, with the role of the social sciences

---

[1] See Offer (2005) and James (2007).

in generating new conceptions of belonging and association. I trace the 'quiet revolution' in which early social scientists helped generate a new relationship to the enchanted landscape which broke from literary, Wordsworthian motifs of rural romanticism.

I begin with an account of the importance of the 'enchanted landscape' in contemporary Britain, drawing on my own research as well as other recent studies. I then move back in time, to the 1950s and 1960s, deploying interview material collected during these years to show the hesitant emergence of a new kind of identification with landscape, one of which the social scientists were midwives.

1.1 TWO NARRATIVES OF CONTEMPORARY BELONGING

Today, two narratives of belonging to place, 'nostalgia' and 'elective belonging', compete with each other for attention. In the former, one's place of residence appears to have lost its magic; in the latter, one's place of residence is seen as embodying magical qualities.

Nostalgia is an account of how one's place has moved symbolically and culturally away from the values prized by its residents. Here are two examples from elderly residents of Cheadle, a middle-income suburb located near Stockport in Greater Manchester.[2]

> Yes, it's lost the 'villagey' feel. We still call it the village, Cheadle village, but anybody that's moved in here (more than) fifteen years ago call it the village. Everybody knew everybody... because my parents come from a two up two down environment, it was still neighbours over the fence. The lady who unfortunately has now died, but moved away and retired, I used to call her aunty. I could wander into her house, my mum and her always had a cup of tea at 11 o'clock in the morning, it was the old values and that's how I was brought up. That's changed, everybody keeps themselves to themselves now. In my teenage years I used to go drinking in Cheadle, I would never drink in Cheadle now.[3]

> I don't know, my roots are here, I love the village, I find it very sad now that all the shops are closing down, the shops I knew as a child, as a young woman, all my life.

> *Is that a recent thing?*

> Well it's happened over a period of years, because we had a cinema, we had everything here in Cheadle, but people like me and the girls and young men I went to school with who are now my age, we all went to the pictures, we did things together, and we had what we called the Moat Bar, where we went for dinner say on Sunday afternoons, a congregation of all of us, we'd meet at Bailey's Milk Bar and it was lovely.[4]

---

[2] These interviews were conducted in a project with Gaynor Bagnall and Brian Longhurst. See Savage, Bagnall, and Longhurst (2005) and the further discussions in Blokland and Savage (2008).

[3] Savage, Bagnall, and Longhurst (2005, Interview C13).

[4] Savage, Bagnall, and Longhurst (2005, Interview C15).

This kind of nostalgia is not to be taken at face value. It takes its reference to the past not literally, but to stake a contemporary claim. Thus, Talja Blokland, in her study of a working-class neighbourhood in Rotterdam, has skilfully explored how nostalgia surfaces in conversations between socially similar neighbours, as a means of creating contemporary social boundaries: it defines a group of 'us' who remember, opposed to the recently arrived who do not.[5] This kind of 'boundary work' distinguishes 'insiders' and 'outsiders', becoming a resource for the relatively underprivileged to counter the moral claims of the newly arrived. Reading nostalgia in these terms, highly divided 'communities' can nonetheless represent themselves in later years as being cohesive and unified.

This nostalgic view is, however, a minority view. When Gaynor Bagnall, Brian Longhurst, and I conducted 182 in-depth interviews in and around Manchester between 1999 and 2001, we were struck by the dominance of an aesthetic and ethical relationship to place which we termed 'elective belonging'. This invoked the joys, delights, and passions for one's location.[6] Far from lamenting the loss of community, most people we interviewed waxed lyrical about where they lived. They were clear that they did not live in a faceless global environment, but in a particular place with its own identity, meaning, and 'aura', with which it was immensely important for them to claim affiliation. The history of the place in which they lived was not as important to them in making these associations as the way in which they could claim that the place belonged to them through their conscious choice to move and settle in it. This was a landscape construed predominantly as a personal map, a sense of the landmarks which mark their own journey. It is predominantly an aesthetic and ethical rendering of the landscape. It is aesthetic in so far as it was important to claim beauty, and ethical in so far as it involved making a statement that one exercises responsibility through 'putting down roots', and thereby choses to affiliate one's identity with a specific location.

What is going here? This evocation of an enchanted landscape is a sign that individuals are able to appreciate particular places because of the richness of their own geographical repertoire. The ability to value places is dependent on having a wide enough set of reference points to allow comparison and evaluation. Such values depend on personal, intimate contact, yet also the deployment of an abstract geography premised on experiences of travel and more generally what Arjun Appadurai calls the mobility of the imagination.[7] Hence, a strange oscillation between belonging and not-belonging, where deeply felt love of place can go hand in hand with a sense of the fragility by which one is connected to it.

---

[5] Blokland (2003).

[6] Our account of this orientation to community is fully elaborated in Savage, Bagnall, and Longhurst (2005), and the account here is inevitably compressed. This book also contains an account of how our concept of elective belonging relates to other perspectives on local identity developed by post-war anthropologists, sociologists, and geographers—which is a point I return to later in this chapter.

[7] See Appadurai (1996).

By standing alongside, rather than inside, any particular location, judgement can more easily be passed. The landscape evoked is one which is defined by physical, rather than social markers. Visual and other sensory perceptions are crucial, whereas the values, attitudes, and interests of other local residents seem less important, unless they intrude unduly. People bracket out those who live in the place as irrelevant to their own apprehension of it. This can be rendered humbly as recognition that others living in the location have their own values which may well differ from theirs. Or it can lead to a sense that making a choice of where to live is vital for the modern individual to locate their stake in the world. In these cases, we can detect a motif to place and community living which is that of Simmel's stranger, someone who 'comes today and stays tomorrow'. These 'strangers' are united in their wide-ranging cultural geography, the recognition that they can choose to live in one amongst other places, and that this choice is highly telling and evocative for them. And, like the stranger, they never fully feel they belong, even whilst making their strident claims to place.

These two forms of nostalgic and elective belonging invoke change and mobility. Both are dependent on the ability to provide an account of one's rationale for living in a certain place. They are defined in relation to each other, two opposing ways of situating people around contested stakes of place.

What is the relationship between these two accounts of belonging? Is one an historical residue? What kinds of resources do people draw on in articulating their sense of locality in these ways? One way of examining these issues is to draw on evidence from a sample survey, a key research instrument whose distinctive history I examine in Chapter 8, and which offers the scope to assess the typicality of patterns across the nation. During 2002–6, I was involved in a research project, *Cultural Capital and Social Exclusion*, which conducted a national survey of 1,564 respondents, twenty-five focus groups, and forty-four qualitative interviews examining people's cultural interests in the area of visual arts, music, reading, television and film viewing, and sport and leisure.[8] This comprised the most extensive study of people's cultural tastes and interests ever conducted in the United Kingdom.

A minor part of this study involved an interest in people's relationship to where they lived. This could not be tapped by the survey itself, which only contained the address of the respondents, and which was then anonymized so that we were only

---

[8] The account below draws on Bennett et al. (2009). The research team for the ESRC project *Cultural Capital and Social Exclusion: A Critical Investigation* (Award no. R000239801) comprised Tony Bennett (Principal Applicant), Mike Savage, Elizabeth Silva, and Alan Warde (Co-Applicants), David Wright and Modesto Gayo-Cal (Research Fellows). The applicants were jointly responsible for the design of the national survey and the focus groups and household interviews that generated the quantitative and qualitative data for the project. Elizabeth Silva, assisted by David Wright, coordinated the analyses of the qualitative data from the focus groups and household interviews. Mike Savage and Alan Warde, assisted by Modesto Gayo-Cal, coordinated the analyses of the quantitative data produced by the survey. Tony Bennett was responsible for the overall coordination of the project. I do not report here the main findings of the project, for which see Bennett et al. (2009).

able to work with broad descriptors of where the respondents lived. However, in our forty-four qualitative interviews we did ask about people's attachment to home and locality. Twenty-two of these interviews were with respondents who had also filled in our nationally representative survey so that we were able to relate their accounts and plot their relationship to their survey answers.[9] These qualitative interviews began by asking about respondents' reasons for living in their current house, and about how satisfied they felt in their current job, then probed their tastes in the areas of music, reading, cinema, television, eating, and sport (in some cases asking them to amplify responses they had given in the survey). The interview then closed by asking them how they felt about their appearance and their home. I have used all parts of the interview, but a question at the start about the reasons why they came to live in their current house and one towards the end asking them to identify their 'dream home' are especially thought provoking.

Even though this was not a major part of our study, some of our interviews epitomize 'elective belonging'. Ian and Cherie's autobiographical account ruminates on how they came to live in an historic northern town, emphasizing both contingency and choice. Ian ruminates,

> How did we come to [here] then? Jane and I first met in 1984 working up in Fort William in Scotland and we did a season there together, we started going out together and when we left at the end of the year, she went home to the west coast of Scotland and I came back down to Leeds because my mother lives in Leeds. And we decided we wanted to work together again the following season so the three places we'd earmarked that we thought we would like to work was [here], Chester or Channel Islands and [here] was the nearest one to Leeds, I hopped on a bus from Leeds one day and came up, did the trawl round the job centres and I got myself a job at a hotel [here] and started in the February 1985 and Cherie came down about the June or something, a few months later wasn't it?

Here we see another example of the routine ways that social scientists 'cover their tracks'. There is a discrepancy here between my decision to anonymize the precise location in which Ian and Cherie lived, and the passion which this couple had for their adopted city. For, even though Ian and Cherie had no local 'roots' [here] (he being Welsh, and she Scottish), they both chose to put down roots [here], a city which they now completely, gushingly, identified with, in its particularity and specificity. Their work was bound up with the leisure and tourism industries, and they lived in a 'period' Georgian flat in a fashionable terrace. In talking about their dream home, they sought to make even stronger claims on their city's historical features.

> Cherie: We'd not live in this barn! I would love to have a really, really old house, not out in the countryside, in the town, a town house, a really, really, old, old house you know, about 14th century, that's what I would like.

---

[9] The remaining interviews were carried out with partners of survey respondents, or with individuals drawn from atypical groups for which we did not have representatives from our sample survey.

Low ceilings and beams?

Cherie: Yes, and all sorts of funny little bits that you walk up to and down to, and that's what I would love. Do you know [here] at all, you know the water tower at [bridge], the river, the old water works, you know where [...] bridge is?...well there's a tower there that was actually a water tower and it's about 15th century and they've just announced that they're turning it into flats and I'm not normally an envious person, but I'd sell my granny to buy one of those flats they're actually advertising it internationally, it's gonna go for a fortune, it's gonna be really something I think.

So that would be not for what they're doing in terms of all the modern fittings but the history of the building?

Cherie: It's Grade 1 listed, they're actually gonna have to do it with like the Civic Trust and things so it's gonna be done in keeping, a property like that would be fantastic....We have a friend that actually rented an apartment, when you go up along the [road] there's an opening on the left hand, [here] is full of these little hidden properties, you don't know anything about and it's a lovely kind of arcade, it's in towards a lawyer's office and there's a wrought iron balustrade and you go down and round it, there's this fantastic huge Jacobean house building that's in flats and the back garden overlooks...doesn't it and when Anne had her apartment, we went to visit, when you went inside it there was an enormous staircase, it was as wide as this whole room with huge stone balustrades that went right up and up and then divided in two, fantastic place it is. To have something like that, I don't mean the whole house, just a little bit.

We see here a strong claim on place, seen as a fusion of aesthetic, emotional, and instrumental attachments. The spatial scale of interest is remarkably miniaturized. Specific streets and buildings are identified as being of special significance and convey aura. Yet what we also see is the difficulty of rendering the specificity of this place in an interview format in which – following best practice – identifying detail is removed and hence specific locations are anonymized. The interview, it seems, elicits accounts whose revealing particularity is then effaced.

The data from the sample survey does not permit a detailed account of attachment to specific places: it deploys the abstract geographical space of the nation, region, and area. Yet it is possible to be inventive. We can link these in-depth interviews to survey responses so we can see how their 'elective belonging' is associated with their survey responses concerning their cultural interests. To do this, we can place these individuals in a cultural map, in which they can be located close to others who are similarly culturally positioned. Figure 1.1 uses multiple correspondence analysis[10] to show the relationship between a large number of variables measuring people's participation in, and taste for, music, reading, eating out, sport, the visual arts, television, and film. Figure 1.1 locates the

---

[10] The principles of MCA are fully explained in Bennett et al. (2009). It is useful to note that it was championed by Pierre Bourdieu, who saw it as a means of conducting the kind of field analysis which he saw as an alternative to positivist variable-based analysis. I return to the value of field analysis in later chapters.

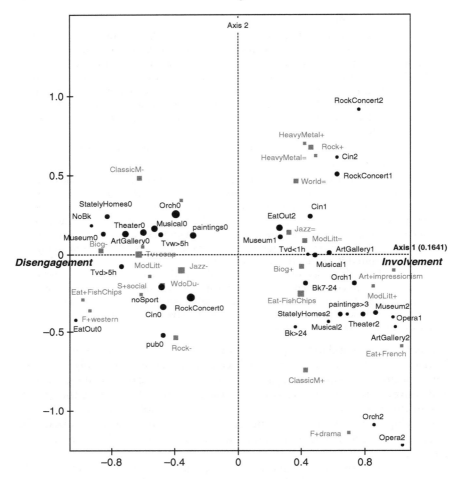

Figure 1.1 Multiple correspondence analysis of Cultural Capital and Social Exclusion survey: axis 1

Source: Bennett et al. (2009).

coordinates of each of the variables which contribute significantly (i.e. above the mean) to the variation between different activities and tastes. Like any map, the further apart that the variables are, the more they are distant from each other: those who eat in French restaurants tend not to eat in fish and chip shops. To aid interpretation, variables concerning participation are marked as circles, and those to do with taste are squares. The size of the variable indicates the numbers of people who fall into a given category: thus we can see that more people like soap operas than modern literature. When a participation question has 0 it means that something is never done, when it has 1 it is occasionally done, and a 2 means it is frequently done. When a taste question has a minus sign this means it is disliked, a positive sign indicates it is liked, and an equals sign indicates neutrality.

Figure 1.1 reveals that on the first, most salient, axis, most of the likes and forms of participation are on the right-hand side, and many dislikes and lack of participation are on the left-hand side. To be more specific, on the left the only positive values are for liking Western films, social sports, fish and chips, and watching more than five hours of television a day. On the right-hand side, there is only one negative value, for not eating fish and chips. The actual range of tastes and forms of participation which appear on the right-hand side are varied. The most extreme right-hand location is for attending the opera frequently, followed by eating at French restaurants regularly, going to orchestral concerts, to the theatre, and to rock concerts, and liking impressionist art. These activities are counterposed most powerfully with eating fish and chips, never eating out at all, having no books, and never going to museums. In short, we see that the most significant division holds apart those who take part in the forms of cultural activity that are represented in this axis and those who do not.

We can see this map as differentiating between those who appear engaged – according to the questions which we used to construct our map – and those who are detached. This cultural map is also socially uneven. On the right-hand side are socially privileged and relatively affluent professional and executive classes,[11] who are actively engaged in attending museums, art galleries, musical concerts (both orchestral and rock concerts), and who are avid readers of books. On the left-hand side of the first axis are those who are culturally disengaged, at least in terms of their formal participation. These predominantly comprise the less-affluent working classes and those with fewer educational qualifications.

We are able to assess whether interviewees drawn from different parts of this axis report varying attachments to place, and how it might be associated with elective belonging and nostalgia which I have discussed earlier (see Figure 1.2).

We can see that Cherie is located towards the bottom right of Figure 1.2, amongst the culturally engaged middle classes. Many of the individuals on the right-hand side also exhibit a similar kind of aesthetic and ethical 'choice' in their place of residence. James, a university lecturer from a Welsh city, talks about his identity as an 'urban' person: 'I do love having a corner shop in the High Street and the cinema and all these things'. James and his doctor wife were doing up their Edwardian house, with immaculate attention to detail, with each room having its own ambience: 'I think that's an interesting thing, say you go into one room and you get a certain atmosphere and, you know? So, I think it's important to have artworks around'. His wife developed the same theme. 'I mean, we're really happy here....I can't imagine anything more even if there was no, it's in the, it's inner city and, and yes, people that are really nice and I can't imagine wanting anything more than this, really'. Jenny, having been brought up in Glasgow, had moved out to rural Scotland, because 'it was quite a nice place to bring up the kids and we decided to have a family. And we've more or less been

---

[11] We discuss the class characteristics of this group in detail in Le Roux et al. (2008).

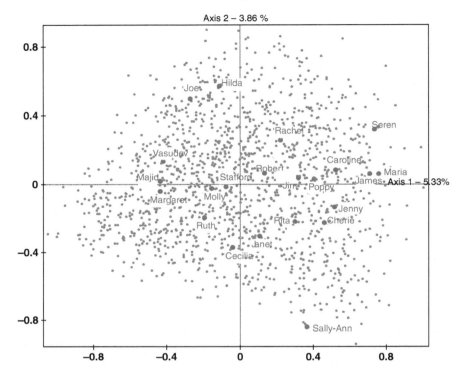

Figure 1.2 Cloud of individuals – axes 1 and 2
Source: Bennett et al. (2009).

here ever since'. Maria, a housebound teacher, dreams of a larger, more expansive house, though in the same semi-rural location that she now lives in. Seren, a middle-aged social worker, originally from England, 'lives in Wales out of choice'. Janet, a middle-aged hostel warden, originally from Scotland, now lives in North-West England and would not move again. When asked about her dream house, she reported that 'Actually I think I've got what I want. I've got a house with character and a nice....I suppose if you could plonk it somewhere in the middle of the country it would be nice'. Her husband had a similar view but for him a move of 100 metres off the busy main road would be enough to constitute a rural retreat. Sally-Ann, an elderly 'doctor's wife' had lived in her current suburban house for forty-nine years. Like Maria, she had been brought up nearby, but had moved out to the countryside because 'we just wanted our own space'.

It appears that those who are culturally engaged according to our cultural map also evince a sense of investment in place which links aesthetic and ethical values and an emphasis on 'choice'. None of the individuals above refer to historic or accidental reasons for living where they do. This evidence chimes with much research on urban gentrification, showing that an aesthetic rendering of residential place is increasingly important, and we can see that this concern is not just found in central urban locations.[12] Despite their differences, the culturally engaged middle classes are highly vested in their place of residence, which they claim to have actively 'chosen', and which conveys a great symbolic meaning.

Nostalgic refrains are rare amongst those we interviewed, the main exception being Robert, from Scotland, who is also on the right-hand side of Figure 1.2. He was unusual in the intensity of his attachment to his hometown. The interviewer notes that

> He kept mementoes of [coal town] in an old bureau, and showed me a poem about a mining disaster of 1939. 'I love [coal town]' he proclaimed. And you could see why. His life had been spent there, his family had been part of the history. His pseudonym was borrowed from his grandfather, a footballer for [coal town] who had gone to play for Bolton Wanderers in England.

When asked about his dream house, Robert had a lot to say.

> I think it would be a country cottage. I think, because I love animals and I love plants and I think, I've seen…country cottage that you could actually make into your own and – seclusion would be great, just hearing water running and – I think that's – we could have that, we could have that, but again, you need company.

> *You could have had that some years ago if you had wanted rather than buy this, you could have moved out.*

> Me and Betty was always talking about going to St Andrews and we always liked the area, every year we went for a fortnight but we seen a house in Langlands Road, and it was just near the football pitch. There's a wee football pitch…she thought it would be ideal.…We liked St. Andrew's, it would have been ideal because I love it, (you can leave) your door and you can walk any road.

We see here the spatial separation of ideal, fantasy, location from where Robert actually lived. The difference between Ian and Cherie, and Robert lies not in their balance between abstract and particular spatial referents, but in the extent to which these could be reconciled. Both exemplify a different kind of enchanted landscape, albeit one which has varying coordinates. For Ian and Cherie, a [historic northern town] itself figures as an intense space where their desires and actual daily lives can be reconciled, whereas for Robert his fantasy space was separated from where he actually lived. Ian and Cherie could lever abstract evocations about 'history' onto specific locations. Ian wondered about choosing to live in 'that little Dutch house up by [neighbourhood]'. Cherie responded, 'Yeah, that's a strange little house isn't it', to which Ian tellingly replied, 'It's a strange house up there, yeah. Something with history, something with character'. Here notions of history and character, whilst appearing to evoke particularity and specificity actually operate as highly general and abstract terms. Robert, by

---

[12] See Butler and Robson (2003) and Jager (1986).

contrast, loaded his fantasies onto St. Andrews, a city eighty miles distant, and which he knew he would never have the opportunity to move to.

Ian and Robert might be assumed to be fundamentally opposed in their attitudes to place, yet Figure 1.2 reveals that they are actually not so far apart. Both have the capacity to define the landscape in enchanted terms. There are, however, a large group of individuals located on the left-hand side of Figure 1.2 who do, however, exhibit different relationships to place. These, it turns out, are people living in the midst of a location in which they were born and bred, and who are strongly vested in their current location in which they are irredeemably thrown. This is a different way of experiencing place and belonging from that which the culturally privileged exhibit.

Margaret and Frank, located firmly on the left of Figure 1.2 were living on their family farm, close to where had been born and brought up. They were completely steeped in this enterprise, Frank having built the house in which they now lived. Unlike Ian and Robert, Margaret found it difficult to articulate a view about her ideal home before finally coming up with an uncertain, though rather beautiful, aspiration.

> *Do you have an ideal, this question about an ideal home. If money wasn't a problem, if you could have a house anywhere, or an apartment, what would you choose?*
>
> Margaret: Well I would have to think what Frank would think. I'm quite happy here, the only thing is . . .
>
> *here's me trying to tempt you away with all this money*
>
> Margaret: No, no, we have enough here. No, no I'm quite happy here, the only thing that I would do is I would definitely love the back tarmacked but that's gonna cost a bomb to do that. I would love that tarmacked, I would love the whole house finished, I would because we've still got a lot to do until the house is finished. I would love this finished and I would like a pond.
>
> *RJ: A pond! Is the pond in the back garden?*
>
> Margaret: Yes
>
> *RJ: Has it got animals?*
>
> Margaret: No, I would just like a pond with like old stone round it, and a bit of greenery round it. There doesn't have to be anything in it.

Margaret does not identify an imagined geography, but when forced focuses on her home, in all its practical accomplishments and individuality. And this sense of being thrown into place is a common response from those towards the left-hand side of Figure 1.2. Hilda was still living in the Northern Irish town where she had been brought up and could not imagine moving anywhere else. 'Oh yes I would have to stay here', she replied to the question about her dream house. Cecilia, living amidst her family in a working-class area of a large Welsh city, could not imagine moving anywhere, her fantasy being to buy the house next door and knock it into hers. Molly ruminated on the beauty of her hometown, and could not imagine being anywhere else. Unlike Ian and Cherie, this account emphasizes the given-ness of place, the lack of ability to possess more of it. These are accounts of dwelling in a place which defines one's life. They present themselves in passive terms, not choosing their location, but literally placed by it: 'I love it in the summer time,' Molly reports. 'Beautiful views in the summer time. But really bad in the winter now, you couldn't get out. Like you couldn't get out to the shop or anything'. Like Edie also born and bred in a Home Counties village, she imagined fantastic locations for her dream house (Florida for Molly, Majorca for Edie), yet this is a desire born of the recognition that it would not and could not happen in reality.

It should not be thought that these respondents did not have an aesthetic attachment to where they lived, but rather that it deployed different kinds of motifs from that of the elective belongers with their concern to command and own space. Margaret's response is evocative.

> I would just like a pond with like old stone round it, and a bit of greenery round it. There doesn't have to be anything in it.... I just like the look of water, if you under-stand what I mean. I think water is actually relaxing, even you know, do you know what I even love too? I remember the time going in the car at night and listening to the rain beating on the tin roof and thinking oh, or just, I'm lying in bed, so cosy listening to the rain, it's so relaxing, I love that, I just think it's so relaxing.

In place of the active investment displayed by Ian or James, Margaret's account is of her enjoyment of passive relaxation listening to the sound of rain on her roof.

Attachment to place turns out to be a crucially loaded affair. We can discrimi-nate, in the broadest terms, between those who choose and are vested in place, and those who are thrown into, and dwell in it.[13] Nostalgic accounts turn out not to stand in contrast to those of elective belonging but appear as caught between these two orientations. How do we understand the power of this politics of land-scape? And how do we identify the process which creates this relationship to place? Let me now leave the staple social science resource of the survey. I return to this, in a different register, in Chapter 8. But let me pursue my interests in the interview method, examining how earlier social scientists have used interviews to examine these issues.

1.2 THE 1960S: DWELLING IN THE LANDSCAPE

Since the late 1930s, a series of studies conducted by social scientists asked people what they thought about living in their current residence. Let us work back in time, and let us return to the streets of Huddersfield, where we left Brian Jackson, fifty years ago, bravely trying to doorstep reluctant working-class couples. Aware of the cultural gulf between his hometown of Huddersfield, and Cambridge, Jackson was fascinated by how he could render his hometown to offer an alterna-tive understanding of English society to that which was offered by bucolic images

---

[13] The importance of dwelling is developed by Ingold (2000).

of the English Home Counties. What was this home? In his first book, with Dennis Marsden, *Education and the Working Class*, which made his name, it was Marburton, an anonymized northern town. Shortly afterwards he decided he needed to name the town, which the Penguin editions (which sold over 100,000 copies) identified as Huddersfield. His next book *Working Class Community*, even more explicitly focused on the city, revelling in its 'otherness', deliberately evoking the capacity and richness of its working-class bonds as a means of challenging middle-class stereotypes.

> [W]hen you hear them, these voices are Yorkshire, deliberate, authorative within their worlds. This book is an attempt to exemplify why they matter, why we should hear them. They are all working class voices – the mill girl at the dance, the plumber with his vision of 'brotherhood', the labourer climbing out of the bathroom window.[14]

The records of his study include a number of unstructured interviews he conducted with young working-class couples.[15] He asked about how the couples felt about living in Huddersfield. Some representative accounts he obtained ran as follows:

> Well, I think I'm proud to have been born here. I think I've warm feelings about it. I'm not ashamed to the place anyway. The place where you're born is different from anywhere else, isn't it? I think down south, I should be frightened to live down there (No. 1 husband)

> Whenever I've been down south, I've always felt inferior somehow. I've always felt that everybody down there knew a lot more than we did. They're always much more up to date, aren't they (No. 1 wife).

> No, I don't think either of us likes the place very much. It's just that we live here, family ties I suppose. And it's so difficult making a move, I don't think we'll move out, but I wouldn't say we were proud to live here. Not a bit.... If anybody asks you where you come from and you have to say Huddersfield, well you feel a bit uncomfortable. Your heart sinks. I don't know what it is. I think perhaps it's the speech, the way you talk. (2)

> I've never thought about it. It's alright I suppose. I'm not bothered. Well, when you go away a lot of people have never heard of it. (3)

> ...and then you see living in Huddersfield you are bound to feel a bit differently about it, aren't you. It's your home town, and you know so many people. It's not friends, no, it's not people you go out with, but people you meet in the street and knowing where to go, knowing where everything is. And having a house and a secure job. That's a lot really to give up (4 wife).

> well it's as good as the next place, isn't it. (The chief thing they valued the town for, was work. They felt that they never fear for a job living in a place like this. They weren't particularly proud of living here) (6 husband).

---

[14] Jackson (1968).

[15] These do not actually appear to have been used in the book itself, or at least, they are not cited.

Well it's alright. It's alright for work, shouldn't say I was thrilled about it. Don't misunderstand me, I don't mean that we dislike the place (8).

Well I'm proud to be Yorkshire, not Huddersfield particularly, but I'm proud to be a Yorkshireman. To me, Yorkshire is the county. I think anybody coming from abroad, when they think of a county they think of Yorkshire, don't they. You think of people as being tough (10).

Well, we're not that proud Huddersfield, we're a bit more proud than we might have been a few years ago, now that Huddersfield's more on the map. One or two things have happened here. We've the choirs and the choral society, people know where Huddersfield is, they don't say Huddersfield, where's that. (11).[16]

Huddersfield at this time was a prosperous, industrial town, with a strong engineering sector and a significant textile industry. Jackson drew attention to the remarkably vibrant civic life – though he did not dwell on the fact that this was only for men. This was based on the popularity of working men's clubs, bowls, brass bands, and the like. Yet this active civic involvement went hand in hand with people's own, rather downbeat, account of what it meant to live and belong. This is not, it would appear, an enchanted landscape, but rather evokes the dwelling perspective. In the quotes above, the young couples do not draw on a developed or elaborated comparative frame of reference in making their judgements about living in the area, nor can we see fantasy or desire wrapped up in their accounts. There is little evidence of a developed cultural geography where respondents feel willing or able to compare specific features of Huddersfield with other places salient to them. No other places (other than the county of Yorkshire and 'the south') are mentioned. Huddersfield is, simply, where they live, the place that their life is centred on.

The main criterion for assessing a place is whether it offers people the chance to live a decent life. The familiarity of living in the city gives residents a sense that they belong in the place, albeit ambivalently. In the way emphasized by many post-war anthropologists, having kin in the area explains why they are there and gives a rationale to their relationship to place in terms of their dwelling.[17]

Residents are aware of how Huddersfield might be seen by outsiders, and feel that, on the whole, it does not measure up. Their articulation of who these outsiders are is unclear, though there is a sense that they are southerners. For most respondents, it is not clear what the actual location is of such outsiders, but there is simply an implicit sense that Huddersfield is not the 'centre', but part of a stigmatized periphery. This is a model in which a local insider is juxtaposed to a generalized but powerful 'centre' from which these residents are excluded. The dominant moral claim which is allowed within this way of thinking about place is one based on local patriotism or more precisely 'pride' (as with interview 10). One cannot just leave Huddersfield behind, and therefore one has no option but

---

[16] All quotes extracted from Jackson (1968, box C5).
[17] See Edwards (2000), Strathern (1981), and more generally, Savage, Bagnall, and Longhurst (2005).

to champion one's place in the scheme of things, however limited one ultimately recognizes your local belonging to be.

There is good reason to suppose that these kinds of embedded attitudes to place were not unique to Huddersfield. In the later 1960s, Richard Brown conducted a series of extensive studies on Tyneside shipyards. Although these were primarily workplace based, they were remarkably thorough, including ethnographies of many of the shipyard trades, and semi-structured interviews with large numbers of workers. One question asked the shipyard workers to say whether they had ever thought of moving south for work. Most respondents replied tersely in the negative. They had never thought about it. 'I'm settled and happy'; 'I like being in a rut'; 'born and bred here – know almost everyone to nod at and many to talk to'.[18] But more telling are the accounts of the one-third who would be prepared to move, the vast majority of whom could only identify two reasons for doing so: firstly the higher wages and secondly the weather.[19] Only two could identify a personal connection, or a specific location that would attract them. There was no developed emotional or aesthetic geography. The appeal of the money, and the weather, was dependent on the fact that they were both abstract qualities. Like the Huddersfield case, the generic 'south' was defined in the absence of any specific knowledge of particular locations which might make it up.

The accounts elicited by Jackson and by Brown's associates tally with that dissected by many post-war social scientists. This is the dwelling of those 'born and bred', where family affiliations define one's place.[20] It is not a form of belonging that lends itself particularly to discursive articulation. It reminds me of the attachment I encountered when, travelling in rural North Carolina in the mid-1990s, our car broke down. Making conversation with the mechanic who towed it to a local garage, I asked him whether he enjoyed living in his area of North Carolina. It was an easy form of small talk for me, a privileged academic, but it became clear from the look he gave me, and his stilted reply, that he had never given the matter any thought. Place, as it seems to have been for the Huddersfield and Tyneside respondents interviewed by Jackson and Brown, was simply where one lived. You did not really like or dislike it, you just lived there.

It therefore appears that the evocation of an enchanted landscape was unusual amongst these Northern working-class respondents. But these are not necessarily typical, of course. During the middle years of the twentieth century people did, of course, move, and in large numbers. It was never the case that this apparent kinship-based attachment to place meant that the population was stable and immobile. Historians have demonstrated the huge population shifts in twentieth-century Britain, especially from the depressed areas of Ireland, Southern

---

[18] SN 5514, Cases Jo08, Pl15, p. 122.

[19] Of the 31 per cent who wanted to move south, 14 per cent, that is, nearly half of these, mentioned money as the main reason and 7 per cent mentioned the weather.

[20] See notably Strathern (1981) and Edwards (2000).

Wales, and Northern England to the relatively prosperous South and Midlands. But as well as these large-scale population shifts, which meant that the majority of those interviewed in Luton by Goldthorpe and Lockwood in the early 1960s had not been brought up in the area but had their roots in Ireland, Scotland, and Tyneside, there was also routine mobility entailed by occupational cultures. Railway workers and bank workers could all expect to be moved between posts. Most professional and managerial forms of employment expected workers to move, if only because it was rare for vacancies to be found for the upwardly mobile in their current location.

These reasons explain why contemporary social scientists argued that there was a major cultural divide between the mobile and the immobile, the 'locals' and 'cosmopolitans', and the 'burgesses' and 'spiralists'. The multifaceted nature of this divide has been a main theme of post-war social science, registered in the work of Ronnie Frankenberg, Colin Bell, Norbert Elias and Scotson, Margaret Stacey, Ray Pahl, and Marilyn Strathern.[21] But what sort of a divide was it? It was, to be sure, a class divide, in which the mobile middle classes were pitted against the predominantly working-class locals. But, more subtly, it was a cultural divide. Incoming migrants wanted to become locals, often trying avidly to join whatever local associations they were permitted to, but this often only confirmed them as outsiders. Working-class locals sought to offset their social inferiority by investing in the moral status that they claimed on the basis of their long-term residence. Locals needed outsiders, as strangers, to deal with, and mediate irreconcilable local conflicts, whilst outsiders needed locals in order to define a 'real' community whom they could try to identify with. Perhaps, then, the spiralists are akin to the migrants, like those on the right-hand side of Figure 1.2, who have chosen to move and are now strongly vested in place.

We can get intriguing clues about the kind of local identifications of the mobile by revisiting Ray Pahl's studies of the 1960s, which explicitly focused on the sociological implications of spiralism. Pahl was the first sociologist to focus on the implications of large-scale corporate mobility, with white-collar workers and managers moving around the country. Numerous interviews with corporate managers, located in suburbs throughout the country and overseas, reveal an attitude to place which was relatively little interested in the distinctive qualities of particular towns, but embraced generic qualities, of the ideal village, suburb, or town.

> Having once moved from my home town I am quite happy to go wherever my husband's work may take him. I have found no real disadvantages in our moves, but I have found many advantages. I have learnt to make friends much more quickly and easily, and I look forward to seeing and living in different countries. There is also the point that in moving about one's children are less likely to develop a strong dialect. In fact, I tend to feel sorry for people who spend their whole lives in one town.

[21] Frankenberg (1957), Bell (1968), Pahl (1965), Stacey (1960), and Strathern (1981). See the discussion in Savage, Bagnall, and Longhurst (2005*a*, chapter 2) and Crow and Allan (1994).

In general, these spiralists were relatively unconcerned with the particular place in which they lived. These accounts are concerned with identifying the kinds of generic amenities and facilities available. In one unusual example where there was reference to the particularities of place, it presented as a mysterious, opaque location, to which they had no real access.

> In Royston, the longer we live here the more it seems that Peyton Place has nothing on Royston. It seems as though the lack of community ties leads almost to immorality unless one is very strong willed. It stems from the fact that most of them are 'travelling' men, able to develop other liaisons, with the wife free of the children for the most part of the day and perhaps night and little to occupy their minds – are susceptible to other attentions.

This construction of their local environment as a kind of mysterious zone that was only knowable through defining it in terms of a soap opera indicates the lack of concern with auratics of place. This all seems a world away from the loaded and possessive reflections of those interviewed in the more recent period. Consider the further examples from a Mass-Observation directive conducted in 1995 which appear so different from the accounts generated by the 1960s' researchers.

> (Leighton Buzzard) has a boring image to people...they forget the beautiful Dunstable downs, Warden Hill...but most important of all, I like it here!

> We like living in Sheffield very much. The Peak District is within 10–15 minutes drive from where we live. Manchester, Leeds and London are easily accessible and we have two theatres and a good concert hall available. The presence of two universities helps to ensure a lively cultural atmosphere and in general we find the people friendly.

In the 1960s, by contrast, respondents spoke above all of institutional attachments as their main means of connecting to place, tied to a loose sense of regional attachment. One woman trumpeted her enthusiasm for the project of moving, after having stated that she initially found this difficult when she was first married.

> I now look forward to our moves (present home 5th in 10 years of marriage) and the advantages of exploring new surroundings, the challenges and changes a new house brings and making new friends.
>
> Disadvantages
> 1. Being left with children and responsibilities of moving and selling house etc whilst husband is whisked away to follow his employment in the new area.
> 2. Finding suitable education facilities (R.C.)
> 3. Leaving friends
> 4. Not being able to form any permanent attachment to any club, society etc so not being able to hold responsible positions in these establishments.[22]

---

[22] SN 4864, Pahl Interview 67/24, paraphrasing in the original.

This is a revealing ordering of concerns. There is no worry about retaining access to a place with its particular associations and memories, the bearer of desires or treasured values. Even though Pahl was prescient enough to draw out the symbolic power of the 'village in the mind' as a cultural beacon to the middle class, it appears from his interview data that it is the generic 'village in the mind' which is appealing. Place matters in terms of its ability to offer appropriate institutional and associational support to the domestic housewife, expected to move in pursuit of her husband's career. Thus, one wife characterized her current location in terms of its capacity to offer potential friends. I 'have only just moved to this neighbourhood', she reported, 'but (I am) quite likely to make as many friends here as elsewhere'.

> My husband spent two years at a Scottish branch of his firm. The community was more tightly associated and therefore there were greater opportunities of meeting other wives and families than in the London area.…Moves have always been to mutual advantage. Last but one move was unpopular because the weather was so bad and cultural stimulation negligible…local hospitality alleviated much of the boredom. But we would not have gone had the position been permanent.[23]

For this woman, location surely matters, but as a site from which certain activities are possible: it needs to offer the potential to make friends, some kind of cultural stimulation, and it helps if there is good weather. This interest in the weather, which seems endemic in the sources of the time, is almost entirely absent amongst those we interviewed in the later 1990s. Is this because global warming and better heating means that the desire to escape a harsh winter has lost its hold? One of my enduring memories of being an undergraduate student at York in the late 1970s, having spent my childhood in London, are the freezing cold winter nights.[24] Possibly. But the weather was never so different between different parts of England. More likely, the weather is evoked as an abstraction, a means of differentiating places according to principles that are not themselves place specific. Other than the appeal to the weather, any kind of aesthetic or emotional ties to place are striking by their absence. A terse dialogue between one husband and wife illustrates this connection well. The husband could think of three reasons for having moved in the past, '[firstly] to move from the profession; secondly to widen experience; thirdly the preference of being a big fish in a small pond with the security of a large organisation behind me'. All these reasons were work-related and centred on his career prospects. However, his wife then intervened that, 'I don't want to move particularly. Nice house. Good school. Neighbours not so friendly'.[25] Even though, unlike many of Pahl's sample, she did want to stay put, it was the quality of house and schooling rather than aesthetic

---

[23] SN 4864, 67/24.

[24] The centre of the University of York campus contains an artificial lake which froze regularly. It was common for us to take shortcuts to classes by crossing it. I am told that today the lake hardly ever freezes.

[25] SN 4864, Pahl Interview 65.

judgements which were paramount. Another wife thought that her husband should move jobs and house because 'both of us are ambitious and require to progress in this life...if it is in the best interests of my husband I do not mind moving from place to place every so often'.[26] Another reported that she enjoyed 'moving, as this inevitably means promotion for my husband. It means I can change my ideas about the structure of our home, and we can usually buy a better house. I meet new people and this does provide new interest for me. Because of these moves, if I didn't like a place I need only regard it as temporary'.[27]

What we see in these accounts is the evocation of an impersonal world of social contacts, neighbours, and friends, who could in a sense be located anywhere. Once again, this is very different from those we interviewed in the 1990s, who identified particular people who mattered to them, who were located in specific places. People could name best friends, many of whom lived at a distance, but this place from which they were located itself formed part of the enchanted landscape. The kind of landscape envisaged is not just a physical landscape, it also encompasses social relations and conceptions. I now want to explore these connections in greater detail.

In one respect then, there is not much difference between the orientations to place of the Huddersfield and Tyneside working-class locals, and the new mobile spiralists. Both were founded on a restricted cultural geography and functional orientation to place. Both were rooted in fixed, patriarchal, family forms, in which unthinking subordination involved a resignation to place. Elective belonging is not simply, therefore, the product of the expansion of the middle class or of suburban life. Its roots are more complex, and also more interesting.

1.3 THE ORIGINS OF ELECTIVE BELONGING

In 1960, the anthropologist John Nalson, conducting fieldwork for a PhD in rural North East Staffordshire, was struck by its depressed state. The farming industry was declining. Few outsiders wanted to live there. There was a steady drift of people from the land. However, revisiting in 1976, he noticed a distinct change. Middle-class 'offcomers' had chosen to move to the relatively cheap houses in a landscape seen as attractive. Nalson took the unusual step of holding himself responsible for this transformation.

> In the late spring of 1960 Bill Watson who was supervising my PhD work, visited me in the field. North Staffordshire was at its best – the sun was shining and the views were breathtaking. The local pub had good beer and a convivial and colourful local clientele. Bill decided that the area was ideal for a summer cottage.... Subsequently to Bill Watson's sojourn in the district, Max and Mary Gluckman bought and renovated an old farmhouse.[28]

[26] SN 4864, Pahl Interview 67/21.   [27] SN 4864, Pahl Interview 66/10.
[28] Nalson (1982, 71).

Noting that Watson and Gluckman were the first middle-class residents to move into this area, Nalson tellingly concluded that

> In contrast to the predominantly economic motives of the full and part-time farmers moving on to farms...the Manchester academics, and the business and professional men who followed them in the sixteen years from 1960 to 1976, all appeared to be seeking a congenial and aesthetically pleasing rural locale somewhat remote from the populations and pressures of large urban centres.[29]

This kind of shift, which Nalson identifies as a 'quiet revolution', was found throughout Britain, and has been much studied by subsequent researchers interested in the process of rural gentrification.[30] There are numerous precedents for wealthy people moving to attractive rural locations, but these tended to be staged and managed affairs. When Portmerion became known as the 'Greenwich Village of Wales' in the 1950s, this was due to the deliberate attempts of Clough Williams-Ellis to create an intellectual community separate from other local residents.[31] The same is true of other artistic colonies which were formed in earlier periods. Gluckman and Watson, by contrast, wanted to belong, after a fashion, even if from benches of a country pub on a summer afternoon. We get a glimpse here of how the orientations of middle-class spiralists moved away from seeking a retreat, bounded from the outside world, and instead sought out their own place in the country. In this subtle shift, the research practices of social scientists are themselves implicated in the very social changes which interest them.

This process is tellingly revealed in Bott's intensive studies of twenty London households, the richness of which lies in the wealth of detail the interviewers recorded about the households. A particularly interesting part of this work was when the researchers reported on the reference groups which mattered to the couple. Bott and Robb conscientiously recorded details of every group which appeared to be of interest to the couple, whether these were abstract social groups, particular individuals, or indeed places. The results now make fascinating reading as an account of the interests of the proto-social scientists who were drawn to the research. We are bequeathed a stunning source for reflecting on the cultural geography of twenty London households in the early 1950s.

There are a few differences compared to the accounts elicited by Pahl, Jackson, and Brown. We can even detect evidence of 'elective belonging'. One young middle-class husband and wife were both university graduates. Mr Bullock was a research economist and enthusiastic Labour Party activist. They had moved precisely to their 'village in the mind'.

> After marriage they decided the kind of place they wanted to live in, looked around until they found just the right place, moved in 3½ years ago. They live in a 16th century cottage on the edge of what was once a village green, next to the churchyard and a short distance away from, and out of sight of, a main road...the house is completely furnished, chiefly in the new but simple and plain furniture that enables them to give the air of 'period' furnishing. They have emphasised this in various

---

[29] Nalson (1982, 72).   [30] See Newby (1980).   [31] Emmett (1964, 26).

ways particularly by highly polishing the floors, and ceiling beams, off-white distempered walls, and considerable use of horse brasses etc in decoration

This is the kind of account that James, or Ian and Cherie, could have provided over fifty years later. Bott goes on to talk about their relationship to their neighbourhood.

The only close neighbours are those living in the other two cottages. These are old people. Contact has been friendly but slight and the Bullocks have no wish to extend it. They have no complaints about these neighbours, they just aren't interested in them. More distant neighbours are seen vaguely. A few of them achieve reality as members of the local Labour Party or as prominent opponents of this, but most of them are lumped together as conservative, stuffy, members of the Residents association, not worth bothering about.[32]

Contrast this with another, working-class household, the Newbolts. This family was one of the few to be clearly from the London working class.[33] Around this one case, Bott constructed her account of the working-class family, characterized by its wide-ranging social networks and its high degree of gender demarcation between husband and wife.[34] Bott's notes record that the (Newbolts) are a 'solid working class family' strong in building and furniture trades. She goes on to note

Neighbourhood: this is a relative term, meaning sometimes all of the East End, sometimes districts within it, and sometimes a street or two. They do not feel at home outside of the area. They feel that everyone knows everybody else in the East End whereas outside it is impersonal 'They say we are rough but I think it is the best place there is. Everyone is friendly. There is no life in the West End compared to the East End. They drink champagne and we drink beer. When things are la-di-da you feel out of place'. Only go outside East End on set occasions, to the zoo with kids, to Southend, hop picking, Trafalgar Square to see Christmas tree, to C and As.

She goes on to note that

'Home' for this sort of family normally means one or two streets, but there is a wider area where they feel at home, consisting roughly of Hackney, Bethnal Green, Mile End, Bow and Shoreditch.[35]

This seems to have parallels with the accounts produced by Jackson about Huddersfield and by Brown's associates about Tyneside, as well as with our more

---

[32] SN 4852, Bott Interview 10.

[33] Indeed, this single household was fundamental to the argument developed by Bott which distinguished the gender-segregated social networks of the working class with the more integrated relationships of the middle-class couples.

[34] Bott has herself, in a personal communication, noted that she felt able to use the evidence from this one family as the frame for her account of the working class extended family because her contacts with the Institute of Community Studies, and the work of Young and Willmott had also turned up other families of similar type.

[35] SN 4852, Bott Interview 7.

recent interviews of who 'dwell' on the left-hand side of Figure 1.2. Bott and Robb's notes reveal that these different relationships with place were also bound up with different kinds of social identification. The Newbolts in fact were a difficult family to research. They broke off their involvement in the study before they underwent psychological tests, partly because they were introduced into the study by almoners and were always hesitant about their involvement. Yet we can take the Baldocks who also were rooted in East London as a parallel. They did not abstract social groups from their spatial location.

> The reference here is much more to place than to people...the district is the place where they belong and feel at home, that neither wants to move from. In considerable measure it is her family's home....When they talk about the district as a whole they imply that the people who live there are pretty good, looked down upon by the outside world, and especially social workers, but nevertheless basically admirable people....At times one gets the impression that they are compelled to stay in the district and to be patriotic but are able to do this only by associating themselves with the place and dissociating themselves from the people.[36]

This embeddedness went hand in hand with a sensitive social geography in which groups were necessarily located in specific places. They

> deny the existence of social classes except as figments of the imagination of social workers and other 'misguided people'. However, they were happy to talk about 'West Enders' – identified with upper classes, includes ideas as 'wealth, extravagance, immorality, Mayfair, Piccadilly, high living, etc'...at the same time he tends to join with her in stressing the idea that there are no social classes and everybody is the same as everybody else.

By contrast, the Bullocks, with their social science credentials, and with their elective belonging, are much better able to articulate an abstract conception of social groups, removed from the landscape, as it were. Their salient reference groups included 'Democrats': 'These are people who perform certain kinds of activities, obeying certain rules. It is hardly an exaggeration to define democrats as people who have the same ideas as the Bullocks and use proper committee procedure to put these ideas into action'.

The Bullocks also had a clear view of who 'people like us' were, which were deemed to be 'various friends and acquaintances'. 'The characteristics of these people seem to be that they are intelligent, young, socialists, politically active, mildly unconventional....They would like to extend the people like us group over a very considerable number of the population'. Bott tellingly includes the following comment:

> In all their discussions on social organisations, politics, etc, I do not remember a single occasion when they referred specifically to the actual individuals affected in this way....He talks about his political views in largely intellectual terms and the same applies to his personal relationships. Everything is reduced to a rather flat

---

[36] SN 4852, Bott Interview 11.

unemotional level....Very much in line with this is the impersonal nature of most of his relationships. He seems to see people in terms of their official roles. They are committee members, chairmen, conservatives, property owners, but not real people.[37]

We see here in remarkable detail how the ability to 'abstract' from place, so that one can stand outside it and judge it aesthetically and ethically, is associated – at least in the Bullock's case – with the ability to define an abstract language of social groups, plucked out from the landscape and the people who inhabit such a landscape, who become defined in terms of their abstract, social, political, and psychological characteristics.

This point is interesting for a further reason. The Bullocks were nascent 'elective belongers', they were Labour Party activists, and he was also a social scientist. As with the migration of the Manchester anthropologists to North Staffordshire, social scientists appear themselves to be key agents in championing a certain way of thinking and relating. As noted in the introduction, in fact most of Bott's sample had interests in social science and were political activists.

We can go back even further in time, to Mass-Observation, which gives us a final resource to reflect on the complex history of the enchanted landscape. Three months before the Second World War, in 1939, Mass-Observation sent a directive to a panel of 'observers', asking them to write in about why they chose to live in their current area of residence.[38] The results are revealing. Even though Mass-Observation encouraged its members to account for themselves, few Mass-Observers were able to give anything other than a mundane account of the reason for their place of residence. For the vast majority of Mass-Observers, even though they were relatively privileged and advantaged, residence was not a matter of choice. Many younger correspondents were still living in their parents' homes (14 per cent of the total). For many, their residence was a simple product of the location of their work (18 per cent). The answers are often terse in the extreme. 'I live in Knightsbridge because my parents do'. 'I have had no choice but to live in Taunton'. 'I live here because I have to. No reasons. No motives. My father moved here – I followed'. Another Mass-Observer noted that his residence was for three reasons, '(a) convenience for work and my weekends at home, (b) quiet yet accessible, (c) within my income range'. Another lived in London 'by necessity'; a third, 'lodged here, met my husband here, he worked here at colliery, got a house here'.[39] In all these cases, residence was largely presented as a fact of life over which one had no, or limited, control.

Amidst these predominantly functional responses, there are a few more purposeful accounts of choosing to live somewhere (eight cases, or 5 per cent in total). Especially amongst those who live in larger cities, there was a sense that people could choose a district (the term which was always used in preference to

---

[37] SN 4852, Bott Interview 10.

[38] All the extracts below are from M-O Directive (A), with a total sample of 174 cases.

[39] M-O (A): These cases are from Brunel, Cameron, Cornhill, Ditmas, Devivar, and Dawson, respectively.

the contemporary term neighbourhood) to live. The criteria used to assess the areas are usually seen as the attributes of the place itself, rather than as reflecting the values and ideas of the correspondents, abstracted as it were from the spatial environment. 'It is a "superior" district and therefore we are amongst our own class (as superiority goes in Leeds)', one young woman tartly remarked, who then embellished this by noting her desire to move out of a Jewish quarter where she 'felt like a foreigner'. A further consideration was the quality of the 'air'. In a period before the Clean Air Act, when the universal use of coal for heating meant the high presence of smog, we are reminded of the environmental differences between those areas of cities where the prevailing winds and proximity to the countryside entailed better prospects of clear and less-polluted air. As an extension of this concern, being close to the country was itself often seen as desirable. In nearly all cases, it is the generic countryside which is venerated: there are few references to particularly scenic countryside spots or precious places.

Only two Mass-Observers report in terms which are similar to those of contemporary 'elective belongers', who – as it were – speak across time. These accounts stand out because of their far more elaborate narratives about their local attachments. One middle-aged female teacher wrote about her love affair with Chepstow:

I suppose that in the first place one does not live in a place entirely from choice. Economic conditions play a large part…it was the boom in work which brought me here just after the war. It was my everlasting love of nature and the beauty of the district which made me decide that it was a good place to live in. Chepstow in those days was a clannish little place and strangers were not very welcome, but so much new blood has since flowed in with a fluctuating ship yard population…it now seems a much more friendly little place.

But one thing I am certain, that I do live here now because I like living here. After my husband's death I went to teach in Blaenavon, a mining area. How my heart ached for the green and the trees of Chepstow.

I like this small country town because I am a free and easy person and like being friendly with everybody. Here the policeman, the publican and the busman are my friends…here you can mix with all classes without losing caste. Therefore your outlook on life can be much more versatile. I like teaching in the country because of necessity I must rise early and catch a bus which lands me in the wide open spaces at 8 am thus giving me the opportunity of breathing good pure air.…I like teaching country children because they come into school for the first time completely unspoiled. I like living where I can see green trees and hear the singing of birds and the changing seasons.…I like to know that I have one of the world's beauty spots at my door and yet when I wish to seek the excitements of big town life, I know that Cardiff, Gloucester and Bristol are within an hour's journey – even London itself can be reached in 2½ hours.…I like the free and easy life I manage to live here, no one notices idiosyncrasies in dress when so many holiday people are about.[40]

The terms of this discourse are striking. Recognizing her distance from the local community, she is thereby able to position herself as hovering over the landscape,

[40] M-O (A).

so to speak. Her valuation of Chepstow is integrally related to her account of the possibility that she can travel elsewhere: there is no other person who mentioned five other places in the course of her account. As with the Bullocks, we see that the ability to refer to abstract social groups as well as psychological tropes is concomitant with her sense of belonging: she can talk of social classes, occupational types, and she is also able to describe psychological states. And yet, even here, we see that she is of her time. The prefatory remarks in which she notes the limits of choice are revealing too. More than this lies her sense that she is a loner, not part of a community of others like herself who have chosen to live in Chepstow, but one of an unusual kind. This is the major point of contrast with the later generation from the 1990s who are aware that it is now normal to elect to belong.

The other exception was a middle-aged writer, who had given up his job to move to the seaside.

> For the first 35 years of life I lived in a manufacturing town (Luton) and grew to hate it, and during the last ten years or so I knew quite definitely what I wanted. It was to live in a Cornish or Devon village, on an estuary which had plenty of trees nearby; I longed for the sea, for the quietness of a village, to get away from the town. The opportunity came, I had to make a change, and I selected this village, which provides in full measure for the things I desire most. I am, in the Wordsworthian manner, a lover of nature. I hate the noise and bustle of modern life and perhaps like the alleged ostrich I can see here less vividly the ominous sights. A cowardly action, but I have no faith in future life and this village life I embrace almost passionately. I still get an emotional thrill from being here and not in a town.[41]

Again, we see the evocation of landscape, the insistence on solitariness, and in this case on being a backward-looking romantic. In 1939, he clearly identified the future as one of anonymous urban development, with which he positions himself as being out of kilter.

What we see, by their own words, is the way that both these individuals mark themselves out as being unusual. His use of literary allusions as a means of justifying his taste is indicative of the power of humanistic, and not scientific, motifs.

1.4 CONCLUSIONS

I have in this chapter traced the increasing enchantment of the landscape during the second half of the twentieth century. A landscape which during the middle years of the century was seen as functional and constraining has increasingly been seen as an object of fantasy and desire, hope and escape. Those few hermits

---

[41] M-O (A).

of the middle years of the twentieth century have now become part of a large social group. I have argued that this 'enchanting of the landscape' is associated with wider cultural change. It involves construing the social as separate from the spatial so that one can talk about abstract social groups as entities plucked out of place, and hence depends on a broader process by which advantaged individuals feel able to locate themselves as outside of place, able to fix on, and choose, where they want to live. This is a discourse of strangers. Yet in another way, this process also involves reducing the abstract qualities of the air, the weather, and money, all of which were identified as constraints in earlier periods, to ones which are clearly located in specific places.

I have also elaborated how the social sciences were part of this process of generating new conceptions of the landscape. The very practice of writing, teaching, research, and intellectual labour itself generates new capacities for belonging. It is not incidental that the only two Mass-Observers in 1939 who embody the 'ur-state' of elective belonging are a teacher and a writer. Those from Bott's sample who respond emotionally to place are social science researchers. The association with a particular political vision is also clear: the politics of elective belonging involves a concern to make a different place to live a matter of political concern. The decision to move, to put down roots in a particular place, is implicated in a political perspective, it announces a set of possibilities in people's thinking, and it literally puts those possibilities in place. This is not to claim that a particular social group, in this case social scientists, are somehow acting 'alone': rather, as I explore in later chapters, they are part of a wider infrastructural nexus which mobilizes distinctive methods and expertise. The increasing capacity to evoke social divisions and social groups sets apart a middle class vested in 'choice' from a working class which remains located and thrown in the landscape.

Finally, we can see how one method, the interview, produces rather different kinds of account in various time periods. This suggests that we need a fundamentally historical account of methods, one which sees both the research repertoires themselves, as well as the resources available to interviewees – and interviewers – as the product of their time. It is by reading the absences and subtleties of different accounts that we can gain a sense of how complicit researchers are with the very business of change and identity.

Part I

Technical Identities and the Rise of Social Science

2

1938: The British Intellectual and Highbrow Culture

In the early 1960s, in a celebrated paper, Perry Anderson lamented the weakness of the British social sciences, seeing this as a characteristic failure of Britain to embrace change and modernity.[1] He was writing, however, at precisely the time that an unprecedented expansion of the social scientific apparatus was taking place in Britain, driven in part by the concern to modernize. Yet despite the increased attention on intellectuals and experts of various kinds, it still remains normal to emphasize the tensions between the world of intellectuals, associated with the arts and humanities, and that of instrumental concerns, linked to business and science. Stefan Collini's important recovery of the role of the British intellectual, in his *Absent Minds* is a case in point, as it largely recounts the familiar pantheon of names associated with art and culture: T. S. Eliot, R. G. Collingwood, George Orwell, A. J. P. Taylor, and A. J. Ayer. In this chapter, I argue that this misconceives the role of technical identities as offering a distinctive managerial conception of knowledge and expertise, one that has proven powerful in post-war Britain. My aim in this chapter is twofold. Firstly, I critique those perspectives – notably that associated with Pierre Bourdieu, but which would also apply to Collini – which assume that the intellectual position is fundamentally one based in the humanities. Secondly, I show how in the middle years of the twentieth century we can detect an increasingly clear rejection of what was deemed the snobbish and elitist refrain of 'highbrow culture' and an increasing enthusiasm for a different kind of intellectuality, one bound up with science, technique, and skill.

2.1 INTELLECTUALS AND SCIENTISTS

Let us start with Pierre Bourdieu's inspiring excavation of the historical and social role of the 'intellectual'. Rather than take the intellectual as a self-evident social category, he insists on the need to understand how intellectual

[1] Anderson (1964).

practices are a form of social endeavour, embodied in social relationships, and demanding certain forms of apprehending, relating, and knowing. His refusal of the temptation for social scientists to reify the social world, with the attendant assumption that variables can be isolated and measured as if they are objective categories, leads him precisely to avoid positing objective, measurable definitions of specific phenomena.[2] Instead, he prefers a relational analysis, which lays out the distribution of agents and their practices in 'social space', so that the distances between them can be delineated as if they were a map. This kind of field analysis is precisely the approach which I used in Chapter 1 in exploring the 'cloud of individuals'.[3] It is not incidental that in evoking this form of analysis, Bourdieu himself exemplifies a landscaped approach to analysis, where social space is seen as if it were geometric space.[4]

Bourdieu emphasizes that throughout history a prime tension can be detected between those with resources (or 'capitals') and those without.[5] Using survey evidence, as well as documentary sources and interview data drawn from France in the 1960s, he insists on the way that this tension is marked in the cultural appreciation of different social groups, with the educated middle classes exhibiting a taste for the 'legitimate', sacrosanct, forms of culture, which are largely out of the reach of the working classes. He sees this fundamental divide as the product of the 'aesthetic disposition', which is defined as follows:

> A generalized capacity to neutralize ordinary urgencies and to bracket off practical ends, a durable inclination and aptitude for practice without a practical function (which) can only be constituted within an experience of the world freed from urgency and through the practice of activities which are an end in themselves, such as scholastic exercises or the contemplation of works of art.[6]

However, around this fundamental divide, Bourdieu also emphasizes the existence of a second tension, which cross-cuts it. On the one hand lies what he terms the 'pure' aesthetic, which is characterized by an embrace of the modernist concern with the dominance of form over function.

> An art, which, like all Post-Impressionist painting, for example, is the product of an artistic intention which asserts the *absolute primacy of form over function*, of the

---

[2] So, for instance, Collini's refusal (2006, 57) to use Bourdieu's concept of cultural capital because of its 'narrowly economistic notions of "competition" and "positional strategy"'.

[3] See the discussion of these issues in Bennett et al. (2009, especially chapter 2), and more generally on field analysis, see Martin (2003) and Weininger (2004).

[4] The issue of the relationship between physical and social space is explored briefly in Savage, Bagnall, and Longhurst (2005) and in 'elements of the descriptive turn'. The relationship between Bourdieu's sociology and the field theory developed by Lewin in the mid-twentieth century is explored in later chapters.

[5] 'The primary differences, those which distinguish the major classes of the conditions of existence, derive from the overall volume of capital, understood as the set of actually usable resources and powers – economic capital, cultural capital and also social capital' (Bourdieu 1985, 114). More generally on the concept of capitals, see Savage, Warde, and Devine (2005).

[6] Bourdieu (1985, 55).

mode of representation over the object represented, *categorically* demands a purely aesthetic disposition which earlier art demanded only conditionally.[7]

This leads to an aesthetic of the modernist avant-garde, championed by intellectuals and artists, seeking the purity of abstraction. By contrast, wealthy 'industrialists' embrace a different aesthetic, one which still repudiates routine everyday experience, but through an embrace of the leisurely and luxurious, whereby they 'incline towards a hedonistic aesthetic of ease and facility, symbolized by boulevard theatre or Impressionist painting'.[8] This is the aesthetic of 'conspicuous consumption', of lavish display.

Over certain issues, intellectuals and industrialists may make common cause,[9] united in their shared rejection of the everyday world of the popular and vulgar. However, when they feel less threatened by this plebeian world, and especially in their relations to each other, these internal tensions come to the fore. These relations are therefore not to be understood as rigid class divides, whereby people are clearly lined up in strongly bounded camps. Rather, by construing the social as a contested landscape, he draws attention to the routes, ruses, and feints involved in battles over the land. It is in this spirit that we can reflect on cultural dynamics in twentieth-century Britain.

At the outset, the fundamental issue posed by the peculiarities of the British is the extent to which we can usefully demarcate the tension between the modernist and the leisured aesthetics. Bourdieu's account can be said to be thoroughly French in its insistence on the cultural distinctiveness of 'intellectuals', taken to be representative of cultural modernism, from the industrialist 'bourgeoisie'.

> The contrast that is drawn between the 'intellectual' of left-bank taste and 'bourgeois' or right-bank taste is not only an opposition between the preference for contemporary works and the taste for older, more consecrated works.... It is also an opposition between two world views, two philosophies of life,... the centres of two constellations of choices.[10]

Christope Charle has provided a valuable historical rendering of this point, through his excavation of the role of the Dreyfus case for announcing the presence of French intellectuals. In response to the alleged perverting of evidence by the military authorities in the indictment of the Jewish soldier Dreyfus in 1894, Zola, in his famous 'J'Accuse' letter, inspired a group of self-styled 'intellectuals' to write public letters denouncing the machinations of clerical and militaristic authorities. By identifying themselves as intellectuals in the public realm, they created a new, heroic, and enduring identity for themselves as thorns in the side of the established,

---

[7] Bourdieu (1985, 30).   [8] Bourdieu (1985, 176).

[9] It is important to see Bourdieu's categories here as roles, rather than as fixed occupational groupings. In some cases, these roles do indeed become crystallized as occupations, to the extent that we might treat occupational groups as shorthand for the role itself, but we should not assume that this is always the case.

[10] Bourdieu (1985, 292).

backward-looking, bourgeoisie. This process of self-identification, Collini claims, marks out a distinctively French concern to venerate the radical intellectual, which persists throughout the twentieth century, with the result that later writers such as Sartre, Foucault, and indeed Bourdieu himself feel they need to live up to this image of the critical intellectual.

There has been an enduring tendency to see this distinctively French elevation of the intellectual as the norm from which other nations deviate. This is the central allegation of Perry Anderson's influential critique, which rests very much on the alleged absence of 'great' critical intellectuals in the French manner.[11] However, Collini rightly argues that in fact France is utterly exceptional in witnessing this kind of intellectual identity. In Britain, as in most other nations, intellectuals were not formed at such odds with the dominant, 'bourgeois' culture. Eminent British intellectuals, from John Maynard Keynes through George Orwell, A. J. P. Taylor, R. J. Collingwood, Isaiah Berlin, and Freddie Ayer are much more closely folded into the bosom of the bourgeoisie, even allowing for their occasional 'gingery' statements.[12]

In the British case, the modernist aesthetic seems to be much more closely reconciled with the leisurely aesthetic than one might suppose to be possible from the pages of *Distinction*.[13] One might trace this close affiliation back, certainly to the Victorian period, where the powerful reaction against utilitarianism led to a determination by the educated middle classes to celebrate both the importance of pure art and the ability of elite groups to enjoy and appreciate it in leisured circumstances. This is nowhere more marked than in John Ruskin's house at Brantwood on Lake Coniston, with its famous turret from where the great romantic could calmly contemplate nature.[14] By the early twentieth century, the reconciliation between these two motifs is no more clearly announced than in G. E. Moore's clarion call for the 'Ideal' which deemed ultimate value to lie in 'the pleasures of human intercourse and the enjoyment of beautiful objects',[15] where the former might be taken to represent the leisurely aesthetic and the latter the modernist one. In a similar manner, Gordon Fyfe has explored the resolution of tensions between aristocratic and professional visions of art, which had led to significant conflict between the Tate Gallery and the Royal Academy during the first half of the twentieth century. Declining aristocratic fortunes from the later nineteenth century forced the nobility to operate in alliance with more academic

[11] Anderson (1964).

[12] On these figures, see Ignatieff (1998) on Taylor, and see Burk (2000).

[13] On contemporary cultural dynamics, see Bennett et al. (2009). Whereas Bourdieu shows that there is an important division between wealthy industrialists and well-educated intellectuals, we found that this opposition was much less significant in the British case. This is because, in the United Kingdom in 2003, the well educated and the wealthy tended to overlap in a distinctive 'professional and executive class'.

[14] I remember my son, Bardy, being very interested in Ruskin's motif 'There is no wealth but life' which was amply displayed during a visit we made to Brantwood. After absorbing this idea with great interest, he quizzically asked me, 'But if he thinks that, why did he live in such a big house?'

[15] See Skidelsky (2003, 89).

professional interests, leading to 'the forging of an aesthetic partnership between the state, the professional class and a declining aristocracy'.[16] The cultural authority of the aristocracy was incumbent on their accepting the cultural writ of professional art curators, who themselves were in turn attracted to an aesthetic 'which naturalised the gulf between the elite and the masses (and which) had an affinity with the developing Mandarin culture of the Civil Service'.[17] Here, Jon Agar has shown how ideas of technique were deployed to mark out the elite intellectual 'generalists', from the lowly administrative grades, whose job it was to apply technical procedures. In a similar manner, Donald MacKenzie has shown how leading Victorian medics, biologists, and statisticians were drawn to a statistical theory which differentiated groups according to their worth, and can be seen as associated with an 'intellectual aristocracy'. In all these ways, technical and scientific identities were subordinated to a humanities-oriented intellectual elite, nurtured in the private schools and Oxbridge.[18]

Early modernist pioneers did occasionally articulate a more direct opposition to the aristocracy in a manner which has certain resonances with Bourdieu's model. The leading poet Ezra Pound expressed the view on the eve of the First World War that 'the old aristocracies of blood and business were about to be supplanted by "the aristocracy of the arts"'.[19] However, as Jonathan Rose and John Carey[20] note, this hostility to the leisured aristocracy was small beer compared to the loathing directed towards the uncultured 'masses', and during the course of the early twentieth century this fusion of modernism and gentility gathered strength in opposition to 'the great unwashed': the archetypal, though undoubtedly caricatured instance is Bloomsbury, which championed both the modernist avant-garde, famously through the literature of Virginia Woolf, and also the embrace of the leisured, aristocratic ideal as its necessary concomitant. The case of John Maynard Keynes is instructive here. Probably, the single most influential intellectual in twentieth-century Britain, his economic theory was intended to shore up Edwardian civilization in the increasingly turbulent capitalist conditions of the period after the First World War.[21] His emotional geography is worthy of note. His London base was 46 Gordon Square, the heart of Bloomsbury, where he lived close to his fellow 'Bloomsberries', Vanessa Bell, Duncan Grant, and the Woolfs, from where he walked to his office in the Treasury during the week. Most Friday nights he took the train to Cambridge, where he was Fellow at Kings College, and spent the weekend serving on college committees (which met on Saturdays), and socializing with his family and friends, before returning to London on Monday morning. For three months of the year, he lived in his

---

[16] Fyfe (2000, 157).   [17] Fyfe (2000, 154).

[18] Agar (2003) and MacKenzie (1981). See also Annan (1999).

[19] Rose (2001, 435).   [20] Rose (2001) and Carey (1992).

[21] Keynes's passion is best revealed by his attack on communism, part of his critique of Soviet Russia: 'How can I adopt a creed which, preferring the mud to the fish, exalts the boorish proletariat above the bourgeois and intelligentsia who, with whatever faults, are the quality of life and surely carry the seeds of all human advancement' (quoted in Skideslky 2003, 372).

farmhouse at Tilton in Sussex, also close to the Charleston estate colonized by the Woolfs, where he could live out his miniature vision of the rural estate. Through these routine journeys powerful symbolic connections were forged, traversing rather than separating the corridors of power, academia, and the art world.[22]

Of course, Keynes's case also reveals tensions between these worlds. Although he was clear about his advocacy of modernist art, his artistic friends in Bloomsbury did not always trust, or even entirely respect, his worldliness. Once Keynes's career as economist flowered, he was treated more warily by his Bloomsbury friends and (former) lovers. Although it is clear that Keynes saw himself predominantly as searching for the means to preserve Edwardian upper-class culture through sound economic management, this is not how his friends regarded him.[23] His shift from his homosexual early years in Bloomsbury circles to a marriage seen by some of his friends as all too convenient, was further testimony to this.

The result of this alliance between modernism and gentility was to place cultural tensions within a hierarchical formation, whereby they overlapped with class resentment. In England, following from the American example, cultural distinctions in the interwar period were framed through the discourse of 'high-', 'middle-', and 'lowbrow' taste, in which highbrow taste was treated with some suspicion and never secured easy legitimacy for itself.[24] Collini brings out how even those who were generally identified as highbrows, such as Leonard Woolf, could not own up to a straightforward highbrow identity but had to treat the issue facetiously, and by contrast, the vigour of a range of writers (such as J. B. Priestley and Arnold Bennett) emphasizing their 'middlebrow' credentials.[25] In Jonathan Rose's words,

> In the first half of the twentieth century, two rival intelligentsias squared off against each other, competing for audiences and prestige. One was middle class, university educated, and modernist, supported largely by patronage and private incomes; the other was based in the working and clerking classes, mainly Board school graduates and the self educated, more classical in their tastes, but fearlessly engaged in popular journalism and feature films.... One was inspired by Marx, Nietzsche and Freud, the other Carlyle, Dickens and Ruskin.[26]

Rose does not bring out the distinctive geographical locations from which these two brows wrote. The 'middlebrows' were irredeemably provincial, but in a way which lauded the qualities of the provinces, seen as more virtuous and down to earth than the metropolitan and estate heartlands of the highbrows. The location of the best known makes this geography very clear: Arnold Bennett, from

---

[22] These details of Keynes's residences and journeys are derived from Skidelsky (2003, 256, 361, 657) and passim.

[23] Perhaps the classic 'snipe' to this effect is Virginia Woolf's recollection of Keynes in 1920 'like a gorged seal, double chin, ledge of red lip, little eyes, sensual, brutal, unimaginative. One of those visions that came from a chance attitude, lost so soon as he turned his head. I suppose though it illustrates something that I feel about him. That he's read neither of my books' (quoted in Skidelsky 2003, 259).

[24] See McKibbin (1998, 478f).   [25] Collini (2006, 114).

[26] Rose (2001, 431).

the Staffordshire potteries, whose literature was situated among the Five Towns; Neville Cardus, from Rusholme in Manchester, who as a music and cricket correspondent of the *Manchester Guardian* lauded his provincial roots; and J. B. Priestley, from Bradford, who set his work in the industrial North and through his journeys around the nation. In all these cases, their location was not incidental to their work: the same even applies to metropolitan middlebrows such as Richard Church, who hailed from suburban south London and was intent on countering the north London, anti-suburban ethos of Bloomsbury. Whereas Bourdieu depicts a tension within the dominant classes between intellectuals and industrialists, in Britain, the 'battle of the brows' reveals a hierarchical split between the genteel upper-middle- and lower-middle-class cultures.

In Bourdieu's later work, he introduces the idea of 'technical capital' – the idea that those who have technical expertise command certain resources and capacities.[27] Here he hints at the disruption which technical expertise, as distinct from that based on literacy and cultural resources, might pose to his account. Embedded in products and artefacts, technical expertise was historically embedded within the middle- and lower-brow world of 'trade', notably in skilled manual production. The capacity to know how to mobilize machinery and use tools usually involved theoretical as well as practical knowledge and carried its own status with it. During the nineteenth and twentieth centuries, the genteel middle-class culture recognized such technical prowess whilst also demarcating and domesticating it. The practice of scientific research and professional engineering was incorporated into a gentlemanly form, marking it off from the routines of practical craftsmen. There were also notable scientific intellectuals, perhaps most importantly, H. G. Wells, who was simultaneously a 'middlebrow' science fiction writer, a sociologist, a socialist, and a highly visible public figure. Yet, during the twentieth century, the importance of the scientist and technician began to be elevated in ways that were to challenge and ultimately break from this gentlemanly mode. New mechanisms, devices, and repertoires from the later 1930s involved a new kind of critical intellectual identity, which distanced itself from references to the middlebrow and which championed a new, scientific, emphasis positioned as a critique of gentility. In so far as we can see the appeal of science as lying in its formalism and abstraction, these scientists came to exemplify the 'intellectual' wing in Britain, in contrast to the French case where intellectuals were more clearly linked to the art, critical, and literary worlds. It is to the emergence of this technical identity and its challenge to gentlemanly culture that I now turn.

2.2 MASS-OBSERVATION: THE FORMATION OF THE INTELLECTUAL AS SOCIAL SCIENTIST

Mass-Observation is the most studied, and arguably the most important, social research institution of the mid-twentieth century. There are currently two

[27] Bourdieu (2002).

major approaches to its historiography. The first focuses on the distinctive visions and cultural politics of its diverse founders, the anthropologist and later Melanesian museum curator Tom Harrisson, the surrealist photographer Humphrey Jennings, and the poet turned sociologist Charles Madge. This explores in broad terms its politics and institutional achievements, its role in developing an iconoclastic surrealist social science of everyday life, and its longer-term legacy in pioneering anthropology 'at home', and qualitative research such as that which was to lead into life history.[28] Nick Hubble has recently drawn this work together to repudiate the disparagement of Mass-Observation by established anthropologists and sociologists by restating its subversive, revolutionary intent, identifying it as the practical application of the anti-auratic cultural politics advocated by Walter Benjamin. 'M-O founders were convinced that if the individualist democracy of the 1930s could be culturally combined with a working-class collective identity, a classless society could come into existence.'[29]

A second approach uses the vast amount of data collected by Mass-Observation as raw source material for social and cultural historical analysis. Historians of the Second World War have found this an especially valuable source material in recovering popular views of the war, which demonstrated a higher degree of popular scepticism towards the Churchill government than was previously assumed to be the case.[30] More recently, this source material has been deployed to study mid-century popular attitudes to sex and sexuality, and most importantly, anti-Semitism and racism.[31] An important aspect of this latter work has been to publish some of this data so that it can inform popular as well as academic understandings of social change. Simon Garfield's recent post-war and wartime diaries, as well as the diaries of other Mass-Observers, have been especially influential here, and Kynaston has recently deployed this material extensively in his account of *Austerity Britain*.[32]

Although this use of Mass-Observation material has valuably allowed popular narratives to inform historical research, it fails to address the fundamental issue of who the Mass-Observers actually were, and how we can read the processes by

---

[28] For examples, see Jeffrey (1999), Marcus (2001), Sheridan (2001), and especially Hubble (2006). A key aspect of this discussion concerns the need to remedy the 'neglect' and 'disparagement' of Mass-Observation by later social scientists. Whilst such a pleading may have been warranted twenty years ago, it is now abundantly clear that the source is now recognized as a major resource.

[29] Hubble (2006, 226–7). On Benjamin, see his (remarkable?) claim that 'Benjamin would have supported and understood the ideas behind M-O ... indeed Benajmin goes further than the founders themselves in expressing the logic of M-O, by arguing that mass audiences are replacing the function of the critic' (p. 122).

[30] Calder (1992), Addison (1975), and Summerfield (1988). A key aspect of this discussion concerns the need to remedy the 'neglect' and 'disparagement' of Mass-Observation by later social scientists.

[31] On the former, see Stanley (1995a) and on the latter, see Kushner (2004).

[32] Garfield (2004), Kynaston (2007), and Jolly (2001).

which their accounts were elicited.[33] Extending the contribution of Dorothy Sheridan, Penny Summerfield, and Liz Stanley, I champion a third way of examining Mass-Observation which is to focus on its 'audience', where we take this to be people who contributed to it – by writing diaries, day reports, letters in response to directives – as well as those who read its work. Here, we can take a lead from those writers who have argued that we need to see Mass-Observation as a social movement, which mobilized large numbers of people.[34] Well over 300 wrote diaries, and there were over 3,000 on the panel who responded to directives in its early years. Involvement could be labour intensive and time consuming, sometimes involving the daily keeping of diaries or writing long letters in response to directives. Why did the Mass-Observers do this? What did they want out of their involvement? What kind of statement were they making through their activism? Focusing on the diarists, Hynes argues that they were 'largely young, single, provincial and lower middle class, "the lonely bored livers of unexciting lives"'. Jeffrey is critical of this condescending interpretation, and argues instead that they 'volunteered to work for Mass-Observation because they wanted to be of some use in the fight against fascism and against official neglect of ordinary people'.[35] Hubble takes up this theme by suggesting that the early Mass-Observers were seeking to transcend established class divisions, and arguing that both its methods, which conflated the researcher and the researched, as well as its identification of the 'mass' as both the object and the vehicle of study, precisely marked this tension. Hubble traces a lineage to an alternative literary culture, consisting of exponents of critical intellectualism, schooled on H. G. Wells and through literary and social journals such as Ford's *English Review* and *The New Age*. This group of scientifically oriented intellectuals were, however, relatively weak in the earlier parts of the century: Mass-Observation was a vehicle which gave them their chance.[36]

None of these writers, however, has looked in detail at the directive responses (rather than the diaries or observational studies) to consider the identities of those involved. The Directive was a distinctive method pioneered in 1939, which asked Mass-Observers to write an open-ended letter in response to questions generated by Mass-Observation. Internal analyses of directive replies to one of the first questions which they asked, regarding Mass-Observers' social class identities, indicated that 15 per cent saw themselves as working class, 22 per cent as upper class, and 52 per cent as middle class. Given what we know of class identification in the middle years of the century,[37] this amounts to a massive over-representation of the upper as well as the middle classes, and does not suggest that they saw

[33] This is a particular problem with Kynaston's deployment of Mass-Observation, which treats these accounts at face value and does not explore how they were produced.

[34] See, for instance, Summerfield (1985).   [35] Jeffrey (1999, 29).

[36] On the earlier role of scientific culture, see Parrinder (2004, 20): 'the new scientifically and technically trained elite never became a political force, and remained largely invisible'.

[37] The standard source here is Glass (1954), admittedly based on survey responses conducted shortly after the Second World War.

themselves as 'marginal'. Looking at the recorded areas from which they wrote, large numbers lived in the South of England, and there is no obvious evidence of a provincial bias.[38] To be sure, as I discuss later, considerable numbers of these Mass-Observers identified with left-wing political causes, but by contrast, their interest or sympathy with ordinary people seems much less marked. What drew them to Mass-Observation, I argue, was their commitment to an emerging 'intellectual' identity. More precisely, by becoming Mass-Observers, writing diaries and responding to directives, they were identifying themselves as a kind of technical, 'social scientific' intellectual. This was largely a new species in the British context, and could not readily be classified within the familiar terms of 'high-', 'middle-', or 'low-' brow (terms which they only rarely used). To this extent, Hubble appears correct that the early Mass-Observers were indeed part of a rethinking of social relationships.

Detailed examination of the responses of 1939 to the directive asking about class identities indicates how intellect was seen not to be the property of the upper classes alone. Many correspondents emphasized that you could find intellectuals from different classes, and the working class was not, by and large, inherently 'un-intellectual'. The widespread commitment to a form of Labour and socialist politics meant that they embraced certain kinds of educated, politicized 'working class' people as the kind of person with whom they would want to associate, and who might also be 'intellectuals'. A good example is the following case, where one Mass-Observer insisted that he was

> Middle class, not of the weekly wage earning variety or of the private business or landed section but belonging to the monthly salary variety, whether employers be public authorities, universities, etc or private business. More exactly than this, however, I feel I belong to the section called the intelligentsia (which of course, over-laps partly into the 'working class' and into almost the whole of 'the upper class'), a group of people who have had university education, or at least, some form of higher education....I feel it is here a question of conditions of life and background interests and outlook rather than money that matters with this intelligentsia.
>
> I am very much at ease with working class who are left wing and therefore are or crave to be 'educated' and have serious interests....I am embarrassed with working class people who are only interested in football, racing, etc because I can't talk about these subjects.[39]

However, we should not be too sanguine about the revolutionary potential of this call to the intellectual. Most Mass-Observers were happy to use class idioms and were mainly seeking to redraw them, as a critical response to aspects of 'middle-class' culture.[40] Interestingly, the upper class was rarely the target of this kind of

---

[38] Mass-Observation Directive (A). See the appendix for further details on this, and all subsequent M-O directives. Not all writers indicated their address, so firm quantitative evidence cannot readily be supplied.

[39] M-O (A), JGC.

[40] It should further be noted here that Kushner's study of the Mass-Observers' views on ethnicity at this time also indicate the strong hold of racist views, especially around anti-Semitism and the need to prevent miscegenation.

criticism, and many sections of the middle class were also exempted (if only because Mass-Observers were usually frank enough to position themselves clearly within it). Furthermore, although overt hostility to the working class was limited, this was in large part because their world was seen as not very salient to their concerns.[41]

One emblematic account can be used here. When asked in 1939, three months before the onset of war, what kind of people he felt comfortable dealing with, one young man noted that he felt

> most at ease with well read, travelled and life experienced members of the techni-
> cally trained classes – usually secondary school, night school, educated £5 a week
> men. But they must be 'hard boiled' – no time for the mugwump. Feel embarrassed
> with classes of £8 a week and over and also with the very low, ignorant, poverty
> stricken classes – labourers etc.

> Example: when first came to live in this house, used occasionally to spend evening
> with local public school acquaintances and invite them in return. Do not do so
> now. Was bored, when not definitely irritated by shallow 'small talk' apparently
> customary in such circles. Embarrassed by inability to sustain such a conversa-
> tion. Rendered taciturn by doubts of the reception of my bolshie and tough
> minded views on life and things would receive. Embarrassed by references to
> expensive hobbies and purchases I could not afford – motoring, golf, flying,
> tourist trips, good dances of dinner jacket 10/- ticket type, etc. could not be
> amused by their footling ideas of humour and jokes and failed to make them
> laugh with my own sardonic and cynical and rather improper comments on love,
> marriage, politics and 'class distinctions'. These people were not exactly
> mugwumps – they'd travelled and they'd experienced hardships. But their whole
> attitude was different because they had never experienced actual and desperate
> poverty – destitution.

> Further example: railway carriage full of labourers. Discussion of 'Thetis' subma-
> rine disaster. Was embarrassed as soon as I opened my mouth to join in discussion,
> because they stopped speaking, stared at me. Conversation became stilted and fell
> off. Violent contrast between my accent and theirs. Uncomfortably noticed glances
> at my neat shoes, collar and tie, etc.[42]

A number of aspects are worth noting here. Firstly, the absolutely easy and straightforward way in which he recounts these incidents. There is no sense of embarrassment about the fact that he had difficulties in relating to particular social groups, and that he preferred certain kinds of people. It is a very different discourse from that which I found in my research with Gaynor Bagnall and Brian Longhurst in Manchester in the later 1990s where there was a domi-nant ethic that 'one should be able to get on with anyone', and people were rarely

---

[41] Here it is likely that there are important differences between directive writers, whose involve-ment with Mass-Observation was limited to their writing letters, and those involved more actively, for instance in the observation of the masses, who might have been more likely to challenge cultural boundaries.

[42] M-O (A), C1.

keen to draw attention to their unease when they were with certain kinds of people.[43]

Secondly, we see a double negative reaction, to both 'labourers', and 'public school' acquaintances. The ordering and detail are telling. The public school boys are mentioned first and he unravels his displeasure with them in more detail, and in more subtle, and also more heartfelt ways, than he does with the labourers. He is a complete outsider to the labourers, with no point of contact. He is more attentive, however, to the possibility that he could have been like his old public school friends but for his own individuality, experiences, and values. He is ultimately more fascinated by them than he is by the labourers. Nonetheless, this order of priorities is revealing in showing how this nascent intellectual identity involved a separation from staid middle-class identities as well as a repudiation of the world of labourers.

But, thirdly, what we also see is a nascent identity as part of the 'technically trained class', one which lacks the privileges of the professional middle classes, and which evokes a different kind of identity from that of the humanities-oriented 'gentleman'. This is not an isolated response: another Mass-Observer identified as part of a 'scientist' class which he saw as isolated from other classes. As Nick Hubble notes, the idea of encouraging such a 'technical' class was itself close to the aspirations of the founders of Mass-Observation. It was also to be a theme of George Orwell in his influential advocacy of a form of classless English-ness in his essay 'The Lion and the Unicorn'.[44]

We should not exaggerate the numbers who defined themselves in these 'technical' terms at this point – it remained at best a protean identity at this stage. Nonetheless, the Mass-Observers staked out, through their very involvement a commitment to research and inquiry were questioning a 'gentle' identity and groping towards a new sense of themselves. In staking out this vision, it is striking how two common spatial motifs were invoked in this 'boundary' work. One involved reacting against 'county' society and the other was a reaction to the 'suburban' middle class. In both cases, claiming intellectuality was related to a repudiation of a fixed spatial location. In a thoroughly Bourdieusian sense, intellectualism involved abstracting from location, creating what Timothy Mitchell in a different context calls a 'locationless logic'. It required the lifting of expertise away from the physical landscape in which gentlemanly status was held to reside.

The refrain against county was a direct repudiation of the perceived un-intelligence of the aristocratic, landed ethos. Thus one Mass-Observer claimed to be embarrassed to deal with the 'rather haughty type of person, county or aspiring to be county, who looked through me', whilst another was distressed

---

[43] I remember my surprise when one respondent (a skilled manual worker) actually stated openly that he preferred the company of school teachers to other kinds of people.

[44] Reprinted in *Orwell's England*(2001). This essay appeared after the Mass-Observation directives discussed above, so there is no possibility that the Mass-Observers were responding to Orwell's cue.

by the 'very class conscious, army people and county people who ask at once, "who is she?"'. She went on to say that 'The only class I ever feel awkward with is the "county" class – hunting, shooting, fishing, hard drinking'.

If the intellectual identity involved peeling off from the world of 'county', this was still less heartfelt than the horror of suburbia. Here, intellectual identities found common cause with the metropolitan vision of Bloomsbury and the modernists. Suburbanites were defined disparagingly as 'the ultra respectable lower middle class'. This anti-suburban sentiment crystallizes very clearly with a nascent intellectual identity in the words of a 29-year-old librarian who, when asked his class identity, replied:

> I am embarrassed by and (and can't even stick) the suburban, bridge playing, motoring, and West End theatre going people, not university educated...who think they are being highbrow by reading Charles Morgan and Cronin and going to hear Charles Laughton, who cultivate 'an accent' and mispronounce French badly, who have possibly read translations of whipper-snappers like Pierre Loti and Maetternich but who gape at you blankly with a kind of asinine British stare when you remark to them, over the garden wall, that we appear to be doing exactly what Voltaire recommended – cultivating our gardens, and who thought, when Chamberlain quoted Shakespeare, that the quotations were both felicitous and correct.[45]

This is clearly a heartfelt set of prejudices. The locations brought to bear in condemning the non-educated middle class range widely, from the West End to the suburban garden. Yet we can also sense that this specific reaction against the experiences and tastes of the suburban middle class is born from a certain familiarity with their lifestyles. He may not be as different from those who have read Pierre Loti as he might like to think or hope. Given the ambivalence of these boundaries, becoming a Mass-Observer was itself a means of demonstrating one's difference through a commitment to writing, research, and self-reflection. What we therefore see is the evocation of a particular kind of intellectual identity that departs from the 'sanitized' version, and which locates it in the citadels of the university and the monthly salary (so ruling out pretty much all of Bloomsbury and the highbrow cultural establishment).

What we see is a sense of breaking from spatial constraints which are also social restraints. The appeal of the country, nearly always seen as an abstract space of freedom, rather than as a peopled, worked, and weathered landscape, lies in its status as a repository of 'escape'. One highly unusual Mass-Observer, who worked in industry as a manager of a weaving factory, identified this powerful current in semi-ironic terms. Recognizing himself as a member of the 'industrial lower middle class' he went on to note ironically, that 'isn't it a heavenly strata of society?' Warming to his theme, a stream of invective followed, setting off the staid qualities of his hometown with the 'freedom' that the countryside offered.

[45] M-O (A), JGC.

In a place like Bradford, culture counts for very little. Small organisations, civic theatre etc – for promoting culture are run by upper middle class cliques, pseudo highbrows, whose affectations are rather intolerable.... I'm most at ease with the working class. Find it difficult after 10 minute conversation with my neighbours to fall into their futile talk of bourgeois values: weddings of local mill owner families, bridge parties, etc. I'm at ease with anybody who loves the country, music, poetry, with anybody who listens eagerly for a new viewpoint. My wife and I hate curtains, so neighbours think we're eccentric. They love to stay at home, proud of their suburban home and garden. We love to get away from it in our extravagance, the car! They love to chatter about 'housy' things, painting, each other's children, empty gossip. We want our baby to kick its limbs on the top of some moors, and to come to consciousness to the accompaniment of bird song, waterfalls, lovely music. They want pictures (cinema) dances, socials, which although we can imagine might be very valuable, seem to us here as impedimenta. God preserve us from our industrial lower middle class.[46]

We can read, then, the accounts of the 1939 Mass-Observers as seeking out an intellectual space, one which did not reproduce existing class divisions, but which creatively sought to use Mass-Observation to distance itself from gentlemanly, artistic, highbrow motifs in favour of a more 'technical', scientific intellectual vision, one concerned to free itself from fixed spatial location. This current reworked political tensions within the modernist aesthetic between those wedded strongly to political Liberalism (such as Keynes) and those attracted to radical, Marxist politics. The appeal of Marxism to the modernist intellectuals, especially in the 1930s, is well known, with figures such as W. H. Auden, Anthony Blunt, Christopher Isherwood, and numerous others ostensibly rejecting the aesthetic aristocracy in favour of a commitment to communism. The Mass-Observers had very little affiliation with Marxism or Communist politics, which they often saw as part of the elite cultural reflex they were trying to avoid. One person, for instance, did not feel comfortable with 'middle class communists who are anxious to be proletarians'. Their commitment to the Labour movement was anchored around the idea of a planned, rational government, which was at one with their vision of the intellectual, and had little time for the utopianism of the communist vision.

From this point of view, the rise of Mass-Observation was indicative of a new kind of intellectual formation which challenged conventional hierarchies and especially the importance of the 'brow' distinctions. They did not identify as 'elitist' highbrows, but nor were they satisfied with writing from the 'middle-brow'. Here Mass-Observation was part of a larger movement. The sudden success of Penguin paperback books was a case in point. Founded at roughly the same time, 1936, Penguins broke from a gentlemanly culture relying on either expensive hardbacks for a respectable readership, or discounts for the mass market, and offered new paperbacks at the cheap price of 6d. Shortly after their inception, and in view of the difficulty of gaining rights to publish fictional work

---

[46] M-O (A), C2.

in paperback form, the publisher, Allen Lane, began to commission Pelicans, non-fictional works covering science, current affairs, and the nascent social sciences. This kind of factual documentary writing was easier to commission and had no extensive hardback equivalent to compete with. The success of the paperback in this format is worthy of note: it is one of the few examples of consumer innovation in which the British preceded the Americans who were much more hesitant in taking up the paperback form.[47]

It is not coincidental that when in 1946 Mass-Observation asked its correspondents to talk about their paperback book collection, nearly all respondents identified having a large stock of Pelicans and social science books. Of those who were prepared to give details, the average number of paperbacks identified was forty-four, but this understates the figure since it was impractical for those with very large collections to provide full lists. But, more interestingly, only a handful of those with paperbacks had no social science books amongst their collection.[48] One observer did not give a list but noted that 'most of the paper covered books are Penguins and Pelicans. The subjects range from biography to politics and social conditions. When I used to teach current events I bought every Penguin that came out about India, China, etc.... psychology, science, town planning are included'. The range of social science books which the Mass-Observers held was remarkable, ranging from the Pelican stock of Sigmund Freud (easily the most popular 'social' scientist amongst them), the anthropologist Margaret Mead, James Burnham (whose book *The Managerial Revolution* which proclaimed the replacement of the owners of businesses by a new managerial class no doubt struck a hopeful chord with many Mass-Observers), 'technical', and of course Mass-Observation books. There were a smattering of references to the books of G. D. H. Cole and R. H. Tawney, and it was common to stock reference books on town planning, local government, sex education, health, world affairs, and social insurance. Several Mass-Observers made a point of buying Government Reports, especially the Beveridge Report.[49] One had even purchased the 'Clapham Report on Social and Economic Research' (on which, see Chapter 4). There was, however, no evidence that Marx was read, let alone the canon of sociologists such as Durkheim or Weber who were to frame sociological thinking from the 1960s and who were still mainly untranslated into English.

---

[47] See Lewis (2006).

[48] M-O (B). Only four had no paperbacks. Eleven said they could not provide a full list. Only three of the remaining twenty-one who list their paperback books reported no social science titles. Those who had more books also reported higher numbers of such titles. A good example of the relationship between hardbacks and paperbacks is provided by one observer who had the time and energy to provide a complete list of both. Her 252 hardbacks contained only seventeen fiction and twelve economics and politics titles. Her 169 paperbacks included thirty-four economics and politics and fifty fiction titles, indicating how such formats were generated by the paperback itself.

[49] M-O (B). Six of the twenty-one with social science titles had Freud, four Mead, and three Burnham. One observer noted that 'If the Stationery Office publishes a pamphlet or small book on anything I am interested in, e.g. health, national insurance, company law, I should get it... if anyone else such as Penguin published some other view on the same subject I should get that also'.

Was this interest in the social sciences new? Jonathan Rose's study of popular audiences for reading in the earlier twentieth century suggests that it was. The educated, 'intellectual' working class examined in Sheffield in 1918 were familiar with natural scientists (Edison, Darwin, and Watt) or with literary and cultural figures (Dickens, Milton, Ruskin, and Shakespeare), but no social scientist with the exception of Herbert Spencer was mentioned.[50] Amongst the autodidact South Wales miners, a survey of nineteen miners' libraries catalogues between 1903 and 1931 found that the social sciences accounted for only 5.3 per cent of book stock.[51] The partial exception was amongst the Workers Education Association, which, revealingly, overlapped with the culture of Mass-Observation, and which had also grown considerably during the 1930s. In 1938–9, 58.4 per cent of its classes were in the social sciences, with a strong orientation towards economics.[52]

This emerging intellectual scientific group increasingly lost contact with modernist literature. For instance, *Penguin New Writing*, set up in 1940 to publish a diverse blend of little known and experimental writers, became increasingly stilted during the war years and lost most of its circulation by the end of the war and was forced to close.[53] This was, in short, a group increasingly committed to the cause of applied social research as part of their intellectual identities. By the eve of the Second World War, we can see the emergence of a distinctive intellectual group which reacted against the leisured world of the industrialists, but not, as in Bourdieu's France, by taking up the role of the artistic and cultural avant-garde (who, in the eyes of the Mass-Observers, were too closely associated with the 'aristocratic' world), but instead by adopting the role of the technician and the scientist. Vehicles such as Mass-Observation, the WEA, the Left Book Clubs, and Pelican paperbacks were vital in elaborating the infrastructure which permitted this group to articulate itself. The Kantian aesthetic, in so far as it existed, now rode under the banner of science and administration as well as art. This was a group which was to seize on the opportunities for technical and scientific expertise elaborated in the military regime of the Second World War to carve out a distinctive place for itself in English society.

---

[50] Rose (2001, table 6.1)   [51] Rose (2001, 248).   [52] Rose (2001, 294).

[53] See Hubble's revealing quote (2006, 207–8), of one Mass-Observer who shows resentment at its loss of novelty and focus on working-class characters.

3

1954: The Challenge of Technical Identity

In Chapter 2, I traced how the new Mass-Observers of the late 1930s forged an intellectual identity attracted to the scientific ethos. In this chapter, I will explore how this vision melded into a clearly social scientific one by the 1960s. My argument will be that the changing relations between the middle and working classes encouraged amongst the former both a rejection of the gentlemanly embrace, which was seen to be out of keeping with the meritocratic tenor of post-war Britain, and a new interest in rational planning, which was to prove receptive to the social sciences. This recognition leads us to understand cultural change in the 1950s and 1960s less in terms of the widely discussed mobilization of literary and cultural figures, famously in the figure of the 'angry young men', and more in terms of the less visible yet ultimately more significant assertion of 'soft' scientific values.[1]

In developing this argument, I take my cue from David Edgerton's emphasis that we need to understand social change in twentieth-century Britain not through the lens of the supposed rise (and then fall) of the welfare state, but in terms of the obduracy and persistence of the 'military–industrial complex'. Conventionally, the rise of the social sciences has been linked to the growing welfare state, through its historical association with social work and education.[2] However, Edgerton rightly insists that it is the military imperative which has been fundamental to twentieth-century British history, and I want to show how it shaped the social scientific vision as it developed during the post-war years. Rather than a fundamental concern with welfare, I want to argue, the social sciences were shaped by a managerial concern, strongly indebted to cultures of war, mobilization, and demobilization. This argument runs parallel to Nikolas Rose's emphasis on the way that the post-war social sciences became critically involved in new projects of 'governmentality' that sought to 'rule through freedom'.[3] Rooted in the prominence of psychology, which had come to the fore

[1] For examples of accounts which focus on literary and cultural history, see Sandbrook (2004) and Marwick (1996).

[2] This is particularly true in Halsey's history of British sociology, which invokes a 'political arithmetic' tradition concerned with governance and welfare. I return to contest this account in Chapter 4.

[3] Rose (1999*a*).

during the war years and was to have major influence thereafter, Rose shows how these intellectual currents framed a science of the individual which was also a science of society. The project of managing democracy involved the creation of 'responsible' individuals who were capable of self-regulation and thus automatically aligned themselves to the social order of neo-liberal democracies. The social sciences, therefore, do not merely respond to a changing external environment but are themselves implicated in new forms of governmentality, regulation, and social imaginary.

3.1 THE SECOND WORLD WAR AND THE REMAKING OF CLASS RELATIONS

In his account of the decline of Mass-Observation after the war years, Hubble attributes its loss of momentum to the hardening of class divisions.

> The trend of bringing the politicised sections of the new middle and working classes together by showing everyday life as a site of public contestation was reversed as workers were relegated once more to the resistant sphere of the everyday.... The general effect on society was the re-introduction of firm 'working class' and 'middle class' stereotypes which had been losing their rigidity in the late 1930s.[4]

The hardening of class divisions in this period has been commented on by several historians, mainly around the theme of a middle-class backlash, as they reacted to a Labour government committed to social welfare and economic redistribution. McKibbin has examined the reasons why the middle classes felt under attack.[5] Servant keeping declined dramatically. Many amongst the middle classes could not keep motor cars in the way they had between the wars. In terms of income, white-collar workers lost ground to manual workers of all kinds: manual earnings rose 141 per cent between 1937 and 1949, whereas the incomes of higher professionals rose by 88 per cent. Evidence on social mobility suggests bleak prospects. Although Glass, reporting the first-ever national survey of social mobility carried out in 1949, draws attention to the way that the professionals predominantly self-recruited (with 48.5 per cent of professional men themselves being sons of professional fathers), his findings also offered much less cheery news. Slightly less than 50 per cent of the sons of professionals had non-professional or managerial jobs. Perhaps most tellingly of all, in the sample there were more fathers who were professionals than there were sons, indicating that prospects for these groups had actually retracted during the difficult interwar years.[6]

---

[4] Hubble (2006, 206).   [5] McKibbin (1998).
[6] It is important here to recognize the implications of the difference between absolute and relative mobility rates, for which see Goldthorpe (1987). In 1949, given that there were so few professionals

Within professional and managerial ranks, there was an emerging gap between the more technically oriented middle classes and the more established, gentlemanly groups. The technical, scientific cadres had expanded considerably as a result of wartime policy. Between 1931 and 1951, the number of scientists, army officers, and engineers rose from about 100,000 to nearly a quarter of a million. By this time, they easily outstripped the 'gentlemanly' professionals in accounting, medicine, law, writing, and the church, whose numbers rose more modestly from 160,000 to 200,000.[7] The professional, scientific, and technical corps of the civil service rose from 6,500 in 1929 to 23,100 in 1950 (by which time it easily outstaffed the 'gentlemanly' administrative corps of whom there were only 3,000). The administrative cadre of the civil service saw its income rise by 28 per cent between 1938 and 1950, whereas the post office engineers saw their pay rise by 107 per cent. Structurally then, the new technical wing of the intelligentsia emerged from the war in an unprecedented position. Edgerton thus argues:

> The state research corps was just one part of a hugely expanded scientific and technical effort associated with the warfare state. This warfare state, not the welfare state, had the decisive influence on the wartime and post-war development of the British university. The university became a much more scientific place, and a more masculine place than it had been before the war.[8]

Edgerton's insistence on the rise of the masculine, scientific middle class challenges the influential accounts of cultural change which see the old highbrow modernists achieving much more complete cohesion and dominance than ever before in the years after 1945. In the later 1940s, the collapse of the 'middlebrow' ethic and the renascence of the modernist highbrow, institutionally supported by a much better resourced state apparatus, is often seen as making the years between 1945 and 1955 the 'golden age' of the modernist cultural establishment. In *Our Age* (Lord) Noel Annan, Cambridge don, intellectual historian, first vice chancellor of the University of London, and leading cultural broker between the 1950s and the 1970s, offers a strident defence of the power and value of this modernist, gentlemanly establishment which he pointedly called *The Generation that Made Post-War Britain*. Expanding on the definition provided by the don Maurice Bowra, he saw this as a generation consisting of 'those who make their times significant and form opinion'. 'It goes without saying that he expected them to come from the upper or middle classes, to grow up in public schools, and

---

in the labour market (slightly under 3 per cent of Glass's sample, for instance), the fact that 38.8 per cent of the sons of professional fathers were themselves professionals marks a very striking over-representation, as Glass emphasizes. However, this should not blind us to the fact that in absolute terms, a large number of sons of professional parents were downwardly mobile. As Goldthorpe (1987) brings out, by 1972, when the Oxford Mobility Study was conducted, in absolute terms, the proportion of sons of his social class 1 who were downwardly mobile had declined, though only because of the greater opportunities for them to move to professional and managerial jobs.

[7] Figures derived from Edgerton (2006, figure 4.1). In fact, the modest rise in 'gentlemanly' professionals was nearly entirely accounted for by the rising number of accountants.

[8] Edgerton (2006, 148). See also Harrison (2009).

go to Oxford or Cambridge. He should have added the London School of Economics. These were the three places where ideas fermented'.[9] Annan identifies what he sees as their progressive characteristics: their liberalism, their bohemianism, their commitment to artistic and intellectual values, and their central role in creating core post-war cultural institutions.

These were the years when a cultural apparatus was formed which allowed modernist artists to achieve unprecedented economic security. One of Keynes's last acts before his death in 1946 was to preside over the formation of the Council for the Encouragement of Music and the Arts (CEMA) in 1942, which was to become the Arts Council, and then succeeded in placing his Bloomsbury contacts on the commissioning panel whilst marginalizing the Royal Academy establishment.[10] More important than this was the formation of the BBC's *Third Programme* in 1946. Whereas highbrows between the wars had largely scorned the radio as vulgar and plebeian, there was growing interest in the post-war years in using it as a means of disseminating cultural values, partly as a result of its wartime importance as a vehicle of communication, and as Collini emphasizes, it also became a lucrative source of funds for the intellectuals themselves, with the fee of 20 guineas for a learned talk being amongst the best possible at the time.

In his famous paper in *Encounter* in 1955, the American sociologist Edward Shils was to identify how these developments marked a new, post-war fusion between the intellectual and aristocratic worlds. He argued:

> The re-establishment of amicable and harmonious relations between the intellectual and British society has really been the unification of the intellectuals with the other groups of the ruling elite...the culture which has now regained moral ascendancy is not an aristocratic one in the sense that it is the present culture of an active aristocracy...it is the culture traditionally inspired by those classes, the culture appropriate to certain institutions allied to these classes...it is pluralistic culture within itself; it has room for politicians, for sportsmen, for travelers, for civil servants and judges and barristers and journalists, for artists and writers of different persuasions. It is an unbourgeois culture.[11]

At one level, this can only be read as an astonishing piece of chutzpah. It is a breathtaking manoeuvre to define aristocratic culture as somehow open to everyone. What Shils stages, however, is a hugely important intellectual move. Rather than representing the aristocracy as a 'traditional' social group, to which unthinking, habitual fealty is due, he portrays it as a thoroughly 'modern' group, whose intellectual and cultural properties mean that there are rational reasons for valuing it.[12] Shils thus announces the death of 'traditionalism' in intellectual culture, and instead indicates how the merits of the aristocracy, just like any other social group, need to be evaluated pragmatically. It is for these reasons that he sees the aristocrats as preferable to the bourgeois philistine. Certainly,

[9] Annan (1991).   [10] Skidelsky (2003).   [11] Shils (1955).

[12] He is thus, knowingly or unknowingly, repudiating one reading of Weberian sociological views, which were to be reiterated in the 1960s by Perry Anderson, that the aristocracy were somehow a 'traditional' social formation.

this reaction against bourgeois culture was designed to appeal to the 'intellectuals' of Mass-Observation, as a rallying cry for the technicians and scientists to find common cause with the elite groups they had previously disdained. Notably, he holds out a subtle blending of an ethic of leisure, relaxed consumption, gentlemanly pursuits, and high culture as the reward for this calling.

> continental holidays, the connoisseurship of wine and food, the knowledge of wild flowers and birds, acquaintance with the writings of Jane Austen, a knowing indulgence for the worthies of the English past, an appreciation of "more leisurely epochs", doing one's job dutifully and reliably, the cultivation of personal relations – these are the elements of the newly emerging British intellectual class.[13]

Shils was not himself part of the reconciled gentry elite that he describes. He was American. He was a sociologist – indeed, he was a figure in the emergence of the quantitative, managerial, psychologically focused social science that was championed in the United States during the Second World War, and which Nikolas Rose identifies as representative of new forms of governmentality.[14] As Collini rightly points out, Shils's account needs to be read as a call to arms, rather than an effective demonstration that an actual reconciliation has actually taken place. It is, in short, a piece of cold war propaganda. Moreover, it is distinctly mischievous, since whatever limitations it may have as a 'sociological' account of the post-war intelligentsia, it is a very apt pen-portrait of Stephen Spender, the editor of *Encounter*, the new (CIA-funded) journal in which Shils's article appeared. Spender is emblematic of the reconciliation of the intellectuals with the aristocracy that Shils claims is characteristic of post-war Britain: having been a member of the Communist Party in the 1930s, when he rejected living in England and migrated, like his peers Auden and Isherwood, to other parts of Europe, Spender later returned to England, became a pillar of the literary establishment, took on extra commissions, and graciously accepted visiting professorships from American universities to pay for his children to attend private school (like Keynes, Spender had given up his youthful homosexuality in favour of respectable marriage and family). One might, in fact, argue that Shils misses out the third major player in his advocated reconciliation between the intellectuals and the aristocracy, the American educational and security apparatus which allowed the post-war intelligentsia unparalleled access to its largesse.[15]

Spender's own formulations about the cultural politics of the post-war years are revealing here, since, like Shils, he redraws the aesthetic battle lines in different formation from those of the 'brow wars' of the interwar years. In order to encourage rank-and-file intellectuals not to be intimidated by the genteel

---

[13] Shils (1955).

[14] See Rose (1999*a*). Rose's general arguments will be taken up in detail in the following chapters.

[15] Unless they were Communists of course. The peripatetic Marxist historian Eric Hobsbawm did not manage to get a visiting professorship there until 1960, and then only courtesy of one of the few powerful Marxist American academics, Paul Baran, and the fact that the US Consulate forgot to ask him whether he was a Communist. See Hobsbawm (2002, 389–90).

'high brows', he expanded the boundaries of the modernists. An early editorial sees him distinguishing two artistic camps. The first were those haunted by 'renascence ghosts', and included Wilde, Lawrence, and Forster whom he identifies as seeking to articulate the great aspects of past culture informing contemporary social life. Against this group, Spender defined the 'modernist establishment', characterized by Tennyson, Dickens, Baudelaire, Proust, Joyce, and Eliot who seek to construct a pure 'inside' world, 'because they think there is something irredeemable about the "outside" modern materialist one'. This distinction between 'contemporaries' and 'modernists' (with the latter being the group that Spender supports) was taken up elsewhere, but strikingly, Spender sought to include within the modernist camp writers conventionally seen as part of the middlebrow, notably Dickens. He thus seeks to draw wider boundaries and encourage the movement of middlebrows into it. In addition, Spender wanted this modernist group to take up its worldly mission. To be sure he recognizes that they must accept – in true Eliot mould – the world as 'grim and doomed' and seek 'ordering an inner world of the mind, outside time and history'. At the same time, he insists that young artists need to sign up for a worldly form of the pure aesthetic, 'we hope they remember that the idea of a renascence, though expressed by individuals with a personal passion, is also social. It aims at transforming the outward living scene, the Modern City, and not just at creating the interior world of "cerebral" art.' Spender, thus, clearly articulates the need for an institutional shell to nurture his broadly defined modernist elite, and it is here that the appeal of the gentry resides.

There was also an unremarked spatial politics around this lobbying for a dominant gentry, with a central plank involving the disparaging of the kind of 'provincialism' that had proved such fertile soil for 'middlebrow' culture. One of the central calls of *Encounter* was the clear and definite cultural authority of London, and the absolute limits of provincial culture. A major feature of Shils's argument is premised on the lack of a credible cultural alternative to the metropolis as cultural heartland. For even when the 'alienated' intellectuals engaged in their European jaunts in the 1930s, he notes, their emotional capitals ranged from Moscow, Baghdad, Paris, Berlin, Los Angeles but

> it was in any case not London. It was certainly not Manchester or Bristol or Liverpool or Glasgow ... the movement towards London in the twenties and thirties was not merely a demographic fact. It was associated with the assertion of the cultural supremacy of London society – and with it, of Oxford and Cambridge – over the provincial centres.[16]

This theme of the absolute dominance of Oxbridge and London was to be marked in Shils's own biography – he was one of the few sociologists to be employed there and, as we have seen, forms a central part of Noel Annan's ode to his generation. The disparaging of 'provincial' middlebrow culture was an important feature of

---

[16] Shils (1955).

this current. It was further announced in A. J. P Taylor's essay on Manchester published in *Encounter*, which was intriguingly the first of a series on major 'world cities'. Taylor (in the early 1930s a lecturer of History at the University of Manchester, but since 1938 ensconced, though not always comfortably, at Oxford), emphasized how Manchester, the 'last Hanseatic trading city', had at one time offered a credible urban alternative to London. He emphasized how Manchester had pioneered the professional orchestra (the Hallé), the liberal newspaper (the *Manchester Guardian*), and the liberal free trade ethic that predominated in the Victorian age. He was emphatic, however, that during the twentieth century this vision had collapsed, marking the end of the city's cultural writ.

The call to mobilize intellectuals to the gentry involved both carrot and stick. It offered a wider-ranging set of cultural referents than had been allowed within interwar highbrow culture and so offered the potential for an extended group of intellectuals to claim it as their own. However, this inclusion was also premised on an absolutist cultural geography which permitted no challenge to the metropolis. How did this appeal to the technical intelligentsia which had begun to define itself through Mass-Observation and related means in the pre-war years? Initially, it appealed strongly, for this group shared, in general, class resentment against the loss of status in the face of what they saw as a harsh government intent on improving the lot of the working class at their expense.

A strong sense of the insecurity of the Mass-Observers is evident from responses to a directive in 1948 asking Mass-Observers to identify the 'six main inconveniences of modern living'. Like numerous others Britons of the times, they identified rationing, transport shortages, food shortages, and housing.[17] However, it is not clear that the middle classes were particularly hard done by through these measures, and it is the tone of their responses that is more significant. Running through their replies, what is apparent is that it was less the mere inconvenience of rationing so much as the loss of 'style'. It was not the lack of food itself, so much as the fact that one had to queue, that it was 'monotonous', and that shops had an 'independent' attitude. It was not only the fact of rationing, but also the 'bother of collecting coupons'. These inconveniences not infrequently burst out into social prejudices of various kinds, concerned with 'the relative decline, in short, of middle class purchasing power compared with that of the masses', against 'the insanity of many public servants', or 'the economic costs of pampering uninteresting classes of people'.

This sense of loss of status and grace was attributed in large part to the way that bureaucratic regulation associated with post-war reconstruction seemed to

---

[17] M-O (D). See generally, Zweininger-Bargielowska (2001). It is interesting that in general she does not dwell on class differences in reactions to rationing. My analysis of M-O replies indicates that thirty-nine out of fifty-three identified food-related inconveniences, thirty-eight griped about transport (including queuing, cost of petrol, transport restrictions), and twenty-nine about housing shortages or overcrowding. There was a total of twenty-six concerns about social, moral, or civil issues, such as the lack of civility, the lack of domestic servants, the attitude of public servants, and bad manners.

eliminate the 'personal' factor by which the middle classes had traditionally commanded status privileges:

> the lack of civility one meets with in shops, restaurants, and all places where one pays out money and expects service, but seldom gets it.
>
> [S]ecurity seems to have gone to Hell. I am of course referring to social security. Inspectors can come into one's home to see if you are starving...or are responsible for causing television interferences. One can't build a house without a tremendous amount of form filling.... The things we took for granted... have just been forgotten during the war years...and we take it for granted that people can search your home.[18]

Interestingly, this sense that formal regulation stripped away the informal status of the middle classes created a strong anti-working class feeling. Thus, the doctor mentioned earlier went on to say that 'I feel the present government to be actively and dangerously hostile to me personally, and to my standards of life and thought which I have always considered to be superior to the masses. I am resentful of ignorant men making pronouncements concerning me and aesthetic values'.[19] Certainly, in contrast to the relatively benign view towards the workers which characterized the 1930s Mass-Observers, remarkably intense hostility became more apparent in the post-war austerity years. It is very evident in the Mass-Observation diaries collected by Simon Garfield, where the appeal of the 'pure' world of quality is internalized, even by relatively disadvantaged households, as a utopian projection of a better world, and contrasted with the contamination of the post-war working class.[20] For Maggie Joy Blount, an aspiring Slough clerk, keen to get on, but ultimately able only to subsist by letting out her house to holiday makers,

> middle class dissatisfaction with the government seems to be increasing. All the professional people I hear of are gravely uneasy. We seem to be in a tangle that only gets worse and which will never unravel.[21]

For Blount, this concern is linked to a politics of the pure aesthetic.

> Why not change the emphasis from wealth, power, importance, (aggrandise-ment) to cultural and spiritual things – from quantity of possessions to *quality* of possessions? This seems to me much more important. I think if we did, we could contribute something of much importance and value to the whole world. I have a feeling that our people, the ordinary, hum drum classes from the middle-middle downwards have more in them of potential creative ability, imagination, initiative, character and inherent wisdom than in any other race in the world.[22]

Similar sentiments were expressed in responses to directives, notably those in January 1949, which asked people what value they attached to the continued existence of the middle classes?

---

[18] M-O (D): 4201.   [19] M-O (D): 1371.   [20] Garfield (2004).
[21] Garfield (2004, 375).   [22] Quoted in Garfield (2004, 17 March 1947).

This is where the social revolution is most hitting me. It is the subjective emotional factor which was always forgotten when the left intellectual (and I was verging on that myself) was arguing pre war about 'raising the status of the masses'....It is a most serious upsetting factor in everyday life to find that *one has less money to spend* than people who educationally, socially, culturally – and even morally – are in some degree or other one's inferiors....It is, in some ways, hard to keep up the pretence of the 'good life' when one sees people (skilled engineers, etc) who have so enormously benefited by the change in the social structure riding about in cars and buying (the mark of the new rich) television sets....It is only by holding firmly onto good standards in matters of cultural taste (how priggish this sounds!) that one can still feel that there is a difference between me and the masses.[23]

How priggish indeed! But there is no doubting the power of this appeal, even for apparently 'modern' affairs. Consider, for instance, the most popular driving manual of its day, written in 1952. Tellingly entitled *Car Driving as an Art* (and hence, not a matter of technique), it concludes by appropriating the putatively modern motor car to a very old, venerable, practice, that of driving horse vehicles. 'Manners and nothing else are at the root of really good roadmanship, and motoring at its best is so enjoyable that it is worth much unselfishness. As in days of old a man had to look after his horse, so the really good driver must look after his car and will be repaid in full for his trouble.'[24] Here we have, in all its splendour, Shils's vision of the intellectual class shifting into the comforting embrace of the gentry, chased by the spectre of a newly prosperous and assertive working class. As this working class became more visible and was seen as more powerful, so the tensions within the middle and upper classes receded as common cause was found. And indeed, opinion polls reveal that whereas the working class remained relatively divided in their support for the Labour Party, the upper and middle classes swung behind the Conservatives almost completely. In 1951, the Conservative lead over Labour amongst the upper middle class almost reached its arithmetic ceiling, 82 per cent, and the lead was also very strong for the middle class (46 per cent in 1951, to reach 60 per cent in 1959; the figure in 1945 was 38 per cent).[25] For one female civil servant, such was her despair about post-war conditions that when asked in September 1948 for her views on the main inconveniences of modern living, she replied:

I have given up hoping for physical security. I shall be surprised if I or my children die quietly in prosperous beds, but I value such security as I have, mainly economic....I have become less egalitarian than I was three years ago. I am growing to think that there are always enormous differences in endowment and achievement between individuals and that is not a bad thing and should be fostered. Equal opportunity, yes but there it stops.[26]

Accounts such as these endorse Tony Judt's[27] insistence on the immediate post-war years in Europe being ones of major perceived crisis and insecurity. There was

---

[23] M-O (D): 83.   [24] Davies (1952, 174).   [25] See Bonham (1954).
[26] M-O (G): 040.   [27] Judt (2005, 5).

little sense, amongst the Mass-Observers of the later 1940s, that this was a period of hope or consensus. Several correspondents identified the idea that the middle class was declining as testimony to the popularity of this trope. For some, this then slides into an attack on the working class.

> Of course I know it is often said with complete superficiality that the middle classes are being destroyed or crushed out of existence.... This is nonsense. They are being enlarged to include groups of members who would not formerly have been members. In fact England is well on the way to becoming a wholly middle class community. The vulgarity and well fed quarrelsomeness, the acquisitiveness, the ostentation the essentially bad 'genteel' manners of former lower and middle-middle classes are spreading quite alarmingly. The naturally polite simple spoken dignified artisan or labourer, though he was dirty and coarse in his home and often brutal to wife or children... is fast disappearing. Instead we have middle class louts and minxes... it will take another generation after that to develop a modicum of education, culture and real refinement such as belong at present to a very small number of professional people and some of the former aristocracy.[28]

This is a revealing quote. This woman, a doctor and novelist, clearly articulates the sense of middle-class decline. She disputes it, but in terms which see it as being vulgarized and contaminated by the 'mass', before finally holding out the hope for its resurrection through the educated role of professionals and (some) former aristocracy. This, clearly, is grist to Shils's mill. The cultural poles here are now firmly fixed between 'high' and 'low': there is no effective 'middle' (brow or otherwise) to act as a culturally countervailing force in and of itself.

This sense of disgust which was evinced towards the working class is evident in considerable numbers of Mass-Observation accounts in the later 1940s.

> I so regret the apparent ending of the middle classes' way of life – the shabbiness, the lowering of standards and the general 'anything goes' attitude of today which is so prevalent... it all boils down to the fact that I resent the rising of the lower classes, and yet in my heart I think I realise that their previous way of life gave them little opportunity to rise above their circumstances.[29]

And yet despite the power of this cultural reaction, Shils is wrong in seeing it as leading to a full-blown embrace of gentry ideals amongst the intellectuals. We can also see a new kind of cultural identity forming in the writings of the Mass-Observers, which departed from this gentry vision in its embrace of the techno-cratic ideal. This was a vision of the Mass-Observers who, recognizing the post-war travails of the intellectuals as for the middle classes as a whole, and sharing in the reaction against the now powerful working class, sought to define themselves in terms of bearers of a new 'national' project, a grouping whose role was to mediate between the warring parties of workers and gentry, to act in the national interest as some kind of third force, using the forces of reason and science. This vision departed from the old gentlemanly highbrow vision by

---

[28] M-O (G): B1371.   [29] M-O (G): D1246.

defining more pragmatic, 'worldly' justification of their role and importance. A similar vision was articulated theoretically in Karl Mannheim's account of the intellectual, but it is also striking how far a similar sentiment was – uneasily and uncertainly – embraced by a significant number of Mass-Observers as they sought to make sense of their post-war problems.

In responding to the directive about their views of the middle class, one can find a differentiation between a small number of Mass-Observers who were sceptical of the value of the middle class, who saw them as declining, and who positioned themselves as advocates of aristocratic values, and the somewhat larger group who saw that the middle class did have a necessary role, as 'buffers' between the other classes, and as the distinctive bearers of what is increasingly identified as a 'national' mission. Most Mass-Observers saw it as necessary to understand the role of the middle class in relation to the working class.[30] The minority who took a critical view of middle class values and defended the gentry ideals tended to be pessimistic and might have even held the working class, the honest labourer, as a preferable figure. One observer distinguished a particular group of the middle class who had 'supreme cultural value' because of its association with the gentlemanly professions.

> There is the class, risen from the working class, and as I have said, largely composed of technicians, and there is the middle class which fills the professions – the doctors, clergymen, lawyers, architects, school masters, and the like – and which I think has supreme cultural value. We must preserve this class at all costs if we are to preserve culture, as distinct from the amassing of facts, and technical knowledge.[31]

Yet, in fact, this kind of patronizing 'middlebrow' reading of the middle class was very much a minority view.[32] There was a much more commonly held view of the middle class as managers of the nation, as 'responsible for moral and social progress', and as 'the most reliable, intelligent, industrious and law abiding section of the community'.[33] Sometimes this account could be mobilized into an anti-aristocratic idiom,[34] but more commonly, it was yoked to a view of the middle classes as 'buffers' or 'backbones' of the nation, the only group with the capacity to unite and lead an otherwise divided society.

---

[30] M-O (G): Fifty-two (64 per cent) mentioned the working class in some form, and only twelve (15 per cent) made no reference to them.

[31] M-O (G): C115.

[32] M-O (G): A maximum of five responses have some evidence of this kind of account.

[33] M-O (G): G105 and H137.

[34] For instance, from M-O (G): 1873, an anthropology student who thought that the upper classes 'are liable to have their lives mapped out for them, they've no need to plan your life independently for yourself'. Or M-O (G): 1689, who thought the upper class 'are practically non existent now and they are in any case an artificial and despised group'. The political implications of this view are made apparent in the testimony of M-O (G): 842: 'As a class the rich consider themselves to be born leaders. They have wealth enough for luxury, wealth enough to be able to ignore the fact that they live in a society. They do not as a rule work for their living; they have time to waste on fads. It is clear that such a group of self indulgent people can not be permitted to exist in any reasonable society'.

In its function, as the backbone, it holds the whole structure of society together. It produces from its ranks the professionals, those who lead, heal and teach.

The wealthy are engaged in either making or spending.... On the other side the working classes are so absorbed in beer and football that they have not time, nor inclination, for the finer things of life. On the whole I think it important for us to have a healthy core in our national life and that core is the middle class.[35]

The language is instructive here. To be sure, we see a defence in terms of culture, morality, or aesthetics, which partly criticizes the cultural elitism of the gentry vision, but it is more common to sidestep this framing and adopt a more techno-cratic account, where it is the 'function' of the middle classes within the national commonwealth which is paramount. Within this framing, the intellect is valued more in its managerial importance than for its aesthetic or ethical orientation.

The middle class have provided practically the whole intellectual and directive ability that has raised the UK from its position under the Tudor and earlier regimes as a second rate agricultural and pastoral country supporting a small population to that of the great industrial and mercantile power which it was, and still is, in great part.... I am a patent agent by profession and I know what I am saying when I state that practically the whole of the great mass of invention which has formed the basis of this industry has been made by *middle class* people.

... whatever organisation there is in the country, the managerial and intelligentsia part of our class will be much in demand.[36]

The notion that the middle class was the 'backbone' of the nation, or the 'buffer' between social classes had a long history.[37] It is notable that this vision was oriented towards a national, rather than an imperial, perspective. None of the Mass-Observers so much as mentioned the empire as a salient entity, even though in 1949 the British Empire decolonization had hardly begun. It was now a vision of a managed nation that was being championed, in which the middle classes were the main source of 'the intelligentsia, the cranks, the social reformers, in general people who have original ideas' and where 'we badly need the culture and the social service of (middle class) people with some education and some leisure'.[38] But this was also an account which could at times lend itself to a remarkably assertive identity which was in no doubt of its moral superiority over both workers and aristocrats.

We provide the majority of the brains, and beauty to the community. We talk the King's English and not old Ford argot, we provide the administrators from foremen up to directors, the technicians, the majority of the artists and actors. We do not include at one end of the scale the unskilled labourers, the mechanics and artisans. At the other end we exclude the spivs and the aristocrats. In fact we are the vast majority of the intelligentsia and as such *must* survive.[39]

---

[35] M-O (G): R1567 and 158.   [36] M-O (G): 4164 and 403.
[37] Notably Wahrman (1995) on the construction of the early nineteenth-century middle class as standing between two warring parties.
[38] M-O (G): 1873 and F547.   [39] M-O (G): 994, a 28-year-old furniture designer.

We can clearly identify here a deeply felt insistence on the role of the middle class as bearers of rational modern planning, focusing on the role of technicians and scientists. Some did this explicitly by drawing on technocratic measures such as IQ tests in demonstrating their superiority. Others expressed a preference for a more scientific bent to their work, such as a musical writer who wanted to link this 'more to sociology'.[40] This approach could at times verge on a full-blown social scientistic analysis, as for one 60-year-old researcher, who reported in somewhat forced but nonetheless distinctively social scientifically correct prose that a 'managerial and cultural minority' was 'indispensable for national stability'.

> If my account of the personnel of the middle classes is correct, nowadays, particularly that the common features of the mc personnel are (a) higher education (b) special technical training and experience (c) responsibility for planning, organising, legislating, administration. The middle class enjoy reasonable security of tenure as against the short term threat of dismissal common among the wage earners: their type of life is more cultivated, they have on the whole, more varied interests particularly of a more intellectual type.[41]

This was the same refrain as that of a Mass-Observer who urged a 'greater realisation on the part of higher management of the advantages of market research'.[42] What we see amongst the Mass-Observers is the early crystallization of a scientific and technical aesthetic. A key battleground was over the identity of the professionals, of which there were fifteen mentions, compared to five for technicians, and five for managers. Professionals had one foot in a gentleman camp, but could also exemplify more technical skills, hence acting as an important rallying call for a 'respectable' and culturally legitimate technical group. The politics of this vision and its association both with an old provincial middlebrow orientation and with an emergent social science identity is clear in the following case.

> As a student of social science at college I could write a great deal about the continued existence of the middle class but much of it would be a repetition of what Patrick Geddes and Lewis Mumford have already written....I think the middle class are the real political power in this country – and like JB Priestley – I think the 1950 campaign of the Labour Party will attempt to woo the middle class on the one hand, and placate the working class on the other. Among the middle class I include clerks, civil servants, teachers, administrators, technicians, doctors, dentists, solicitors, and so on. A body of people whose professional contact with the working class is such as to earn their respect.[43]

This discussion about technical identities is not just, or even predominantly, over which occupational groups were more significant. It rather was about an ethics of expertise which saw its role as 'making things explicit' so that they could be

---

[40] M-O (D): 125.   [41] 729.   [42] M-O (D): 1876.
[43] 180, a 25-year-old student teacher: 'We should not perhaps over do this'. We can also find the words of a research worker who found his job 'too structured' and aspired to open a tea shop M-O: (D): 237.

planned and rationalized. It was avant-garde, after a fashion, but its embrace of the pure aesthetic was not in terms of Bourdieu's abstract art, but in terms of the appeal of science – including social science. Its identity drew on certain conceptions of professionalism, but did not dwell on its 'gentlemanly' character, playing more attention to its association with the technically trained, working class. It was also a force that thought it had history on its side. One confident young man, even in the midst of the gloom of the later 1940s, had no doubt at all about his prospects.

> I am a student of sociology. I am doing the work I have always wanted to do, and I find it enthralling…my wife is doing the same thing in the same place – we both have wide interests outside our work (although insofar as sociology covers all activities, one cannot ever discard the scientific attitude, whatever one is doing) – film, especially classics, the theatre, modern art, and poetry.[44]

Even at a time when sociology was hardly taught, it offered to this young man the vision of a centred life embracing culture and science.

3.2 TECHNICAL IDENTITIES

How significant were these technical identities? Since the social science sources I am using are actually involved in the formation of this group, they are highly biased. Yet, as I have argued in the Introduction, their bias is a fundamental part of my story. But we can pursue our examination further by returning to Elizabeth Bott's research, examining her household members in depth, to give us a greater sense of the stakes involved in claiming technical identities in an early 1950s austere London. To repeat the point I emphasized in the introduction, these are not a representative sample, but one which was elicited through their interest in research and indeed the social sciences. We are, therefore, well placed to examine in detail how technical identities were organized.

There are only two households where survival of the gentlemanly modernist formation embraced by Shils can be found. The saddest of these are the Bruces. Mr Bruce was part of the old intellectual aristocracy, and he shared in its post-war (mis)fortunes. It is not incidental to my theme that the researchers, Bott and Robb, dwell critically on the Bruces' 'confusions', and their sense of being out of place in 1950s England.

> [Their] confusion is part of a general feeling of being out of place which he repeats in many other situations – the move from Scotland to England at the age of 6, his experiences at school, his moves from job to job, his lack of knowledge or interest in social and political affairs. Social discontinuity is part of the ordinary upbringing for children of professional parents.…But Mr B already felt he had

---

[44] M-O (D): 2024.

lost his background in his early separation and each fresh bit of change empha-
sised his feeling of belonging to no one and nowhere.[45]

Mr Bruce's grandparents were Scottish, who later came to live in England. His
parents had spent time in India. Mrs Bruce's mother was half Swedish and half
Norwegian, and she had married an Englishman. 'Both the Bruces feel that
they are perpetual strangers, belonging partly to several worlds and wholly to
none.' Having been to a 'crammer' and with the financial support of his parents,
Mr Bruce had succeeded in gaining a Cambridge degree in modern languages and
had then 'dithered' with archaeology and teaching. However, he had failed to
secure an established professional position, and having moved in and out of jobs,
including working in advertising for the record company HMV, he had finally
been forced to earn a living as a routine civil servant, buttressed by an attempt to
do serious writing in his spare time. The field notes go on to report that

> in spite of what we feel to be his considerable gifts, he seems never to have been
> moderately successful either in maintaining a good level of orthodox job responsi-
> bility, in his critical writings, or in original creative work.

The Bruces had a strong class identity, which Bott interprets as a defence mechanism to deal with their downward mobility. It is noteworthy that this class identity was linked to their evident spatial isolation. They believed in the innate
superiority of their cultural values, seen as being inalienable even when, in occupational and economic terms, they are in tougher times.

> They identify themselves with the upper middle class which they define in terms
> of occupation and 'cultural' attributes. Throughout their discussion of social
> classes they stressed the importance of cultural attributes at the expense of more
> material factors...in spite of their current difficulties they seem to feel that they
> are personally securely placed in the upper middle class and that no amount of
> financial or occupational disaster can really dislodge them...both the Bruces are
> proud of belonging to a distinguished family, and both feel that to some extent
> they have let their ancestors down. They are below the norm occupationally but
> they have a very genuine love of the artistic interests which they attribute to their
> family and to the upper middle classes....They used the same cultural idiom to
> express themselves....They both identify themselves with the upper middle class.
> To them, this means a public school education or its equivalent, practice of a
> learned profession, absence of 'accent', possession of certain qualities such as good
> manners, interest in art and literature, belief in sexual equality as a natural part of
> civilised behaviour.

Compare this account with Spender's vision of modernism. 'Progress produces
material benefits but it is only in the alive intelligence of the imagination that these
can be related to significant values...in England the real benefits accomplished
by the welfare state have produced an unprecedented spiritual malaise.'[46] Spender's 'moderns' (who include Joyce, Lawrence, Eliot, and Woolf) 'feel that their

---

[45] SN 4852.   [46] Spender (1963, 58).

responsibility towards themselves was as artists and not as money makers producing consumer's products'.[47] One can almost sense the appeal of this modernist vision to Mr Bruce, as he comes home from his unrewarding, mundane day job and gets out his typewriter. This sense of 'culture' as a kind of bulwark, or compensation, for current travails is indeed a major current of middle-class writing and self-identity of the time, and of course, was shortly to be critically exposed in Raymond William's pathbreaking *Culture and Society*.

The Bruces were, however, unusual amongst Bott and Robb's respondents, who as I showed in the introduction were predominantly drawn from a more technical formation. Only one other household had any kind of gentlemanly leaning, the Woodmans'. Mr Woodman had also been to Cambridge University and he was working in a secure professional job. Both he and his wife were interested in the arts, and strongly supported 'creative' activities. They evoked bohemian identities and had a strong belief in gender equality between husband and wife. Yet, rather like the Bruces, they also displayed a revealing lack of cultural confidence. This was in part due to the 'difficulties' of Mr Woodman's homosexuality, which had caused marital strain, and which Bott thought symptomatic of a broader pattern of drift. Bott rather gloomily records that 'Mr H seems worried chiefly about his occupational future, his homosexuality, and what Mrs H will do when the children are older. Mrs H seems to feel that when the children are more independent there will be little point in continuing the marriage'. Yet, Mr Woodman, unlike Mr Bruce, did not just look to gentry and, because of his working-class background, evoked the identity of a craftsman, seeking to legitimize himself by reference to practical, craft values.

The other respondents were much more concerned to distinguish themselves from 'arty' intellectuals, and defended a more punchy and 'hard-boiled', technical self-identity. Even though they were mostly upwardly mobile, and had not been to university, they were more confident and self-certain, with little of the private agonizing and self-doubt that were evident for the Bruces or Woodmans.[48] They were concerned to champion a kind of technical and practical intellectuality. Consider Mr Hartley, a building surveyor from a rural background, and Mrs Hartley, a secretary. In the discussion about their 'reference groups', they differentiated between 'intelligent people' (like themselves) and 'intellectuals' whom they saw 'as stuffy people who read books but never did anything practical'. Alternatively, Mr Redfern, a skilled instrument maker, for whom, the field notes record, the 'technical' 'is almost the most important thing in the world, his greatest achievement and his main hope for the future. In every way it is superior to his past and to his family background…he talks about his work at greater length and more enthusiastically than about anything else'.

---

[47] Spender (1963, 76).

[48] This is not to say that they lacked psychological anxieties, neuroses, and uncertainties. Indeed, Bott and Robb's notes are full of these. The point here is that they nonetheless were able to make a public showing of their confidence and certainty and in particular did not seek to enrol Bott and Robb into their own perceived misfortunes.

For Mr Redfern, this technical identity embraced some aspects of the intellectual role, whilst he rejected its gentlemanly aspects. He thus saw himself as one of the 'practical people', who were the ones who really get things done. 'They have a lot of theoretical knowledge at the back of their ability but primarily they are concerned with getting on with the job.' On the other hand, graduates and professors 'are definitely non-practical people and are to be despised as such'. This did not stop him from defining himself as one of the 'educated knowledgeable people'. A similar set of identities is apparent for the 'Cs', whose work 'involved a high degree of mechanical skill together with some theoretical knowledge. He lays particular emphasis on the theoretical knowledge...but obviously gets his greatest immediate pleasure in the job from mechanical skill'. Mrs C 'has a strong desire for work with some kind of intellectual aspect and feels that office work is the antithesis of this'. She went to training college but does not seem to have been attracted to working with children, 'rather it seems to have been more of an opportunity to be in an intellectual atmosphere, learn history, and prove that she really has a brain. Has thought about doing archaeology'. Mrs C, we learn from Bott, had a positive view towards intellectuals, but not 'in the high powered sense but well educated, cultured people in general, especially university graduates and university teachers'.

Mr and Mrs Salmon were civil servants. His interests in social science included classes in economics, whereas she was interested in psychology. Robb felt a passionate personal involvement with and interest in this couple. What was their vision of life? They identified with 'people like us' which

> includes young couples living in suburbs and with children, normally buying their own houses. Occupationally it covers minor professions (executive grade civil servants, teachers, etc) and self employed small shopkeepers (e.g. a hairdresser). These people should be easy going and informal, but not unconventional.... They should give their children a good education, but it is unnecessary (perhaps undesirable) for them to be over-ambitious themselves...they should be capable of taking an interest in books, music, etc, but again, not enthusiasts.

Several middle-class households sought to elevate their own position through associating their own activities with the ethos of craft and skill. One painter 'seems to consider himself a craftsman, if one can distinguish a craftsman from an artist'.

What we see in this kind of orientation is a partial crossing of class boundaries. Just as with the post-war Mass-Observers, there is a persistent concern to distinguish oneself from a certain kind of 'high-powered' intellectual, identified with purely arty concerns, and instead defend a different version of intellectuality, which allies it with technique, practical application, political commitment, skill, and science. We can see how this appeal reaches down into the world of skilled manual labour and the handicraft tradition, whilst it could also appropriate aspects of the professional and academic educated identities. It is thus able to flourish in the social democratic climate of the post-war years, whilst also defending a role for the intellectual as manager. It is emphatic in its concern to repudiate the modernist identity of artistic withdrawal from the contaminated city. Indeed, to invert Spender's terms, it was an identity of 'contemporaries', rather than 'moderns', of those who seized the present as theirs. It is for these reasons that, in the immediate post-war years, science fiction writing took off as a popular genre of narrative writing, and evidence showed that it appealed especially to professionals and intellectuals as a means of telling modern parables in the name of scientific discourse.[49]

3.3 CULTURAL CHANGE AND THE EMERGENCE OF THE MODERN 'MOVEMENT'

It is useful to consolidate our discussion by returning to Bourdieu's account of the tension between industrialists and intellectuals, which I introduced at the start of Chapter 2. I have emphasized that his account is rooted in the contrast between an urban, middle-class world of 'culture' and a rural, working class, and peasant world of 'nature'. However true this might have been in 1960s France, this fails to recognize the way that in England, with its long history of a skilled urban working class, steeped in practical skills and its own form of craft intellectualism, cultural oppositions and identities were framed around contests over skill and expertise. I have suggested that we should not overemphasize the post-war revival of the gentlemanly cultural elite which might be seen as embodying Bourdieu's critical intellectual artistic avant-garde. Although elements of this can be detected, it failed to engage a younger audience who were more attracted to skill and science. Consider the case of the novelist John Fowles, who was to become the last major Europe-oriented British novelist during the 1960s and 1970s following the success of *The Collector* in 1963. Privately educated, with his degree in French from Oxford in 1949, snobbishly anti-suburban,[50] and dedicated to the craft of writing, one might have supposed him, if anybody, to be attracted to the arty intellectual ethos. And indeed, in the early 1950s, he did admit to his 'aristocratic dream-projections. For example, I have day dreamed of seducing Princess Margaret...to imagine a future in the most aristocratic (aesthetically and socially and artistically) of worlds'.[51] And yet, ultimately even he was more impressed by the appeal of a technocratic clerisy. Shortly afterwards

---

[49] See Finer (1954) and Gerlach and Hamilton (2003), who date this current to the 1950s. I am grateful to Nick Hubble who alerted me to this point. In his autobiography, the leading English post-war science fiction writer J. G. Ballard reports his father's preoccupation with science, as marked by his veneration of Wells.

[50] 'The evening platitudes in the hotel drawing room...stifling...and the sad, weary downfall of the English middle-class stress. What they all speak is common ground – rationing, dogs, children, illnesses. All departures away from common ground dwindle into silence', John Fowles (2003, 114).

[51] Fowles (2003, 96).

(influenced by the London School of Economics political scientist Harold Laski), he recorded a change in his political views and 'what I dream of is an oligarchy of left wing intellectuals, who are cold and dispassionate and scientifically philanthropic, who could do something about the causes of ignorance'. By 1956 he was noting his passion for 'books as documents. More and more it is the psychological, sociological, anthropological, historical values I see in books'.[52]

The pessimism of the post-war cultural modernists should not, therefore, be seen as representative of broader cultural developments in post-war Britain, as Jonathan Rose does, when he argues that in the 1950s, modernist ideas began to feed into working-class culture: 'the modernist mood of disillusionment, disaffection, dissent and dissonance would gradually permeate popular culture and eventually trickle down the social scale'.[53] Rather, we can detect a striking growth in confidence during the 1950s of a full-blown alternative to the modernist establishment in the form of 'progressive' technical identities. It is not incidental that their disclosure demands the use of distinctive sources. This group took on aspects of an 'avant-garde' in its concern to ask new questions, push back boundaries, and disrupt old orthodoxies. However, it did not take the form of pushing the 'pure aesthetic' further, as Bourdieu expects, and was scornful of the pure aestheticism of the 'moderns'. Rather, it emerged in opposition to the modernist establishment by championing an interest in the 'ordinary', the 'real', and the 'natural', in the name of a practical capacity to act in the world. This, I argue in later chapters, was the moment of a nascent social science which was both produced by, and itself helped to form, these new middle-class identities. Therefore, rather than Bourdieu's account in which intellectual identities oppose themselves to the 'culture of the necessary' associated with the popular classes, in the British case, with its long history of skilled, craft production, the intellectual could be reconciled with the technical and the practical. It could do this through an evocation of the role of science to explain, be practically important, and 'make things transparent'. A central moment in the recognition of this distinctive identity was in the later 1950s, when C. P. Snow's essay on 'two cultures', with its famous insistence on the separation of the worlds of art and science, was published, leading to huge debate and controversy.

A recognition of this technocratic current is important in allowing us to place cultural developments in a new light. A crystallizing moment in the idea of the emergence of a new cultural order was the formation of the 'angry young men', associated with John Osborne, Kenneth Tynan, Colin Wilson, and John Wain, which burst into prominence with the production of Osborne's *Look Back in Anger* in 1956. This movement, with its candour and scorn for the modernist establishment,

---

[52] Fowles (2003, 139, 384).

[53] Rose (2001, 456). See also Tony Judt (2005, 206–7), who notes that in the post-war years 'cultural commentators were absorbed by intimations of failure and deterioration' and cites T. S. Eliot and Cyril Connolly.

was seen as ushering in the radicalism and self-discovery of the 1960s.[54] Subsequent debate about the significance of this group has spluttered along. Some are amazed that figures of such apparent intellectual mediocrity could play such an important role, with particular scorn being directed at pop-philosopher Colin Wilson, whose self-pitying existentialism soon seemed to boil down to a few clichés about mental effort and the 'peak experience'.[55] Were they really that angry? And, given their renowned misanthropy and bloody-mindedness, could they ever be identified as part of some collective movement? These objections miss the point. It is the audience, as much as the actual writers, which are interesting. The production of *Don't Look Back in Anger* in 1956 was the tipping point in which new middle-class identities could announce themselves on the national cultural stage.

The appeal of 'opening up' and refusing convention was to have widespread appeal. When the sociologist Ray Pahl researched new lifestyles in Hertfordshire suburbs in the early 1960s,[56] he interviewed a young housewife who explained her disenchantment with her suburban neighbours in ways that annexed suburban antipathy specifically to Osborne's plays. On this estate, she said,

> People are afraid – frightened of invasion, it is important to 'keep the house clean, keep personal affairs to themselves, keep respectable'. When I first came here after about 6 weeks I had a great urge to run down the street stark naked shouting four letter words just to wake them up...sometimes I feel disloyal – I'm nice and charming to these people and then I come home and say 'ugh'...sometimes I feel – you know, God! – these people: husbands, the telly, bed – just what Osborne was screaming about. I'm not content. I'm knowing, despairing, neurotic – low moments, high moments...yet who knows what's going on behind that front door....Terrible things.[57]

This quote, from the same date as Betty Friedan's *Feminine Mystique*, whose publication in the United States was to have a powerful impact on feminism, speaks to the way that Osborne communicated to a particular audience the value of being 'naked'. It also reveals a new and fascinating fear: that danger does not necessarily reside in foreign places, or even in the morally disreputable districts of British cities, but possibly just next door. It is in the ordinary and the mundane that menace lurks. But it is also by seeking to go beyond the 'nice' that one can be true and authentic. Mrs B1 told Ray Pahl how she met her husband.

> He looked the cleanest and safest of a lot at a party. He fascinated me because I thought he was rude but he speaks his mind. I was 'nicely' brought up. In my mother's life you never mention sex, religion and politics.[58]

---

[54] Booker (1970).

[55] See Colin Wilson's autobiography which makes it clear that he sees the defining lesson of his work as elaborating the 'peak experience', manifest in the seemingly trivial incident of his sense of relief having navigated a snow drift in his car: 'I have not fallen into the negative position of believing that all life is an illusion. It seems to me quite clear that certain things can be achieved. I have described in this book the experiences that led me to this belief, for example the intensification of awareness I reached when driving back from Sheepwash through the snow' (Wilson 2004, 384).

[56] See further my discussion of the interview method in Chapter 7.

[57] Pahl, SN 4877, Mrs B.   [58] Pahl, SN 4877, Mrs B1.

It is this appeal of looking behind appearances, and challenging 'niceness' which explains the power of the popular English science fiction of the period, in the hands of John Wyndham and (somewhat later) J. G. Ballard. This distanced itself from the pure technical fantasies evident in American science fiction to elaborate an 'inner space' within an all too immediate dystopic future based in the suburbs and small town sites of post-war Britain. Ballard was clear that science fiction was a deliberate attack on the modernist novel, through its concern to deploy the everyday – understood as a site of scientific intervention – as both menace and promise.[59]

John Wyndham's *The Midwich Cuckoos*, written in 1957, is characteristic of this sensibility. The action here centres on how, in a quintessential English village in the Home Counties, aliens seize control for a day and impregnate all its child-bearing women with their progeny. The ensuing drama reveals the failure of the traditional 'county' apparatus – the church, the local gentry family, the women's clubs, even the local doctor – to understand the nature of the alien threat in their midst and devise a strategy to resist invasion. Bumbling attempts by the local squirearchy to pull the villagers together in the spirit of self-reliance, and teach the alien children to grow up as part of local society fail as the alien children round on, and kill, anyone who threatens them, even if unintentionally. Ultimately, the local squire has to resort to a suicide bomb to remove the threat. The narrator is the one who shows his ability to understand through his own writing, but also more particularly as a social observer, an amateur ethnographer, who is paid by the police and government to keep a watch on the village.

This sense of the social researcher as having the capacity to intervene and mobilize the everyday in the face of the breakdown of hypocritical traditional society is even more marked in Wyndham's *The Day of the Triffids*. Scientists secretly develop a walking plant, the triffid, which is initially farmed to produce remarkably high-quality vegetable oil, but can kill humans with its vicious sting. Although for many years confined within agricultural compounds, the plants break out following a meteor shower, the brightness of which blinds most of the population. In the moral breakdown which follows, as blind people stumble help-lessly around and are mercilessly attacked by triffids, the few sighted survivors plan how to respond. It is now technocratic experts who must lead: 'to hold our own, to make any use at all of the knowledge in the libraries we must have the teacher, the doctor, and the leader, and we must be able to support them while they help us'.[60] And, it turns out, social scientists are key. The longest speech in the book is

---

[59] On Ballard's conception of inner space see *Miracles of Life* (Ballard 2008, 192), and for his critical relationship with modernist literature, see p. 166 of the same book.

Writers of so-called serious fiction shared one dominant characteristic – their fiction was first and foremost about themselves. The 'self' lay at the heart of modernism, but now had a much more powerful rival, the everyday world, which was just as much a psychological construct and just as prone to mysterious and often psychopathic impulses.

This kind of framing of a critical present has huge importance in defining the tools of post-war English critical writing, for instance in the early novels of Ian McEwan, and played an important role in popularizing the emerging genres of television, for instance *Dr Who*.

[60] Wyndham (2008a, 204).

attributed to 'Dr E. H. Vorless D.Sc, of Edinburgh, Professor of Sociology at the University of Kingston', who insists that old genteel morals (such as marriage) have no place any more and that a purely eugenic and functional orientation is required to 'conserve the race'.

> it will not be easy: old prejudices die hard. The simple rely on a bolstering mass of maxim and precept, so do the timid, so do the mentally lazy – and so do all of us, more than we imagine....What we offer is a busy life in the best conditions we can contrive, and the happiness which will come of achievement against odds.[61]

We therefore need to broaden our interests away from the specific concern with 'angry young men' (there had been plenty of these before), to recognize the broader emergence of a critical culture of exposure, of seeking to make the everyday and mundane explicit or 'transparent'. These are precisely the values which the anthropologist Marilyn Strathern sees as a fundamental and enduring feature of English middle-class culture itself.[62] The modernist intellectuals believed they were culturally superior to others, but would not dream of announcing this openly – consider the refusal of Bloomsbury to own up to the highbrow label that everyone else thought they epitomized; their sexuality was bohemian, but they would never openly identify as homosexual or gay. Its cultural values were precisely embedded in the hidden and implicit codes they used amongst themselves, which were, decidedly, not to be shared with a wider audience. There were no formal 'criteria' to apply to join the Cambridge Apostles, one of their main forging grounds.

The cultural power of exposure was evidenced by the huge appeal of an article written in 1955 by the aristocrat Nancy Mitford in *Encounter*. This formally sought to differentiate members of the aristocracy from the uppity ranks of the upwardly mobile in terms of the apparently trivial issue of how the vowel 'U' was sounded. Everyone knew that the gentry spoke differently, but Mitford dared say this openly. This issue of *Encounter* sold out, her article was published as a pamphlet, and then as a book – along with other contributors to the debate she sparked off – which sold 40,000 copies within a month. The importance of the battle lines drawn around this issue are revealed by the subsequent debate on 'U' and 'non-U' which raged in the pages of *Encounter*. Tellingly, Evelyn Waugh, whose intellectual project, somewhat like Shils's, was also to resuscitate the aristocracy as cultural beacon, but in a coded, understated way, resented this explicit naming of social difference. Gently chiding Mitford, he asked her,

> Were you surprised that your article on the English aristocracy caused such a to-do?...Class distinctions in England have always been the matter for higher feeling than national honour, the matter of feverish but very private debate. So when you brought them into the open, of course everyone talked, of course the

---

[61] Wyndham (2008*a*, 117f).

[62] Strathern does not evoke an historical account of these terms in the way I attempt here, and sees them as enduring facets of English culture. I explore the relationship between anthropology and sociology further in Chapter 6.

columnists quoted you and corrected you.... Should delicacy have restrained you? Your friends anxiously ask. There are subjects too intimate for print. Surely class is one? The vast and elaborate structure grew up almost in secret. Now it shows signs of dilapidation.[63]

Waugh here appeals to the gentlemanly refrain 'one does not talk about class', and that if one does it shows that there is a 'chip on your shoulder'. Yet of course, paradoxically, by writing in *Encounter*, Waugh was himself talking about class in the way he claimed he wanted to avoid. And so, despite himself, he cannot avoid coming up with his own 'take' on the matter.

[T]he basic principle of English social life is that *everyone (...) thinks he is a gentleman.* There is a second principle of almost equal importance: *everyone draws the line of demarcation immediately below their own heels*, the professions rule out the trades: dentists, vets; doctors, dentists; the services, the professions; the household brigade, the line regiments; squires, squireens, ... it is essentially a process of ruling *out*.

Of course, as my analysis in this chapter has shown, Waugh does not appreciate that the gentlemanly ideal had lost considerable currency in the previous twenty years. Nonetheless, we see here how the intellectualism involved in talking about class conveys a certain momentum of its own. Once the cat was out of the bag, it could not be put back in.

The new scientific and technically minded, of which the 'angry young men' were only one minor part, believed in stating things directly, 'as they are', by way of a direct response to this culture of complicity. Naming, calling 'a spade a spade', categorizing, and revealing invoked a different, putatively 'immediate' and 'direct' world, in opposition to the hidden, implicit codes where things were supposed to be left unsaid. It was in this spirit that the Consumers Association, formed in 1958, recruited 47,000 members, mostly from professional ranks, in its first years and became devoted to rigorously testing new products to reveal any hidden flaws they might possess.[64] But, although this was a game which appealed to scientists, it was possible for the poets, writers, and artists to join in. Kingsley Amis commented that 'things like novels in England... had been the preserve of what we'll call the public school upper classes'[65] and sought a new kind of 'immediacy'. This movement did not embody a language of class, but a language of the 'everyday' and the ordinary. We see the championing of new art forms, seen as 'close to nature', or 'spontaneous'. Jazz, notably, appealed to young men such as Kingsley Amis or Philip Larkin, drawing on racist motifs of the spontaneity of 'black music'. We see the concern with attacking the pretensions, sophistication, and 'taste' of the cultivated modernist establishment. Rather than the neutral marker of culture, such work was now seen as 'stuck up', aloof, and snobbish. A new kind of culture, supposed to be close to people's lives, or everyday life, was called for. Part of this call involved a new claim for the importance of male sexuality, seen not as an issue of cultural construction, but as a 'natural' desire.

[63] Waugh (1955).   [64] See Hilton(2003, chapter 7).
[65] Sandbrook (2004, 163).

Philip Larkin, whose poetry was central to the 1950s 'Movement' and helped create a new audience for his 'ordinary' down-to-earth verse, is a case in point. As he noted in a letter to Robert Conquest in 1959:

> Kermode[66] patronises Kingsley (Amis) and I in the *Spectator* in course of a review on *myth*. Trouble with blokes like K, is that they have, as salaried explainers of poetry, a professional interest in keeping poetry hard and full of allusions. To my mind either you don't believe your myth, in which case it stinks your poetry up, or you do and call it something else. Myth *means* something untrue doesn't it....I'm not interested in things that aren't true
>
> — — — — — — — —
>
> — — — — — — — —
>
> ...I turned around and showed
>
> My bum to Kermode...[67]

The writing of the Angry Young Men is often interpreted condescendingly.[68] However, its quality is not the important point here. In some respects, literature was not at the heart of this new cultural positioning. This call to make things transparent, to refuse myth, to tell it 'how it really is', and to understand 'ordinary' lives was also at the heart of new currents in the social sciences, and it is by understanding the cultural significance of the social sciences that we get a better understanding of the nature of this movement. It is not incidental that when the influential literary critic and 'broker' Karl Miller edited an influential collection of writing from 'the Movement', he included extracts from Young and Willmott's *Family and Kinship in East London,* from Hoggart's *Uses of Literacy,* and perhaps most revealingly of all, a book review of the 'gifted young sociologist' Hannah Gavron's study of *The Captive Wife,* alongside the usual literary suspects ranging from Sillitoe to Larkin, Amis, Osborne, and Lessing. It is revealing too that Kenneth Tynan, the subversive theatre critic, recorded interviews with radical American sociologist C. Wright Mills, as well as economist J. K. Galbraith, in his notorious television documentary criticizing American affluence, 'We Dissent', which led to his being hauled up in front of the United States Senate Internal Security Subcommittee.[69] Noteworthy also is that Colin Wilson's diatribe, *The Outsider,* was indebted to David Riesman's critique of mass society.

---

[66] Frank Kermode was an associate of Stephen Spender and was to edit *Encounter* with him in the 1960s.

[67] Larkin (1999, 307–8). More generally see Connor (2004).

[68] While American and continental writers flirted with existentialism, absurdism, and general bohemianism, their British counterparts were widely regarded as 'middle class, anti-Modernist, nostalgic, introverted and politically uncommitted' (Sandbrook 2005, 165).

[69] See Tynan (1994, 248f).

We should see this new identity not as the product of a specific occupational group so much as a sensibility which travelled across a wide variety of occupations and social milieux. This having been said, it is not incidental, perhaps, that Colin Wilson himself had been a laboratory technician as well as a factory worker, and was to dabble in psychology, or that Philip Larkin was a librarian whose first patrons was the Mass-Observer and sociologist Charles Madge.[70] Yet Osborne was from a more literary and artistic background. The appeal was for a particular kind of vision of intellectual engagement which insisted on the need to unravel and 'tell it straight'. This could readily embrace cultural concerns with 'realist' theatre and socially committed writing. And, as I will show in later chapters, it was also a clarion call for social science.

Evelyn Waugh realized well enough the politics of 'exposure', as his riposte to Nancy Mitford made clear, where anticipating Michel Foucault's critique of surveillance and normalization by a decade or more, he noted that,

> there is an unwholesome contemporary appetite – the product, perhaps, of psychiatry and the civil service – for categories of all kinds. People seem to be comforted instead of outraged when they are told that their eccentricities entitle them to membership of a class of 'psychological types'. They are inured to filling in forms which require a 'description' of themselves and their houses.

We might, therefore, be advised to see the 'angry young men' and related cultural movements as only one, rather small, part of a large cultural identity which proclaimed the values of science, technique, and transparency – and in which the social sciences were to be key agents. It is in these disciplines that we might better locate the intellectual current of which the 'angry young men' were a part – and the next chapters show how we should understand the origins of post-war sociology in the context of this remaking of British cultural relations.

CONCLUSIONS

In this chapter I have argued that we can trace the development of a distinctive intellectual current in the post-war years, which repudiated the gentlemanly concern to be implicit, and replaced it by a determination to make transparent what were deemed to be social and cultural truths. It is unhelpful to regard this new group as 'progressive'. Their politics were complex. They were chauvinistic, misogynist, and nationalist. They veered between left- and right-wing outlooks. Rather than seeing this group as the simple product of social changes, for instance those associated with the expansion of new industries, bureaucratic structures, or the welfare state, or as the product of new kinds of political or cultural regime, I have emphasized how they emerged through dispute with older cultural formations. Table 3.1 heuristically outlines the oppositions I have elaborated here.

---

[70] See Larkin (1999, 161–2).

Table 3.1 Contours of the British middle-class cultural formation, 1950–70

Key features	Gentlemanly	Technical intelligentsia
Social background	Upper (middle) class	Upwardly mobile
Spatial politics	Metropolitan	Provincial
Born	1880–1920	1920 onwards
School education	Private school	Grammar school
University Education	Oxbridge	Any university
Archetypal discipline	Humanities	Social Science
Career	Academic, gentlemanly professions, civil service	Academic, applied professions, technical occupations
Cultural model	Gentleman	Professional
Aesthetic	Modernist/aesthete	Realist/'ordinary'
Sexuality/gender politics	Bohemian	Heterosexual/misogynist
Mode of presenting cultural values	Implicit	Explicit
Politics	Pacifist/internationalist	Chauvinist
Spatial orientation	Europhile	Anglophile
Quintessential cultural group	Bloomsbury	Angry young men

This new formation thus challenged the terms, notably those associated with high-, middle-, and lowbrow, which had defined previous cultural relationships, and used the idioms of science, the 'natural', the immediate, and everyday to offer a different kind of cultural claim. Emerging out of interwar 'middlebrow', this technical intelligentsia had, by the later 1950s, seized the intellectual high ground and offered an alternative mode of thinking and doing compared to the gentlemanly, modernist, cultural establishment. Rather than seeking to elevate culture in opposition to the grubby work-a-day world, they instead sought to mobilize the everyday, to seek immediacy in the here and now. They did this in the name of science, practicality, and technique. Rather than rooting their expertise in the historical canon, they seized the moment, the 'now-time', perceived as cut free from historical moorings, to announce their authority. This mobilization of the present was to have huge significance in associating this current with the deployment of the social sciences, as I go on to show in Part II of the book.

4

1940: The Resurgence of Gentlemanly Expertise in Post-war Britain

There were few academic social scientists in the late 1940s. They had a limited research infrastructure. However, it would be a profound mistake to draw the conclusion that the social sciences were somehow absent or weak.[1] Rather, they occupied a small but strategically important niche within a 'gentlemanly' academic culture, in which their jurisdiction lay in their moralizing accounts of evolutionary development. I use the term 'gentlemanly' advisedly to emphasize three key points: firstly, their complicity to what Cain and Hopkins see as the distinctively British 'gentlemanly capitalism', in which commerce, trade, and empire dominated over manufacturing and industry.[2] Secondly, to insist on the sexual politics in which masculine authority, linked to the male role of head of family and household was paramount. Thirdly, to note the insertion of this expertise within a broader gentlemanly infrastructure of elite schools, universities, social organizations, and labour markets.[3]

In this chapter, I want to show that there was no easy progression from this gentlemanly social science to the 'new' social sciences of the 1960s. The tension between the modernist aesthetic and technical identities that I have discussed in Chapters 2 and 3 had their counterparts within the social sciences themselves. The older, gentlemanly formation had to be actively contested and defeated in order for new ways of conducting the social sciences to gain ground. In the first decade after the Second World War, there was actually a strengthening of gentlemanly social science.[4]

---

[1] This is the argument of Perry Anderson in his celebrated paper 'Origins of the present crisis'. See the critical discussion in Collini (2006) and Edgerton (2006) for recent reviews of this argument in keeping with the arguments I develop here.

[2] Cain and Hopkins (2001). I do not have scope in this book to explore in detail the relationship between the cultural and social issues I examine here and economic changes in Britain, but my account is compatible with those who emphasize the power of finance capital within British capitalism.

[3] See more generally here, the important arguments of Joyce (forthcoming).

[4] My account is in part dependent on Rose (1999a), as well as his collaborative work with Peter Miller on the history of the Tavistock Institute, yet it will become clear during the course of the chapter that I offer a somewhat different interpretation of events.

Fundamental to this shift, I argue, is not simply theoretical innovation, or the accumulation of knowledge in substantive research areas, or indeed the professional institutionalization of social science disciplines, but the deployment of new kinds of methods as tools by which academic social scientists claimed access to, and jurisdiction over, the social. In so far as gentlemanly social scientists conducted empirical research in the earlier years of the twentieth century, they mainly did so either through the documentary analysis of sources or through observation by 'cultivated' observers. This was a research culture in which historians and anthropologists commanded the empirical high ground. There was little role for the narratives and statements of 'the researched' to count for very much. Quantitative analysis remained largely within a census enumeration tradition. During the 1950s, this emphasis on observation was increasingly challenged by an insistence on eliciting 'direct' accounts by the researched themselves, especially through survey responses to questionnaires, and narratives produced by interviews. Rather than mediate social knowledge through the library and archive, or through the visual gaze of the educated, cultivated observer, it was instead gleaned 'directly' and inscribed into various kinds of narrative. A central feature of this new research culture was a concern with sampling: it was no longer imperative to map whole populations: one could delineate an account of social relations by talking to just a few people.

I begin by illustrating the dramatic changes which took place between 1955 and 1965 in the conduct of sociological research, before considering in greater detail the role of visual observation for the gentlemanly social sciences. I indicate how its preoccupation with personality and normalization was dependent on the unquestioned moral authority of the educated researcher. In the second part of this chapter I show how this gentlemanly social science prospered in post-war conditions, leading to a reviving synthetic sociology based at the London School of Economics (LSE). I finish by noting how the expansion of the LSE brought tensions between sociology as a specialist discipline and as an overarching evolutionary synthesis to a head.

4.1 THREE MODELS OF SOCIAL RESEARCH

Consider the following research report examining the characteristics of young men turning 18 years of age in a London suburb. It is not a famous piece of research and has not been cited by later authors. Nonetheless it was published in the leading *British Journal of Sociology* (BJS), founded four years before by a young group of ambitious sociologists at the LSE, undoubtedly the dominant group of their time.[5] Two extracts from the conclusion, where its authors Logan and Goldberg distinguish in ideal typical form the characteristics of two very different kinds of 18-year-old boys, are indicative of the article as a whole.

[5] This is not a lone example. For other similar kinds of framings, see Castle and Gittus (1957).

[T]he most mature young man was well developed physically: he had got over the 'spotty' stage and was shaving regularly. He had passed the adolescent phase of frequent masturbation and seminal emissions were now mainly heterosexual. He understood readily what was required of him in completing the questionnaire and could comment sensibly on it. His career so far showed a consistent pattern...he was growing towards independence of his family, he was handling his own money, buying his own clothes which were no longer adolescently flamboyant...he was fitting in smoothly at his place of work and he was pulling his weight there as a man...he was no longer shy with girls. In short, this young man knew what he was capable of, what he wanted and where he was going.

However, at the opposite extreme

was a child who had scarcely reached puberty. His body was underdeveloped and his fat was 'chubby', he had hardly any hair growth on his face, very scanty pubic hair and underdeveloped genitals. His voice was soft and unbroken, masturbation was infrequent and with scanty emissions. He was semi-literate and still read comics, he had difficulty in understanding and filling in the questionnaire, he was befogged by the interview...he had little idea of himself, and did what he was told both at home and at work: the future had little meaning for him.[6]

This is a telling example of a particular mode of going about social research, one familiar from Michel Foucault's account of the formation of the human sciences, with his emphasis on the power of 'gaze'.[7] Let me unravel some of its key features. Firstly, consider the role of observation. To be sure, questionnaires and interviews were used, but in these concluding passages it is clear that the data from these are ultimately less revealing than the researchers' observation of the way these were interpreted and answered by the boys themselves.

Secondly, we see the close relationship between social and medical knowledge, the weaving together of physical, social, and moral characteristics: one's appearance was a central signifier of not only your dress sense or personal hygiene, but your entire social and moral being. Undergoing late puberty is not just a physical process, it is also a social and moral marker. Thirdly, we see no conception of the individual, as if this could be abstracted from sex. Sex itself is the central focus of anxiety, with worries about the regulation of 'appropriate' sexual activity (not too much masturbation and not too little, clearly a fine line to tread!). Sex appears problematic because it is not amenable to direct visual observation; it takes place 'behind the scenes' and therefore unsettles the pre-eminence of visual inspection. Indeed, this worry about pathological sexuality is more marked than concerns with race and immigration or juvenile delinquency. Even the liberal *New Society*, which in the early 1960s was publishing sympathetic articles about black immigrants, could publish a paper about homosexuality noting that 'the homosexual is permanently debarred from fulfilment in his most intimate personal life....He will probably remain

---

[6] Logan and Goldberg (1953).   [7] See variously Foucault (1977, 1979).

unsatisfied at the core of his being', and that homosexuals need to 'make the best of a bad job'.[8]

Fourthly, we see issues of moralization and normalization not just resulting from the findings of the study, but as integrally related to the procedures by which knowledge is gathered. There is no recognition in this paper that these adolescents are agents in their own right, but rather an unquestioning assumption about the existence of a normal adult male state – to which some move more easily than others. Finally, we see how moralization depends on an account of personality, so that social research depended on eliciting and arraying accounts of the person. What we see in this study are core features of the gentlemanly social sciences that held sway in the early and mid decades of the twentieth century, and still highly visible in the later 1950s.

Consider now two other research projects, written in the same period, which were to prove much more influential in the later history of sociology. Elizabeth Bott's book *Family and Social Network* was published in the same year as Logan and Goldberg's study, and has proved to be the most cited work of British social science published during the 1950s.[9] This was also a project which was based on intense observation, with its repeated home interviews with its twenty selected households. It continued to have a very clear foot in the moralizing and medicalizing tradition, nowhere more apparent than in the culture of the research team which consisted in holding detailed case conferences on each of the households in which their psychological, emotional, and social states were extensively discussed. The respondents themselves were not present at these meetings and did not have the opportunity of giving their own views. Yet when we read the field notes, we can see important differences from Goldberg's study. There are occasional references in the interview notes to observational features – whether the respondents were attractive, whether the children were well behaved – but on the whole, neither Bott nor Robb was very interested in the visual array of the households or their members. What they were interested in, however, was the 'hidden' psychological states of the respondents, attributes which were held to lie behind surface appearances and which needed to be elicited by other means, namely the probing, face-to-face interview, as borrowed from the practice of psychotherapy. Their notes are littered with their reflections on the psychological attributes of their respondents, extracted from their interview discussions. Here are three examples:

> Mr F's control and domination of his wife in various ways is no doubt a more loving and tolerable form of her mother's domineering ways. In escaping from her mother she has not lost the security involved in being controlled.

> While his peaceableness seems to be largely a kind of obsessional attempt to keep order and control in a world that threatens to get out of hand, I think hers is more

---

[8] Kelvin (24 January 1963); for a contrasting and more sympathetic account of the black migrant, see James Berry's paper about returning to Jamaica from England, *New Society*, 7 February 1963.

[9] It has well over 1,000 citations in the Social Science Citation Index, four times as many as its nearest rival, Lockwood (1957). A fuller account of Bott's work and its relationship to the post-war social sciences is published in my paper 'The enigma of Elizabeth Bott'.

of a depressive reaction to a situation which seemed to offer extremely limited opportunities for satisfaction.

He has a feeling of deep dependency on women which seems to be inextricably tied up with aggression towards them. All this makes him feel anxious and guilty. He feels impotent and at a loss in unfamiliar unstructured, emotional situations. His usual defences do not work. He feels completely potent and in control of himself, others and impersonal forces when he is in a situation where aggression and destruction are positively sanctioned and in which he is bolstered by the support of homosexual relationships. Being the pilot of a big bomber is his idea of bliss.[10]

There are no visual cues in any of these references which are instead to the 'deep' psychological complexes of the men concerned. This is the world of Nik Rose's 'psy-sciences', where the observer uses psychological expertise to elicit an inner, hidden state, and through this mechanism constructs new notions of democracy and the 'self'.[11] But there is a further paradox here. When we read Bott's published book, rather than the field notes of the project itself, none of these kinds of psychological discussions appear in its pages: it is the stated social identities of the respondents, and their reported social connections that are given pride of place. The overt psychologizing has given way to the language of social relationships, roles, networks, and norms, the evidence for which is extracted from people's own accounts. And, rather than psychology's distrust of stated narrative, with its insistence on reading behind what is said for its refusals and absences, and for the role of the 'unconscious', the form of what is said is now given much more importance. Something seems to have happened between the fieldwork of this project, in the early 1950s, and its writing up, which transforms the relationship between psychology, narrative, and observation.

This paradox deepens when we move forward to the early 1960s and consider John Goldthorpe and David Lockwood's *Affluent Worker* studies, the most influential British sociological study ever conducted. Its insistence on the continued role of class division even in affluent society shaped British sociological debates ever after. Methodologically, the book is famous for its pioneering use of questionnaire methods, and its published work relies overwhelmingly on reporting cross-tabulations of questionnaire responses. This study is dramatic in part because none of the previous generations of social researchers had thought it necessary to attend to the attitudes and practices of working class households in such elaborate detail. In its design and conception, this study had also residues of the observational tradition. This is especially true of the home interviews: it is intriguing to consider why the research team, with its interest in work and employment, thought it was necessary to interview at home at all, and why wives were supposed to be present on these occasions. After all, and notoriously, the study only used the accounts given by men in reporting its findings. Reading the interview notes, we can see that the home interview was important in part for

---

[10] SN 4852.   [11] Rose (1999*a*).

allowing the researchers to conduct a visual inspection of the home surrounds, to get a sense of the 'context'. Visual observation remains important, though now as part of the research background. Here are some examples, drawn from the interview notes:

> Wife childless, she has made the house the working class equivalent of 'twee'. Lots of wrought iron and canary yellow. Horrible large non functional glass ornaments, elaborately arranged plastic flowers and lots of draped muslin.

> Very plebian atmosphere. Husband a big, moustached, sweaty reference to a sort of faded style of male glamour, with toothbrush moustache of the Flynn variety and long oily black locks. Sleeves rolled up, and semi-hearty. I got the impression he'd been 'a bit of a lad' before marrying. Definitely a working class flavour to everything they said and did.... Wife a very ordinary girl, just unmemorable in every way.[12]

None of this observational material gets into the finished volumes – and, indeed, it would now appear cringeworthy if it did. These notes are 'asides', apparently the private, semi-amusing reflections of members of the research team to each other, but not deemed the 'stuff' which social science itself is made of. Here the contrast with Logan and Goldberg is revealing, where these kinds of observations, albeit in more sober terms, were central to the analysis. Yet even as internal asides, we now see that the classifications that intrigue the researchers are not those of personality type but those of social class, fashion, and celebrity. Appearance is now the marker of class, rather than of personality. Whether or not class matters to the respondents, it certainly matters to the sociologists. In one case, the interviewer was struck by the apparent 'un-working class' nature of the interview.

> Mr and Mrs X all dressed up to 'receive' me. She constantly called me Mr... which no one ever does. The interview began in a restrained, middle class, manner, but this disappeared rapidly as the questions got more searching.... Mrs X tall and domineering and flirted a bit with me as the interview progressed.... They were the first couple I've had who were in any sense middle class.... I imagine that coming to Luton had increased their contact with the working class (Eastbourne strikes me as a petit bourgeois town)... they used a variety of phrases which reminded me of the aggravating little remarks Wells used to put in the mouths of his lower middle class characters, bridge phrases like 'plus the fact', 'in actual fact'... but even though they were bourgeois, they didn't quite correspond to the conception of the w class bourgeoisified.[13]

This particular interview had obviously been the subject of a lot of discussion amongst the research team. There was a note on the cover of the file from another team member: 'definitely bourgeois. You should find it interesting.'

There was nothing new in social researchers huddled round their notes discussing the characteristics and general worth of their subjects behind their backs. What is new is the way that this profiling is now explicitly done in the name of class, and not in terms of personality type. And what is also interesting

---

[12] SN 4871 Box 9, Interview 77 and Box 10, Interview 130.   [13] SN Box 9, Interview 105.

is how references from literature and the media – Errol Flynn and H. G. Wells – inform such observations. But, the published work itself refuses to use any of the ethnographic material and stakes out its case solely on the basis of questionnaire responses. What we see here is a reworking of what counts as evidence, and what parts of the encounter between the researcher and the researched are viewed as salient to the formation of knowledge of the social, and how the balance between visual observation, elicited narratives, and responses to survey questions is being reworked in favour of the latter two.

What happens, in short, between the 1940s and 1960s is the redefinition of the kinds of legitimate devices that social scientists can put to work, and in particular the downplaying of visual inspection and the proliferation of elicited narrative data, details of which are abstracted from the individual and defined in terms of social relationships. In this process, the relationships between psychology, anthropology, and sociology are contested and remade, and the jurisdiction of the social sciences redefined.

4.2 THE GENTLEMANLY SOCIAL SCIENCES IN POST-WAR BRITAIN

Rather than see Logan and Goldberg's study of young men growing up in a London suburb as a throwback, it is important to recognize that up until 1955, this gentlemanly tradition was in the ascendant, and had indeed actually expanded in the years since 1945. Their study was premised on the ability of researchers to position themselves apart from, and in a position of unassailable moral security over, those they researched. It was thereby dependent on claims to cultural hierarchy on behalf of an inherently superior cultured elite, an 'intellectual aristocracy' to use Noel Annan's terms.[14] Patrick Joyce has examined some important features of the power of this 'administrative' cadre of governors. He emphasizes the production of its habitus in public schools and in Oxbridge, and sees the reform of the public schools as about the formation of a distinctive administrative ethos.

> The old idea was that one could only be a free man if one had experienced freedom in youth. In the old order boys seem to have been neither inherently good nor inherently bad: in the new order, Thomas Arnold struggled against what he called 'the bond of evil' of the small boy group. In England he felt he was surrounded by a 'mass of evil' that had to be reformed. This evil was at once a social evil, requiring social action to make school society a social community, but it was also in particular a sensual evil in the boys, something requiring action on the senses and the body. Again, the training of the flesh is seen to go hand-in-hand with the training of the mind. As Basil Willey saw, Arnold's great gift was to make ideas real, realising

[14] See Annan (1999).

the Christian Society at Rugby in practical terms, the terms of the training of the whole person.[15]

This concern with differentiation from 'evil' was a powerful impulse behind a powerful gentlemanly social research apparatus. During the nineteenth century and in the early years of the twentieth century, 'gentlemen' used their bases in local statistical and charitable societies to pioneer influential forms of social research, and which were to be prominent vehicles in urban governance.[16] All the major social science surveys which were to be canonized as progenitors of scientific sociology before the 1940s were bankrolled by private 'philanthropic' benefactors, including considerable largesse from the United States.[17] Even the state, which backed up this prodigious voluntary effort through the census and related intelligence gathering, such as through local medical officers' reports, relied on gentlemanly support, for instance through its Royal Commissions, which relied overwhelmingly on evidence given by amateur 'experts'.

The fact that empirical social science was dependent on private funds, and that such resources were only forthcoming when the benefactors concerned could place their own 'stamp' on the work is clear enough in the pioneering poverty research of Booth and Rowntree. These surveys deployed visual technologies to construct sociocultural maps of poverty and respectability. Their investigators were trusted, professional agents, who using their detailed knowledge derived from face-to-face observation, could classify households 'reliably'. Booth interviewed 400 school attendance officers to elicit their notes on every family they worked with. He then did further 'wholesale interviewing' of police, rate collectors, sanitary inspectors, school teachers, Charity Organisation Society investigators, hospital almoners, trade union officers, agents of sewing machine manufacturers, 'together with individual personal observation of particular streets and even particular households when exceptionally required'.[18]

Rowntree's study of York was more ambitious in implementing a house-to-house canvass from a specialist researcher, though he also consulted local dignitaries. This was a minute inspection of household circumstances and budgets – though the accounts given by the researched were not taken at face value: 'in some cases there was a disposition to give incorrect information, but experience soon enabled him to distinguish between truth and falsehood, and in doubtful cases the facts stated were checked by neighbours and others'. The detailed house registers include information on the architecture and visual array of the house (the number of its rooms, whether it has a yard, toilet facilities, and so forth). Its columns for remarks are dominated by visual impressions: 'house dirty, very little furniture'; 'wife and house dirty and untidy'; and

[15] Joyce (forthcoming).   [16] See Yeo (1996).

[17] The Clapham Report specifically highlighted the funding of Booth, Rowntree, the Webbs, and the (often American) research foundations (e.g. Rockefeller, Pilgrim, Nuffield, Leverhulme, Cassel, Carnegie, Commonwealth, and Halley Stewart). See also Stone (1947–8).

[18] See the discussion in Webb and Webb (1932).

such like. This tradition was therefore closely allied to that of 'household inspection' institutionalized in the practice of social work and religious practice, which was predominantly conducted by middle class, usually unpaid, women. The work of the Statistical Societies fitted into this form, as did that of the Sociological Society founded in 1903.[19] From their unassailable position, it was possible for cultivated observers to pass judgement on household morality, not by taking the views of household members themselves as a primary piece of evidence, but rather by a holistic moral assessment based on visual dissection, cross-checked with the accounts of influential notables.

By the post-war years, however, the central role for elite patronage on which this endeavour had relied was called into question. Wealthy plutocrats were thinner on the ground. The increasingly corporate structure of the British economy, where joint-stock companies replaced small privately owned firms, meant that interest in this kind of social investigation faltered. That private funding for research which did exist, changed its form, as it was increasingly funnelled through trusts and foundations which reduced – though it did not eradicate – the autonomy of the patrons. The Nuffield Foundation (formed in 1943), the charities associated with Joseph Rowntree (formed originally in 1904), and the Leverhulme Trust (dependent on a bequest in 1930) remained significant benefactors of social research, but placed their funding on a more formal, academically mediated, footing. New corporate bodies found it less important to conduct social research. In the mid-1960s Ray Pahl, teaching senior managers as tutor in the Cambridge Madingley extension classes, a pioneer form of executive training, attempted to enlist his managerial students in support for research on the rise of the managerial 'spiralist'. Many managers, evidently impressed by Pahl's charisma and enthusiasm, tried their best to lobby their companies to fund Pahl's endeavours. However, not a single company could be persuaded to part with any money to fund the research. In the end, Pahl had to resort to begging letters to his university dean for the limited resources which allowed him to write *Managers and Their Wives* with Jan Pahl. The gentlemanly social sciences lost one of their main supports, and it was not clear what the alternatives were in the absence of sustained public funding.

The post-war fortunes of the British Academy are a revealing indication of the changing powers of gentlemanly social science and its capacity to reform itself through an embrace of the public purse. Formed in 1903 specifically to promote the arts and humanities, the British Academy had by the middle years of the century become a major institutional force, a repository of the British imperial mission, through running 'British Schools' in Rome, Iraq, Athens, Egypt, Ankara, and Jerusalem. It was involved in elections to University Courts,[20] and in running several trusteeships of learned bodies. Yet its president embraced post-war

---

[19] Though see Osborne and Rose (2004), who see the spatial politics of the Geddes group associated with the Sociological Society as more ethical than that of the Booth.

[20] *Proceedings of the British Academy*, 1946, reports nominations to Hull's court, for instance.

austerity in gloomy mood, uncertain about the values of humane learning and pessimistic about the prospects for cultivation.

> [T]he peace came, but it brought disappointment. We have realised that it is easier to destroy than to rebuild; that we may dissipate in a few years material and spiritual treasures which it will take decades, if not centuries, to restore.... In such a world, what place is there for a body like ours...? None at all, some would assure us. Scholarship, learning, humane letters are doubtless an admirable adjunct to life in periods of peace and security; now they are an irrelevance.... There is observable everywhere a terrible coarsening and hardening of moral fibre. Slovenly usages of all kinds are corrupting one of the noblest parts of our British inheritance, the English language, and not English only... it may be doubted whether more than a comparatively small minority of men are at any time capable of the highest cultivation. Certainly it is easier to preserve a high standard in a limited than in a wide community of culture, and the first result of any educational extension is inevitably a decline in quality. This, though regrettable, is no more than the price which must be paid for social justice.

This pessimistic and elitist attitude was similar to that which we have encountered amongst Mass-Observers of the time. Yet it was short-lived. Only a few years later, the British Academy had pulled itself out of its depression and launched an impressive campaign to enhance its role and status as custodian of humane learning in post-war conditions. Skilful managerial moves were made. In 1950, discussions with the Treasury persuaded the Chancellor to end all its direct subsidies to educational bodies, and give a block grant to the British Academy which would henceforth administer the entire budget to learned societies and causes. Even in austerity conditions it persuaded the Treasury to double its budget, and by 1951 could report that it was able to disburse £40,000 a year. By the mid-1950s, it had persuaded several foundations, such as the Nuffield, to invest monies in it so that it could support its publication programme.

Part of its revival was due to an effective strategy of incorporating enough of the gentlemanly social science community to prevent its alienation and possible peeling off. Institutionally, this was through its section which recruited Fellows in the area of 'Economic Science' (significantly relabelled 'Economic and Social Science' in 1945), though this one section competed with eight others representing Fellows in the arts and humanities. Nonetheless, this was a route to incorporate leading economists, and the net was steadily cast evermore widely, with the election of anthropologists Radcliffe Brown and Evans Pritchard, and the LSE sociologist Ginsburg in 1954. The terms on which this inclusion took place are telling. The official British Academy obituary for Keynes in 1949, written by his fellow economist Pigou, began not as one might expect with his achievements in probability theory, in economics, or with his role as wartime statesman, but with his contribution to the arts (especially his role in building the Cambridge Arts Theatre). Pigou's obituary went on to emphasize that Keynes 'believed in that now tarnished watch-word "culture".... The chairman of C.E.M.A. must be seen as a disciple of "A gentleman of Oxford" and of the author of *Culture and Anarchy*.[21] Through such means, no doubt, other British Academy Fellows could feel common cause even with an economist. As late as 1949, the President of the British Academy could rail against the fact that 'science and economics are claiming, as against the humanities, an ever larger place in education and public esteem', apparently forgetting that he was supposed to be representing the interests of economists.[22]

It is not incidental that economics could be embraced, even if agonistically, within this gentlemanly formation. At this time, it derived its intellectual power not from any concerns with gaining empirical information, but in interpreting 'economic' information provided by powerful agents, especially from official records. At this time, economics did not celebrate its technical expertise in any marked way, but rather based its jurisdiction on being able to interpret 'macroeconomic' indicators derived from trade reports and economic data. Keynes, the most powerful economist of the middle years of the century, exemplified this kind of approach both in his person and in his economic theory.

By the early 1950s, the British Academy demonstrated a diplomatic concern to promote the social sciences, so long as they stayed in their place. When Charles Webster was elected president in 1951, he emphasized that 'not only the humanities but the social sciences are amongst the disciplines which form our body...in my personal view it is to the advantage of both the humanities and the social sciences to be as closely associated together as is possible'. Webster began insisting on the practical value of research in the humanities and the social sciences and supported rather than criticized the welfare state as a positive development.[23]

The fortunes of the British Academy reveal how a gentlemanly formation was able to regroup in the later 1940s, seeking to recast itself as cultural leader. It was thus part of Shils's post-war revival of the modernist gentry that I have discussed in Chapter 3. Crucially, it allowed a role for the social sciences, so long as they 'knew their place', within an academic structure dominated by the older humanities. This form of gentlemanly social science was personified in the example of the anthropologist Geoffrey Gorer. Because of his prominence as a prodigious reviewer in the broadsheet press, he was the most publicly visible social scientist of the immediate post-war years, though he is not a person whose reputation has endured. Having been educated at Charterhouse and Cambridge, where he graduated in classics and modern languages in 1927, he spent time at the Sorbonne,

[21] *Proceedings*, 1946. Pigou's remarks are, of course, perfectly apt, as my discussion of Keynes in Chapter 3 makes clear.

[22] *Proceedings*, 1949. See his further remarks '...I may surely say that without impropriety that science and economics are not in themselves an adequate foundation for a rich and vital civilisation...the academy is a body of scholars, not of written or creative artists as such; but it is, or ought to be, the national centre and focus for humanistic studies'.

[23] 'We live now in what can be called without irony a welfare state. The national dividend has been redistributed so that the material needs of the people can be cared for in a manner impossible in previous generations....I hope that we shall be able to demonstrate the practical wisdom of increasing the contribution of the State to the interchange of knowledge between scholars' (*Proceedings*, 1954).

Paris, and in Berlin where he penned popular fiction to make his living. At this point, his interests were indeed predominantly in literature, but this changed in the 1930s, following his absorption in the writings of the Marquis de Sade and the psychology of the 'abnormal', which led him to become interested in psychology. During the 1930s, he also became acquainted with anthropological research as he spent time in Africa, leading him to write a popular book *Africa Dances*. During the war, he spent time at the Institute of Human Relations in the United States, where he became preoccupied by mental illness, leading to an unpublished work, 'The World of Tom Madden', tracing the onset of schizophrenia through a detailed case study. He became increasingly attached to the cultural anthropology associated with Ruth Benedict and Margaret Mead, and followed their lead with studies of the psychological roots of different forms of national character.[24]

Gorer's interests marked a mix of anthropology and psychology, fused in his public, gentlemanly persona as a public intellectual. He did not hold a university appointment, but used his country house base (at Sunte House, near Haywards Heath) as his intellectual base. His model was that of Charles Darwin, a century before, or Keynes. Like Darwin, Gorer also relied on an extensive web of correspondence for information and for establishing his public persona: he corresponded with not only many of the leading social scientists of the day (he was a particular friend of Margaret Mead), but with all the leading literary and cultural figures, including W. H. Auden, Kingsley Amis, Sonia Orwell (widow of George), Ivy Compton Burnett, Cyril Connolly, E. M. Forster, Victor Gollancz, Malcolm Muggeridge, and Stephen Spender. Apart from his private income, Gorer was reliant on commissions from the press, and the highpoint of his career was as late as the 1950s, when he used his associations with the press to generate a new kind of popular social science.

Gorer is an interesting case as someone who forged a new alliance with the press as funder of social science research. On the basis of his accessible account of American national character,[25] and having later written on the Russian national character, the editor of *The People* asked him if he would be prepared to write an equivalent study of the English national character to appear in serial form in its pages. Having initially demurred, Gorer then suggested that the newspaper take responsibility for commissioning, and then analysing, a national survey of its readers. This suggestion was enthusiastically adopted by *The People*, and in 1950, Gorer issued an appeal to its readers to apply for a postal questionnaire which they could then fill in and return. The paper was overwhelmed by 14,605 requests for the survey, and by the end of June 1951, 10,524 responses had been sent in. The survey was coded and analysed by Hollerith punched cards which permitted Gorer to base his analysis on 503 cross-tabulations. His book, published in 1955, represents the first ever sample survey-based account of English culture. His theoretical framing was entirely based on a particular form of Freudian

---

[24] See Mandler (2009).   [25] Gorer (1948).

psychology, allied to a loose kind of anthropology of the American 'culture and personality' school, where the youthful formation of personality was seen as linked to the control of drives.

> To my mind, then – and I may still add, now – the central problem for the under-standing of the English character is the problem of aggression...in public life today the English are among the most peaceful, gentle, courteous and orderly populations that the civilised world has ever seen. But from the psychological point of view, this is still the same problem: the control of aggression.... This absence of overt aggression calls for an explanation.[26]

Subsequent chapters of his book focused on friends and neighbours, going out, growing up, love, ideas about sex, marriage, children and child rearing, law and order, religion, and the supernatural. Understanding the social and cultural could only be revealed through the framing concerns of personality and psychology.

Gorer's case shows how gentlemanly social science could use its interest in the normalizing and pathological to take on a wide number of topics, embracing new kinds of research methods in the process. Nonetheless, what is striking is Gorer's distance from the research process itself, and his reluctance to define himself in terms of his own methodological skills. He was absolutely clear that he knew nothing about how to analyse the data presented to him, presented himself as a bumbling innocent about research methods, and defined his expertise as the cultivated interpreter of the evidence.

4.3 SYNTHETIC SOCIOLOGY AND GENTLEMANLY EXPERTISE

Gentlemanly social science had a particular understanding of sociology. It did not see sociology as a specialist subject, with its own intellectual agenda, but rather saw it as a unifying thread combining in grand synthesis a kind of evolu-tionary account of the rise of civilization, one that was congenial to the gentle-manly world view. This kind of synthetic evolutionary sociology could act as a kind of clearing house in which more specialized historical and geographical studies could be integrated. It is for these reasons that Perry Anderson's argu-ment that sociology was historically weak in Britain has been decisively rebutted by intellectual historians who have emphasized its enormous cultural power, when conceived as a broad project rather than as a specialist subject of its own. Lawrence Goldman has shown how in the middle years of the Victorian period the 'Social Science Association' emerged as one of the most influential lobbying bodies of the day, with considerable popular appeal as well as significant intellectual clout. It forged links between social scientists and the state which sociologists in other nations wished to copy.[27]

---

[26] Gorer (1955, 13).   [27] See Goldman (2002).

It followed that sociology was not a predominantly empirical subject, though it could be associated with the considerable social research programme of nineteenth- and twentieth-century Britain. Victorian reformers and statisticians had already clearly defined the existence of a 'social' realm and the importance of 'social' policy without any need for recourse to a specialist discipline of sociology. By the early years of the twentieth century, knowledge of the social was routinely produced by a plethora of institutions: local authorities, intent on producing 'social cities',[28] governments, in their 'social reform' projects, especially those associated with Edwardian welfare provision. Of particular importance here was the rise of the local social survey during the interwar years, with around forty a year being conducted by the 1930s.[29] These were organized around gentlemanly concerns with observation, where the Sociological Society, founded by Geddes and Branford in 1903, played an important role. This enjoyed elite patronage, had limited connections to academic institutions, and drew on community studies using observational methods in the LePlay tradition. Middle-class observers descended on towns and observed what they saw. This could take the form of field reports on towns which they 'surveyed', such as Chester, with a particular interest in the use of visual methods, with a large and comprehensive photographic collection of urban and rural landscapes, comprehensive plans and charts of houses and towns, and the novel use of 'thinking diagrams'. The Sociological Society continued throughout the middle years of the twentieth century from its London base, but could not compete with the rather different vision of social research imagined in Mass-Observation and was increasingly run by a rump of old affiliates of Victor Branford.

It was in this sociological spirit that we need to understand the developments of the post-war years. In particular, the formation of the British Sociological Association (BSA) in 1950 was seen not as the birth of a new specialist area of academic inquiry so much as the reassertion of a more gentlemanly form of inquiry. At the outset, sociology was seen as the synthetic subject allowing discrete branches of inquiry to be united into an evolutionary model. Jennifer Platt has shown how the BSA was critically dependent on the patronage and support of non-sociologists, including anthropologists, economic historians, political scientists, and economists. Prestigious academics from other disciplines – Gombrich from art history, Eysenck from psychology, G. D. H. Cole from politics, and Asa Briggs from history – were very happy to publish in the new BJS.[30] By contrast, it was unusual for papers written by empirical sociologists to be published in its pages. A frequent refrain in the more synthetic theoretical papers of the BJS was the perils of empirical research when not interpreted through the right, sociologically informed, theoretical lens.

We get some indication of this synthetic, evolutionary sociology by looking at the contents of BJS. The decennial index for the first ten years of the journal (1950–9) allows us to detect its most prominent reference points of the time. It is

---

[28] Joyce (2003).   [29] Bulmer, Bales, and Kish (1992).   [30] Platt (2003).

true that classic 'sociological' theorists commanded most interest, with Marx being cited twenty-one times, exceeding Weber's sixteen, and Durkheim's fourteen references.[31] However, of more contemporary writers, anthropologists and psychologists dominated. Radcliffe-Browne is mentioned eleven times, Freud ten, Malinowski eight, and Evans-Pritchard seven along with the psychologist Kurt Lewin. The contemporary sociologists Talcott Parsons and Robert Merton also gain seven mentions. Of the most cited disciplines, there were seventy-three references to anthropology, sixty-four to social administration, forty-three to psychology, but only twenty-one to history, eleven to politics, and four to economics. This was clearly an interdisciplinary sociology oriented fundamentally to anthropology and psychology, in both of which subjects concerns about personality and culture were marked. Bastide noted the fusion of personality, culture, and society.[32] Arnold went so far as to argue that 'sociology in the end is identified with social psychology or even individual psychology'.[33] It was from psychology that sociologists were interested in the use of quantitative measures, as evident, for instance, in Eysenck's use of factor analysis in his study of political attitudes.[34]

This close association between psychology and sociology also explains the popularity of Parsons's structural functionalism and Hobhouse's evolutionary social theory as the dominant theoretical orientations of the day. Parsons's synthetic concern to link personality with social structure attracted much interest,[35] and indeed Parsons's delineation of the overlapping interests in the social, cultural, and personality were the theoretical justification for the alliance between psychology, sociology, and anthropology, which characterized the gentlemanly vision of the social sciences.

Hobhouse's preoccupation was with a science of 'character'.

> Hobhouse's political philosophy was centred on his ambition to improve 'character'...the Aristotelian ideal of the fullest possible development of each individual's powers, which depended on two beliefs: first as they unfolded, the powers of each person in all their variety were mutually reinforcing: secondly, each person's full development was assisted by the full development of the powers of other people, in their immensely greater variety.[36]

Reform was thus seen as a moral project, whereby the focus was on raising the standards of those who could not lead an appropriate life, and was couched within an ethical, collectivist frame.[37] This kind of sociology reached its apogee in the work of T. H. Marshall and R. H. Tawney, with their concern to extend citizenship, both in meaning (so that it included social as well as legal and civil rights) and in scope (so that the working classes were included within its frame).[38]

---

[31] It was not until the publication of Giddens (1971) that Marx was claimed as part of a sociological canon. Before this period, he was regarded as a sociological 'outsider' even if his ideas had some relevance for sociology.

[32] Bastide (1952).   [33] Arnold (1955).   [34] Eysenck (1951).

[35] For example, Sprott (1952) and Halsey (2004).   [36] Dennis and Halsey (1988).

[37] See Dennis and Halsey (1988) and Halsey (1996).   [38] T. H. Marshall (1951).

No clearer example of this can be found than in Marshall's celebrated essay 'Citizenship and social class', which led to the still influential discussion about the difference between civil, political, and social citizenship. What is usually forgotten is that Marshall begins his essay with an account of how his sociological framing compared to that of the economist Alfred Marshall, who had famously asked under what conditions workers could be gentlemen. Rather like the Mass-Observers I discussed in Chapter 3, Marshall realized that in the post-war years of a socialist government, this question would no longer carry much legitimacy. He therefore subtly changed it by replacing gentlemen with citizens. Through this intervention, he took up a core moral concern of gentlemanly social science yet placed it in a frame deemed more appropriate to its age.

Within this kind of sociology, the social did not exist as an autonomous realm, with its own self-determining forces and powers, but rather as the context in which individuals could best develop and prosper with citizenship being fundamentally a moral and cultural affair.

> They thus become part of an individual's personality, a pervasive element in his daily life, an intrinsic component of his culture, the foundation of his capacity to act socially and the creator of environmental conditions. (Right to Welfare, 141)

It could certainly be argued from within this tradition that the popular classes exemplified stronger moral character than the elite classes, as if their character had been hardened by the practical difficulties they had encountered during their lives. But there was no conception that moral values were fundamentally at odds with or in contestation with dominant governing ones. The fundamental issue was to extend consecrated values to everyone, to ensure that a common national social order could be achieved. This was a project which united the social sciences other than economics, which was portrayed as a philistine, amoral discipline. 'Social scientists apparently are doubtful whether economics are even social.'[39]

Just as the cultural circles associated with Stephen Spender and *Encounter*, the BSA was preoccupied with forging American connections. Under various auspices, all the leading American sociologists were invited to come to Britain at this time, and most saw it as important to be active in British sociological circles: visitors and speakers in the 1950s included the doyens of the time: Merton, Parsons, and of course Shils, whose article in *Encounter* was to be of such moment in promoting the idea that the intellectuals were becoming reconciled with the gentry. Living up to his own precept, Shils moved to Cambridge, abandoned to a large extent his quantitative, psychologically focused sociology, in favour of functionalist accounts of the monarchy and the British consensus.

The kind of sociology that the early BSA exemplified, therefore, was that of the administrative advisor to the powerful. All its major exponents, without exception, made great play of the value of sociology for policy makers.[40] The first

---

[39] Arnold (1955).   [40] See Bulmer et al. (1986).

conference of the BSA was on the 'Uses of Sociology' and attracted 250 delegates. McCrae proclaimed the 'fact that sociology is now deeply implicated in the public practice of doing good'. T. H. Marshall noted in his remarks on the BSA conference in 1953 that 'Economics was the first of the social sciences to be enticed from its ivory tower into the dust of the arena during the great depression of the thirties, and others followed during WW2. Now we are all in it up to the neck. And the problems we set ourselves to discuss at this Conference arise because we *are* being used, not because we are *not* being used'.[41]

Today, it seems difficult to divine what use the kind of idealist, synthetic sociology which was paraded in the pages of BJS could be to anyone, and certainly not to policy makers. There is plenty of opinion, but very little 'evidence'. And this is precisely the point. Sociology as a specialist, empirical discipline had not been invented. What sociologists were trying to do was to define themselves as guardians of the moral administrative project, as gatekeepers between mundane producers of social knowledge, the empirical social researchers of various kinds, and the public world of powerful elites. In this respect, they drew on the definition of sociology which saw it as a form of knowledge that could bring together insights derived from all the branches of social knowledge, from anthropology, psychology, and political economy. They were the ones who could put detailed research in context, explain how different social parts fitted together, and provide a rounded view of the social order. This explains the popularity of such synthetic theory as that of the American Talcott Parsons, where sociologists could seek to relate together facets of the social such as the personality, the cultural, and the social into an overarching social order.

The issue for sociology, therefore, was how it could claim some distinct knowledge of the social and how it could find a distinctive jurisdiction of its own in what was a very crowded field? What exact knowledge of the social did sociologists have which all kinds of other experts did not? It would be singularly unhelpful to tackle this question from the point of view of what sociology later became. It is clear that sociologists were not at all well placed to claim any kind of empirical expertise in the actual practice of social research compared to the traditions of social work, for instance, with their painstaking routines of household visits. Sociologists looked singularly ill-equipped to go into the field. Nor was their much promise in proclaiming methodological skills: the social statisticians and the civil servants responsible for the census and other surveys clearly commanded the high ground here. And, those attempts by sociologists to conduct empirical research had not exactly covered themselves in glory: the town survey movement associated with Geddes was both expensive and became increasingly embarrassing as it degenerated into an exercise in pointless voyeurism.

What we see here, is that sociologists' claims to jurisdiction, as for much of the early twentieth century, lay in their concern to be a kind of gentlemanly court of appeal: to be men of learning who were able to synthesize knowledge of the social at a higher level, so putting more specialized results of empirical research into

---

[41]   T. H. Marshall (1953).

broader perspective. This explains the pre-eminence of writers such as Hobhouse, Ginsburg, Sprott, and MacCrae in these years. These doyens of sociology, incumbents of its most senior positions in their times, today are virtually unreadable, and it seems difficult to understand their appeal and the seriousness with which they were treated. What they offered was a way of reconciling all the messy and disparate knowledge of the social produced at the time, in a kind of overarching synthesis, united by a commitment to a broad evolutionary and progressive view.

4.4 CONCLUSION

I have argued that we can best understand sociology in the immediate post-war years as caught up in, and indeed a significant part of, a realignment of intellectuals to national values, and to a gentlemanly social science. A fundamental feature of this kind of sociology rested on its non-empirical claim to jurisdiction. It could not in any obvious way claim jurisdiction over the 'social' itself – which might appear to be its 'natural' provenance. By the middle years of the twentieth century, social knowledge was so widespread that it was not located in any one discipline: at least four disciplines claimed knowledge of the social in some form or another. The discipline of social work had developed a well-tried method of eliciting social facts through the institution of case work and household visiting; social anthropologists, following the lead of Malinowski, used their ethnographic expertise to advance their own claims over social structure; whilst, as Rose has shown, psychologists played a key role in the development of social research. 'Social studies' itself, easily the most numerous of the social sciences, had considerable sway. Whilst later generations of sociologists might condescendingly see 'social studies' as amateur sociology, this was simply what it suited sociologists to believe: there was, in fact, a sophisticated body of knowledge about the social which resided under the label of social studies. And there were also numerous social investigators of one kind or another: journalists, novelists, artists, or even just flâneurs and voyeurs.

We should not view sociology in the immediate post-war years, as precursor to a specialist discipline. Rather, we see the consolidation of a gentlemanly sociology, anchored at the LSE and in the newly founded BSA, that took its cue very much from the moralizing gentry project. Taking the value of contemporary civilization for granted, they saw their role as seeking means of extending citizenship and civilization to wider groups in the population.

Yet within this project, one unresolved question was whether one needed specialist sociologists to pursue moral sociology. And if so, what form should this specialist discipline take, and how should it relate to other social science and humanities disciplines. By the early 1960s, this issue was becoming one which mobilized interest in the highest possible places. In 1962, the revered classicist and Oxford don Maurice Bowra became president of the British Academy. He was not an obvious ally for sociology. Yet even he recognized, for the first time, the possibility of a distinctive specialist form of sociology, rather than a subject which was distributed across all branches of learning.

> Other subjects, of more or less recent growth, have come into existence not by the extension of familiar fields but by cutting across them. Sociology is perhaps unlucky in its hybrid name and in the difficulty of finding a precise definition of its activities, and partly for these reasons it does not receive everywhere the serious attention it deserves. Yet the study of human society is not to be despised or neglected, and the sociologist deserves credit and gratitude for the persistence with which they have fought their cause. Their subject cuts across history, anthropology, economics, religion, geography and psychology, but that merely means that it is a new and independent approach to matters which have not hitherto been fitted into any single sector of organised learning. Just because they are studied from fresh angles in this way, these matters assume a new significance and illuminate the fields of learning which they invade.

Grudgingly, uncertainly, but ultimately supportively, Bowra had identified the rise of a distinctive, specialist kind of inquiry. The year 1962 was to be an exciting one for sociology.

5

1962: The Moment of Sociology

In this chapter, I trace the remarkable, yet little appreciated, institutional rise of sociology within the academic social sciences during the 1960s. My main aim here is to show how sociology was directly implicated in claims to modernity and novelty during this period, and to show how we can see it as a social movement, concerned to challenge traditional forms of knowing in the name of a new, rational mode of expertise which embraced science. I show how this intervention was able to avoid an overt political framing, presenting itself instead through the neutral cover of scientific discourse, which through this very same process came to be implicated in a new kind of rational national discourse. In Section 5.1, I examine the emergence of *New Society* in the early 1960s as a prime source for this moment, and in Sections 5.2 and 5.3, I show how the character of the university system was fundamentally altered by the rise of the post-war social sciences, notably through the way they challenged the authority of the arts and humanities.

5.1 *NEW SOCIETY* AS SOCIOLOGICAL EXEMPLAR

The year 1962 saw the launch of a spanking new weekly journal, *New Society*. Its novel cause was to promote popular social science to a wide audience of policy makers, educated professionals, and the broader reading public. Numerous weekly journals pitched at this audience already existed, but none of them had ever seen the propagation of the social sciences as their main concern.[1] They either took their cue from interests in 'culture' and especially literature and the arts (e.g. *New Horizon, Encounter, Twentieth Century*, and *The Listener*), or they were framed by particular political standpoints (*New Statesman, The Spectator, Universities and Left Review*, and *The Reasoner*).[2] Sociologists had occasionally contributed to these journals, but had never defined their terms of reference.

---

[1] The partial exception is the journal *The Economist*, founded as long ago as 1824, but which had long become a journal of informed commentary rather than specifically social scientific journalism.

[2] Perhaps the nearest forebear was *The Nation*, under Keynes's editorship from 1923 to 1931, which was strongly influenced by Cambridge economics. Even here, however, the journal was first

In this respect, little had changed since the early twentieth century, when Ford's *English Review* published novelists such as H. G. Wells, John Galsworthy, Arnold Bennett, Henry James, and Ezra Pound along with liberal intellectuals such as Leonard Hobhouse. The ground had shifted only slightly since the publication of *Encounter*, which began as late as 1954.[3] Despite its concern to contribute to social and political affairs, it published only a handful of social scientists (notably the American sociologists Edward Shils and Daniel Bell, and the English anthropologist Geoffrey Gorer). Its tone was firmly set by intellectuals from the arts: in its very first issue, it published Virginia Woolf, Leslie Fiedler, Christopher Isherwood, Edith Sitwell, Cecil Day-Lewis, Albert Camus, as well as its editor, Stephen Spender.[4]

The emergence of *New Society* was therefore remarkable. It immediately set out its stall in distinctive tones, with an almost missionary zeal for the role of the social sciences in contributing to national prosperity and social advance. Here, influenced by the success of the *New Scientist* which had been published since 1956, it took its cue from the natural sciences, rather than the arts and humanities, through this process wresting humanism away from the arts, into the court of the social sciences. In its first issue, it proclaimed:

> as natural science has shot ahead, so more and more people have come to feel that man has been left behind in its wake...human relationships, among both small groups and society at large seem painfully inadequate. We simply do not *know* about other people, or even about ourselves...the great need is to bring as many good minds as possible to the study of society.[5]

Its readership rose to 60,000 a week within a year, placing it on a par with its more illustrious competitors. Conservative government ministers – including Enoch Powell, later to become infamous for his 'rivers of blood' speech,[6] but at the time of writing a relatively well-respected education minister – vied with each other to contribute in its pages.[7] It ran regular features on 'Work and Business', 'Progress and Problems', 'the Arts in Society', 'Out of the Way', and 'Welfare and Policy'. Its meteoric rise marked a unique moment for sociology, testifying to the crystallization of a distinctive interest in gleaning knowledge of social life and social relationships in areas that had hitherto been ignored.

and foremost the organ of Liberalism, and also contained a large literary and cultural component (much of which was recruited by Keynes's Bloomsbury connections). Its failure in 1931, linked to falling circulation, and its subsequent merger with *New Statesman* is an indication of its ultimate weakness. See Skidelsky (2003, 318f).

[3] See Chapters 2 and 3 for a discussion of the influence of *Encounter* during the 1950s.

[4] *New Society*, 1(1), 4 October 1962.

[5] *New Society*, 4 October 1962, pp. 3–4 (italics in the original).

[6] This speech, made in 1968, articulated social and cultural concerns about black immigration and led to a major racist backlash. See Sandbrook (2006).

[7] Interviews were regularly conducted with cabinet ministers (e.g. Home Secretary in issue 1 and the Education Minister in issue 2). Several of these also thought it worthwhile to publish original writings in it, as with Education Minister Edward Boyle's extended review on Karl Popper, 12 September 1963.

Its mission depended on looking to academic social sciences for leadership and inspiration. It enrolled all the major academic figures: during just its first year, it enlisted a remarkable 'hall of fame' to write in its pages. Many senior sociologists of the time, including LSE professor T. H. Marshall together with John Madge and Barbara Wootton contributed.[8] Yet what was more striking was the interest given to new kinds of empirical social research being done by new 'up-and-coming' researchers. John Goldthorpe and David Lockwood produced early reflections on their *Affluent Worker* studies which were to shape future debates about stratification and inequality. C. C. Harris, whose study of working-class families in Swansea was to be pivotal for shaping family sociology, was featured, as well as the reflections on working-class life in Dagenham by the influential community sociologist Peter Willmott, who was already famous through his book with Michael Young *Family and Kinship in East London*. Yet, though sociologists were championed above other disciplines, the anthropological studies of Isobel Emmett, Ronald Frankenberg (shortly to become professor at Keele), Jack Goody, Raymond Leach, and Peter Worsley were all seen as worthy of full-length articles. Those applying social science insights to business were well represented. The anthropologist Tom Lupton, shortly to found the Manchester Business School, elaborated his shop floor ethnographies that were to place the study of business on a new footing. Allan Flanders introduced his new and sympathetic account of shop stewards which was to pioneer the emerging discipline of industrial relations. Tom Burns precised his distinction between organic and mechanical management systems that was central to his book *The Management of Innovation*, whilst Ronald Dore reported on his comparison between Japanese and English factories. When, after a few months, *New Society* decided to commission a special series of articles on social theory, John Rex wrote the first, on Durkheim. The social historian Asa Briggs wrote about his history of the BBC.[9] And so it goes on.

Yet we also get a sense of the paper's aims by considering who did not write for it. Celebrated figures from the 'New Left' – Stuart Hall, Edward Thompson, and Raymond Williams – were absent, though Eric Hobsbawm did write about his interest in bandits. Rather than an overt left-wing political framing, evident in the social science of Mass-Observation which had emerged in tandem with the culture of the Left Book Clubs in the later 1930s, this was a social science which presented itself as rational, neutral, and objective – and thereby better able to be politically efficacious. Here, the contrast with the *New Statesman* is instructive. The house journal of the intellectual Labour left, with a circulation somewhat higher than *New Society*, it continued to look towards the literary establishment

---

[8] Wootton published in issue 1, Madge 22, Marshall 1. Other senior sociologists such as Donald MacRae, Marie Jahoda, or David Glass wrote letters, but were not commissioned to write articles.

[9] These writers contributed to the following issues of *New Society*: Briggs (7), Rex (8 and 26), Lupton (7), Dore (4), Harris (9 and 21), Frankenberg (23), Burns (18), Emmett (17), Goody (7 and 28), Leach (1 and 12), Worsley (3), Young (3), Goldthorpe and Lockwood (3), Flanders, (20), and Willmott (23).

for sustenance. It occasionally reviewed social science books (Garry Runciman, Chelly Halsey, and John Goldthorpe being prominent reviewers during the 1960s), but social science research never obtained the kind of prominence that literary figures such as J. B. Priestley, Malcolm Muggeridge, Kingsley Martin, and Frank Kermode routinely commanded. Its sense of intellectual priorities was revealed by the kind of books it highlighted as being of interest to its readers on 24 September 1965. These included forty-two works of fiction, thirty-seven works of literary criticism, thirty-four history books, twenty-six autobiographies, but only thirteen works of politics and nineteen listed under science and social science. This was the kind of political culture which nurtured a figure such as the leading left-wing MP and future Labour Party leader Michael Foot, a celebrated author on literary figures such as Hazlitt and Blake, yet someone who knew virtually no social science or economics at all.[10]

The moment of Mass-Observation, around which interests in social research, left-wing intellectual politics, literature, and the humanities could combine, had clearly fragmented. A particularly important aspect of this fracture lay in the role of economics, which was during the early part of the twentieth century the most powerful and visible mode of social knowledge. No economists wrote for *New Society* or for *New Statesman* as they increasingly trod a more specialized and professionalized path. Even the expanding discipline of political science took on a relatively low profile. Although the literary establishment was absent from its pages, *New Society* was clearly interested in 'culture'. Its first issue bemoaned the lack of funding for the opera. The gay experimental novelist Colin MacInnes wrote a regular column on the arts. *New Society* wanted different terms of reference from the arts, since they believed they had a superior orientation to the literary and cultural brigade: thus, anticipating arguments made by cultural studies in later years. Raymond Williams and Richard Hoggart were both taken to task for being 'ill at ease' with popular culture. 'The spread of academic sociology', it went on to say, 'is likely to alter this situation. If America is any guide, we should soon have no shortage of researchers providing "neutral" studies of popular culture'.[11] It championed critical cultural analysis, for instance of the highly influential Daily Mirror cartoon strip, Andy Capp, which it attacked for portraying the working class in condescending terms.[12] More particularly, it took

---

[10] See Morgan (2007). Intellectual figures such as Dennis Healey were also part of this humanities-oriented current. Other Labour leaders, such as Crosland and Wilson, were more closely affiliated to economics.

[11] Gross (1962). For representative examples of this kind of cultural intervention, see Barker's edited anthology (2006).

[12] Having noted that 'Andy lives with his wife, Florrie, in a Tees-side, terraced, two up, two down rented house' (p. 29), Geoffrey Canon goes on to note that 'Andy Capp is commonly described as callous, mean, a boor, a bully, a wastrel, and a drunkard'. Canon resists this reading, commenting that 'Andy is socially inert – he doesn't want to know, he's idle and selfish. Is he a betrayal of socialism and the trade union movement? Well, first, given the truth that practically everyone wants to earn a living, why shouldn't working class men have the right and chance of being layabouts? This is not a middle class prerogative. Secondly, Andy is a fantasy anyway...' (*New Society*, 15 November 1962).

its stock from a concern with delineating what ordinary everyday national culture was in Britain in a post-imperial situation, when the political choices of free market capitalism on the one hand, and communist dictatorship on the other, both seemed unattractive. In trying to find a new way, even a 'third way', *New Society* sought to enlist the social sciences in the project of eliciting everyday culture: 'we are unlikely to escape from our dilemmas and to move ahead until we have a clearer picture of what we believe to be the right pattern for us. To paraphrase Churchill, what sort of people do we think we are?'[13]

The journal was, above all a proselytizing force, concerned to create a space for a new kind of sociologically oriented empirical social science, perceived to be an objective and rational study of everyday issues. An important feature of its manifesto was to strengthen sociology itself. Perceiving this to be weak in Britain, it looked admiringly towards America, reporting in glowing terms on the annual conferences of the American Sociological Association which attracted several thousand delegates.[14] It lamented the lack of public funding for social science research and campaigned for a Social Science Research Council.[15] It pioneered new models for promoting reader involvement and engagement. After only six months, it conducted a survey of its readers, as a means of demonstrating the scientific value of survey methods. Swamped by 7,344 replies, it took some weeks to analyse its findings.[16] In self-important tones, it asked the leading social scientists to comment on the survey results.[17] Such was the originality of this kind of user survey – now an utterly standard marketing method – that it announced grandly that the results were discussed in the (Conservative) Cabinet. It even pioneered the use of geo-demographics, in its own ironic reflections about the extent to which it was read in Hampstead, centre of the progressive bohemian intelligentsia.[18]

Above all, it saw a particular need for sociology. Reflecting on its first year's success, it proudly boasted,

> Our appearance seems to have coincided with something of a sociology boom.... There is the increasing readiness of departments as the Home Office and the Ministry of Housing to see that policy depends on knowledge ... in the

---

[13] Kelvin (24 January 1963, 4).

[14] See T. H. Marshall's report on the American Sociological Association conference in Washington in the inaugural issue, salivating over its insistence on the need for '*objective* social research as a basis for social planning' (Marshall's italics), *New Society*, 4 October 1962.

[15] McLachlan (1962).

[16] The questionnaire was distributed in *New Society* on 21 March, with the results published on 9 May 1963.

[17] A remarkable range of no less than thirty-four social scientific commentators were enlisted to reflect on its findings in issues 32–34. These included Hans Eysenck, Eric Hobsbawm, Edmund Leach, W. J. M. Mackenzie *New Society* (issue 32, 9 May 1963), Donald MacRae, Guy Routh (issue 33), and Asa Briggs, Michael Young, and Tommy Wilson (issue 34, 23 May 1963).

[18] *New Society* on 20 December 1963 revealed that no less than 8.3 per cent of the paper's readers lived in London NW3.

universities, especially the new ones, the social sciences are coming very much to the fore...both press and television are showing a mounting interest in either pop sociology or something nearer to the real thing. (This rise of interest ...) probably...has a good deal to do with the evident need, with increasing change, for society and its institutions to have some system of criticism built into them. The social sciences provide it. And collectively they tell us that the first of the social sciences, economics, reveals only a part of the truth about man and his motives; that affluence is not enough.[19]

We see here, in miniature, the crystallization of a managerial identity through the mobilization of social science and, more particularly, a nascent sociology: the concern – bordering sometimes on desperation – to gain the ears of public administrators; the argument that the social sciences were a tool for reflexive, critical knowledge, especially necessary in changing conditions; and the view that they stand opposed to economics, even though somewhat paradoxically economics was also a social science. A key emphasis here was on how the social sciences were themselves implicated in the formation of a new mission of national 'greatness', one which no longer rested on imperial power and economic supremacy, but on individual self-realization.[20] Sociologists were not just commentators on social change. They were themselves markers of a new rational modernity.

This early, heroic, moment of *New Society* was short-lived, and even by 1964 its articles took on a less messianic, more pedagogical character. By the mid-1960s, its commitment to the social sciences as a social movement was already waning. Even so, *New Society* remained a key reference point for social scientists well into the 1970s, and continued to publish biting commentary. Following the fraught 1974 General Election, in which the Conservative government was defeated by the Labour Party in the aftermath of a bitter mining dispute, Ray Pahl and Jack Winkler wrote an article saying that it made no difference who won the election, since corporate managerialism would continue. Pahl later recalled that it

> just went everywhere! It just whistled round the world! It was reprinted in Japan and America, and you name it, it went all round the world! And Sir Keith Joseph wrote a rebuttal in *The Times*, a major article, a turnover article in *The Times*, to say that this was terrifying to him, that this was happening, and he was determined to stop this. And he set up his own research group...(in '75 or something) avowedly in response to this thing that we wrote....And that was the beginning of the Thatcherite project. That his response to ours, was one of the main stimuluses, so he said, to thinking, 'We must stop this spread of corporatism.'

[19] *New Society*, 3 October 1963.
[20] See especially Kelvin, 'What sort of people – II': 'the concept of greatness, as it affects Britain, has undergone a fundamental change...past greatness was seen to have depended on power: economic strength, military power and empire: future greatness was seen to depend on the educational standards of the people, achievements in arts and science, with economic strength in third place' (p. 11).

Although Pahl possibly slightly overstates his responsibility for the rise of Thatcherism, his anecdote is nonetheless a revealing indication of *New Society*'s power to frame political discussion.[21]

The moment of *New Society* thereby testified to a decisive role for the new discipline of sociology to command the intellectual limelight. Until the later 1950s, the cultural power of academics based in the arts and humanities was paramount: they formed nearly all of the most significant 'public intellectuals' of their day. They achieved this position not just through their control of the traditional canon of scholarship, but also through their ability to encompass contemporary issues and concerns. Their past informed the present and framed the future. It is not incidental that when, in 1957, the two leading historians of the day publicly vied for the 'top job', the Regius Professorship of Modern History at Oxford, they did so as contemporary historians. A. J. P. Taylor's radical political commitment and left-wing intellectual identity was marked. He was soon to become famous for his book *The Origins of the Second World War*, which analysed events leading up to the outset of war in 1939, which took place just twenty-two years before his book was published in 1961. His successful adversary, Hugh Trevor-Roper, was a gentlemanly intellectual, associated with *Encounter*. He was, thus, quite prepared to take on left-wing critics of aristocracy, even using their own social and economic sources.[22] His commitment to relevance was evident in his popular book on Hitler's last days in his Berlin bunker, which had taken place just two years before his book was published in 1947.[23]

When it came to exploring social change in the later 1950s, it was academics from the humanities who informed debates about contemporary affairs, through arraying them alongside relevant historical reference points. Raymond Williams's reflections on cultural change in *Culture and Society* and *The Long Revolution* fed into political debate and social commentary, and Richard Hoggart, originally a literary specialist, became a widely discussed figure with his influential *Uses of Literacy*. After founding the Centre for Contemporary Cultural Studies at the University of Birmingham, he moved to a senior position in UNESCO in the 1960s.[24] The work of historians Eric Hobsbawm and Edward Thompson also

---

[21] In private communication, Ray Pahl emphasizes the importance of the journal for giving a sense of identity and visibility to new generations of social scientists. More generally, on Thatcherism as a response to what was deemed to be left-wing social science, see Welshman (2009).

[22] See Trevor-Roper (1953).   [23] Taylor (1961) and Trevor-Roper (1947).

[24] Williams's stature as a fundamentally literary intellectual has recently been restated in Dai Smith's biography which emphasizes the importance of his fiction to all aspects of his thinking. Hoggart himself noted the ultimate pre-eminence of Williams's literary work in commanding debates on social change, even though he clearly realized the breadth of interest in the topic.

There is an extraordinary sense of social change in the air today, and this has inspired a considerable amount of work by people who did not think of themselves, when they began to write, as part of a common 'movement'. They were relating to a common climate. We can see the results in, for example, some of the 'Angry Young Men' books, in the publication of the Institute of Community Studies, in my own *The Uses of Literacy*, in *Conviction*, in the *Universities Left Review* and in *The New Reasoner*, here too, *Culture and Society*'s importance can be indicated: of all the work done on this theme during the present decade, it is the most solidly based and intelligent. (Smith 2008, 458)

attracted huge public interest. Only the maverick social scientist Michael Young enjoyed influence on this kind of scale, and tellingly, Young was only an occasional academic.[25]

Yet we can detect an important shift during the 1950s and 1960s in which the position taking of these intellectuals. Whereas social scientists mainly sought to present themselves as somehow 'above politics' (even when articulating distinctive political programmes), historians and literary critics who sought a public role increasingly did so on the basis of a political identity. E. P. Thompson and Eric Hobsbawm were quintessentially socialist historians. Hugh Trevor-Roper, John Vincent, and Maurice Cowling were Tory historians. Raymond Williams could not be other than a socialist literary critic. In short, the stature of such intellectuals depended less on their being custodians of the canon than on their role as political partisans. We see the deep legacy of this transformation clearly marked by the 1990s, where the relative absence of intellectuals from the arts and humanities in contributing to public debate about contemporary issues is remarkable. Those who remain prominent in the public eye do not command authority on the basis of their academic expertise on contemporary affairs, but through their knowledge of earlier historical periods or with respect to the arts narrowly defined. Simon Schama's influential, televised, *History of Britain* tails off during the twentieth century, and especially after the Second World War. It is not incidental that Collini's own encyclopediac study of twentieth-century intellectuals falls off after the 1960s. There is no British equivalent of the Palestinian American literary critic Edward Said, whose work directly addressed contemporary Middle Eastern politics.[26]

How was it, then, that during the 1960s, for a brief moment, sociology seemed so pressing and so important? To understand this, I need to examine the structure of the academic social sciences further.

5.2 SOCIOLOGY AND THE SOCIAL SCIENCES IN 1949

There remains a temptation to read the existence of specialist sociology further back in time than is truly warranted.[27] In fact, as I argued in Chapter 4, sociology did not really exist as a specialist academic subject until the 1950s. Part of the reason lay in the general weakness of the social sciences anyway.[28] The Clapham

---

[25] Young had an appointment at Cambridge in the early 1960s, but this was after he had established his reputation with the Institute of Community Studies.

[26] Perhaps the nearest equivalent is the historian Ross McKibbin who writes regular columns on contemporary politics in the *London Review of Books*. It is telling that Perry Anderson, who might also qualify for this role, is now Professor of History in California.

[27] For instance, in Kent (1981) or Halsey (2004).

[28] See the discussion in Beveridge (1946), and notably the contributions by Beveridge and Bernal, and Vol. 2, 1, 1947 on 'The social sciences: a symposium', notably the papers by Simon, G. D. H. Cole, and F. S. Stone.

Report, which reported to Parliament in 1946 under the brief of considering 'whether additional provision is necessary for research into social and economic questions', and in particular whether there should be dedicated public funds to support social science research reported in sombre tones.

> at present, in some branches of the social sciences, permanent workers are so scanty and are so heavily pressed by multitudinous and conflicting claims – teaching, departmental and university administration, scientific conferences, public committees and the like – that they find it hard to give more than a few hours a month to research. In such a state of affairs, it would be an expensive waste of effort to plan larger schemes of co-operation. The first thing is to provide more high-grade workers.

Certainly, the statistics provided by the Clapham Report are striking. About 42 per cent of the 1,116 university professors in 1939 were in the arts and humanities; 27 per cent were in the natural sciences; 16 per cent in medicine; and a paltry 5 per cent in the whole of the social sciences, covering anthropology, economics, sociology, social psychology, social science, economic history, commerce, and politics. Only 3 per cent of university funding for research went to the social sciences, most of which was geared to the 'big three' clusters of the arts (28 per cent), the natural sciences (25 per cent), and medicine (23 per cent). Leaving aside salary costs, a grand total of £7,551 was available for academic research in the whole of the social sciences in 1939. It was for these reasons that the Clapham Committee argued that it was more important to put public funds into developing social science teaching departments than into supporting funded research. It is noteworthy, however, that some contemporaries detected the recommendations of the Clapham Report as the product of gentlemanly intellectuals based in the British Academy who were keen to keep the social sciences weak.[29]

And indeed, the immediate post-war years saw the dismantling and erosion of social research. Mass-Observation had flourished during the war years, largely due to government largesse, but then lost its government funding, was squeezed out by market researchers, and folded by the early 1950s. Of its two founders, Tom Harrisson was regarded as a crank by his fellow anthropologists, who saw his lack of formal qualifications debarring him from serious claims to academic status. He left England to become a museum curator in Sarawak.[30] The other, John Madge, took up poetry, before venturing back as Professor of Sociology at Birmingham University in the later 1950s. Because of the war, no census was conducted in 1941, the first time since 1801 that it had not been conducted on a regular decennial cycle. The Sociological Society itself was practically defunct by the 1940s.

---

[29] Richardson (1947). See also the comments of *New Society* itself, which noted that on the committee itself: 'there was not a single practising sociologist, anthropologist or psychologist among them, while the emphasis on economic interests was strong' (25 October 1962).
[30] See Heimann (2003).

In the immediate post-war years, the academic social science infrastructure was little stronger than in 1939.[31] Table 5.1 enumerates the size of the social science disciplines in British universities in 1949–50. There were only sixty-eight professors in the entire social sciences (slightly more than in 1939), and a total of 352 lecturers, including a large number of the most junior grade of assistant lecturer, who would not normally be expected to undertake research. Within this general scarcity, it is the almost complete absence of sociology, the disciplinary dominance of economics, and the institutional power of the LSE which command attention.

Table 5.1 reveals that only economics (sometimes twinned with politics through the study of political economy, as at Oxford and in Scotland) existed as a coherent discipline. Economics was the only social science which had broadly equivalent standing within universities to subjects such as geography, history, literature, or the teaching of languages.[32] About 231 staff, well over half of the total social scientists in Britain, worked in economics, or economics-related disciplines, and this was the only discipline where numbers of staff could rise to double figures, as they did at Cambridge, Bristol, Leeds, Manchester, Oxford, and the LSE. This was the one discipline which hosted a significant number of academic journals, and where an academic infrastructure of disciplinary conferences operated. This subject was strongly dominated by Cambridge, Manchester, and the London universities, with one-third of the total academic economists working here. This having been said, nearly every university had to have some economists – it was the only social science which was nearly obligatory.

Leaving aside the special case of economics, all the other social sciences were institutionally weak, and especially sociology. Only two universities had specialist sociologists, the LSE and Oxford (which only had one, Donald MacRae). This was somewhat weaker than politics (at Aberystwyth, Belfast, Edinburgh, and Glasgow) and anthropology (at Cambridge, Edinburgh, LSE, Oxford, and UCL). More common, and in some ways more telling, were the popularity of general departments of otherwise undefined 'Social Studies', in which there were seventy-seven staff scattered across the nation. Here, Liverpool stood out, beating the LSE into second place. In addition, there were academics in other policy-related fields, notably town and country planning, stretching to accountancy and commerce. This was clearly a very different academic world from that which existed in the United States, where large sociology departments, with distinguished graduate schools, were already entrenched and were hosting large and comparatively well-resourced research schools, for instance at Chicago.

Table 5.1 also reveals clearly the utterly distinctive nature of the LSE in 1949. It was the only university where sociology existed, and, intriguingly, the only one where economics was not the numerically dominant social science. Twenty-nine per cent of all English university social scientists, other than economists, worked at the LSE. The next highest concentration of social scientists was at

---

[31] See also the comments by Cole (1947).
[32] See Simon (1947) and Cole (1947), for further discussions.

Table 5.1 Academic positions in British social science disciplines, broken down by university, 1949–50

University	Economics	Social studies	Politics/anthropology/ sociology	Other
Aberdeen	1P 8L (a)			Acc 1L
Aberystwyth	1P 5L		1P 1L Pol	
Bangor	1P 4L			
Belfast	1P 7L	4L	1L Pol	
Birmingham	1P 3L (g)	1P 3L		Acc 1P 1L Econ History 2L
Bristol	1P 14 L			
Cambridge	2P 23L (a)		1P 4L Anth	
Cardiff	1P 8L (f)			1P 1L Industrial Rel
Durham	1P 4L (a)			
Edinburgh	2P 6L (a)	5L	2L Anth, 1L Pol	Acc 1P 5L(d), Bank 1L
Glasgow	1P 6L (a)	6L(e)	2L Pol	Acc 1P 1L
Kings, Newcastle	1P 7L			Acc 1L T&CP 1P 8L
Leeds	2P 12L	1P 4L		
Liverpool	2P 6L	1P 16L (h)		Commerce 2L
London – UCL	1P 9L (a)		1P 5L Anth	T&CP 1P 2L
London – LSE	3P 12L	1P 13L	1P 4L Anth, 2P 5L Soc, 3P 7L Pol and PA	Acc 1P 1L, Bank 1P 1L, Commerce 3P 3L, Crim1L; Demog 1L
London: Bedford Coll		1P 4L (d)		
Manchester	6P 15L (i)	4L		Acc 3L T&CP 1P 3L
Nottingham	1P 4L	1P 4L (k)		
Oxford	1P 4L (a)		2P 4L Anth, 1L Soc, 2P 6L Pol	Crim 1L
Reading	4L (a)			
St Andrews	1P 3L		2 Pol	
Sheffield	IP 6L	1L		Acc 2L
Swansea	1P 3L	1L		
Exeter	1P 6L			
Hull	1P 6L (j)	3L		
Leicester	1P 3L (j)	2L		
Southampton	8L	2L		
Total	36P 195L	6P 71	26 Pol, 24 Anth, 8 Soc	

Notes: P = professor; L = all grades of lecturer, including assistant lecturer and academic staff.
Acc = accounting, Pol = politics, Anth = anthropology, Soc = sociology, Crim = criminology.
(a) Politics and economics/Political economy
(b) Located in the Bartlett School of Architecture
(c) Economics and commerce
(d) Including actuarial science

(*cont.*)

(e) Social and economic research
(f) Economics and social science
(g) Including economics and institutions of the USSR
(h) Includes four dedicated research workers
(i) Includes five dedicated research workers
(j) Economics and commerce
(k) Social administration

Source: *Commonwealth Universities Yearbook: 1949–50.*

Manchester (with 32 social scientists), Cambridge (30), Oxford (27), and Liverpool (27). I have shown in Chapter 4 how the LSE's sociology was part of an evolutionary, gentlemanly social science, one which was not highly oriented towards empirical research. This was more generally true of social science at the LSE. It is true that its most famous director, William Beveridge, insisted on the need for factual knowledge, and that the LSE was occasionally involved in important empirical research[33] (notably the *New Survey of London Life and Labour* in 1929 under Bowley's influence). But its leading figures mainly gained their reputation in other ways as eminent public intellectuals who could use their Holborn stage to intervene in public affairs. Harold Laski was a celebrated teacher and political activist in the Labour Party.[34] Its sociologists Hobhouse and Ginsburg specialized (if that is the right word) in evolutionary social and moral theory which had little or no empirical content,[35] and its historians such as R. H. Tawney conducted historical analyses – albeit pertinent to social democratic concerns of the times. Despite its origins in the Fabian politics of the Webbs, its cultural power resided in not being politically partisan – its first Director, W. A. S. Hawkins was a loyal Conservative and its most famous Director, William Beveridge, an ardent Liberal – but in its general centrality to government and administration. Much of the early demand for its courses came from students pursuing vocational training, notably in the railways. It had strong links to the colonial civil service, and played an important role in teaching the first generation of leaders and civil servants of newly independent ex-colonial nations after 1945.

Even the more empirically minded of LSE sociologists can be seen as working in this formation. On the face of it, demographer David Glass specifically avoided

---

[33] Beveridge's four claims (Beveridge 1946) are that the social sciences should be seen as sciences, not humanities; that they needed to work from facts rather than deductive categories; that 'their common subject is man in society'; and that they need to be emotionally detached.

[34] Tellingly, even Dahrendorf, in his official history of the LSE, plays down the importance of Laski's scholarship.

[35] As David Lockwood tellingly noted in comparing Cambridge in the early 1960s with the LSE in the 1950s:

And I think the difference from the LSE was that the idea of doing research, especially empirical research, at the LSE at that time, apart from Glass...it wasn't looked on as really important, whereas I think, at Cambridge, there's much more of a scientific ethos. (Interveiw with Paul Thompson, p. 37)

questions on personality, and followed the Webbs' advice in asking only about basic factual information about household composition and income. Yet his inaugural lecture in 1950 explains his own concern with politically engaged sociology:

> Social research is particularly required first in the formulation of policy and secondly in the testing and advancing the implementation of policy....It is the contention of this lecture that provision should be made within the structure of government for social research applied to the assumptions of social policy and to the implementation of social policy.[36]

Through this framing, we can see how the moral character of the gentlemanly social sciences could be reworked within a progressive political vision. This dominance of the LSE can best be understood as the institutional vehicle for elite, administrative, social science, with its close embrace of Whitehall, leading intellectual circles, and the press. It was through rupturing the LSE's monopoly of sociological expertise that the expansion of the specialist discipline became possible. Let me turn to consider how this happened.

5.3 THE FALL OF THE LSE AND THE EXPANSION OF SPECIALIST SOCIOLOGY, 1949–70

Halsey's influential account of British sociology emphasizes that a process of diffusion took place whereby the LSE influence migrated outwards and influenced the development of post-war British sociology.[37] This is part of his more general emphasis on the persistence of the traditional liberal university, which he sees as continuing to define the mission of the modern university even in the radically expanded system which was introduced from the 1960s.[38]

> [D]espite the present clamour for expansion and change, it is worth emphasising that the university also has fundamentally conservative functions for the culture of the society of which it is a part. It is the task of the university to preserve and

---

[36] Glass (1950).

[37] Halsey and Trow (1947) and Halsey (1992). Halsey's importance partly derives from his role on a series of influential commissions during the 1960s on the future of higher education. For an extended discussion, see Chapter 9.

[38] See notably Halsey (1992). His account is in line with Annan and Shils. Halsey and Trow (1947, 214–15) quote Shils approvingly as follows:

The modern British universities, which in scholarship and science take second place to none in the world have...been belittled in their own eyes. They have never had a place in the image of the right life which has evolved from the aristocratic, squirearchical, and higher official culture...if a young man, talking to an educated stranger refers to his university studies, he is asked 'Oxford and Cambridge'? and if he says Aberystwyth or Nottingham, there is disappointment on the one side and embarrassment on the other.

hand on some of the most highly prized elements of knowledge and belief in the cultural tradition.[39]

Halsey emphasizes the status persistence of Oxbridge (as well as LSE) values even with the massive expansion of universities during the 1960s, and the creation of brand new 'plateglass' universities of East Anglia, Essex, Lancaster, Stirling, Sussex, York, and Warwick, as well as the distinctively modern Open University. Despite the significant increase in student numbers which took place in this decade, Halsey insists that they were folded into older elite values. This was partly because of the way that many academics were trained at the old universities. In particular, he argues that those sociologists who graduated at the LSE in the early 1950s (which included himself) played pioneering roles in the development of the discipline throughout the entire nation. Bringing out the relatively 'provincial' origins of these LSE graduates, and the lack of career prospects at the LSE or in the older universities, he emphasizes how their career mobility, and especially the extent to which they moved to fill chairs at new universities, generated a sense of collective, generational identity as the subject itself expanded. He also emphasizes the way that the LSE's influence arose from newer departments initially teaching LSE external degrees.

Halsey's diffusionist perspective emphasizes the continued power of the old elite universities. Using sample survey evidence from his research on academics, he noted that during the 1960s few Oxbridge dons wished to work in 'lesser' universities, whereas significant minorities of academics from other institutions wished to work at Oxford or Cambridge. Whereas two-thirds of those at Oxbridge thought it is a 'very good place for me', the figures decline to between 36 per cent and 39 per cent at the 'redbrick' universities (such as Leeds or Manchester). His survey evidence reveals that being a College Fellow and Lecturer at Cambridge was a more popular option than being a professor at Leeds or Sussex. He thus emphasized the power of old gentlemanly models of the traditional liberal university.

These influential arguments have generated a conception of the English university which takes the 'excellence' and cultural power of the old institutions – Oxford, Cambridge, and the LSE – as the linchpin of its analysis. Halsey's work focuses on how far these unquestioned values persist into the mass higher education of the later twentieth century.[40] However, this account is seriously flawed. Like his forbear, Shils, Halsey confuses status and reputation on the one hand, with the existence of traditional aristocratic and liberal culture on the other, as if it is a contradiction in terms for the former to exist without the latter. Undoubtedly, modern universities – in all nations, and indeed, internationally – exhibit a strong concern with their 'pecking order' and with differentiating between themselves on the basis of their research and teaching excellence. However, this does not necessarily mean that they adopt the models of the old university. As American

---

[39] Halsey and Trow (1947).
[40] See notably Halsey (1992). Similar interpretations are evident in Annan's account (1991).

sociologist Joel Podolny[41] insists, this concern with status can be understood as produced by thoroughly modern branding and marking devices, and can indeed be enhanced by 'indicator'-based commodified systems of higher education. The cultural pre-eminence of the old universities does not in and by itself indicate the perpetuation of older aristocratic academic values. They could equally well be understood in terms of neo-liberal marketization of higher education.

Two fundamental moments of contestation of the Oxbridge model can be identified. The first was from the mid-1950s, when an awareness that increasing numbers of pupils were staying on at school beyond the minimum school leaving age (6.6 per cent in 1952 to 12.1 per cent by 1960) led to a recognition that demand for student places was increasing. Oxbridge, valuing their intimate cultures, proved reluctant to countenance expansion and saw no need to grow. It was the northern civic universities which laid down the gauntlet, calling for university expansion not in terms of their humane, gentlemanly culture, but in terms of their role in a technocratic state. Lord Simon, Chairman of Manchester University's Council and advocate of the social sciences, issued the clarion call in 1955.

> I do hope that as a condition of the strength and welfare of the country and almost of its survival as a great power, we shall immediately set to work on a great building programme for the universities and on achieving a steady and rapid increase both in total students and more especially in technologists.[42]

This call for a technocratic national mission, deliberately distancing itself from the old imperial gentlemanly culture was even more clearly articulated by Vivian Bowden, Principal of Manchester's College of Science and Technology: 'Scientists and technologists are the missionaries of the modern age. The days when a man might qualify himself to govern the Empire by studying Greek and Latin verse are over.'[43] Manchester's vision for expansion was embodied in its bold precinct development, which deliberately cocked a snoop at Oxbridge architectural ideals through invoking system building and aerial walkways.[44] But by the later 1950s, the cudgel was taken up by C. R. Morris, Vice Chancellor of Leeds, who launched a scathing attack on the values of Oxbridge, emphasizing that their focus on undergraduate teaching undermined their research culture and that therefore 'modern' universities were the ones that valued 'professional scholarship and professional research'.[45] It was certainly the case at this time that staff–student ratios were higher at Oxbridge than in the redbrick universities. Rather remarkably, Noel Annan, now installed at University College in London, conceded this case, preferring to defend the greatness of Oxbridge in terms of their elite teaching function rather than any research qualities they might aspire to.

---

[41] Podolny (2005).		[42] Quoted in Perkin (1972).
[43] Quoted in Pullan and Abendstern (2004, 93).
[44] See Pullan and Abendstern (2004). Perhaps emblematically, the precinct was only partially built and has recently been demolished.
[45] Morris (1960–1, 329).

We teach and know our men. Sit on any committee which receives testimonials concerning students from all universities and you will see how Oxbridge tutors can analyse their men's abilities and characters in a way which their colleagues elsewhere do not begin to rival. This knowledge comes from teaching and sometimes from friendship.[46]

This was a dodgy line of defence at the very same time that influential journalists argued that it was precisely the hold of a gentlemanly establishment, tied together through webs of personal connections, that was responsible for Britain's failings.

These skirmishes were followed up by the cultural challenge of the 'plateglass' universities. Apparently liberal and largely non-vocational, these institutions appeared, on the face of it, to ape the Oxbridge model. They were often based in sleepy cathedral towns (Canterbury, York, Lancaster, and Norwich) and several deployed collegial systems with their Oxbridge hallmarks.[47] They might be thought of as trying to implement Oxbridge intellectualism more thoroughly and profoundly than Oxbridge itself, stymied as it was in the embrace of the aristocratic and gentlemanly structures, actually could. Halsey thus argues that the new universities accepted the cultural writ of Oxbridge and enshrined their liberal gentlemanly academic models. Many of the early vice chancellors and senior academics were drawn from Oxbridge ranks. Even Noel Annan, the quintessential gentlemanly don, doyen of Oxbridge and UCL, played an important role in developing the new Sociology Department at Essex as Chair of its Academic Advisory Committee. More generally, the values of the new curricula were largely non-vocational and non-technical, with a strong emphasis on humanities disciplines and 'learning for its own sake'.

Yet actually, the plateglass universities offered radically different kinds of academic values from those found in the older universities. Public interest in these was such that the first vice chancellor of the University of Essex, Albert Sloman, was asked to deliver the BBC's prestigious Reith lectures in 1963 precisely on his vision for the new university. Essex espoused a limited number of disciplinary fields, with departments to be housed within three schools: physical sciences, social sciences, and comparative studies. Sloman hence redefined the humanities as a form of comparative social science, and placed the social sciences at the heart of its academic structure. In an even greater blow to the arts, those studying in comparative studies were not allowed to study European nations, with their canonical cultural icons, but had to study culture from different continents. This model was similar to that developed in Sussex, which also placed the humanities within comparative regional schools. This orientation was evident in all the plateglass universities, even such as at York which was more enthusiastic about building large humanities departments. Students were often expected to take courses from outside their specialist discipline. Liberal studies

---

[46] Annan (1960–1, 357).

[47] Perkin (1972) argues that the location in small towns was largely contingent owing to the supply of suitable land and labour in these locations.

of science were encouraged. In this innovative milieux, the social sciences were championed as the most appropriate specialist disciplines for modern universities, and within the social sciences, sociology in particular was universally endorsed. All the plateglass universities recruited flagship groups of sociologists, and saw the formation of sociology as central to their identities as modern universities. New teaching methods – notably the seminar, which was imported from America – were a critical response to what were seen as problems both with the Oxbridge tutorial system and with the culture of teaching through lectures as was practised in the civic universities such as Manchester (which was to lose many of its more ambitious younger staff through frustrations with its professorial autocracy).[48] Ian Watt, who oversaw its introduction at the University of East Anglia, emphasized that the seminar allowed appropriately 'research-led' teaching since it depended on students coming to seminar with ideas to share and explore collectively.[49]

Specialist sociology was not entirely the product of these plateglass universities. Leicester had famously opened up its influential department in 1955 and many leading sociologists of the day, including Norbert Elias, Ilya Neustadt, John Goldthorpe, and Anthony Giddens worked there. Its beacon-like status was such that talented English students, such as John Sutherland (later to become Professor of English at UCL), could not find room on its courses.[50] Nonetheless, it was at the plateglass universities that specialist sociology departments prospered. Sociology at Essex University was the classic case. Peter Townsend, who had experience at the LSE and the Institute of Community Studies, was recruited at the young age of 30 to be the first Head of Department through a direct approach from the first vice chancellor, Alfred Sloman, which he saw as a 'huge opportunity both for Sociology and Social Policy, and that, as a young person just developing, I felt I just had to take it. I very much had that sort of attitude, of being bequeathed – as an opportunity which I hadn't bargained for arising for many years'.[51]

Townsend's enthusiasm was related to his criticisms of the LSE, where he had studied as an undergraduate, which he thought was 'poorly managed and very unimaginative and uncreative'. Townsend makes it clear that he did not share Noel Annan's view of sociology as a form of 'social arithmetic'.

> But I wasn't, myself, eager to restrict my work to that of what could be described as social arithmetic. Sociology was far more important and vaunting than that, and was an intellectual and emotional challenge of the first order, because I believed then, as I believe now... that sociology is pre-eminent in some respects in relation to other subjects.

The new sociology departments were able to take advantage of growing political rifts which were evident at Cambridge and the LSE. At the LSE left wing, younger sociologists were alienated by the conservative sociology of Donald MacRae and Julius Gould. Bottomore went to Sussex, Tropp to Surrey, and Goldthorpe to

---

[48] See Pullan, *History of the University of Manchester*.   [49] Watt (1963–4).
[50] Sutherland (2007).   [51] Townsend, interview with Paul Thompson.

Leicester. At Cambridge in the early 1960s, where there was the potential for forming a distinctive sociology grouping, the grouping of Shils, Annan, and Runciman alienated the Young Turks, Goldthorpe and Lockwood. One result was that David Lockwood, the undoubted star amongst the new generation of sociologists, chose to leave Cambridge to take a chair at Essex.

Sociology in the new plateglass universities was energized by strong departmental culture, seen as 'adventurous, pioneering...democratic...intellectually galvanising', and different from that which College or Faculty structures could allow. Ray Pahl, who had been a student at Cambridge and a graduate at the LSE, was similarly emphatic about his excitement at working at Kent.

> One was just jolly pleased to be in what seemed an exciting new development...one began enormously enthusiastic and loyal, and excited about, about being part of a new university project. And it seemed to be, you know, real going back, to think of going back to a conventional university after that, that to go off to some, you know, Manchester or...or Liverpool, after being at Kent, would seem to be losing all the excitement of these very flexible and friendly sort of...well, a new institution, it developed its own pattern. And it was a nice part of the country to be. So we were all happy to just get on with it.

The plateglass universities were much more selective in their support for those disciplines deemed to have markers of old forms of scholarship. No anthropology departments were formed in the new universities,[52] and only at Sussex were significant numbers of anthropologists recruited to the new interdisciplinary schools. Essex, Warwick, and York did not create geography departments, seeing them as throwbacks to colonial Britain. With the exception of Essex, politics departments were much smaller than those in the civic universities such as Leeds, Manchester, and Sheffield. And although there was universal enthusiasm for history, it was those historians who were attracted to social history and more critical social science perspectives who set their stamps on their new departments: Perkin at Lancaster led a new interest in 'social history'. Aylmer at York fashioned an administrative history of evolutionary social change and was joined by the Marxist Gwyn Williams, one of the first advocates of Antonio Gramsci's thinking. Similar currents were evident in history at Sussex. E. P. Thompson's appointment at Warwick was however resonant of the problems that gentlemanly intellectuals faced in the new universities. Celebrated author of *The Making of the English Working Class*, he found the business ties of *Warwick University Ltd* repugnant and retired to his country seat in Worcestershire.

The rise of the plateglass university was hence part of a wider transformation of the disciplinary structure of the university which allowed a much more significant role for the social sciences and which displaced the Oxbridge gentlemanly model in significant ways. It is worth reminding ourselves that this was not universally welcomed. In one of his less well-known poems, Philip Larkin worried about the capacity of the social sciences to defend Britain's military role.

---

[52] See Pritchard (1967).

When the Russian Tanks roll westward, what defence for you and me?
Colonel Sloman's Essex rifles? The light horse of L.S.E.?[53]

There was also opposition from the old guard at the LSE, largely left high and dry by the sociological excitement elsewhere. There, doyen of British sociology, T. H. Marshall, wrote critically of the emergence of a new kind of empirical sociology deploying 'scientific' methods. Turning his wrath on Noel Annan, who was involved in the development of sociology at Essex as well as at Cambridge, Marshall remarked:

> the subject sponsored by the movement, or school of thought, represented by Noel Annan is not scientific sociology…but rather social studies using scientific techniques to collect and present factual information.

He then turned his ire on Peter Townsend, already becoming famous for his use of social surveys and personal documents to research poverty.

> the marriage of techniques cannot give rise to a science. Something more is needed…for technique without science is inevitably driven to what Bales calls the 'flip-flop' type of explanation which is not derived in any way from the research itself nor drawn from a system of theory and ordered knowledge, but is tailored ex post facto to fit the data, even if this means that it must be turned inside out because the facts discovered are the reverse of those anticipated in the hypothesis.[54]

New methods were therefore seen as an abandonment of the traditional sociological mission by the old establishment.[55]

But this hostility to sociology was too little, too late. By the mid-1960s, specialist academic sociologists now played a key role in a much larger social science apparatus. Social scientists had their own Research Council from 1965, its first chairman being Michael Young. Its initial emphasis was on supporting social science disciplines rather than in seeking to support research laboratories or institutes, as was more common in the natural sciences. In 1970, no less than 52 per cent of its budget was for postgraduate grants, and it organized its work primarily through different disciplinary subcommittees. Its budget rose from £2.2 million in 1972 to £105 million in 2004–5, changing from under 2 per cent to (only) 5 per cent of public spending on research councils, most of which was geared towards the natural sciences.[56] The most important shift here was the way that the arts and humanities, the largest single area for research spending in 1939, lost ground. Its share of research spending fell from 28 to 3 per cent by 2004–5.

We can trace through these disciplinary changes by considering the Economic and Social Research Council's review of the demography of the social sciences in 2003–4. By this time, there were no fewer than 14,000 academics in the core

---

[53] Larkin, *Collected Poems*, 172.   [54] Quoted in *New Society*, 1963.

[55] The extreme figure here was Donald MacCrae, who continued to espouse a humanities-based sociology into the 1970s to an increasingly disinterested audience.

[56] Details from DTI Science Budget allocations at <http://www.dti.gov.uk/files/file14994.pdf>.

Table 5.2 Size of academic social science-related disciplines, 2003–4

Discipline	Academics	Research active (%)
Economics	1,530.7	57.0
Anthropology	331	92.7
Politics	1,407.7	79.3
Sociology	1,400	63.1
Social policy	1,773.1	68.4
Social work	812.8	44.8
Psychology	2,871.4	64.4
Town and country planning	677.9	51.7
Business studies*	6,049	45.8
Accountancy	814.4	
Education	5,094.5	42.5
Linguists	574.8	87.4
Geography	1,759.8	73.6
Law	2,600	
Media and cultural studies	1,178.8	
Total	29,213	

*Includes accounting and finance.
Source: ESRC Demographic Review.

social sciences, and up to 30,000 in fields with social science expertise.[57] Table 5.2 shows the proportion of academic researchers working in different social science disciplines in 2003–4. By this time, about 25 per cent of academics worked in the social sciences, only slightly below the numbers working in medicine and health, and in the natural sciences. Academics in the arts and humanities composed little more than 12 per cent of academics, having fallen well behind the social sciences.

Table 5.2 reports the sizes of specific social science disciplines in 2003–4, showing some important shifts from the 1940s. Firstly, we can see the rise of the core social science disciplines themselves. Most of these had expanded to become large groups of academics, the main exception being anthropology, which in the 1940s was the same size as politics and sociology, yet had evidently failed to expand as rapidly as these two subjects thereafter. Within the core social sciences, economics had lost ground, in relative terms, and politics had become the single largest discipline. If the 'social' disciplines of social anthropology, sociology, social policy, and social work are grouped together, they become clearly the numerically dominant part of the social sciences, with over half of the core social science staffing. The most interesting departure from this fold is that of psychology. In 1945, psychology regarded itself as a core social science, where it looked closely to collaborate with its disciplinary partners, but by 2001, it associated

[57] See also Commission on the Social Sciences, 2003–4.

predominantly with medics and to a lesser extent natural scientists. Only in a handful of institutions, such as the LSE or Cambridge, were there echoes of the earlier collaboration.

Secondly, we see the rise of new disciplinary fields which hardly existed in 1945 but which rose to prominence in the post-war years, and were strongly influenced by social science models. The most important of these were in business studies, which had replaced the small-scale teaching of 'commerce' which existed in only a few universities in 1945. There was also a huge increase in the field of education. These applied disciplines looked almost exclusively to the social sciences for their intellectual tool kit (though medical and natural science models had some limited purchase), especially with respect to their research methods. By the end of the century, more academics worked in these fields than in the arts and humanities.

Thirdly, we can see a new group of disciplines emerging as hybrids drawing together the humanities and the social sciences. Area studies, which Wallerstein has shown emerged out of American post-war geopolitical concerns, brought together those with humanities expertise in language and history, with social science concerns with social development, international relations, and politics. Media and cultural studies fused literary and social science interests. Fourthly, we can see the rising influence of social sciences within the traditional humanities. Rather than the previous self-definition of such disciplines as concerned with cultivation and '*bildung*', increasing numbers of researchers looked to the social sciences to justify their expertise. Foremost amongst these was human geography, which largely abandoned its focus on the culture and traditions of fixed regional spaces and forged close relationships with sociology and anthropology and self-identified as a social science. These influences were more contested within history. Here, the post-war expansion of economic and social history and the manifesto for 'social science history' associated with the French Annales school and the Marxist tradition captured the intellectual high ground from the 1950s to the 1960s, but was then challenged from the early 1980s in the face of the resurgence of political, 'narrative' history. Even so, the dialogue with the social sciences was central to debates within history about its identity, its methods, and its concerns. There were numerous other disciplines where we can trace the influence of social science models such as in law, medicine (especially nursing and primary care), archaeology, computer science, and engineering.

The expansion of this social science infrastructure, in a university system that was itself undergoing major growth and transformation took place especially at the expense of the arts and humanities. Although the natural sciences remained dominant in terms of their research funding, and with levels of staffing above those of the social sciences, their cultural authority was considerably undermined by the various critiques of science, especially in the name of ecology and the critique of rationality. By the end of the twentieth century, it is possible to talk of the cultural dominance of this social science establishment. There is a striking lack of reciprocity in the borrowing of ideas between the social sciences and other disciplines. In true imperialist style, social scientists displayed their confidence by extending their analyses into the jurisdiction of other disciplines, ranging from critical analyses of the professional power of medics, lawyers, and other 'experts'[58]; the burgeoning popularity of 'social studies of science'[59]; and the critique of 'ideology' and 'humanism' within the arts disciplines.[60]

5.4 CONCLUSIONS

The second half of the twentieth century saw a profound, though remarkably neglected transformation in the disciplinary base of the academic infrastructure. In place of the demarcation between sciences and arts, the social sciences emerged as a numerically large group of academics, and also as key intellectual brokers between the arts and sciences. Within the social sciences, sociology which had previously been seen as the synthetic social science emerged as a specialist academic subject of considerable size and significance.

There was nothing inevitable about this shift. There is no reason to suppose that sociologists, or social scientists more generally, have some innately superior capacity to understand contemporary affairs. Rather, we need to see this contestation as a political battle. The success of the social sciences in celebrating their expertise lay in being able to separate out the contemporary – the site of social change – from the longer term, hence contesting a more historically embedded recognition of the links between past, present, and future.[61] The rise of the social sciences, as they contest the power of established disciplines, involves forging a vital relationship to claims about the new, and in this process we can see the collapse of an older form of gentlemanly social science, and the formation – halting, uncertain, yet ultimately triumphant – of new discourses of the social as an immanent site of change. Whereas earlier conceptions of change had defined it either in terms of longer-term evolutionary process or through exogenous 'shocks', change could now be detected as immanent within the everyday life of

---

[58] The first critical accounts of professional power date from the 1960s, for a representative and very influential account within sociology, see Johnson (1972).

[59] It is not incidental that the first sociologists to study science did so in the United States, where the social sciences were strongest, yet even here early formulations were deferential. The Edinburgh School sociologists in the 1960s were the first to develop a systematic critical account of the pretensions of scientific knowledge, and this body of work became increasingly influential in the latter decades of the century.

[60] It is not incidental that the boundaries between 'theory' and 'social theory' are thinly drawn. Virtually all the influential theoretical currents (Marxism, Foucault, structuralism, post-structuralism, post-colonialism, etc.) in the social sciences and the arts and humanities are critical of the humanist notions which had underlain the concerns with 'character', 'cultivation', and 'culture' within the traditional arts subjects.

[61] Thus, the influential poet and literary critic Stephen Spender upheld the distinction between 'contemporary' and 'modern' and saw those who only addressed the former as having limited horizons.

the social fabric. Ordinary lives thus became pregnant with change, ripe for social scientific analysis.[62]

This moment allowed an alignment between the new technical identities I have examined in Chapters 2 and 3, and the emergent social sciences to take place. We are still living in this moment. The remaining chapters of my book show how this moment was anchored in a series of powerful new models for eliciting the social in forms of devices – the interview and the sample survey – which were both mundane yet also extremely effective.

[62] For some programmatic remarks on this conception of immanent social change, see Savage (2009*b*), and in more historical vein, the special issue of *Contemporary British History* on the theme of 'Contesting Affluence' edited by Shinobu Majima and myself.

Part II

The Social Science Apparatus

6

1956: The End of Community: The Quest for the English Middletown

During the 1920s, the anthropologists Helen and Robert Lynd, in their study of Middletown, had shown to an eager and receptive American audience how a community study could hold up a mirror to American society. A detailed account of Muncie, Indiana, an obscure, little-known Midwestern town was used not to mobilize anxieties about problem populations but to create conceptions of the 'average American'.[1] The Lynds examined the day-to-day activities of ordinary Americans, at work, at play, and in their homes. Their publications were feted as vital accounts of what it meant to be American, and became lauded as an example of how the social sciences could assist national understanding. As I have shown in Chapter 5, British social research was organized at this time in a very different way, as a means of mapping morally suspect populations. During the 1950s and into the 1960s, the struggle to mobilize an English equivalent of Middletown, to use the community study as a means of defining national identity was to prove a compelling quest – as fraught in its own way as the last major British triumph in exploration – the ascent of Everest in 1953. Where could Middletown be found? Was it English, Scottish, Welsh, or British? Was it located in the metropolitan heartlands of South-East England? Or should it be positioned in the industrial areas of Northern England to represent the nation's industrial status? In the country or in the city? Was it working class or middle class? Whereas the American Midwest acted as a kind of symbolically neutral space detached from the social crucibles of the major American cities, it was not clear what the no equivalent location in Britain.

Furthermore, which kind of expeditionary force was best equipped to find it? It was anthropologists, after all, who had claimed expertise around the kind of ethnographic methods which allowed them to gain knowledge of local communities. Geographers had unparalleled expertise in map-making and in detailed local knowledge. It was political scientists who pioneered local studies in England, through their research on local campaigning and local political alignments.[2]

---

[1] Lynd and Lynd (1929). See the full account of the historical importance of this study in Igo (2007).

[2] See the local studies in the Nuffield General Election Studies, for example Butler (1952) as well as Birch's study of Glossop (1959).

The story I will tell in this chapter concerns the way that sociologists, whose expertise was initially the most limited and most dependent on a moralistic sociology of mapping disreputable populations, sought to muscle in on this quest to find Middletown, through seeing it as a place in transition. Ultimately, therefore, their failure to produce a scientific community study was to be deeply significant in closing down a landscaped vision of social analysis.

We can gain an initial awareness of the stakes involved in the quest for Middletown by considering a singular and instructive case. Bill Williams's account of the village of Gosforth in Cumberland was published in 1956. This was one of a series of community studies which appeared during this remarkable period – with book-length monographs on Glossop in Derbyshire, Featherstone in Yorkshire, two on Bethnal Green in London, Glyn Ceiriog in North-East Wales being amongst them.[3] But Williams was the first to explicitly frame his study as sociological, signalled most obviously in its very title, *The Sociology of an English Village*. Yet in fact, Williams's claims to pursue a sociological study were not straightforward. He had actually been trained in anthropology and geography, being one of the first social scientists to be appointed as a Geographer at the University College of North Staffordshire (Keele). His work drew on ethnographic and documentary sources rather than the kind of sample-based research that other sociologists of the time were beginning to champion.[4] He had interviewed every single inhabitant (with the exception of one, apparently reclusive, household). He had composed detailed maps of the landholdings of every farm, and carefully delineated the kinship structure of the local inhabitants.

What was novel about Williams's work? Perhaps most importantly, he departed from the tradition of studying the Celtic 'periphery', which remained the province of anthropologists. Indeed, his intervention contested the familiar pattern of the metropolitan observer going to the provinces. He was a Welshman looking at England. Williams's most obvious sparring partner here was the Jewish Londoner anthropologist Ronnie Frankenberg whose ethnography of the Welsh village Glyn Ceiriog was published to much acclaim in the same year as Williams's study.[5] For Williams, a sociological concern involved reversing the metropolitan gaze and taking a Welsh perspective on the English. As he reported at the end of his book,

> Although handicapped as an 'offcomer', the analysis of the social structure was much facilitated by the fact that I approached it as a Welshman who had lived for some time in southern England. The contrast between the latter and much of the

---

[3] See the discussion in Cohen (2005). Examples include Birch (1959), Dennis et al. (1956), Robb (1954*a*), Young and Willmott (1957), Frankenberg (1957), and Emmett (1964).

[4] See Chapter 8.

[5] A notable example being his review of Frankenberg's *Village on the Border* in *Sociological Review*, which stated that 'Dr Frankenberg's study is weakest and most cursory in its treatment of religion, devoted to the dichotomy between Church and Chapel. Welshmen, at least, will find it surprising that the author, with his keen eye for social disharmony, sees practically none between the four chapels in the village. Does he speak Welsh?'

social life of Gosforth, and the numerous similarities which exist between it and Wales is particularly striking.[6]

Williams deployed a subtle geography, one which plays off the Welsh against the English but also the southern English against the northern English. This manoeuvre allowed a distinctively northern English location to be seen as intermediate between the two extremes of Wales and the English south. A kind of Middletown.

This geography is associated with Williams's deployment of social class as a major feature of the Gosforth social structure. As he later reported, he first became aware of the English class system during his student days in Aberystwyth, when King's College London had been evacuated to this Welsh capital in hiding, home to a distinctive school of Welsh geography, with strong interests in social anthropology. This work emphasized the value of studying Welsh communities, seen as lying outside English influences.[7] Yet, Williams was intrigued by the contrasts, seeing that the manners of King's students and staff were very different from those that he was used to, growing up in the industrial town of Merthyr. This perception was used to frame his account of the strangeness of Gosforth.

> Wales is a...is a small country, and I grew up being accustomed to friendship networks, work networks, kinship networks and so on. And, of course, when I went to...when I then went to Gosforth, I regarded myself as going to a foreign country, and when I got off the bus in Gosforth, there was absolutely – I don't think I put this in the book, I'm sure I didn't – absolutely a beautiful example of this, which made me convinced I'd come to the right place, because I got off the bus, and there was a woman coming down the road, on a white horse, and she stopped outside the shop – Barnes's shop – and Mr. Barnes came out and said...and actually touched his forehead, said, 'Good Morning, Miss Keene', and she said, 'Good Morning, Barnes', like...you wouldn't do that in Merthyr! And she then gave him her order, and he wrote it down and said, 'Yes, I'll bring it up this afternoon, Miss Keene', and off she went. And I discovered that Miss Keene was actually the Rector's daughter, and the Rector's daughter clearly belonged to a different social class from Mr. Barnes. And I thought, 'Here is the English class system in action!' (LAUGHS) And it...it couldn't be more different from industrial South Wales, where there was a strong egalitarian ethos.[8]

Williams *wanted* to find class divisions in this English village. It confirmed him in his sense of English strangeness. But in this endeavour he relied on American referents. His conceptual thinking drew on American social science, notably Lloyd Warner's *Yankee Town* studies, with their insistence on the importance of class and status divisions. Revealing the power of class in an English village involved importing an American vocabulary.

[6] Williams (1956, 200).

[7] See, for instance, Rees(1951, v), which defends its choice of Llanfihangel as its case study area by noting that 'in spite of its proximity to the English border, the social organisation of the area remains fairly representative of the Welsh uplands generally'.

[8] Williams and Thompson (2008, 97–8).

We hence see the power of two foreign visions of the English, from Wales and from America, crystallizing in the form of a distinctive appeal to sociology. From Wales came an awareness of the power of the English upper classes; from America came the use of a distinctive social vocabulary. The old history of English imperial power in Wales, and the new deployment of a modern social scientific apparatus are thus conjoined.

In this chapter, I trace how these contestations over the English Middletown played out during the 1950s and 1960s, and how they ultimately laid the ground for a new sociology of social change which was able to abstract from the landscape in the name of defining modernity itself. I begin by examining the politics of landscape as it had been mobilized in literary work during the early and middle years of the twentieth century. I show how the contested battles between a provincial middlebrow and metropolitan highbrow carried with them different evaluations of the landscape itself. I argue that these fraught terms defined the arena in which the post-war social sciences operated, making it difficult for them to present an abstracted conception of the English nation. Although sociologists sought to use extensive research on northern England to emphasize the extent of social deprivation and inequality, this ultimately reinforced these long-standing tensions.

In the second part of my chapter, I therefore show that it was unsettling accounts across the Welsh border which was to prove pivotal in mobilizing a vision of the English community as defined not by the metropolitan–provincial tension, but in terms of its class relations. This was an endeavour which both anthropologists and sociologists shared, making it possible to generate – for a while – an interdisciplinary account of the ordinary English. Yet the final part of my chapter shows how ultimately the sociologists sought a new, and profoundly influential, take on the local community. By defining the local as a site of social change, rather than as a location in a wider landscape, they abstracted the local study from its environment, and so mobilized them as displaced exemplars of the nation. This form of analysis, I show, involved the use of sampling, survey, and interview methods, which gave sociologists a distinctive lever to prise change open, and in the process involved the loss of Middletown.

6.1 CONTESTING THE ENGLISH LANDSCAPE

During the middle years of the twentieth century, in a period of national anxiety driven by a sense of the loss of British industrial and imperial power, made visible by the challenge of Nazi Germany, the quest for English national identity reached new heights.[9] This concern to define England was fraught by a recognition of the difficulty of finding points of contact between its contrasting and conflicting

---

[9] Kumar (2003).

elements. George Orwell, whose work was fundamentally concerned with defining a politically progressive Englishness as a counter to the imperial British identity that he detested, was well aware of the difficulties of this endeavour.

> Are there really such things as nations? Are we not 46 million individuals, all different? And the diversity of it, the chaos! The clatter of clogs in the Lancashire mill towns, the to-and-fro of the lorries on the Great North Road, the queues outside the Labour Exchanges, the rattle of pin-tables in the Soho pubs, the old maids biking to Holy Communion through the mists of the autumn mornings – all these are not only fragments, but *characteristic* fragments of the English scene. How can one make a pattern out of this muddle?[10]

One way of making sense was to abstract particular motifs out of the force field identified by Orwell. This was the path taken by British prime minister John Major in 1991 when he cited only the 'old maids' motif in his rendition of Orwell's vision and so forgot about the lorries, factories, state institutions, and pubs. Orwell's own resolution to this anxiety over national identity was to hold open the possibility of a progressive national identity which recognized the reality of the industrial areas, whilst at the same time recognizing the view from outside England, in which even its differences could nonetheless be seen as having something in common.

Orwell's politics was clearly embedded in the wider mobilization of landscapes within literary narrative which during the mid-twentieth century had ended up in a marked stand-off. Franco Moretti, taking his lead from Benedict Anderson, has brilliantly explored how 'the novel found the nation state',[11] through defining its plot lines within the thresholds of imaginary national space. He shows how the desire and fantasy of the novelistic plot in its key phase of the late eighteenth and early nineteenth centuries involved a process of territorial uprooting in which nation resolved local turmoil.[12] Yet by the middle of the twentieth century this national literary idiom was increasingly fractured between highbrow and middlebrow forms.[13] Highbrow novelists set their plots in the metropolitan and estate heartlands of the nation, ignoring the provinces and the boundaries of the nation, increasingly through refusing to situate literature in a definite and fixed location but rather placed in some quarter of geographically unspecified 'deep

---

[10] Orwell, 'The lion and the unicorn', 252. The Penguin edition notes in a footnote that there is an additional source of difficulty to that enumerated by Orwell: his population figures are actually for the whole of Great Britain and not just England. This kind of account of national culture through the delineation of discrete, unconnected facets was not new to Orwell – it was also espoused by Eliot (1949).

[11] Moretti (1999, 17).

[12] 'A striking instance of the problem solving vocation of literature, (Austen's) plots take the painful reality of territorial uprooting – where her stories open, the family abode is usually on the verge of being lost – and rewrite it as a seductive journey: prompted by desire, and crowned with happiness. They take a *local* gentry, like the Bennetts in *Pride and Prejudice*, and join it to a *national* elite of Darcy and his ilk': Moretti (1999, 17–18).

[13] See Chapter 2 for a discussion of these.

England'.[14] Provincial middlebrow novelists on the other hand – like Orwell – insisted on the physical and social reality of the peripheral locations, making the process of abstraction from these locations an act of pain and loss, rather than a marker of national resolution. Within this framing, the journey emerged as the major device for national reconciliation. The appeal of this framing was nowhere better apparent than in the success of J. B. Priestley's *The Good Companions*, which was to become one of the best selling works of fiction during the 1930s and became canonical for middlebrow culture. Priestley relates how a travelling theatrical troupe was assembled from three diverse people each representing a different social type and physical location: Mr Oakroyd, from the weaving sheds of the industrial North; Miss Trant, the colonel's daughter from the Cotswolds, and the defiant teacher Inigo Jollifant, Cambridge graduate and refugee from an East Anglian private school 'crammer'. Through their coming together and travels they defined the nation through navigating its diverse localities. Yet perhaps more emblematic of the tensions which were to unravel was the narrative of Englishness embedded in John Cowper Powys's novels, and notably *A Glastonbury Romance* which treated the Somerset town as template for the class relations and sexual antagonisms of English society. Here the forces of East Anglian rationalism were pitched against Western Celtic mysticism. In a memorable chapter, this relationship is made concrete in a car trip from East Anglia to Glastonbury, in Somerset, which involved an emotional awakening at Stonehenge, quintessentially seen as 'very English' by the book's hero.[15] It was in these ways that the journey, and especially the car journey, became a fundamental marker of English national identity, enshrined most emphatically in the 'motoring pastoral' associated with H. V. Morton and the Shell Guides.[16]

What emerged during the interwar period was therefore a field whereby idioms of deep organic England – based predominantly on images of the rural landscape – stood opposed to accounts of provincial 'real life'. And this transient quality of deep England presented its own problems, for if it could not be located, then how real was it? Attempts to picture the countryside in fixed, real settings were thereby provoked as a means of objectifying the ethereal. The picture book *The British Countryside* dating from the 1950s, is a revealing indication of the cultural tensions this led to (see Table 6.1). Forced with the need to assemble photographs from specific sites, its biases and absences could not be hidden. The large towns and cities are necessarily entirely absent, except on the few occasions that they can be rendered picturesque through evoking primitive associations, as with pictures of the West India Dock in London, or of Aberdeen harbour. Nonetheless, London serves as the gravitational centre of these images, with a clear east–west axis juxtaposing images from the South-East (notably from Kent and Sussex) and the South-West (notably Devon), which between them provide a repertoire of an idyllic rural counterpart to the absent metropolis.

---

[14] On the importance of deep England see Wright (1985).   [15] Powys (1932, 97).

[16] See Matless (1998, 64f).

Table 6.1 Images of British rural life, 1950

	Country folk ways	Town and village	British landscape	Rural crafts	Total
South-West	8	17	11	6	41
South-East	9	19	8	7	44
Home Counties	5	10	5	2	22
East Anglia	2	11	6	2	21
North-West	1	4	5	3	13
West Midlands	4	7	11	2	24
East Midlands	0	7	2	0	9
North-East	1	5	6	0	12
Scotland	3	13	18	6	40
Wales	0	5	11	3	19
Northern Ireland	1	2	3	1	7
Generic	9			10	19

Source: Vesey-Fitzgerald, *The British Countryside in Pictures*.

The main exception to this southern English focus is the deployment of extensive Scottish images, especially in the chapter on the 'British landscape', testimony to the author's insistence that a common British rural identity transcends any national particularity. The dominance of Scottish (and to a lesser extent, Welsh) pictures in the chapter on the landscape has the effect of naturalizing national differences, rather than defining them as social and human concerns. It is however striking that a picture of Princes Street in Edinburgh is the only urban image used in the book, where it sits alongside the much more familiar provincial idioms associated with Cambridge, Oxford, Lichfield, York, and Chester.

Two particular absences are worth drawing attention to. The Welsh feature much less strongly than the Scottish, and many of its images are of English castles built to tame them. Secondly, the relative invisibility of the English Midlands and North is striking. With the exception of a few iconic locations, such as the Lake District (which accounts for all five North-Western references in the 'British Landscape' chapter), references from the county of Lancashire (especially), Cheshire, Staffordshire, Leicestershire, inland Yorkshire, County Durham and Northumberland are neglected. These arenas, it seems, lay outside the force field which defined the British countryside.

It was therefore not accidental that these were the environments that the burgeoning social sciences were to seize as their territory. The invisibility of large swathes of Northern and Midland landscapes within this cultural geography allowed critics to mobilize such places for competing visions of the nation.[17] Orwell brilliantly played on the politics of these symbols in his *Road to Wigan Pier* where he used his sojourn in the depressed Lancashire town as a means of

---

[17] Matless (1998) insists on the modernity of these kinds of rural images.

ruminating on how the class-divided English could learn to understand each other. Wigan pier turned out not to be the kind of seaside pier which one might expect from a southern resort, but actually was a modest coal-loading berth on a North-Western canal. Indeed, Wigan pier turned out not to exist at all – it had been demolished several years before Orwell's visit.[18] In this way, the contrast between ethereal markers of Englishness and fixed physical locations was deliberately mocked, even subverted.

This theme of 'beating the bounds' of Englishness through journeys between its metropolitan yet unspecified core, and its provincial realities became more heightened with decolonization in the post-war years, so making it more difficult for writers (such as Malcolm Lowry, Somerset Maugham, Joseph Conrad, and even Orwell himself) to draw on colonial locations as the dark venues of fantasy, danger, and risk for their educated British protagonists. This intensified the use of provincial England during the 1950s to provide an alternative site to depict the 'dark side' of Englishness. A particularly important development here was the deployment of the social mobility narrative, in which the ethics of 'bright young men' leaving the industrial province became a central motif in the work of Keith Waterhouse, David Storey, John Wain, Shelagh Delaney, Kingsley Amis, and Raymond Williams.[19] Philip Larkin's celebrated poem *The Whitsun Weddings* describing his train journey from Hull to London one 'sunlit Saturday', in which momentous events – 'a dozen marriages' – could take place in close proximity, yet ultimately be only a 'frail Travelling coincidence' with little shared except London as their destination, is one of its most elegiac markers.[20]

We can thus see how mobilizing visions of the English provinces became fundamentally implicated in the politics of abstraction, in which the reclamation of a fixed, situated, and peopled landscape proved the most important repertoire for those resisting the seductions of the modernist establishment who preferred to work with idioms of eternal and ultimately un-located 'organic' Englishness.[21] Yet in both cases, as Moretti shows, this literary exploration involved the construction of a geography of desire and fantasy, abstraction and reality within a unified national space. There was little awareness of the view from outside the national borders, but rather the elaboration of stocks of self-contained national literatures which became defined as representing specific national traditions. By treading lightly on English geography, the highbrow tradition was able to position itself as best able to appreciate and police this high cultural tradition.

---

[18] 'I'm afraid to tell you that Wigan Pier doesn't exist. I made a journey specially to see it in 1936 and I couldn't find it' (Orwell 2001, 217).

[19] See the discussion in Russell (2004, 95f).

[20]   …and none
Thought of the others they would never meet
Or how their lives would all contain this hour.
I thought of London spread out in the sun,
Its postal districts packed like squares of wheat:
There we were aimed.

[21] See generally on the power of the 'organic English body', Matless (1998, chapter 4).

During the 1950s, the politics of landscape was further complicated by the emergence of London as the unique location in which international forces could be conjoined to the national cultural repertoire. Made physically concrete in 1951's Festival of Britain, London became icon to the vision of the modern and culturally dominant, so wresting the claim away from the industrial cities of the north. In this vein Anthony Powell was to write his monumental *A Dance to the Music of Time*, situated firmly in the metropolitan space of London, though intertwined with the usual journeys to Oxbridge and the bucolic rural environment of the Home Counties. But London was also the venue for the South African émigré Doris Lessing to set her *Bildungsroman* of *Martha's Quest* and for B. S. Johnson to develop his experimental novels of the 1960s.

During the early 1950s sociology was also marked by a stand-off between metropolis and heartland, which mirrored this politics of landscape. A renascent sociology based at the LSE with the resources of the *British Journal of Sociology* developed a new concern with the sociology of the nation. In direct contrast, provincial sociologists gathered around the *Sociological Review* championed an empirical sociology of Northern communities. Taking up the pervasive account of the Northern reaches as sites of social problems and social deprivation, a series of important studies began to flesh out in unusual depth the working relationships and neighbourhood life of the English industrial areas.

A key institutional base was the new series of the *Sociological Review*, now established at the University College of North Staffordshire at Keele under its maverick editor Bill Williams. It is not incidental that Keele was keen to promote the *Sociological Review*. Keele was the brainchild of the Oxford don A. D. Lindsay as a means of bringing learning to the working class. It is not coincidental that whereas previous generations of gentlemen dons from Oxbridge had sought to civilize the masses through opening settlements in London, Lindsay, energized by the politics of national landscape which had opened up in previous decades, felt the need to go north, to the Staffordshire potteries. Lindsay's vision emphatically championed social science, though predominantly geographical and anthropological rather than specifically sociological. Keele's acquisition of the *Sociological Review* was a bold attempt to take over the heritage of the *Sociological Society* and position it as rival to the powerful LSE. All its social science professors sat on its reconstituted editorial board which therefore represented a synthetic sociology able to unite its different disciplines.

Working from this provincial location, the *Sociological Review* sought its energy through promoting research on social problems. Here it formed a key alliance with Liverpool, which had benefited from public money made available in the aftermath of the Clapham Report and which, in the later 1950s, could claim to be the leading British centre for empirical social research. With over a dozen dedicated researchers by the later 1950s and funding from the Department of Scientific and Industrial Research, the Liverpool department was the first to develop an empirical research programme into work and neighbourhood relations in Britain.

Research from Liverpool was published in numerous monographs, and also, increasingly, in the *Sociological Review*. During the first eight years of the publication of its New Series, it published no fewer than twenty-two studies of northern cities, mainly detailed case studies of its poor neighbourhoods or its industrial workplaces.[22] By contrast there were only six studies of Britain as a whole, (four of which appeared in the first volume of the New Series).[23] In short, rather than a 'methodologically nationalist' vision, a new sociology of 'northern English urban space' was championed, which played on long-held conceptions of the provinces yet appeared to deploy the latest social science methods to reveal their employment and urban relations.

Simey's vision was explicitly managerialist and technocratic, linked to his background in wartime studies of evacuation, along with his colonial experience at the University of the West Indies. He believed in addressing conventionally defined social problems, rather than choosing to question the terms of debate. He thus promoted an interdisciplinary, social-problem-based programme.

> Many social scientists have therefore turned their attention to intensive methods of enquiry which have brought them into closer relations with the subjects of their researchers...close collaboration between teacher, researcher and administrator is a characteristic feature of the Department's work.[24]

By the mid-1950s, large-scale studies emerged under Simey's leadership, of the Liverpool docks, and then on neighbourhood relations on working-class estates in Liverpool and Sheffield.[25] Both these studies used formal questionnaires and championed a practically applied empirical sociology. The model was a new collaboration in which the sociologist would abandon their role as synthesizer, roll up his or her sleeves, and get involved in empirical research: 'Controlled experiments in industrial relations are still in their infancy but the times demand that the difficulties of conducting them must be faced. In doing so, industry will require the services of industrial sociologists....The future this would open up, of collaboration between the sociologist, the manager, the Trade Union official and the social worker responsible for what is now recognised at last as a very important industrial service, would be a very happy one indeed' (p. 165).

In 1956 Simey joined the editorial board of the *Sociological Review*, as the first academic from outside Keele to be on its board, along with Kenneth Little from the Anthropology Department at Edinburgh. This was part of Bill Williams's attempts to realign sociology away from London towards its provincial reaches. A telling example of his strategy can be found in its reports from 1960 on what it

---

[22] This list includes the first published article by Anthony Giddens, a study of the halls of residence at Hull University, and not one of his better-known pieces.

[23] In addition, there were five studies of locations in the south of England, one in England as a whole, one of Northern Ireland, three of the Midlands, and one in Scotland.

[24] Simey (1953).

[25] Notably Kerr (1957). See the discussion in Todd (2008) and her observations about how this research programme was associated with a discourse on the 'problem family'.

regarded as the leading centres of sociology. The sequencing of these makes interesting reading. It was not surprising that the reports began with the Liverpool Department of Social Studies itself. Attention then switched north of the border, to the department of Anthropology at Edinburgh. Here, it was noted, in the major social science department in Scotland, there was a major programme of research on race relations (involving studies of Cardiff, Manchester, Liverpool, South Shields, Stepney, involving Michael Banton, amongst others), and on Scottish rural life (involving Erving Goffman). Edinburgh's more conventional anthropological interests in West Africa were also presented in terms of challenges to assumed imperial assumptions: 'the question to be asked is not what is "African", or "European", or "transitional", but what is significant in terms of social groupings and relationships'.[26]

It is notable that both Manchester – whose Anthropology Department under Max Gluckman was then at the height of its reputation – and London, were bypassed by Williams.[27] His third report did eventually trek south to the metropolis, but in what must only be seen as a calculated snub, ignored the LSE and went instead to Bethnal Green, and the Institute of Community Studies. This was championed as a centre for empirical social research which rejected a problem-oriented approach and marked a fusion of anthropology and sociology. Finally, in 1962, a report was commissioned from the LSE, but it was telling that this was not the Department of Sociology, but from the neighbouring, and altogether more empirically applied, Department of Social Administration.[28]

This ordering indicates the kinds of sociology which was being championed by the SR: taking its cue from the kinds of social problems that were seen to beset Northern and working-class districts, it eschewed evolutionary sociology in favour of sustained empirical research, where it was allied with the case work expertise of social workers.

This echoed the cultural politics of landscape in which the 'earthy' provinces were situated in tension with the 'exalted' metropolis. Although significant, indeed lauded at the time, this work however remained embedded within a moralizing tradition; one concerned to delineate social problems through the deployment of extensive programmes of research. It did not unravel a Middletown which citizens could define as their own, but instead served up 'problem ridden' Northern cities, and in this sense was ultimately compatible with gentlemanly Southern prejudice.[29] It was unable to rethink conventional research relations, construing the project of empirical study to be the focus of trained social

---

[26] See Scott and Mays (1960) and Little (1960).

[27] It is important to note that relations between Gluckman and the SR were actually cordial, and certainly close enough for him to publish an influential paper, 'The extended case study method', in its pages.

[28] Young and Willmott (1961) and Abel-Smith (1961).

[29] My argument here has parallels with those cultural geographers who emphasize that images of the English North are ultimately coherent within a wider conception of the English landscape as encompassing both garden and wilderness. See Cosgrove et al. (1996).

workers. We need to look elsewhere for bolder attempts to search out England's Middletown.

6.2 SOCIOLOGY ON THE WELSH MARCHES

After ruminating on the dispersion of Englishness and the apparent impossibility of abstracting from its constituent parts, Orwell proceeded by suggesting that only under foreign gaze could the reality of England be distilled.

> But talk to foreigners, read foreign books or newspapers, and you are brought back to the same thought. Yes there *is* something distinctive and recognizable about English civilisation... it is somehow bound up with solid breakfasts and gloomy Sundays, smoky towns and winding roads, green fields and red pillar-boxes... above all it is *your* civilisation, it is *you*. The suet puddings and the red pillar boxes have entered your soul.[30]

Orwell conjures up an ordinary England, one not embedded in ritual or pageantry, or in terms of its pressing social problems, but its enduring 'banal' features. This kind of refrain has been identified by Michael Billig as a central component of contemporary nationalism.[31] How was this banal ordinary nationality to be understood? What are its key characteristics, and what motifs does it command? As Orwell indicated, it was from outside the nation that such ordinariness could best be understood. And so it was that in generating a social science in search of the English Middletown, it was the work of anthropologists, steeped in the cultures of other countries, which led the way. More specifically, whereas the Scottish border was largely impermeable for the English, it was encounters across the Welsh Marches which were to be fundamental to the search for the English Middletown. It was the western universities of Keele, Manchester, and Swansea which were to play the incubating role in shaping a distinctive research vision able to elicit the ordinariness of the typical English town out of its strangeness.[32] It was precisely Wales's ambivalent political situation with respect to its neighbour that allowed it to act as the territory from which to champion a new kind of social inquiry, which questioned the unacknowledged normality of English social relations and instead subjected them to critical, even sceptical, analysis. And, as we shall see, out of this body of work, sociology was to develop the germ of its

---

[30] Orwell, 'The lion and the unicorn', 252–3.   [31] Billig (1995).

[32] It will be clear that my analysis here is indebted to Matless's pioneering excavation of the politics of landscape in the formation of twentieth-century Englishness. In particular, I fully concur with his emphasis that metaphors of Englishness through landscape are predominantly run on 'East-West rather than North-South lines, with the West associated with the spiritual, the mysterious and the Celtic, and the East with down to earth reason and the Anglo-Saxon' (p. 17). However, it is surprising that Matless exemplifies this through the importance of the West Country and Cornwall rather than through the importance of the Welsh encounter.

interest in social change, so that it could define for itself its specific methods and expertise and part company with anthropology.

Keele's significance primarily lay in the role of Bill Williams, whose study of Gosforth I have already discussed. Although important in raising the banner of sociology, this ultimately proved the least ambitious, in large part because it remained attached to the contained local study of whole populations as its prime method. Williams was inspired by Alwyn Rees, the first to carry out large-scale anthropological fieldwork in the British mainland,[33] in his comprehensive study of the structure of economic relations and social ties in a Welsh village. Williams's main innovation was to take Rees's concern to systematically map the social organization of a community, but to use a language of class to analyse such relations, in the process claiming his study as sociological, though this continued to be framed within an holistic framework in which the entire local population needed to be studied.

The Manchester School is the most familiar, and certainly the most mythologized, of the western universities.[34] This anthropology proved sufficiently flexible to embrace a sociological component, with the result that there was no possibility of a separate, bounded jurisdiction for sociology to emerge from this group.[35] Its leader, Max Gluckman was hostile to Evans-Pritchard's influential emphasis on anthropology as an historical subject based in the arts, and instead was well disposed towards sociology – to the extent that he contemplated defining anthropology as a form of 'comparative sociology'.[36] This was one reason why he was determined to demonstrate how the anthropology of the African Rhodes-Livingstone Institute could be shown to have resonance in modern Britain. In striking contrast with Simey's managerial sociology at Liverpool, gestated whilst he was Professor of Colonial Social Policy in the University of the West Indies, this was allied to a critique of colonial dominance. Gluckman's emphasis on situational analysis had clear parallels to the field theory of the Tavistock psychologists, in insisting that the social relations and cultures of African peoples needed to be understood in terms of their social roles, as workers, townspeople, rural dwellers, and so forth, rather than in terms of any supposed evolutionary limitations or innate cultural features. At Manchester this perspective, concerned to link the specific and general through situated case studies, led anthropology to command sway over the social sciences as a whole, which involved deploying not just ethnography but a wide range of research methods seen to be appropriate for modern industrial society.[37] Under Gluckman's emphasis on the 'extended case

---

[33] Rees (1951).

[34] See notably Burawoy et al. (2000), Frankenberg (1982), and Cohen (2005).

[35] The most amusing instance being Gluckman's attempt on several occasions to unilaterally rename the Department as 'Anthropology and Sociology', with porters being summoned to remove the offending signs (Frankenberg, private communication).

[36] See the discussion in Frankenberg (1982*b*).

[37] Cohen (2005, 607) refers to the 'central position which Gluckman had carved out both personally and for the subject among his most influential Manchester peers, including W. J. M. Mackenzie,

study method', ethnographic research on Manchester factories was conducted by Sheila Cunnison and Tom Lupton in the early 1950s, followed by widely influential ethnographic studies of schools by Colin Lacey and David Hargreaves.[38] Even more unusually, quantitative approaches to social research – later to be seen as the province of sociologists and economists – were countenanced,[39] and indeed Clyde Mitchell became one of the major influences in the development of social network analysis during its formative moment of the 1960s.

The Manchester school also traversed the Welsh border, in the form of Ronnie Frankenberg's study of the Welsh village Glyn Ceiriog, *Village on the Border*. This study presented its village – anonymized – as a Welsh Middletown, whose conflicts, notably those between its locals and offcomers, were emblematic of social relations everywhere. Frankenberg positioned Glyn Ceiriog not as a remote rural village, but as an industrial town. Despite its remoteness, he emphasized the links between Glyn Ceiriog and the rest of the world: 'in fact, their (i.e. the villagers) sense of isolation is in most senses an illusion. Geographically, economically, and historically, the village is part of a larger whole'. In part due to Frankenberg's exposure to colonialism, and the serendipitous way that Frankenberg's doctoral studies shifted from the Caribbean to Wales when he was deported from the former on the grounds of his left-wing sympathies, he refused to reify his community.[40] Tellingly, he begins his study with an account of how he reached the village for the first time, so identifying its point of contact with the outside world. Frankenberg's emphasis is on the dynamic nature of village life, with social relations organized as an ongoing process of tension, conflict, and (partial) resolution, rather than as the site of social problems as delineated in Liverpool's Northern sociology. By making the relationship between strangers and insiders one of its central concerns and by exploring how social relations in this Welsh village were not preordained but were performed and dramatized in ordinary venues such as its football club, he was able to deploy ethnography as a device for eliciting the everyday.

Precisely because Frankenberg's account, along with the general approach of the Manchester School, was relatively 'sociological' it proved difficult for sociologists to use these models to define a distinct expertise of their own. Manchester school ethnography could thus be exported to factory studies, proving inspirational in the creation of the Manchester Business School (the first business school in Britain) through the work of its first director, Tom Lupton. Its educational ethnography was a formative influence on Paul Willis's pioneering study of

Dorothy Emmett, Michael Polanyi, Arthur Lewis, and Ely Devons'. See also the account of W. J. M. Mackenzie (1982).

[38] See Cunnison (1982), Emmett and Morgan (1982), Lacey (1970), and Hargreaves (1967).

[39] See Frankenberg, 'A social anthropology for Britain' (p. 28), 'I think it worth mentioning in passing that Gluckman while not attracted to quantitative research methods himself made sure that his students were aware of them, and encouraged his colleagues to pursue them'.

[40] See Frankenberg's introduction to the second edition of *Village on the Border*, as well as Cohen (2005) and Macdonald et al. (2005).

working-class schooling in *Learning to Labour*. And in fact, when sociology did form as a separate discipline at Manchester in 1970, it was not incidental that it sought to define its jurisdiction with very little reference to research on contemporary Britain. It became a leading centre of ethnomethodology and conversation analysis, drawing on American influences of Garfinkel and Sacks, and also retained an active interest in the sociology of development under the leadership of Worsley and Shanin. It was not until much later, in the 1980s, that Manchester sociology began to assert its distinctive account of British society, one which focused on the relationships between cultural and social inequalities, often adopting Bourdieusian insights.[41]

It was therefore Margaret Stacey who ultimately claimed an English Middletown – Banbury – most emphatically for an emergent sociology.[42] Whereas Williams's book remained a study of a remote village in Celtic England, Stacey undertook a more ambitious quest, to stake out Middle England in its deep English heartland, not through a study of a Cotswold village but through an encounter with a modern industrial town. Her study was marked by her experience of anthropology and of living in Wales, but critically involved taking her distance from both of these positions. In this respect, her study paved the way for sociologists to challenge the authority of anthropologists to define and research community.

Unlike Frankenberg and Williams, Stacey's education had not been in anthropology: indeed she had studied at the metropolitan heartland of the LSE. There, she became aware of the stand-off between a moralistic evolutionary sociology and the study of social problems, and wondered how this could be challenged by a sociology of the ordinary.

> That was really why I finally did the Banbury Study. Because I really thought that we needed some empirical data about how 'ordinary people' lived – not these categories who were presenting social problems. And it seemed to me – I wanted to link with the theoretical ideas. And the gap I just found very upsetting.[43]

Stacey too had spent time outside England, working in a factory on Clydeside. Afterwards she taught in the Oxford extra-mural department, involved in setting up WEA classes in Banbury, and was able to enrol her Banbury class members in the study of the town. She was aware that she had to ask permission to do her study to go to Banbury. As she later recalled,

> There was no sociology at all in Oxford at the time... the nearest thing was anthropology. So I muscled my way into the anthropology seminars, and Evans-Pritchard and Meyer Fortes were there at that time....And Meyer Fortes, one day, said to

---

[41] This book is of course a contemporary manifestation of this current.

[42] Stacey returns to Middletown again and again. See Stacey and Thompson (2008, 110): 'I suppose I took the Lynds' *Middletown* and *Middletown in Transition* as models, see also her reference to its "classical" status in Stacey' (1969, 58), and she notes its 'outstanding' qualities in Stacey et al. (1975, 1).

[43] Stacey and Thompson (2008, 109).

me – rather curiously, in view of that whole business about you have to go and do your research work abroad, in another language, that they were quite religious about at one time – he said, 'Will you mind if I come, one day, to Banbury, to do a study of Banbury?' So I said, 'No'. And I sort of went on working there, and I hung about, and no sign of Meyer Fortes. So I went to see him, one day, and I said, 'Meyer, do you remember that you thought of doing a study in Banbury?' And he sort of mumbled, so I said, 'Well, would you mind if I did one? And I've got this class, and they've already done some groundwork and...dah-di-dah'. And he didn't seem to mind, he thought that was all right. So that was how it started.[44]

Stacey was surely the last sociologist who felt the need to obtain the symbolic permission of an anthropologist before beginning a local study in Britain. Her encounter with Meyer Fortes proved to be a defining moment in the parting of the ways between these disciplines. Although her Banbury research was actually carried out between 1949 and 1951, it took nine years for the book finally to be published, in 1960. This delay was due in part to Stacey's move to Swansea, where her husband taught politics. Swansea was another venue for social science investment in the post-war years as a result of 'Clapham money', which had led to a pioneering social geographical account of *Social Change in South West Wales*.[45] Nonetheless, despite these precedents, Stacey was unhappy. As a married woman with children she was not offered a job in Swansea for ten years, by what she perceived as the 'male domination' evident there. Her relationship with Wales was agonistic. She ultimately rejected the Welsh anthropological tradition, represented in the figure of Bill Williams as Head of Department, whom she regarded as intellectually lightweight. Her own position as a woman academic whose career was defined by her husband's position no doubt rankled.[46] It was out of this agonistic journeying between the English Midlands and Wales that Stacey was to forge the tools for a distinctive sociology of community that she hoped would demonstrate the potential of a new kind of modern and scientific research.

In some respects her book *Tradition and Change* relied on the familiar motifs of the landscaped community study, with one of the most beautifully written paragraphs ever composed by a sociologist in her evocation of the Oxfordshire landscape.

> Banbury lies in a country of regularly undulating hill and dale. The hills are level broad-backed ridges, so level that you may look across from one ridge to the next ridge and see the trees on the one beyond that again. A fine day in February is the time to see this country.[47]

Yet, whilst Stacey begins from the landscape tradition, she took a profoundly new angle of attack. Methodologically – because of what she saw as the size and complexity of the town – she did not conduct the kind of intensive ethnography

---

[44] Stacey, 'interview with Thompson'.   [45] Brennan et al. (1954).

[46] In her life history interview with Paul Thompson, Stacey does not refer to the way that her discomforts may also have been related to her sexuality. After her husband's early death, Stacey came out as lesbian and subsequently became a pioneer of feminist sociology.

[47] Stacey (1960, 1).

characteristic of her predecessors. Instead she conducted small-scale surveys and used in-depth interviews, so allowing her to gain knowledge of a place where – as she travelled to and fro – it was not practical for her to know all aspects of it. These methods were also ones which could be used in organized research teams, using her adult education students.

Her main theme was that Banbury was the site of both 'tradition and change', in which she sought to unravel the relationship between new and old, between Banbury as rural market town, and Banbury as new industrial suburb.[48] This was not a new idea, and had in fact been extensively deployed in literary accounts of communities which had predominated hitherto. J. B. Priestley's *English Journey*, written in 1934, ruminating on the author's car journey through the English provinces, concluded by noting the existence of three Englands: the 'Old England: the country of cathedrals and minsters and manor houses and inns', which he ultimately saw as elitist; the 'nineteenth century England: the industrial England of coal, iron, steel, cotton, wool, railways', which ultimately 'had done more harm than good to the enduring England'. Finally as a kind of synthesis to the tensions of the first two, there was the 'new post-war England' of 'arterial and by pass roads, of filling stations and factories that look like exhibition centres', which managed to be classless and democratic.[49] Stacey took up Priestley's argument that these three Englands coexisted within, rather than between areas, through a close study of the different role systems between traditionalists and non-traditionalists which could be detected within the town itself. Intriguingly, this division between old and new was also one between the English and the Welsh, since it was Welsh migrants who moved to Banbury to take up jobs in the new aluminium plant. And Stacey does look to Wales, taken as exemplar of a traditional society, as a contrast with the more complex social relations in Banbury. Even so, her parting words look back to the adaptability of tradition: 'traditional society is capable of absorbing some new customs: what is non-traditional today may well be traditional tomorrow and this new tradition itself open to the challenge of fresh change'.

This formulation drew attention to the juxtaposition of the old and the new within one locale, and with its stress on the complexity of social relations and roles, it indicates the potential for a new sociology of social change, taking up Orwell and Priestley's interest in the progressive landscape. Yet ultimately, this project was to run aground over the issue of what it would mean to do a re-study of Banbury. Part of the Middletown legacy was the view that it should be possible to go back to the same location and examine how far change had taken place through using fresh fieldwork. This idea of researching change through re-study was also familiar within the poverty research tradition.[50] As part of her endeavour

---

[48] 'The purpose of the research was to study the social structure and culture of Banbury with special reference to the introduction of large scale industry', Stacey (1960, v).

[49] Priestley (1934, 372–5).

[50] On London, see Smith (1930–5), on York, Rowntree (1941), and Rowntree and Lavers (1951). See generally, Kent (1981, 103–9).

to champion a professional sociology, Stacey decided not to rely on her adult education class but instead to enrol a larger academic research team, whereby she recruited a team of young, enthusiastic, researchers, Colin Bell, Eric Batstone, and Anne Murcott. Impressed by the Middletown example, she even had these researchers running local courses on the 'Banbury Social Survey', which proved a popular draw and made the project a centre of local attention. Rather solipsistically, an adult education class took students through each chapter of *Tradition and Change* on a week-by-week basis. The book was taught in the local high school, and a whole row of the local library was given over to multiple copies.

For all the admirable planning and ambition which went into the re-study, the follow-up book failed to capture the imagination of its predecessor. There were squabbles within the research team, in part because of professional jealousy, related to different views about how far the researchers should become involved in the lives of their subjects.[51] The problems arose in part from Stacey still being based in Swansea, whilst the other three were living in Banbury, a town which they had no personal connection with and all had ambivalences about living in.[52]

In retrospect, these squabbles were also linked to the tension between sociological and anthropological perspectives. Stacey's idea of the re-study was as a marker for a mature sociology which could measure change exactly, through a commitment to replication. Unimpressed by the fusion between anthropology and sociology at her home Department at Swansea, she enthusiastically moved to the new Department of Sociology at Warwick in 1974. Colin Bell, however, a graduate of anthropology and sociology at Keele who was put in charge of the second Banbury fieldwork, remained much closer to the anthropological perspective.

Whereas Stacey wanted Banbury to be the English Middletown, Bell had a different model in mind. 'Banbury will forever be the social system with which I compare all else. It is my Nuer land and my Tikopia,' he later related. This was not just a matter of his exposure to anthropology at university. Like his undergraduate tutor Bill Williams, Bell's geography was marked by three-way contrasts between Wales, the north of England, and the Home Counties. Going north to study at Keele had opened his eyes.

> Keele also taught me about the North. Don't forget, I am a boy from Tunbridge Wells.... I used Stoke-on-Trent slightly unusually by UCNS[53] standards, like I did go to the Clubs, and I even knew the odd girl in Stoke-on-Trent!... I did some of the mapping of the remaining pot banks in Stoke-on-Trent, so walked through those really benighted, Longton, Fenton, really, really desperate places.... But it was an utterly different experience, and this sounds very patronising, but it was

---

[51] See generally the admirably frank accounts in Bell and Newby (1977).

[52] 'I mean, the second team hated it. They really couldn't bear it. They hated it, and they kept telling me so' (PT interview with MS). Bell, however, refused to admit that he hated it, admitting only to 'ambivalence'. See Stacey and Thompson (2008).

[53] University College of North Staffordshire.

actually quite exotic. I had a feeling about being in a different place. As exotic as going to Swansea was, which I did after Keele. I mean, Swansea was really again, a very exotic place for me.

Bell's postgraduate research on white-collar suburbs of Swansea, was closely influenced by anthropological work on kinship, notably that of Raymond Firth. He was particularly influenced by the arguments of anthropologists about the distinction between locals and cosmopolitans,[54] which he sought to elaborate in a case study of suburban Swansea and relate more systematically to social class. Bell himself was clear that his resulting book *Middle Class Families* was in an anthropological rather than a sociological tradition.

> And that, again, just look at the tradition it's out of, it's not a British sociological tradition, it's social anthropology. It's Clyde Mitchell, another man who came to the seminar and told us what was what! But there I am, working in Swansea, reading stuff out of the Rhodes Livingstone Institute and the copper belt, and this thing on the kalala dance, which is a really massive piece of urban ritual, and I pretentiously talk about that, in the same sort of way as Clyde Mitchell did.

Only hesitantly did Bell himself take on a sociological identity,

> PT: When did you crystallise that it was a sociologist you wanted to be? Because you could have been an anthropologist.

> CB: Yeah, I could have been an anthropologist. No, I think I knew that it was other than a very curious hybrid department, I wasn't a real anthropologist. I hadn't done any foreign language, I hadn't gone somewhere exotic. It wasn't real anthropology. I think I knew it wasn't real anthropology. Nowadays, you know, it looks more real than what most anthropologists do. But it didn't at the time, I think I knew it wasn't. I was working on Modern Britain, and I think I knew I was a sociologist.

The key phrase here is the last: if one is working on modern Britain, one is now a sociologist. We see here how a crucial anchoring of sociology defined in terms of its concern with the new. This is ultimately enough to define Bell as a sociologist, despite all his best endeavours to make Banbury his 'Tikopia'.

We can thus see how the problems of the Banbury re-study lay in terms of an unresolved tension between sociological and anthropological voices. Stacey, seeing herself as the proper sociologist, gave a dressing down to Colin Bell for getting so involved in local affairs that he actively encouraged people to vote Labour rather than acting as a 'detached' researcher. Yet Bell was actually living in Banbury, and indeed with his wife had bought a house there with the financial support of his parents-in-law where they were bringing up two young children. As Bell relates, his second son was actually a Banburian. Stacey was still living in Swansea. Did she have the right to tell him not to get involved in local politics? And behind all this was the model of what they both wanted Banbury to be.

---

[54] Notably Watson, who was the supervisor of Bill Nalson whom I discussed in Chapter 2.

Loads of the trouble there really was, was me not really, really understanding that you didn't have the kind of freedom to do anything you liked. It wasn't your Tikopia, it was Margaret's Tikopia. That's the mistake. Banbury was Margaret's Banbury, and I ought to have understood that. It wasn't my Tikopia, it was her Banbury, and I was living in it.

Stacey finally concluded that 'replication isn't possible'.[55] Whereas she actually lived in the town when she did her first study, where she assembled her research team from other local inhabitants, she came to realize that this situation was only possible in a particular phase of her life, which had now passed. The idea that you can personally stand outside time to conduct a scientific replication was a mirage. Bell's recognition of the impossibility of re-study took a different form: having interviewed many of those whom Stacey had also interviewed in the first study, he found them telling completely different things, indeed denying who they were supposed to be.[56] Bell disbelieved the first study: Stacey disbelieved the second study. In this manner, the paradigm of tradition and change, in which sociology claimed expertise over the question of change could not effectively claim the community study as its key device. Whereas Stacey's first book promised a sociological approach to community, the second proved problematic for failing to find an adequate means of understanding 'change'.

6.3 FROM COMMUNITIES TO SOCIAL CHANGE

During the 1960s the battle to find Middletown reached its climax. What was at stake were two contrasting ways of deploying community studies. Let us consider these. From the industrial North, *Coal Is Our Life*, published in 1957. It was a study of the values and lifestyles of coal miners in Yorkshire, the first anthropological monograph of a 'working-class' community.[57] Written by two anthropologists and a sociologist, it offered an evocative account of work relations and community life in a mining town in West Yorkshire. Their book evoked a deep sense of the isolation of this town. The miners were in, but not 'of' British society. They had their own values which were only explicable in terms of the nature of their work and community relations, and which did not conform to any middle-class norm. Their attitudes to risk, their harsh treatment of their wives, and their sense of fatalism were attributable to the dominance of the coal mines. They were not a social problem to be dealt with in any conventional way, but their presence

---

[55] PT interview with MS.

[56] 'Over half of them denied what was on a piece of paper that we had. And sometimes the job, 'No, I've always worked for the Co-Op'. You said, 'Never worked for the Railway?' 'No. Always worked for the Co-Op'. And Eric and I got thrown by this, absolutely thrown. And we told Margaret about this, and she was in denial about it.'

[57] The book has certainly been canonized by subsequent writers. See its central role in works as diverse as Frankenberg (1966), Clarke et al. (1979), and Crow and Allan (1994).

offered a different kind of understanding of the nature of English society. The first sentence of the book revealingly reads as follows:

> Yorkshire might be described as a microcosm of England in that every type of region in the country, from remote hill farms to industrial towns is represented.[58]

Featherstone was thereby delineated as a part of the whole, embedded in a wider social landscape. Yet, although rendering Featherstone as part of England, rather than the industrial North, it shared fully in the familiar positioning of the Northern industrial landscape as a direct contrast to that of the southerners. It derived its emotional power, rather like Orwell's *Road to Wigan Pier*, as a means of presenting to a literate public a life fundamentally marked by the graft and endurance of hard manual labour.

Consider, by way of contrast, *Family and Kinship in East London* by the sociologists Michael Young and Peter Willmott. This appeared almost simultaneously in 1957. It too was a study of the working class. The choice of London did, however, challenge regional stereotypes. It was a study not of factory and mine, but of neighbourhood and family. In emphasizing the matriarchal and tightly bonded nature of working-class families they initiated a view of the working class as cohesive and communal. In contrast to the ethnographic and observational methods of *Coal Is Our Life* it used qualitative interviews to develop a powerful new model of sociological research. It begins in a tellingly different vein from *Coal Is Our Life*.

> This book is about the effect of one of the newest upon one of the oldest of our social institutions. The new is the housing estate....The old institution is the family.[59]

And, in their first chapter, they then go on to report that

> Bethnal Green is part of the country which has been, in living memory, the scene of great social changes.[60]

We see here, in palimpsest, two different ways in which the case study is rendered as emblematic. For Dennis and his colleagues, the coal-mining village of Featherstone stands as an exemplar of English society, rather in the manner that the central figure in a Russian doll reveals a secret interior, which can only be unravelled through peeling off the outer layers.[61] There is no emphasis on change in their study, which instead emphasizes the enduringly brutal nature of work in mining communities, only marginally disrupted by events such as the nationalization of the industry in the post-war years. Rather, the aim is to examine the internal relationships between the work relations of the coal-mining industry, family relationships, and leisure.

---

[58] Dennis et al. (1956, 11).   [59] Young and Willmott (1957, xv).
[60] Young and Willmott (1957, 3).
[61] The concept of the 'fractal' within complexity theory is an interesting example of how this conception is once again proving productive. For examples within sociology, see Abbott (2001) and for anthropology, see Green (2005).

Although Ashton's life in its many aspects is influenced by innumerable factors, great and small, which derive from 'outside' of itself, the principal lines of Ashton's institutions show an inner consistency and structure one with another. The foregoing chapters suggest that this consistency derives from the social relations of work in the coal mining industry.[62]

Young and Willmott set out their stall in a very different way. Bethnal Green is a venue which is not situated in a landscape but exists as a capsule in which the nature of social change can be delineated.

People are well aware of the change which has come upon them in the course of a few decades. Indeed it is because the comparisons they make between old and the new are so much part of their mentality, the source of much exhilaration and perplexity, and because the influence of the old is so clearly written upon the new, that the contrast properly belongs to an account of the impressions we have formed of present day life.... The old style of working class family is fast disappearing.[63]

It is true that as their book progresses, Young and Willmott point to a rather more complex picture of historical continuity, and argue that the power of the matriarchal family can be traced back to the Industrial Revolution.[64] Yet even this recovery of continuity is integrally related to their focus on change, where certain stabilities are disclosed from a narrative form which focuses on temporal disclosure. If Dennis and his colleagues unravel a hidden secret spatially fixed within the English landscape, Young and Willmott emphasize the historical, temporally embedded, character which endures in a changing environment. For Young and Willmott, the local is a site in which change can be examined, whereas for Dennis and his colleagues, the local is a social miniature.

The divergence between these two perspectives is revealed in one telling sentence at the end of Dennis and his colleagues' book. 'The principal reason for our neglect of the major question of social change, for example, was the clear fact that in a community which is part of a wider economy and culture, the sources of change are operating at a higher level than the functioning of the community itself'.[65] In seeking to define the expertise of anthropology as resting in unpicking the internal relationships between elements in a bounded local community, Dennis and his associates sought to bracket out issues of change. This actually marked a narrowing of the anthropological perspectives: it was, after all, a familiar theme to emphasize the interconnectedness between local and non-local elements – most famously in Radcliffe-Brown's 1940 address,[66] and also, as we have seen, marked in Frankenberg's ethnography. The claim of Dennis and his colleagues might be seen as an attempt to carve out specific expertise for

---

[62] Dennis et al. (1956, 247).   [63] Young and Willmott (1957, 5, 15).

[64] See especially Young and Willmott (1957, 157f).   [65] Dennis et al. (1956, 249).

[66] This includes the famous quote, 'At the present moment of history, the network of social relations spreads over the whole world, without any absolute solution of continuity anywhere. This gives rise to a difficulty which I do not think that sociologists have really faced, the difficulty of defining what is meant by the term "a society"' (cited in Knox et al. 2006). See also the discussion there.

anthropologists in the British context, a means of allowing economists, political scientists, and social administrators to have their say in the large-scale aspects of British society, but to insist on the value of anthropology in providing 'local' insights, especially appropriate in those 'provincial' parts of England where industry dominated. However, by making this move and seeking to establish the importance of anthropological research by focusing on local social relations, the door was left open for sociologists to take the 'bit' of social change firmly between their teeth, and in the process carve out this area as one that was distinctly and uniquely 'their own', one that their neighbouring anthropologists had little say in, or jurisdiction over. This was precisely the baton which Young and Willmott were to take up in their study of Bethnal Green. Located as it was within the largest city in the world, economically dependent on the docks, it was implausible to claim this as a detached, isolated settlement. Instead, it could be seen as a site of change.

The Institute of Community Studies was a powerful advocate of the idea that the local case study could be used to study change. Thus, in yet another journey across the Welsh border, Rosser and Harris's study of Swansea, dependent on the intellectual support of the Institute of Community Studies, was framed specifically in terms of *The Family and Social Change*. Yet it is important to emphasize that this perspective was contested during the 1960s. An important, though largely forgotten, debate took place between those who drew on anthropological perspectives to develop spatialized conceptions of social change, and those who instead preferred to champion abstracted sociological accounts. Frankenberg, drawing on the anthropology of the Manchester School, though now working as Professor of Sociology at Keele, was an important figure. In his book *Communities in Britain* he delineated change as part of a 'morphological continuum' distinguishing rural from urban. In this formulation, 'rural social life is built up out of a relatively small number of role relationships – which are arranged with great fluidity into varied patterns. Urban life makes up for the loss of these by a large number of role relationships and their formalisation'.[67] By portraying social change spatially, as linked to the difference between rural and urban, Frankenberg is able to retain the spatial sensitivity of the landscape tradition.

Undoubtedly the most important figure to work through the tensions of this approach was Ray Pahl, who wanted to develop a spatialized conception of social change. Working as an extra-mural tutor in Hertfordshire, he became intimately aware of the lure of change. 'In local debates "change" became the key theme. But what precisely was changing?' In studying the Hertfordshire suburbs, he relates the tensions he experienced being supervised by Emrys Jones (Welsh protégé of Alwyn Rees) and the Marxist sociologist John Westergaard.

> In a nutshell I was in a mess. Because John Westergaard was empirically rigorous, he saw the world in terms of class, job ratios and employment statistics...while in my other ear Emrys was talking about Welsh villages and the power of the

---

[67] Frankenberg (1966, 282).

London labour market, and how the metropolitan region was always changing geographically'.[68]

For Pahl, the Welsh influence was not about reclaiming an 'essential Welshness' but was concerned with recognizing the power of movement to define place. He was thus more dependent on Emrys Rees's geography than his anthropology.

> Rees appeared to want to retain an essential Welsh culture through the distinctive sets of social relationships that emerged in relative isolation. However, Emrys Jones also alerted me to the danger of equating geographical isolation with social isolation. He had spoken with old men in Tregaron who knew the haunts of Soho and the area round Smithfield Market very well. The drovers of Wales had travelled from the most remote and isolated settlements taking their livestock to market for hundreds of years.[69]

In the end, Pahl failed to resolve these tensions to the satisfaction of the Welsh. 'The examiners of my thesis were Emrys Jones and Bill Williams. When I entered the room for my viva they were engrossed in Tafia gossip which they very reluctantly stopped after a bit to turn to me. Bill was disappointed that I didn't emphasise community over class'.[70]

Ultimately, Pahl's concern to delineate Hertfordshire commuter villages as a 'frontier' of change seemed to satisfy nobody – and certainly not himself. Yet the formulation remains a valuable example of a perspective which insists on the physicality of social change. 'The outer part of the metropolitan region is seen, then, as a frontier of social change, moving over communities and creating, as it were, new places which in turn form the bases for different types of communities'.[71] The idea is, therefore, that the spatial can be made to reveal insights into social change by focusing on boundaries, frontiers, and crossings.

In contrast to this landscaped account of social change, sociologists became increasingly confident in abstracting change from location. The key study here was that of *The Affluent Worker*, where Goldthorpe and Lockwood specifically took up the question of change but analysed it in a new way. This was a study of a potential English Middletown – Luton – that never materialized. What began as a study of community and work relations, not dissimilar in form from *Coal Is Our Life*, ended up being an exercise in industrial sociology. Through this means, the theme of change was wrested from community and in the same process, detached from locale.

Goldthorpe and Lockwood were emphatic that their inspiration lay in taking up the challenge of novelty.

> Against a background of sharply accelerating social change, new issues were opened up and old ones appeared in different forms. In the years in question, economic growth, in North America and western Europe in particular, went rapidly ahead.

---

[68] Pahl (1965, 105).   [69] Pahl (2008).
[70] Pahl (personal communication).   [71] Pahl (1965, 73).

The era of 'high mass consumption' was achieved and the coming of the 'affluent society' was, at all events, frequently proclaimed.[72]

Change was given two decisive twists. The first was through their insistence that affluent workers were a sociological, rather than a social, problem. Compared to the 'problem-based' practice of social research which had been recharged in Simey's Liverpool Department, Goldthorpe and Lockwood took up Bott and Stacey's call that the task of social research was to explain the 'ordinary' features of social life, as much as their problematic ones. In this process, a new role for social theory, in offering a comprehensive perspective on all features of social relations, and not just their aberrant ones, emerged. This proved a crucial moment in which academic sociology could insert its particular expertise into social research in a new and distinctive way. This was the subversive appeal of the idea of studying affluent workers. No one conventionally thought that the existence of increased prosperity amongst manual workers in the new assembly-line industries was a social problem; indeed, quite the reverse. To be sure, a political problem – whether the working-class electoral base of the Labour Party would decline as a result of affluence – was identified by earlier writers.[73] Goldthorpe and Lockwood were clearly keen to engage with these concerns, but on their own explicitly sociological terms. They were clear that the real problem which animated them was the challenge that affluent workers posed to different versions of sociological theory. A dramatic feature of their inquiry was the way they commenced their final volume not by commenting on how their work derived from social problems or political issues, but with a very clear statement of the theoretical starting point of their concerns: 'the debate on the working class…has its origins in the work of Marx and Engels'.[74] This concern with theoretical framing is familiar enough today, but we need to recognize its dramatic novelty during this period. This was a trumpet call for sociology, and for sociological theory, to define pressing questions for research, and in the process to rework what the public, or politicians, might assume to be the 'social problems' worthy of social investigation.

The second, more important twist, was to redefine the role of the case study, to remove it entirely from the landscape tradition, and place it in a new analytical frame. The researchers therefore chose Luton for theoretical reasons, because it represented an 'extreme' case of working-class affluence. They became intimate with the geography of the town, and their field notes reveal that when conducting their research, they in fact conducted a very intensive community study. They mapped the social standing of specific streets, and built up a very clear social and cultural geography of the town. Yet, when one reads the book again, Luton itself largely disappears and the study is presented as a piece of industrial sociology abstracted from its environment. There is no contextual information about the

---

[72] Goldthorpe et al. (1969, 5–6).   [73] Abrams and Rose (1960).
[74] Goldthorpe et al. (1969, 1).

city, no attempt to evoke its landscape, its housing estates, its routines and conversations.

These innovations represent a profound reworking of sociological jurisdiction which we can see, following Mitchell, as premised on a 'locationless logic'.[75] Class becomes abstracted from local social relations and identified as a property of the industrial and occupational structure, itself the product of the division of labour. This permits sociological researchers to define a new kind of expertise ruptured from place. It was thus that community sociologists such as Ray Pahl and Colin Bell saw themselves as being marginalized by this new body of work. Yet it is still possible to detect, in the Affluent Worker studies, elements of the older problematic. Many of the ideal types used by the authors depend on the local community studies which are extensively referenced in the text.

Goldthorpe and Lockwood's work proved so important, then, because it marked the simultaneous fusion of three distinctive features of the new sociological agenda: it addressed the issue of social change head on, it was deductive and rejected the social problem agenda, and it did not rely on a locality-based account. And yet it would be wrong to see the study, which was written up in the later 1960s, as fully formed by these currents at the outset. When the project was planned and designed, it was much more closely allied to earlier currents of work, and it was during its course that its distinctive character became apparent.

6.4 CONCLUSION

The search for Middletown ended in failure. Yet the journeys inspired by the endeavour proved as epic, in their own way, as the quests of King Arthur's knights in dim and distant history which had also taken place in these same territories, on the western boundaries of the kingdom. It was not from metropolitan London that these social scientists voyaged to Gosforth, Featherstone, Glossop, Banbury, or even Luton. It was from the Welsh border that the aim of exposing a strange yet ordinary Englishness was nourished. And, although no one could finally locate Middletown, the germ of a social scientific way of constructing the rational nation was pioneered. For generations until the Second World War, concepts of national identity had been bound up with historical and literary narrative. Yet during the post-war years social scientific measures of the nation came to challenge and ultimately eclipse these. Whereas literary and historical constructions were derived from the metropolitan heartlands and championed the heroic self-conceptions of the nation, these new conceptions came from outside England itself, drawing on a powerful emotional geography which pitted abstracted motifs against provincial reality. And, through finding the intellectual resources to understand the English as strangers, they found means of avoiding the moralistic gentlemanly formation which held sway into the 1950s.

[75] Mitchell (2002).

Perhaps the most important adventure arising out of this quest was that of change itself. Increasingly confident social scientists saw change not as embedded in the landscape but as something which rose above it, which undoubtedly affected people's towns, cities, and villages but which was somehow bigger than any particular place. This focus, on modernity and change, allowed the social sciences to settle its terms with tradition, the arena in which literature and history had defined the locus of national identity and belonging. More specifically, it explains the parting of the ways between anthropologists and sociologists who in the early 1960s had made common cause. By taking up the motif of change which had gained significant currency in the arts and political debate, sociologists were implicated in the construction of this vision of the bursting out of the 'new' and the 'vital' from the shell of the old and redundant. In this way, change came to constitute a central feature of the self-identity of parts of the social sciences, and especially sociology, as it broke from its position within the gentlemanly synthesis and began to articulate a specialist vision for itself. The expertise and jurisdiction of sociology became bound up with its claims to be able to delineate the new and emergent, to the extent that it was not a neutral observer of the changes it explored. Rather, it was implicated in the very processes which it purported to describe.

There was no necessary reason for a sociology of social change to triumph. Initially it was anthropologists, building on their expertise in the study of locality and community, who took the lead in the elaboration of a new social scientific interest in England. Anthropologists were involved in all the major community studies, apart from Stacey's research on Banbury which was to pioneer a distinctive vision of a scientific sociology. It was only during the 1960s that this alliance was to be ruptured through the different temporal sensibilities of the two disciplines: whereas anthropologists championed a spatial, 'landscape' conception of the social, and saw the issue of change as one which had to be interpreted through transformations in the landscape itself, sociologists increasingly wanted to lever change out of any fixed location.

For these reasons sociologists gave up the search for Middletown. As late as 1969 Margaret Stacey saw the study of community as one which was central to the very definition of a scientific sociology. It was only through the study of 'local social systems' that it was possible to challenge 'problem solving research'.[76] She resisted the appeal of the national sample survey, for instance in her opposition to the funding of the Nuffield mobility study.[77] Numerous other sociologists of the period, such as John Rex, Robert Moore, and Ray Pahl were equally emphatic that social relations could only be understood as they were on the ground.[78] For Stacey, central to the scientific method was the ability to compare. Yet it was precisely the failure of the Banbury re-study which revealed the difficulties of this endeavour. She herself chose to redirect her energies to become a feminist medical sociologist, pursuing her interests in community not through studies of

---

[76] Stacey (1969, especially chapter 1).   [77] Goldthorpe (personal communication).
[78] A good example of the power of this kind of thinking is found in Pahl (1970), which contains references to the key sociologists of this bent.

places, but of patients and consumers. Colin Bell and his associates at the new University of Essex ridiculed the concept of community as vague, confused, and flawed.

In revisiting the search for Middletown I am not just making a historical point. For, the elaboration of a vision of sociology as a subject concerned with change abstracted from the landscape remains with us, fifty years later. Indeed, we can see emerging out of the Welsh Marches a distinctive paradox which has haunted British sociology ever since, a quest for the eternal new. No sooner is social change detected than it is immediately left behind by further rounds of change. So it is that Young and Willmott's study, which they thought was about changing families, is today read as an account of the 'traditional', 'stable' family. Young and Willmott were explicit that the kinds of matriarchal extended families they discovered were of relatively recent provenance. Yet, almost from its inception, their account was read as one of 'how things used to be', of the historical pattern which could serve as the benchmark of change. An account of the new is rapidly appropriated as a marker of the old.

We see here a striking feature of sociology as it emerged during the later 1950s, that its own delineation of the new was a means of staking out its expertise in terms of providing definitions of the modern rational nation. This creation of sociology as a new specialist discipline depended on built-in obsolescence, producing knowledge which makes itself rapidly redundant as the newness it establishes in any one moment of time is then seen as that which needs to be left behind by successors. Rather than stabilities, sociology seeks fleeting identities, no sooner established than dissipated. And so it is that when John Urry announced in his introduction to the millennium edition of the *British Journal of Sociology* that 'there is a widespread sense that social-material transformations are occurring round the millennium that indicate a break in the development of human societies',[79] he is largely repeating a well-established mantra that has existed in British sociology since the 1950s. He does not remember that he is following in a very well-worn groove. Here are Rosser and Harris, relating the accounts of 'social and cultural change' given to them by Mr Hughes, from Swansea in 1960.

> He is talking of two radically different worlds.... His use of words is significant: *formerly* they 'stuck together', 'didn't wander off', 'used to cling', 'had to help one another', 'all lived close', 'were all in the same boat'; *nowadays* 'the Mam holds the whole thing together somehow', 'all over the place now', 'always on the move', 'once they're married, they're off', 'don't cling like we did', 'seem to live in worlds of their own'. There is over half a century of rapid social and cultural change between these two sets of statements.[80]

Over fifty years these themes have been endlessly repeated. When read not at face value but historically, they actually point to continuities, to an enduring way of apprehending society.

---

[79] Urry (2000*b*, 1).

[80] Rosser and Harris (1960, 13–14). See also the discussion in Crow (2008) including Colin Bell's reflections.

7

1951: The Interview and the Melodrama of Social Mobility

During the later twentieth century, and especially in the 1950s and 1960s, a fundamental change took place in the use of the interview as a method for generating knowledge. Previously, the interview, enshrined in the professional expertise of doctors, clergy, social workers, and welfare officials, was fundamentally a mechanism for disclosing information, which would allow powerful agents to assess people's right to a claim – whether for medical treatment, welfare, or moral salvation. Claus Moser's canonical account of survey methods, written in 1957, thus emphasized that interviewing did not call for 'special intelligence', nor did it normally demand specialist training.[1] By the later 1960s, however, this had been supplanted by the widespread deployment of informal interviewing to elicit story-like narratives as a means of generating social knowledge. The deployment of interview methods within sociology was especially striking: since the 1950s, at least half the qualitative papers published in the leading British sociology journals used interview methods, and by 2000, a remarkable 80 per cent relied on them.[2] The implications of this development were far-reaching: it meant that narrative was no longer the special province of humanities-based literary scholars, but could be used by social researchers. The narrative form could be proliferated on new audio and visual media, notably on radio and television, as well as in newspapers and magazines.

We need to remember that the use of interviews as a form of popular social research was, during its inception, controversial. Associated with sensationalist journalism, interviews continued to be disreputable down into the post-war years.[3] Writing in 1957, Moser noted sniffily that 'informal' interview methods

---

[1] Moser (1958, chapter 11 and especially 194f). The most important and provocative treatment of the interview remains that of Foucault (1979). His emphasis on the interview as a device for producing confessional accounts, which thus allows the subjects to self-produce their subjectivity, informs the argument of the chapter; yet I also show here the need to be attentive to the historical specificities.

[2] See Halsey (2004, table 10.3). It is not entirely clear how interview methods are defined in this analysis, and the figure is best seen as a 'ballpark' one.

[3] The famous example of interview-based journalism was Henry Mayhew, though it is notable that in this case, as for popular journalism more generally, interviews largely remained only one

were associated with the social researcher Ferdinand Zweig, whose reputation was as a disreputable populist rather than as a scholar.[4] It was only in the later 1950s that the pioneering studies by Michael Young and Peter Willmott, as well as by Elizabeth Bott, provided influential exemplars of how these methods could be used to generate genuine social scientific insight. Even so, both these encountered resistance and scepticism. Richard Titmuss, Professor of Social Policy at the London School of Economics (LSE) noted in his acidic foreword to Young and Willmott's study of Bethnal Green that their use of interviews 'raised some difficult questions of presentation. Ultimately they resolved, to put it simply, to favour readability...this has meant that some chapters now have an impressionistic flavour'.[5] The same lukewarm reception was evident towards Elizabeth Bott, where the reviewer of her book *Family and Social Network* felt that she was using interviews to muscle into the territory of social workers, who ultimately knew much more about how to read interview material.

> There is a good deal which although it is a matter of common knowledge and not a result of sociological or anthropological work is extremely obvious, and it is debateable how far it is worth demonstrating what most people in fact know already. The hard boiled social worker will also be inclined to smile at the naivety with which some of the fieldworkers recount their experience.

The review concluded that the book

> does not add much to our knowledge of the family as a social group.[6]

The idea that the interview could be conducted by the expert social science researcher rather than a professional practitioner was deeply unsettling.

This chapter examines how the interview could be claimed for an emerging sociology, as a means of generating distinctive kinds of 'ordinary' knowledge. Firstly, I argue that the interview provided a mechanism to move away from a concern with whole populations in favour of narratives of specific individuals. I am especially interested in how this involved abstracting individuals from the household in which previous generations of community researchers had invariably placed them, and arraying them in terms of their changeability (and hence manageability). Secondly, I show how interviews were removed from a distinctively psychoanalytic and therapeutic domain on which they had originated, and

---

part of a more ethnographic strategy of defining the 'dangerous underworld' through conjuring up images and scenery more generally. See Walkowitz (1992) and Koven (2004).

[4] Moser (1958, 205). An example of the disrespect with which Zweig was held can be found in Runciman's observations on the conclusions he draws from his interviews. 'It seems harsh to describe them as a string of platitudes but in a sense it could hardly be otherwise.... Zweig is trying by his own account to be, as it were, a true life novelist, and what general conclusions can be drawn from even the best of novels which will not, once stated, be unmasked as platitudes' (p. 88). Runciman concludes that he is a 'sophisticated Mayhew'. *New Statesman*, 16 July 1965.

[5] Young and Willmott (1957, xi). David Lockwood also relates David Glass's scepticism towards Young and Willmott, interview, 25, 30.

[6] Chambers (1958, 187).

were deployed in collaboration with literary narratives in order to provide 'melo-dramas of social mobility'. Thirdly, this innovation was part of a wider masculi-nization of social research, as women interviewers were displaced by men; a process which also involved making women invisible. The struggle for the right to interview in the name of generating ordinary knowledge was a contested, deeply political process.

7.1 INTERVIEWS AND OBSERVATION

In 1932, the doyens of British social science, Beatrice and Sidney Webb, Fabian founders of the LSE, published probably the first-ever comprehensive British guide to social research methods. Their advice for the aspiring social researcher focused closely on the need for observation as the fount of knowledge. Question-naires could be useful, but because they were artificial instruments, they could confuse those who filled them in and mislead researchers.[7] Statistics needed to be approached with caution. However, noting that it had its origins in psycho-analysis, they recognized that the interview

> as a device for scientific investigation...is peculiar to the sociologist. It is his compensation for inability to use the astronomer's telescope or the bacteriologist's microscope.[8]

Nevertheless, their caution about the interview is striking. There is no sense in their account that the interview can reveal aspects of the respondents' identities, values, or personalities. The interview is a means of eliciting information about an institution or situation. It is for this reason that the interview is best conducted not on 'queer or humble folk' but on the 'key informant', the person who has some valued knowledge to impart: 'the person interviewed should be in posses-sion of experience or knowledge unknown to you'.[9] It is essentially an adjunct to the social researcher as observer. And it was in such a spirit that the first research monograph to focus specifically on social change, Brennan et al.'s study of South-West Wales in the later 1940s, based itself on 3,709 questionnaire responses distributed only to religious and trade union 'leaders'.[10]

Within this perspective, what ordinary people 'said' mattered in terms of whether they were aware of their shortcomings and were prepared to atone.[11]

---

[7] 'The printed questionnaire proved a costly and even a pernicious failure. When we handed it to workmen or to employers, in the course of our interviews, their glum looks or stony silence, as they turned the pages of this formidable printed document, convinced us, to put it politely, that the value of our pearls was not appreciated' (Webb and Webb 1932, 69).

[8] Webb and Webb (1932, 135).   [9] Webb and Webb (1932).

[10] Brennan et al. (1954, 80f).

[11] An especially good example being the study conducted in Sheffield in 1919 entitled *The Equip-ment of the Workers* which assessed the moral stature of the working class and how equipped they were to become modern citizens. See the discussion in Cronin (1984). I am grateful to Mark Peel for his thoughts here.

Interviewing methods could thus be placed within a wider programme of social observation, all embedded within this moralistic framework. This gentlemanly social science was concerned to map whole populations located in households which were seen as engines of moral value. Women were assumed to play the pivotal role as custodians and guardians of household morality. During the early and mid-twentieth century, the supremacy of the household as the privileged site for social research was uncontested. Legions of social workers, charity inspection agents, and school inspection officers made it their business to uncover the moralities of households through their scrutiny of domestic interiors. These currents pervaded gentlemanly sociological research, some elements of which, associated with the Institute of Sociology, were inspired by the French sociologist Le Play's insistence on the need to understand the intersection between 'folk, place, and work'. Here, the research device of the household visit and the enumeration of its household budget as the central 'data' for social research became prized.[12] Innovative field studies conducted by the Institute of Sociology, as well as other burgeoning 'field studies' associations saw the inspection of households as a central sociological concern down into the 1930s.[13] During the interwar years the Institute of Sociology innovated within this frame by using a series of detailed household plans, visual records of houses, conventional household budgets, family histories, and pen portraits of the moral quality of the family members.[14]

Identical assumptions were evident in those studies of 'populations' which dominated social research down to the 1950s. Issues of personality and character could not but be understood in terms of inherently male and female attributes. There was no conception of individuals divided into genders – one was either male or female.[15] Women, with their assumed importance as moral guardians, especially through their responsibilities for nurturing and raising children, therefore were central objects of social inquiry, and if anything, their distinctive qualities were seen to require special study; a fact most clearly brought out by the notorious 1908 Report on Maternal Childrearing which publicly aired worries about the declining moral stock of the population.[16] Rowntree's 'classic' study of poverty in York, written in 1901, proceeded from the assumption that it was not possible to abstract the measurement and definition of poverty from the familial and especially the marital characteristics of York households. In listing what

[12] On the role of household research, see Yeo (1996) and Donzelot (1980). Savage (2008c) argues that the specifically gendered aspects of this current of household research remain underdeveloped. On the research on the Institute of Sociology, see the archive of the Institute of Sociology held at the University of Keele.

[13] See Matless (1998).

[14] The most developed survey conducted by the Institute of Sociology was on Chester, in 1929–30. For an example of the Farmer family, see <http://www.keele.ac.uk/depts/cr/fos le play/home-surveys/chester/family-studies/farmer-family/farmer2.htm>. In this case, the notes recall: 'the husband is a quiet capable person: the wife is cheerful and talkative, but "feckless", untrained, and a bad manager. Visitors report that she and the children are untidy and dirty.'

[15] See also, on the need to historicize the concept of gender, Stanley (1995b).

[16] See Szreter (1996).

kinds of households were seen to comprise specific poverty classes, family struc-ture played a central, even defining, role. The researchers take pains to demarcate income from 'male' and 'female' heads of household, and 'male' and 'female' supplementary earnings (chapter III). When calculations are made of the nutri-ents required by households, sex-specific differences in calorific requirements were deployed (chapter IV). Interestingly, when, in chapter V, the focus becomes that of delineating the causes of poverty, issues such as the death or incapacity of the chief wage earner are emphasized, but this is subsequently broken down by whether this concerns men or women. In short, the analysis depends on, and reproduces, sexed accounts of men and women, and refuses to abstract from these to talk about poverty as an 'individual' phenomenon.

Even those researchers who sought to elaborate a more subversive form of social inquiry, such as Mass-Observation, were concerned to distinguish men and women. All its directives were filed carefully by separating out the letters received by sex, and according to their alphabetical surname,[17] so that anyone subsequently reading these directives has no choice but to look at boxes either for men or for women. Mass-Observation also sought to specifically quiz the moral boundaries of sexual decency, by devising questions that forced directive respond-ents to reflect on their attitudes to sex and courtship. Many of the more impor-tant Mass-Observation studies of the early period focused especially on what were thought of as being 'gendered' processes, such as 'pub going', manual work in engineering factories, or public ritual. As Liz Stanley has examined, an interest in sexuality was especially pronounced in Mass-Observation's 'Little Kinsey' which used both qualitative and some rudimentary quantitative measures to examine male and female sexual practices and identities in a period before Kinsey himself published his pioneering studies of sexuality in the human male and female.[18] Stanley brings out how Mass-Observation's controversial methods allowed it to address issues of sexuality in ways which were not possible for more conventional survey methods. Responses to Mass-Observation directives make it clear that many observers were prepared to talk about their sexuality as part of their concern to present themselves as scientific subjects. We might further read the interest in psychology, especially its Freudian elements, as concerned not only with eliciting concerns with the 'self' but also with revealing their sexual-ized nature.[19]

The practices of moral social science were inherently sexualized in a further sense, that they all depended on a gendered division of labour, in which women

---

[17] This practice of separating out directive respondents by their gender has been continued in the recent, post-1981 directives, though the curator, Dorothy Sheridan, has noted that it was never made clear why this system was introduced, and what analytical value it has.

[18] Stanley (1995a). See also John Madge's championing of the Kinsey studies as an example of how British social science could learn from American.

[19] Foucault's inspirational *History of Sexuality* is clearly very important here. His arguments have encouraged interests in general concerns over 'sexuality'. However, at this period sexuality could not be abstracted from male and female bodies, and hence it is male and female sex which might more precisely be emphasized.

were the necessary empirical 'underlabourers', and men were the synthesizers and systematizers. In the late 1950s, no less than 22,000 social workers comprised the routine ground troops in the practice of social research, 95 per cent of whom were female.[20] All contemporary treatises on social work assumed the occupation to be a female one, in terms of its historic 'Lady Bountiful' image.[21] Men, by contrast, dominated the academic positions in universities and the social research institutional apparatus. In 1945 only 2 of the 138 Fellows of the British Academy were female.

In the post-war years, huge anxieties about changing relations between men and women, generated by worries about how demobilized men could adapt back to civilian life and relate effectively to women who had become used to independent living, acted as a spur to innovative research projects. Geoffrey Gorer used a postal survey to probe household and especially marital relations in his book *Exploring English Character*.[22] As Gorer recalled, the initial focus for these studies was centred on sexual and moral relations amongst the English population: of the six topics which he negotiated with the editor of *The People* (who were responsible for administrating the survey), the first two ('you and your sweetheart'; 'you and your husband (or wife))' focused specifically on relations between the sexes. By contrast, interests in work and employment were marginal. There was originally to have been a topic on "you and your boss", but – remarkably in the context of later developments – Gorer argued that 'I did not feel questionnaires were a suitable method for investigating the relationship between employer and employee…so I suggested that "You and Your Boss" be replaced by "You and Your neighbour". Gorer's subsequent analyses invariably compared the patterns for men and women, and the central chapters of his book dwell on the nature of the marital relationship, in its sexual, emotional, and practical aspects. The main picture which Gorer paints was of the low expectations of marriage, and the dire state of domestic relations. About 75 per cent of men and 80 per cent of women enumerated faults with marital partners which presumably were derived from their own observations. A clear majority (58 per cent) of women thought that the worst fault of husbands was that they could be selfish; 29 per cent of men thought that the worst fault of wives was that they were 'nagging'.

This problematization of sex relations was also fundamentally important in the emergence of the interview method, especially through the role of the Tavistock Institute, the interdisciplinary centre founded in 1946 which brought together psychologists with anthropologists, and whose research was strongly oriented around the moral panic of understanding marital relations in the post-war period.[23] The Tavistock was important as the key site in which the qualitative interview was developed, and taken away from its unique psychotherapeutic focus

---

[20] Wootton (1959).   [21] Woodruffe (1962).   [22] See also the discussion in Chapter 5.

[23] My argument here summarizes and precises that which I develop in more detail in 'Elizabeth Bott and the formation of modern British sociology' (Savage 2008c) to which I refer readers who wish to read a fuller account. More generally on the Tavistock Institute, see Rose (1999a).

to being an instrument of wider social scientific value. Its first use was to gauge household and familial relations, where it sought to unpack the post-war crisis in family dynamics. Whereas the Tavistock researchers were confident that extensive programmes of ethnographic and observational work could allow them to analyse factories and work settings, they were less sure how to study household relations in dispersed urban settings. They therefore hit upon the model of the interview as a means of eliciting quasi-ethnographic information. A key figure here was the anthropologist Adam Curle, who worked with the psychologist Erik Trist on a project exploring how demobilized male prisoners of war settled back into domestic civilian life in the 1940s. Curle and Trist noted that the ex-prisoners appeared to psychiatrists to have various symptoms of distress, which did not appear linked to obvious psychological causes. They decided to study the domestic lives of these prisoners to gain greater information about the psychological state of the respondents. Given the difficulty of observing directly in people's own houses, they adopted interview methods. These accounts were then checked by asking friends, neighbours, and employers for their own views about the former prisoners, so that their declared testimony could be cross-checked, and possibly corrected.

Their analysis of the interview material was reported in highly normative form, with ex-prisoners distinguished into three types, 'the settled', the 'unsettled', and 'the norm'. Curle and Trist concluded starkly that the domestic and family lives of most of those they interviewed was very bleak, characterized by intense conflict and tension between husbands and wives. In the 'normal' household, major domestic disputes were commonplace, leading to heated arguments lasting for two hours or more, roughly on a fortnightly basis. However, in a significant minority of 'unsettled' households, relations were much worse, with physical abuse of the wife by the husband and a near-constant state of animosity and antagonism between the partners. Even in the 'best' households, with no overt conflict between husbands and wives, this was not because the partners necessarily saw eye to eye, but rather they had learnt how to laugh off, or in Tavistock terminology, 'work through' their difficulties.

They were absolutely clear about the traumatic state of domestic relations they uncovered in their post-war studies.

> [T]he family of today cannot be regarded as a widely ramified system of organised and positive functional relationships, which form a bridge between the individual (and his family) and society as a whole....For many of those whose restricted pattern of social relationships is associated with feelings of discontent, anger, or bitterness, the marital relationship may be the only social relationship sufficiently real and secure to permit the expression of such hostile feelings to another human being.[24]

This account of the family shattered the complacency of gentlemanly social science with its assumptions about normal household relations. It was also a very

---

[24] Curle and Trist (1947).

different view of the family from that being developed in American functionalist sociology by Talcott Parsons and his associates, which saw the male-headed 'nuclear family' as the appropriate form for modern industrial society.

Ultimately, having raised concerns about marital relations during the 1940s, social researchers withdrew from these issues. We should not simply read this change as due to declining moral anxieties over marital relations as the divorce rate fell in the early 1950s, but see it also as linked to the emergence of new research repertoires. In place of the concern of gentlemanly social scientists to make relations between men and women visible, the use of interview methods came to render these as invisible, as somehow outside the distinctive province of social science. It was now class, and more particularly stories of class mobility, which came to be emphasized using interview methods.

The rise of a demoralized social science was about the active elimination of the kinds of sexual and familial sensibilities from the social science agenda, in the name of the modern and rational study of individuals.[25] This development became complicit with an implicitly (and sometimes explicitly) masculinist social science which explored not the relationships between male and female roles so much as aspects of the public pre-eminence of men, and notably the class relations between them. This development was associated with the use of the interview as a mechanism for revealing hidden sentiments. For, although the interview emerged out of psychotherapy and hence was indebted to the gentlemanly model, during the 1950s it was redeployed as a means of eliciting social information, and through this process the observational complex that lay at the heart of moral social science could be decentred.

It was the work of Elizabeth Bott which was to be central in demonstrating the potential of the interview as a mode of narrating the individual. This is ironic given that her work *Family and Social Network* was fundamentally concerned with the nature of household relationships, on which indeed it developed a highly influential 'social network' perspective. She transformed a problematic of family relations originating out of Curle and Trist's work, and which was focused on eliciting information about the psychological and about the dynamics of marital relations, into an account of social networks and relations. Bott's project was deliberately designed to link anthropology and social psychology. The respondents were expected to undergo psychological tests, conducted by Wilson and Menzies, while Bott and Robb were in charge of the fieldwork. This required intensive household interviews, involving up to twenty visits to each family, in order to work through a detailed semi-structured questionnaire. In Robb's account, the questions asked cover the following topics:[26]

• Detailed social history covering virtually all the descendants of the grandparents of each partner.

---

[25] See generally, Rose (1999*a*) though for my account of how he neglects the role of gender divisions see Savage (2008*c*).

[26] Robb (1954*b*).

- Internal organization of family: diaries of week's activities, main work tasks, with issues such as who does it, who is responsible for seeing it done, how are decisions made, and 'what disagreements are there and how are these handled'.

- Informal social relationships outside family and all connections with friends, relatives, and neighbours.

- Formal relationships with doctors, schools, churches, trade unions, etc.

- Ideology – political beliefs, views on the social structure, changes in family life, and attitudes to money.

The respondents were also interviewed individually to 'check' the interpretations from the psychological tests and give their impressions to Bott and Robb. When the project began, its director, Tommy Wilson, was hopeful that it could be used to generate a psychological–anthropological synthetic analysis of the marital relation. The idea was to develop an holistic account of the psychological and sociological relations between husbands and wives in order to enable a fuller understanding of how families could be successful. The project, however, ended in failure, precisely because the material collected through interview methods could not easily be assimilated into an account of personality and psychological dynamics. As late as 1956 the plan was to write a major monograph, with the psychologist Tommy Wilson drafting 50,000 words on the psychological dynamics of the couples, and Bott writing a series of compressed case notes on each of the households. Bott modestly noted in a letter to her colleague Jim Robb that the Tavistock had also agreed to publish her own work as a 'technical report'. Even at this stage, Bott noted that 'the ambitious scheme of integrating the socio-logical and psychoanalytic analysis has gone by the board', with Wilson's mono-graph simply to comprise annotated case studies. But in fact, even this limited monograph was never produced.[27]

By the time we get to Bott's published work, the interview is no longer used to elicit psychological data which differentiates men and women, but is instead deployed to talk about how individuals refer to norms and roles. She thus took the idea of the 'free' interview which had emerged within psychotherapy, where it was thought that unstructured conversation could allow respondents to reveal hidden, private features.[28] These ideas were also taken up in social work, where the female interviewer was by the 1950s experiencing considerable stress. The regulation and bureaucratization of social work which accompanied the expan-sion of welfare provision threatened to undermine the autonomous judgement of the 'knowing' woman professional and replace it by a purely functional role. More importantly, as Barbara Wootton identified in a controversial account

---

[27] Qualidata SN 4852, file 21.

[28] Robb (1954*a*, 66), who notes that 'many of the freer techniques have been developed by thera-pists and, although these have been used chiefly by them and by social case workers, social science research workers have also shown considerable interest'.

of the challenges to social work in the later 1950s, the rise of affluence problematized the role of the social worker as philanthropic custodian, able to differentiate the deserving from the undeserving poor. In the context of these changes, social work became increasingly influenced by psychological models which defined the expertise of social workers in terms of their ability to diagnose the psychological states of household members and offer appropriate support: 'where an older generation (of social workers) would have spoken of "investigation", the modern social worker writes on *"Diagnosing family situations"*'.[29] Wootton herself was deeply critical of this psychological turn, arguing that social workers lacked the expertise to engage in serious psychological intervention, with the result that the appeal to psychology would simply be a cover for them to impart arbitrary judgements. Wootton's own strategy, in the circumstances, was to define social workers as agents of the bureaucratized welfare state: '[T]he social worker who does for the run of ordinary people what confidential secretaries and assistants do for the favoured few is putting genuine professional skills at the disposal of those who may be properly called her clients.'[30] However, by construing social workers as functionaries, their autonomy and jurisdiction disappeared, and more importantly, the importance of the interview as an encounter was reduced in importance. Her account was therefore bitterly criticized by those who thought she was undermining the autonomy of the social worker as interviewer.[31] It was in this arena of uncertainty about what the interview could actually elicit that Bott was to stake the brilliant claim that it was academic social scientists, and not social workers, who should do interviews and in the process generate distinctive access to the 'social'.

Bott and Robb's use of in-depth interviews sought to elucidate the 'reference groups' of their respondents. Following the example of American social psychological researchers, Wilson's team was interested in the social identifications of the respondents, in the kind of groups which were salient and significant to them.[32] The interview notes contain detailed accounts of the 'negative' and 'positive' reference groups of the men and women, including full details of when these were shared, and when they were segregated. Here we see the interview being used to elicit information about the respondent's thoughts, in ways that were utterly alien to the older tradition of the interview as adjunct to observation, as prized by the Webbs.

How did Bott wrest the interview away from its psychoanalytical context to elicit information which could be used to inscribe social relations? It was here that her concern to explore how respondents understood social class proved important. The Tavistock had no conceptual vocabulary to deal with class, which was largely lacking from their work, even when studying manual workers. Thus,

---

[29] Wootton (1959, 273).   [30] Wootton (1959, 296–7).   [31] For instance, Wilson (1960).

[32] The American influence was mediated by the central figure Edward Shils, who had supervised Robb's Ph.D. thesis, which was to form the basis of *Working Class Anti-Semite*. Bott relates that it was Shils who advised her to work at the Tavistock as he thought it was doing the 'best research in England' (private communication).

Curle and Trist when exploring the norms and values of the resettled soldiers emphasized their self-perception not as members of social classes, but as 'alright', 'just ordinary', 'nothing special', or 'quite respectable'.[33] Trist and Bamforth did not deploy the concept of class in writing their study of longwall coal miners.[34] In this respect, they remained highly anchored within a normative, medical, gentlemanly problematic. Curle and Trist thus argued on the basis of their interviews with resettled prisoners of war that there was a coherent normative structure to their views in which

> a man would be married, have children, and maintain an independent household located in a specific neighbourhood of his 'home town' community in which there also lived, in a similar way, a good many of his closer relatives (...); in this wider community he earned his living as the employee of a particular firm, exercised the rights granted to a person carrying the status of a free individual, and observed the laws and obligations binding on a citizen.

It followed that Curle and Trist identified differences in family forms in terms of the different capacities of families to live up to universally shared norms, rather than in terms of conflicting views about what family life might consist of.[35]

What Bott did was to more fully 'relativize' this kind of inquiry, so that rather than defining one dominant 'norm' to which households aspired with varying degrees of conviction and effectiveness, she recognized that norms themselves were contested and varied. This allowed her to present her families as different types, interpreting such differences in terms of their different social relations, without seeing one kind as morally superior. By identifying the variability of social norms and values, and the way that the researcher needed to explore individuals' own takes on them, Bott provided a rationale for the intensive in-depth interview conducted by sociologists, as a fundamental research tool. Here, she used the concept of class as a means of summarizing these kinds of complex views about their social relations. 'When an individual talks about class he is trying to say something, in a symbolic form, about his experiences of power and prestige in his actual membership groups and social relationships both past and present.'[36] Through this formulation, class becomes a means of linking together disparate attitudes, values, and conceptions of the social. Although there is no reason to doubt her insistence that she was deriving the concept of class inductively, we can also note that the interview itself allows class to be assembled into a narrative which displaces that of the psychological subject. Rather like the concept of network, class was useful in allowing her a way of mediating structure and agency through the elicitation of a narrative account. She reported:

> First I tried to explain differences in norms and definitions of roles in terms of class, then in terms of neighbourhood. Neither attempt was successful, and I gave

---

[33] Curle and Trist (1947).   [34] Trist and Bamforth (1951).

[35] It is instructive that when class is mentioned by Tavistock researchers, as by Menzies (1950), it is only in terms of the sampling ratios derived from different classes, and that class itself does not become an object of analytical interest.

[36] Bott (1971, 163).

up this effort temporarily and turned to the analysis of class ideology. Here it was evident that personal experience and personal needs both conscious and unconscious were affecting people's concepts of class.[37]

Bott claims that her interest in class arose from her own experience, arriving as Canadian, and seeking to make sense of British society in terms of the hidebound conventions that seemed to her to be so powerful. In fact, as her own notes indicate, the respondents themselves did not use the terminology of class to any great extent in discussing their reference groups and identities.

What we see here is a fight over jurisdiction. Since the nineteenth century the task of household investigation through interview had been the province not of academic social scientists but of social workers and visitors. In a manner which broke with the long tradition of social observation, Bott claimed that researchers should, indeed must, conduct their own interviews in order to produce valid sociological insight, and that a study of people's accounts of class could be used as means of unravelling how people saw their social roles. It is not surprising that the social workers sought to defend their own 'empirical' expertise through resisting this move. And, because the Tavistock study separated out the collection of the psychological data from the social data (since the respondents were supposed to visit the clinic to have tests conducted on them), this meant that the household interviews did not cover moral and psychological aspects which were central to the psychological use of interview methods, so much as the social aspects. By a process of serendipity, Bott was left to write up a wealth of field material around the terrain of an emerging 'social'.

We can note that this intervention is very different to that which David Riesman led in the United States at the same period.[38] Riesman also sought to claim the in-depth interview as a valid sociological method, but he did so largely through using it to probe the 'character' or 'personality' of respondents in a way which did not fundamentally break from a psychological framing. This explains why the in-depth interview never became such a significant method in the United States, and why, when it was used, it remained focused on moral concerns.[39] By contrast, Bott mobilized the in-depth interview in the name of more fully sociological framing in terms of perceptions of class.

This move was one which allowed sociologists to define themselves as key agents in organizing often inchoate accounts into coherent form. Bott's example was to prove inspirational here. She emphasized that respondents' views could systematically reveal their sense of class even if this was elliptical to respondents themselves (a move rather similar to the way that the psychoanalyst could interpret their patients' words). In fact, looking now at the detailed reference groups listed in Bott's archived interviews this appears less obvious, so testifying to Bott's panache. What she managed, in fact, through the interview, was the enterprise of lifting social groups out of the landscape in the manner I have discussed

---

[37] Bott (1971).   [38] Lee (2008).   [39] Bellah et al. (1985) or Alan Wolf (1999).

in Chapter 1. They did this in three key ways. Firstly, by bringing out the negative reference groups invoked, they were able to systematically explore how even those respondents who did not talk about abstract social groups could nonetheless be shown to be in differentiated relationships from others. They were thus able to draw out for sociological purposes people's accounts of who they were not. Thus Mr Wraith, a journalist, reported that 'we are unique, unconventional, independent, self assured, doing what we like when we like and caring nothing for other people's opinions'. Mr Bullock, an economist, identified with people who 'are intelligent, young, socialists, politically active, mildly unconventional'. Mr Appleby, a carpenter, identified strongly against 'blokes at work'. This is exactly the way that Bott puts it in her account that 'concepts of class are used for general orientation in the society at large, for placing strangers, and for evaluating one's own position and that of others'.[40] Class does not evoke a sense of collective belonging to a group so much as a means of differentiating and positioning.

Secondly, the concept of class was used to summarize a whole series of cultural distinctions in the words of the respondents, a means of making visible and formalizing what were actually more inchoate accounts. We might see this as a process akin to that which Dirks describes in India through evocations of caste.[41] Only nine of the ninety-nine terms used to define some kind of social reference group explicitly names class as such, and most of these are negative reference groups. Four different kinds of social groups were identified: (*a*) Most powerfully there is a major cultural division with on one hand those with practical, often manual skills (Mr Appleby's enthusiasm for 'people who can do things with their hands', or Mr Redfern's interest in 'practical people'). By contrast those without practical skills, such as intellectuals, graduates, professors, drones, 'hangers-on of royalty' and the like are often singled out for criticism. This might be interpreted, in Bourdieu's terms, as an axis of cultural capital, though we might note, following our discussion in Chapters 2 and 3, that it is the practical which is valued over the intellectual. (*b*) There is also a cross-cutting moral division between the respectable and unrespectable (in which 'criminals', 'spivs', 'fiddlers', 'people who borrow', 'people with dirty jobs') are denigrated, and (*c*) a distinction in terms of authority and power ('bosses', 'those in authority'). By contrast, income and wealth is rarely identified as a salient division, except in so far as it can be made morally significant, through reference to 'people who borrow' or 'the indigent poor'.

We can see in many of these references a continued reliance on nineteenth-century populist idioms,[42] differentiating between a large 'popular' group and 'parasites' (drones, the non-productive, etc.), but these have now been spliced into a more modern language of class, with reference to employers, capitalists, and so forth. Bott's achievement is to link all these complex terms to the overarching importance of class, through her conceptual innovation that 'class is a means of symbolically making sense of everyday power relationships'. My fundamental point here concerns her use of the in-depth interview as a means of registering not psychological, but social attitudes and identities, which could then be

---

[40] Bott (1971, 191).   [41] Dirks (2003).   [42] Joyce (1990) and Lawrence (1998).

linked to the political language of class to render issues of sociological interest. Through this means, both what people say and how they say it becomes of interest to the sociologist.

7.2 MASCULINIZING THE INTERVIEW PROCESS

In this chapter I have argued that the interview is not a 'natural' way of doing social research, but had to be actively produced and championed as a suitable device. This involved a process of competition, in which alternative modes of eliciting social life, for instance through the community study, were contested. A crucial part of this contestation involved the deployment of sex and gender as categories. Interviewing entailed breaking from the practice – enshrined in census, local surveys, and community research – of obtaining comprehensive information on every household member, and their family relationships, thereby fixing on the household as the fundamental social unit. Instead, it focused on the individual respondent abstracted from their context. An essential – though still relatively ignored – concomitant of this shift was a different kind of treatment of gender and sexuality to that which was embedded in moral social science. Rather than the household being a necessary crucible for their formation and intersection, it became possible to extract 'gender' from the household, treating it as a distinctive variable in and of itself.

A key moment here was the growing visibility of men as interviewers during the later 1950s and into the 1960s. In the 1950s, it was assumed that most interviewers would be female: in his influential textbook on survey methods written in 1957, Claus Moser noted that 'since most interviewers are women, I shall refer to them throughout as the female sex'. The normal employment practice of the leading research agencies which conducted interviews, the British Institute of Public Opinion and the BBC Audience Research Department, was to employ interviewers on a casual part-time basis, which was likely to lead to female recruitment. Historically, when men had interviewed, they had normally done so on their premises, as in the doctor's consulting rooms, and it was largely women who were seen as appropriate for home visiting. Yet, in the hands of a new breed of young, male, social scientists, the home interview became a mechanism of eliciting story-like information which could be the stuff of an emerging sociology. The pioneers of the in-depth interview, Peter Willmott and Michael Young, from the Institute of Community Studies (ICS), were especially important models. Willmott and Young had no formal training. 'Our aim was to try to combine something of what we understood to be the approach of anthropology with that of sociology. We wanted ... to study a smallish community in depth. ... We wanted to collect some basic information from random samples and to analyse it with proper statistical care'.[43] Unusually, they were interested not in specific

---

[43] Willmott and Young (1961).

problems, or moral concerns, but 'our original purpose was to study the relationship between the social services and working class family life. The assumption was that policy makers and administrators were *insufficiently* aware of the needs or views of the working class people who form the bulk of the users of social services.' Like Bott, class proved a lever to elicit social knowledge, in a way which seized this from the psy-sciences.

The ICS was unusual in that although it had some similarities with other East End social settlements, it lacked their explicitly moralistic concerns, and in addition, was largely staffed by men. Unlike the division of labour that was deployed at the burgeoning Department of Social Studies at Liverpool University, which explicitly championed a synergy between social workers and social scientists, the founders of the ICS all played key roles in doing their own interviews. The founding work which established Willmott and Young's reputation, *Family and Kinship in East London*, deployed a local individual sample of every thirty-sixth person drawn from the electoral roll, leaving a final sample of 933. This method necessarily abstracted from the household relationships which were their focus, and it was their use of a more intensive sub-sample of forty-seven of these households which contained married couples with young children which was to be more innovative, and which provided all the vignettes and rich quotation which was to prove so influential.[44] The practice of sampling, and hence reducing the in-depth interviews to a relatively small number, allowed Young and Willmott with the assistance of Peggie Shipway to undertake the interviews themselves. They placed unusual emphasis on the fact that they had themselves done these interviews, whilst also providing one of the first accounts of how the relationship between quantitative and qualitative research might be understood.

> The formal 'mass' interview can provide fairly precise quantitative data, within a limited range, about a larger sample of people than can usually be seen in informal, intensive interviews; but the latter can provide richer material.... Certainly in any future enquiry of this kind we would not only write up the results but again carry out a series of interviews ourselves, for we value highly and our own understanding, slight as it still is, has benefited from, the close and continuous contact we have had with the people concerned.[45]

Despite the methodological criticisms that the increasingly confident survey researchers made of the work of the ICS, the use of intensive interviews was to prove an exceptionally important exemplar of how sociological research could be done. Through this means, (male) researchers now had access to individual 'respondents', and a reason to quiz them directly, rather than relying on female social workers or professional interviewers as intermediaries. This intervention took

---

[44] 'Thus all the qualitative data are drawn from the marriage sample interviews, and only the barest skeleton of facts comes from the general sample. The usual procedure of illustrating the hard data with examples is reversed: the anecdotes are illustrated by occasional figures' (Platt 1971, 49f, 51).

[45] Young and Willmott (1957, 174).

place specifically under the banner of class, where the intensive interview was seen as a means of allowing the middle-class male academic researcher to gain some insight into a different, non-intellectual, manual working-class world. It was absolutely essential, therefore, that the subjects on which intensive interviews were first championed were the working class.

The masculinity of this new breed of male interviewers was fundamental to the deployment of story-like accounts which could be used in popular sociology. A further key influence here was that of Brian Jackson and Dennis Marsden, both of whom were also associated with the ICS, and who in 1962 wrote what was to become the first classic work in the emerging 'sociology of education', entitled, *Education and the Working Class.* Using a sample of records of boys from Huddersfield grammar schools, this study concentrated on understanding the problems facing working-class boys in succeeding at school. Tellingly, both Jackson and Marsden were themselves from a Huddersfield working-class background, but had succeeded in going to Cambridge. Jackson himself was an English graduate, and the echoes of Leavis are evident in the references of *Education and the Working Class.*[46] Jackson's later work, *Working Class Community*, is explicit in aligning social research with the tradition of the 'creative artist' whom he identifies in the figures of D. H. Lawrence, L. S. Lowry, and Henry Moore, all upwardly mobile working-class writers and artists.[47] His colleague Marsden studied the natural sciences, having no contact with the social sciences as an undergraduate, and both drifted into social research indirectly, after early careers as school teachers, and through personal contacts with the ICS.

Both Jackson and Marsden appealed to the idea of emotional truth in laying out the significance of their work, and in delineating the power of class as a cultural divide. For Jackson, the appeal of Henry Moore was that, 'He is able to go beyond any position that a sociologist could reach: he records the problem of loss – class makes a gulf across which all the best human flow is lost'. Revealingly, in his later account of the book, Marsden's appeal to 'emotional truth' as a reason for deploying the use of intensive interviews on small samples indicates how this method was akin to fictional narrative accounts.

> Well, you couldn't possibly base any kind of scientific conclusions on that sample of [88] from one Grammar School. But it's never been repeated, and it was enormously successful, it sold hundreds of thousands – although we never made any money out of it. So, at some level, it must be emotionally convincing, it must be coherent. It has a coherent argument, and it performs, I think, one of the ideal functions of qualitative research, which is to explain what's going on....I think it was an extremely good book, and I think it was a book of its time. I think what's amazing is it had such an enormous impact with such a very small sample, but I think it convinces at the level of myth, rather than fact. People set the 'A' level

---

[46] For example, Jackson and Marsden (1965, 242). Note also that Jackson and Marsden note approvingly that 'an excellent book to read on the same theme' is Williams's *Border Country* (1960) (though his work of literary criticism remains unreferenced, see p. 280).

[47] Jackson (1968, 14f).

question as, 'Criticise the methodology'. That's nit-picking. It's not about that. It's got a kind of emotional truth, and captures a moment.

This appeal to 'emotional truth' reaches out to a literary tradition, for instance that celebrated by Raymond Williams and Richard Hoggart, yet it allowed this idea to be wrested from the world of literature and placed in the context of what could instead be rendered as social truths, seen as related to narratives of social class, differentiation, and mobility. It could also be extended away from the study of the upwardly mobile, to studies of the immobile working class, the experience of which could then be rendered as the salient 'other' to that of the upwardly mobile. This appeal resonated with the social realism of early 1960s television, film, and literature, and with the masculine 'hardness' of these cultural forms. The extent to which these literary models figured in the interviewing of the early 1960s is also apparent from the field notes of the Affluent Worker study.

> It's a plot. Graham Greene and Michael Young created this couple on a dark and stormy night, with DH Lawrence as marriage guidance counsellor they gave up the struggle to be anything but fiction of a lurid kind. The wife looked like a golden haired consumptive. She was cloying in manner, though her general appearance was of a soiled waitress.[48]

On other occasions, the interviewer notes deliberately evoke a literary style in seeking to conjure the image of the interview.

> A gloomy young pair who sat in silence, almost dozing....The wife was a fat little middle aged young woman and the husband looked younger, but just as care-worn...they gave no hints of having a wide network of friends and I should think their social life is restricted to a few shifty visits to and from kin. Really there's nothing to say about people like this. They hardly gave the impression of living at all. Just being here. Sets of clothes moved around by lumps of flesh.[49]

Sometimes the evocation of misogyny, psychology, and the literary form through the interview experience are even more apparent. The account is self-consciously ironic, recognizing the power of the interviewer, in rather a similar mode to a literary writer able to exercise power through the processes of inscribing.

> I have never come across a marital relationship like this! This couple live an almost completely isolated life, brooding over the defects of others, especially those with noisy children or who otherwise disturb the calm tenor of their world. I suspect they are in a terrible psychological mess. Or maybe they're absolutely happy. These things can be so curious. Anyway they're both under 40 but they're old. I bet she never lets him have it. 'Stop it, its vulgar'....He is completely and absolutely dominated by her. He's got no spine at all, she answered practically every question....Fortunately I'm not in a literary mood or this attack could go on for chapters. Mind you in a way it was quite a pleasurable experience seeing them wriggle on the end of probes, like hideous, trapped little insects. I think they regarded my visit as an honour, in the end, not an impertinent incursion. The hypocrisies I suffer for this project. Being honest about this makes me feel like a right bastard.[50]

---

[48] Luton Interview 178.   [49] Luton Interview 166.   [50] Luton Interview 162.

Who needs to read D. H. Lawrence when socio-sexual dynamics can be so power-fully evoked by the interview experience? The masculinity of the household interviewing is best revealed by Ray Pahl's research on suburban life in the English Home Counties in the early 1960s. Fresh from his studies at Cambridge and the LSE, Pahl wanted to find out about the secret world hidden behind suburban curtains, recalls his experience of interviewing women in Hertford-shire. Adopting the challenging style of interviewing which was frequently used on television, he saw himself as agent provocateur, concerned to probe conven-tion and unsettle respondents. The way that a 'posh' and confident young man could unsettle women who were not used to being asked personal questions by strangers is clear from the transcripts. One interview ran as follows:

> *How does your husband like living here?*
>
> He's not fussy – he doesn't much mind where he lives. He's not terribly social – he likes to come home and settle down for the evening...
>
> *What things do you really look forward to?*
>
> I don't honestly know? I tend to live from day to day. I'm not looking forward to the baby getting older...but I do look forward to the complete family...(four) is a reasonable number. Not too many. And they'd be reasonable companions for each other. It's as many as we could possibly afford
>
> *Do you prefer the company of males?*
>
> Yes, perhaps I identify myself more with males than females (confusion) what sort of Freudian thing are you going to make of that. I don't know what I mean
>
> *(What about your) Husband?*
>
> I suppose he uses the home mainly as a resting place and an eating place. He enjoys his home life but...what am I trying to say? I think I'll go and make a cup of tea, I'm thinking. I've done more talking than I've done for ages.[51]

Pahl's own later account of this research is revealing in demonstrating the sexual and gendered stakes of male researchers such as himself seeking direct access to women's accounts.

> And I remember...they'd got these nice little boxes in Stevenage, which they filled with little ticky tacky, you know, like Pete Seeger was singing, 'Little boxes, little boxes, little boxes on the hillside', and I scared the wits out of them. I said, 'Why is it so important', I said, 'Imagine you've just got the new television', which was just coming out, 'or a new table, and little Willy down there takes his car and goes 'Whoooosh' right across it, with a big scratch'. And they all went white, you see, and winced! And I said, 'Now, why is that so important? Because it's just as good a table. Why does that scratch worry you? What is it about that?' And, you know, 'Is it right, do you think, that you should be the person that makes sure that every-thing's clean? And what about this...why do you clean? And what's the importance of cleaning? Why is the house so much a kind of object? You know, when, in fact the kids might be happier with more muck', you see. So I really got them upset, and they came back and said, 'You know, we didn't sleep for two nights. I was talking to

---

[51] Ray Pahl, interview.

my husband about this', and I realised it was dynamite!...I just stumbled on dynamite, that there was this tension between the women who were getting fed up being housewives, and I just somehow put my finger on the button....And, you know, I was scared, because then they said, 'Well, you've upset us so much, our husbands want to come along and see this man that's upsetting their wife'. So I ran a thing for the husbands, and had a lot of trouble. They didn't take to it like the wives did, at all. They thought, you know, they were very suspicious.[52]

Pahl later claimed that he was influenced by Friedan's *Feminine Mystique* and was deliberately using the interview as a means of provoking a feminist response. In any event it is clear that the interview was far from being a neutral research method. He took up a particular interest in gendered roles in his book *Managers and Their Wives*, written with his wife, Jan Pahl, which interviewed both husbands and wives, and took the nature of their relationship as a specific focus of the research.

What these young male sociologists were all doing was presenting interview evidence as a means of eliciting 'real', sometimes shocking accounts, which provided narrative drama. It was a means of challenging boundaries of respectability and convention by laying on the table the voices which had historically been seen as irrelevant. It is not incidental that this use of interviews took place at exactly the same time as the censorship ban was lifted on D. H. Lawrence's *Sons and Lovers*. Nothing need now be kept covered up. It was precisely in this way that interview methods began to be taken up by newspapers and journals in this period. The progressive left-wing *New Statesman* began to use the occasional interview with 'ordinary' people in the mid-1960s, specifically as a means of eliciting shocking accounts. An interviewer introduced a 'very swinging girl' in 1965, 'she crosses long brown legs – narrow shoulders and big arse. Straight black hair and jagged cut fringe. She's a beauty'. Her account ran as follows:

[I]f I fancy someone I go to bed with them, they don't have to court me or spend money on me or make me any promises...I enjoy sex much more if I hate someone, yes, I get a great kick out of having sex with someone who I've no respect for – I feel they're there for my pleasure. I get a great kick out of the first night flinging off my clothes, I suppose I'm an exhibitionist. I'm showing off my body.[53]

Here, the interview method could be used to displace the responsibility for the production of salacious material to the interviewee rather than the interviewer or journalist. This highly sexualized quality of interview methods was also present in more academic settings. Dennis Marsden, who like Pahl also enjoyed interviewing women, was also insistent on the way that men were legitimate interviewers.

I was a bit miffed later on when the Women's Movement started, in the early seventies, claiming that only women could interview women, and all that Feminist research bollocks.

---

[52] Pahl, interview with Thompson.   [53] *New Statesman*, 15 October 1965.

PT: You don't accept the idea that only women could interview women?

DM: Well, how could I, you know? I mean, I'd had women in writing and saying, 'You've absolutely caught my story'. You know, that *Mothers Alone* had illuminated their life.

The important point here is less the personalities and styles of the male interviewer and more the way in which the interview could elicit an essentially male 'melodrama of class mobility' as the centrepiece of the interview. The focus here was on the scholarship boy, the upwardly mobile working-class man and his exciting story of mobility and advance, contrasted with the confined woman, trapped in the housing estate. These were, of course, an enormously powerful cultural repertoire during the later 1950s, echoing the themes of the realist literature of Alan Sillitoe and John Wain, as well as in their cinematic adaptations, and in academic currents through the remarkable interventions of Richard Hoggart from Leeds, and Raymond Williams from the Welsh borders.

Both of these had been relatively marginal figures, working in provincial adult education, before they produced their major works, *The Uses of Literacy* and *Culture and Society*, respectively. As Robbins discusses, the use of such narrative devices inherently constructs mobility as an ambivalent process of loss as well as advance, so rendering the original working class in positive terms.[54] These writers still defined themselves against the social sciences: Hoggart invoked his own autobiographical reflections as itself an acceptable means of dissecting culture, and in the process pitched himself against social science: 'this book is based to a large extent on personal experience and does not purport to have the scientifically tested character of a sociological survey'.[55] He is definite that it is through the humanities, and especially English – and not social science – that class can be understood; 'it is some novels, after all, that may bring us really close to the quality of working class life'. This is a similar concern of Williams, with his focus on registering the emotional truth of his own trajectory spanning the Welsh valleys, with his signalman father, his exposure to Leavis's English at Cambridge, and his later work in the South-East (at Hastings and Oxford). Dai Smith has recently emphasized how far Williams fused his literary criticism and his creative writing, seeing them both as integrally concerned with rendering the experience of male class mobility something which could be narrated. Yet for both writers, rendering experience through this kind of mobility narrative provided the potential for a social scientific framing.

It is on the basis of these models that it became possible for the melodramatic male mobility narrative to then be elicited, at first hand, through interviews with respondents themselves. It is interesting to note here that many of the early male interviewers – Jackson, Marsden, Goldthorpe, Lockwood, Pahl, Bechoffer, and

---

[54] For a valuable discussion of how the upward mobility story has been a vital device in literary narrative, though usually in a form which equates mobility with the act of narrating itself, and renders such mobility as ambivalent, see Robbins (2006).

[55] Hoggart (1957, 9).

Young – had either studied or worked at Cambridge, the bastion of Leavisite English. It was this generation who were to champion the new deployment of the intensive interview, by the use of 'rags to riches' narratives of change and social mobility. Through this process they appropriated narrative for an emerging sociology.

This deployment of everyday narrative did not meet with universal approval. J. B. Priestley, doyen of the literary middlebrow which had previously laid claim to the ordinary and everyday, took up his pen to bemoan the use of 'factual' accounts. Emphasizing that he wanted 'to keep well out of the sociologists' status symbol world', he mourned what he saw as the loss of the place of fiction in the public mind, whose place had been usurped by 'ghost written memoirs, biographies, tarted up history and sodden slabs of sociology'. Stridently, Priestley tried to turn the clock back by insisting that it was only novels that can bring people 'closest to his fellow countrymen of these 1960s', and emphasizing that a stranger to Britain would be better off ignoring 'opinion polls and all this documentary stuff' and instead should read '20 or 30 decent novels'.[56] Priestley thus recognized that the nature of reportage and narrative had itself been redefined.

7.3 CONCLUSION

By the early twenty-first century the interview came to enjoy wide legitimacy as a key social science method. This chapter has shown that this was not always the case, and that it took a long time for it to be granted this status. In some nations the qualitative interview failed to gain the cultural power which it came to possess in Britain. With a few notable exceptions, American sociologists did not come to rely on qualitative interviews in the same way. Partly drawing on the influential model of David Riesman's interviews which had enjoyed a mass audience in the 1950s, as well as the popularization of narrative accounts in Studs Terkel's journalism, interview-based studies were deliberately designed to have a wide public appeal. Alan Wolfe's study of middle-class American values, or Robert Bellah's account of American attitudes to community, all reported very large numbers of interviews, typically several hundred, but deployed these within a form of serious journalism which largely avoided theoretical reflection.[57] The qualitative interview in American sociology was never given as much pre-eminence as either the survey or the ethnographic study.

In Britain, by contrast, the interview was given greater importance as the vehicle for a new mode of sociological expertise, but this could only take place once it had been wrested out of the hands of applied professional service workers to make it available for the new social sciences. This process had a crucially

---

[56] J. B. Priestley, 'Fact or Fiction', *New Statesman*, 6 January 1967, p. 9.
[57] Terkel (1997), Bellah et al. (1985), and Wolfe (1999).

important component in making the stated values and identities of research subjects of interest and importance to sociologists, and hence allowing a distance from normative assumptions based on assumed moral values. It permitted a space for respondents to talk in their own terms, and for researchers to mobilize such accounts as critical alternatives to dominant social values. Yet it also marked a new kind of masculine expertise, which challenged the previous role of women as interviewers. It told the male melodrama of the upwardly mobile, an issue which it had in common with the literary currents of the day. The interview, therefore, marked a specific fusion of literary and social scientific concern. And the masculinity of this story of social mobility was itself a vital aspect of the interview, with predominantly male sociologists being especially important propagators of the technique in the 1950s and 1960s.

These observations explain the distinctively gendered issues around the deployment of interview methods. By the later 1960s academic feminism emerged within the social sciences, linked to the practices of consciousness raising and using narrative methods as a means of reasserting the power of women talking to other women. Most accounts of feminist politics emphasize how it was part of a wider challenge to conventional social norms which took place during the 1960s. The evidence from this chapter suggests a somewhat different interpretation, one which sees feminism as a response to the emergence in only the previous decade of a powerful masculinist social scientific current, one which did not draw attention to household relations or the visible role of women as moral guardians, but defined them at best as foils to upwardly mobile men. This new social science also involved contesting women's roles as interviewers and intermediaries. The assertion of a distinctive feminist kind of social research, and the need for women to talk to women can best be seen as a counter-mobilization against this current.

Interviews could take many more or less structured forms. During the early 1960s the qualitative interview emerged as a major research repertoire, a status which it has retained in later decades. Yet it was the use of the structured interview as a mechanism for eliciting the sample survey which was to have the greatest short-term impact in the 1960s. It is to this story that I turn in Chapter 8.

8

1941: The Sample Survey and the Modern Rational Nation

Up until the 1950s, many teachers, most educationalists, and nearly all politicians envisaged educational research as a mildly interesting and marginal activity, suitably carried out in the small back rooms of a few universities, supplemented by one or two projects of a more comprehensive nature carried out by NFER; an activity justifying very little financial support and one with little or no relevance to the formation of educational policy or the development of educational methods. The periodic reports of the Central Advisory Council – that typical British method of providing the basis of educational progress and development – formulated their recommendations by the time-honoured method of canvassing opinion and seeking a consensus. Recent reports, however, have demonstrated a revolutionary change. Crowther, Robbins, and Plowden were not content with merely canvassing opinion – an important part, but only a part, of the decision-making process – they proceeded to seek out facts, and where facts were not available, to commission research to discover them. The consequent interest in the authority of these significant reports has been obvious to all.[1]

In 1964, a Labour government, led by Harold Wilson, was returned to power after thirteen years of Conservative rule. It defined itself as a modernizing government, committed to sweeping away the corrupt and backward looking 'Establishment', which critical commentators had vigorously argued, to a receptive audience, still held the levers of power. This aristocratic formation (personified by the elderly, even doddering, figure of the old Etonian prime minister Alec Douglas-Home), which had been identified as a modern, dynamic force by sociologist Edward Shils just a few years earlier, was now seen as a spent force, holding back the possibilities of a modern and progressive nation keen to rid itself of its dated imperial image.[2] Claims to modernity now lay with a technological current, brilliantly mobilized by Harold Wilson's Labour Party, whose zeal for modernization was personified most aptly in the formation of a Ministry for Technology, led by the arch technological enthusiast Tony Benn, and which came to employ 39,000 staff by the later 1960s.[3]

---

[1] NFER Annual Report, 1967–68: quoted in Griffiths (2003, 50).
[2] See Sampson (1962), and the general discussions in Savage and Williams (2008a). For Shils, see the discussion in Chapter 3.
[3] See the ribald commentary in Sandbrook (2006, 308f).

Yet, although the flagship projects of this technological moment – from the hovercraft to Concorde – are well known, its more mundane deployment of new social science methods have been much less appreciated. Yet, central to this modernizing moment was the extensive deployment of a new method for gaining social data – the sample survey. This became a crucial technology for defining the modern rational nation and the project of the new state.[4]

Let us consider the example of the Redcliffe-Maud Royal Commission on Local Government which sat between 1968 and 1969. It reported on how to rationalize the 'hotchpotch' of local government which had not been subject to significant reform during the twentieth century.[5] The Local Government Acts of 1888 and 1894 had distinguished between Counties, County Boroughs, Municipal Boroughs, Urban Districts, and Rural Districts. For those in a County Borough (effectively, large towns and cities), one local authority provided all municipal services allowing a strong commitment to municipal autonomy. By contrast, if one lived in a rural area, County Councils provided some services and District Councils provided others. The boundaries of counties were themselves largely unchanged since the Middle Ages, despite the huge shifts of population and the rise of large cities subsequently.[6]

These historically anachronistic arrangements were ripe for scrutiny by a modernizing government. Redcliffe-Maud, in its search for 'functional effectiveness', argued for the value of unitary authorities, in which every resident – whether in a large city or a small village – only had to deal with one local authority. They also supported the rationalization of local authority boundaries to avoid huge units and remove small ones. Their deliberations were aided by, indeed dependent on, the authority of the social sciences. Enlisting the expertise of the political scientist L. J. Sharpe, Redcliffe-Maud conducted three national sample surveys to gather the appropriate empirical basis for its recommendations. Firstly, a survey of local authority councillors was conducted, showing them to be over-represented by elderly and higher status men. Elements of an 'Establishment' could be detected in local government. Secondly, a local elector survey explored the extent to which citizens were confident in the decisions of their local council and revealed a worrying degree of apathy towards local government.[7] Thirdly, a local community study was used to examine what kinds of boundaries were meaningful to local residents, and was influential in indicating in large urban areas at

---

[4] For more general accounts, see Bulmer et al. (1986) and Wagner et al. (1991), though neither of these brings out the significance of particular research methods.

[5] The term 'hotchpotch' is precisely that used in the semi-official account of local government reform, Redcliffe-Maud and Wood (1974, 24). See also Sharpe (1980).

[6] 'The administrative county of Lancashire contained 2.2 million people (. . .) almost a hundred times larger than the population of Rutland. Devon's 1,650,000 acres could be contrasted with the 53,000 acres of the Soke of Peterborough. Many of these counties had boundaries which could be traced back to Medieval times or even earlier' (Redcliffe-Maud and Wood 1974, 25). On Rutland and the politics of English melancholia, see Matless (1998, 274).

[7] 'Sample surveys showed that few citizens knew even the name of their councillor, let alone the range of services for which he (sic) was responsible' (Redcliffe-Maud and Wood 1974, 3).

least, local citizens did not have parochial attachments to specific districts or neighbourhoods.[8] This finding was used to demonstrate that the people preferred generally smaller-scale units of local government.

Although we should not exaggerate the impact of specific research findings on the particular policies recommended, the use of sample surveys allowed scientific and rational data to be mobilized as a means of generating knowledge seen as fit for modern government.[9] In this process, it could also deploy alternative mechanisms for revealing 'popular' feeling which bypassed the accounts of elected representatives themselves. In this manner, the sample survey was a lever which could be used to produce new information that had the power to remake processes of local political deliberation, and all in the name of science and rationality.

In this chapter, I explore the dramatic rise of the sample survey as an instrument of modern rational governance. Beginning in the 1920s, consolidated during the war years through the institution of the Government Social Survey, and culminating in Harold Wilson's 'modernizing' Labour government of 1964–70, the survey came to occupy a central role in producing knowledge fit for governance. If we follow Benedict Anderson's arguments about the way that modern nationalism arises from mechanisms which produce a national 'imagined community' out of discrete and fragmented monads, we can see how important the sample survey becomes. Anderson notes how narrative serves to link disparate experiences and incidents into a coherent national story during the nineteenth century, so creating a romantic modern nation, in which history and literature play a central role in defining national identity.[10] The sample survey also provides a mechanism for linking observations on a very small number of people into an account of the nation. However, rather than relying on narrative, it deploys the scientific language of sampling error, units of stratification, and confidence levels. The survey thus mobilizes a rational statistical account of the nation in which the truth of the nation is guaranteed not by storytelling but through the protocols of science itself.

In this chapter, I therefore explore how the sample survey brought with it fundamental new possibilities for discerning national social structure. Yet I want to demonstrate that this emergence was fraught and untidy, and that there was no simple 'unrolling' of a coherent and unified sample survey method, for instance through a 'political arithmetic' tradition.[11] In fact, we can detect competing fragments in survey methods, which could well have led in different

---

[8] See Sharpe (1980, 29f).   [9] This cautionary view is argued by Sharpe (1980).

[10] See Anderson (1982) and the discussion in Moretti (1999). The same idea is central to the important analysis by Desrosieres (1998) in a chapter insightfully entitled 'The part for the whole'.

[11] Teleological accounts of the survey tradition were exemplified at the time by Jones (1949) and Abrams (1951). They were later systematized in the arguments of A.H. Halsey, who identified the survey as a key component of a tradition of 'political arithmetic' which originates in Petty's work in the seventeenth century and is elaborated and expanded with the use of sample survey analysis during the twentieth century. For a further discussion see Osborne, Rose, and Savage (2008).

directions from those which became dominant in the 1960s modernizing moment. I bring out the tensions between four major issues in the following paragraphs.

Firstly, derived from the 'psy-sciences', the sample survey was crucial for elaborating a social account of the 'developmental individual'. Whereas gentlemanly social science focused on the individual necessarily situated in the environment of his or her household and locale, the survey plucked individuals out of this immediate context, arraying their attributes in isolation, and established the abstract features and correlates of individual development through the statistical manipulation of variables. I will show how many early surveys focused on the individual in their developmental capacity, notably through the early use of panel or cohort studies, the first of which dates to 1946, with the National Child Development Study beginning in 1958. A particular feature of this interest was the sample survey's importance in eliciting the active role of 'intelligence' within the social order, and so it helped produce the social scientific habitus itself. The sample survey thus helped generate a new conception of the modern engaged citizen.

Secondly, the sample survey brought with it a new interest in the nature of social groups themselves which allowed 'variable centred' conceptions of the social to command provenance. We have seen how earlier social science, indebted to field analysis and to the observational method, found it difficult to isolate and abstract social groups. By contrast, the sample survey proved a mechanism by which the characteristics of even obscure social groups could be delineated through defining their aggregate characteristics. I show that down to the later 1960s, it remained more common to conduct a sample survey on a specific group, often in a particular location, than on a national random sample, and that we can therefore see the survey as being an important device for eliciting social categories as meaningful ones.

Thirdly, the survey encapsulated the nation itself. In the wake of de-colonialization and the loss of empire, surveys could provide core indicators of the 'state of the nation'. Unemployment rates, the cost of living, inflation, increasingly depended on the deployment of survey findings which were critically conducted within national boundaries. This is a story therefore of how the sample survey becomes a central feature in the deployment of what later social scientists have defined as methodological nationalism.[12]

Fourthly, and crucially for the themes of this book, the sample survey embedded conceptions of change as endemic to it. Whereas earlier generations of researchers had examined change through comparing separate documents or observations, survey researchers developed the means to analyse change through the internal manipulation of survey data. They were thus able to take up the widely heralded interest in change but promise a scientific rendering of it. This, I shall argue, remains the enduring legacy of the survey method.

---

[12] Urry (2000a) argues that sociology needs to go beyond a concern with national social structures and the assumption that nations are containers for different national societies. Although his argument is powerful, he does not draw out the historical foundations for the association between nation and society, which are powerfully dependent on the use of survey analysis.

8.1 THE SAMPLE SURVEY AND PUBLIC OPINION

The idea that a sample of a few can be mobilized to generate an account of a whole society is both old and new. On the one hand, sampling theory, with its roots in probability theory, has a long history, dating back to seventeenth-century dice games, and the main principles of sampling as applied to surveys had been worked out during the later nineteenth century.[13] The first significant application of sampling methods in England was in A. L. Bowley's much acclaimed 1915 studies of poverty in five English towns, which came to influence other studies, notably the re-study of Booth's London poverty survey in the later 1920s (which conducted a sample of 1 in 50 individuals under Bowley's direction) and Rowntree's re-study of poverty in York in 1935.[14] From the 1930s, sampling became more widely used, notably in opinion polling which was imported by Gallup from the United States in 1938. In government research, sampling was first seriously used in 1923 by the Ministry of Labour to study the characteristics of the unemployed, and then more widely in the later 1930s to examine cost of living, along with wages and income.[15]

Thomas Osborne and Nikolas Rose have provided an insightful account of the significance of the sample survey in their claim that the phenomenon of 'public opinion' was dependent on the rise of the Gallup poll. Before polling, ideas of public opinion had been biased towards the articulate middle class, yet the concern of democratic politicians to articulate representative opinion led them to champion the poll as a means of defining democratic and representative public opinion. The rapid take-up of sample surveys in market research and wartime government inquiries led Osborne and Rose to argue that '[b]y the end of the Second World War, then, it appears there was something of a consensus on public opinion; that it exists, that it can be measured, that it is related to action, that it is important for all kinds of political and non-political decision making, that it can be ascertained by research technologies, and so forth'.[16]

Yet we need to be attentive to the fact that opinion polling remained relatively disreputable in Britain, and that there continued to be considerable scepticism towards the value of sample surveys for eliciting opinions and attitudes. The issue is partly about timing. If Gallup's successful prediction of the 1936 presidential election was seen as a triumph for these new methods in the United States, the appropriate British comparison is with the experience of the 1945 General Election. Although the opinion polls predicted a large Labour victory throughout

---

[13] See MacKenzie (1981) and Desrosieres (1998).

[14] Smith (1930–5) and Rowntree (1941).

[15] The most useful accounts of the early pioneers of sample surveys remain Moser (1958, chapter 2), Abrams (1951, chapter 3), and Jones (1949). I do however take issue with the interpretation of these authors regarding the development of sample surveys below. Other useful overviews remain; see also JRSS (1949).

[16] Osborne and Rose (1999).

the campaign, no significant commentator believed them, and it was a huge shock when Clement Atlee's Labour government was elected in a landslide. Although opinion polls were conducted during the election campaigns of the 1950s, they only appeared in the *News Chronicle* and *Daily Express* and continued to make significant mistakes (for instance, in predicting a Conservative electoral majority over Labour in 1951) and by no means enjoyed paramount status until Harold Wilson's Labour government of the 1960s, where poll-watching was elevated into an art form.[17] In the 1970 Election polls dominated media coverage as never before, yet their failure to predict the victory of the Conservatives led to a committee of inquiry to assess their failure.[18]

But even more than this, the very idea of opinion polling remained disreputable. During the war, the attempt to study morale using surveys had caused considerable unrest because it was assumed to breach privacy (leading to popular denunciation of 'Cooper's snoopers') which led the Government to fall back on Mass-Observation with their more ethnographic and qualitative emphases to learn about civilian morale.[19] A further reason was the association of the poll with the grubby world of commercial market research, in which the survey was deemed to be an American device for the spread of commercial values. This link was made most concrete in the form of Mark Abrams, who was both a pioneer of market research and the most strident advocate for the sample survey. Although influential, especially in his denunciation of what he saw as the idiosyncratic methods of Mass-Observation, he was in his turn regarded as suspect for his lack of scholarly credibility.[20] Even those sociologists who aspired to the American model of scientific social science did not necessarily see the sample survey as important. John Madge, whose book *The Origins of Scientific Sociology* was a plea to British sociologists to learn from America, chose to laud only one survey-based exemplar: Stouffer's 'American soldier' project. Most of his book concentrated on American excellence in community studies, interactionism, and psychological

[17] See, for instance, the exchange of views between Mangus Tunstile and Frank Teer, *New Statesman*, 5 May 1967, p. 618.

[18] See Butler and Stokes (1969, 13): 'the polls have...provided the political parties with the tools of market research – although, in Britain at least, these have been used only slowly and tentatively'. The Nuffield election studies of the 1950s indicate that polls were often publicized in national newspapers, but it is instructive that they were still seen as an 'alien' technology: 'Despite the limited accuracy of their predictions in 1951, the influence of opinion polls is likely to be increasingly important in future elections, and it is to be hoped that a greater understanding of their utility and of their limitation will develop than was revealed in most of the comment on them made both by newspapers and politicians' (Butler 1952, 240). For other remarks on the slowness of the British to take up sample survey compared to the Americans, see Moser (1958), Miller (1983), and Bulmer et al. (1986, chapter 6).

[19] Duff-Cooper was Minister for Information in 1942, see the review by Claus Moser (1958) of Abrams's *Social Surveys and Social Action*: 'no more than ten years ago, official surveys tended to be greeted with cries of "snooping" by the press and general hostility by the public. Now the work of the Government Social Survey, of market researchers, of Gallup Polls and of academic social surveyors is more widely known and generally received with serious consideration'.

[20] See Abrams (1951) and for the wider relationship to Mass-Observation, Liz Stanley (1995*a, b*).

testing, and resisted strategies which simply enumerated social phenomena.[21] So it was that, in making their case for a proper sociological account of the 'affluent worker', Goldthorpe and Lockwood took as their point of departure the limitations of poll evidence which they thought did not allow attitudes to be placed in adequate context: 'it can only be concluded that the findings of class identification studies conducted via poll-type questioning are of very little sociological value'.[22] Here they were largely reiterating the suspicion of such methods which often surfaced in the journals of the time. One correspondent to the *New Statesman* parodied the means by which knowledge could be extracted through such apparently contrived means.

> Sir – some weeks ago an extremely well spoken young lady called at my home and asked me to identify certain personages whose names she read out to me from a printed questionnaire. Among the names was George Brown[23] whom I correctly identified as a xylophone player as I know him to be a member of the Archie Jones percussion band (still, as far as I know, entertaining around the pubs of Stockton).
>
> I was also asked about other characters, some of whose names I did not quite catch. However I dealt with these questions to the best of my ability including one on 'who are the Beetles?' which I left unanswered as I realised that pollsters usually include 'trick' questions in their surveys to ensure that informants are giving genuine answers.
>
> I can also change water into wine and ride a bicycle with no hands.[24]

Although there was considerable scepticism towards surveys in the United States as well as in Britain,[25] the academic social sciences were considerably more enamoured with survey methods. Lazarfeld's championing of variable-centred analysis commanded the social science high ground by the 1950s, and political scientists such as Ronald Inglehart promoted the analysis of attitude surveys from the 1970s.[26] British attempts to tap public opinion using sample measures were more spasmodic. One high point was the concern of the Younger Committee on Privacy (1970–2) which used a survey to gauge popular attitudes towards privacy. However, as Rhodes reports, partly because it took so long to obtain the survey findings, the Commissioners had mainly made up their minds on the basis of other deliberations and finally noted that 'survey and other evidence confirmed "what a few moments intelligent reflection makes obvious"'.[27] Attitude surveys were not widely deployed in the United Kingdom outside commercial

---

[21] Madge was thus critical of the survey research of Alfred Kinsey for conflating causal and descriptive strategies. See Madge (1967, 24f).

[22] Goldthorpe and Lockwood (1963, 144).

[23] Brown was at this time Home Secretary in the Labour government.

[24] Letter by A. M. Hedges, *New Statesman*, 8 October 1965.   [25] See Igo (2007, chapter 4).

[26] For an example of the power of this work in the United States by the mid-1950s, see Hyman (1955).

[27] G. Rhodes, 'The Younger Commission', cited on page 117. The survey is discussed in some detail by Bulmer (1979).

marketing, and it was not until 1983 that the British Social Attitudes Survey was set up, which even then remained relatively little used by academic social scientists. Bulmer's discussion of the limited salience of attitude polls and the disjuncture between people's expressed opinions and their actions is typical of the scepticism that most academic social scientists maintained towards opinion polls.[28] This suspicion of polling and market research was made concrete in the critique of quota sampling methods, where interviewers sought to interview enough respondents from particular kinds of group, rather than through fully random methods.[29]

In fact, up to and including the period of the Second World War, documentary data collected on whole populations continued to enjoy more pre-eminence than sample survey evidence. The introduction of National Insurance legislation in 1911 meant that every individual in a registered occupation had a central record kept on file, allowing the systematization of labour statistics. The extension of this scheme in 1920 meant that interwar labour statistics were based on complete administrative data, though on some occasions samples from this were drawn.[30] In 1939, on the eve of war, a National Register was created with no less than 65,000 enumerators recording every person resident on the night of 29 September at their residential address. This register was to be the basis for wartime identity cards. This database on the entire population was kept up to date through being linked to records of death, birth, enlistment into the armed forces, demobilization and removal to other parts of the United Kingdom (which was notified through migrants reapplying for ration books in their new area of residence). In addition, the Ministry of Food kept complete files to allow them to administer rationing. Complex decisions about how demobilization from military services was to be conducted in a planned manner depended on the deployment of records such as these.[31] Similarly, the formation of the National Health Service in 1948 opened the possibility of analysing medical records of the entire population in a systematic way.[32] Jon Agar shows how the development of early (predigital) computing machinery, in the form of Hollerith punch card machines, went hand in hand with this utilization of administrative data, since they were seen to

[28] Bulmer (1986, chapter 6).

[29] See Claus Moser's comments in response to Gray and Corlett (1950, 200), '[I]t is not appropriate that surveys the results of which administrative action is to be based should rely on a method of sampling which is so likely to lead to bias. The chief attraction of quota sampling is its cheapness and although this probably explains why it is still used a great deal by commercial organisations, I think the social surveys changeover to random sampling is greatly to be welcomed.'

[30] See Jones (1949, chapter 7).

[31] See generally, Moser (1949, 233f), who argues that the greater deployment of such lists in Britain compared to the United States explains why sample surveys were less significant. John Wishart, 'Statistical aspects of demobilization in the Royal Navy', discusses how such records were used in practice. All servicemen had an index card recording an occupational and an industrial code, their area of residence, code number, whether they were married, and their scale of pay. They could thus be demobilized according to the strategic importance of their occupation.

[32] See the discussion in Cotton and Heron (1948). Actuarial statistics continued to be dependent on the recorded cause of death on death certificates.

provide the technological basis for the handling of large data bases.[33] In short, at least until the later 1940s it was not obvious that the sample survey was actually needed as it appeared that technological advances would permit the more extensive deployment of administrative records.

8.2 DEFINING SOCIAL GROUPS AND INDIVIDUALS

Until the 1960s only government and market research companies had the infrastructural capacity to administer and analyse surveys using large numbers of interviewers, analysing the data using large amounts of clerical labour, and deploying the most sophisticated mechanical and early mainframe computers of their day. For these reasons, by the 1960s, government surveys, organized within the Office of Population and Census, represented the gold standard. The key step in the formation of this governmental nexus is widely recognized as being the formation of the Government Social Survey (GSS) in 1941. Under its aegis, the number of surveys conducted rose steadily from the later 1940s, with 64,000 interviews being conducted in 1946 rising to 110,000 by 1949.[34] By this period, between 250 and 300 part-time interviewers ('mainly women') were employed by the GSS to conduct research for various government departments.

It is striking that at this stage, surveys were not used to provide aggregate accounts of the national social structure. This remained the province of the census and administrative data sources on the whole population. Rather, surveys were used to delineate the characteristics of particular social groups which could be abstracted, lifted out of their geographical location, through the sampling process.[35] Thus, the first official use of sampling methods, in 1923, involved using National Insurance records to sample the unemployed, scattered throughout the nation and hence largely impervious within many local studies. These could then be identified as a coherent social group in their own right through sampling mechanisms.[36] This interest in defining social groups through sample surveys continued, when, in 1937–8 the Ministry of Labour conducted a sample survey specifically on the expenditure of 10,000 'working class' families. Detailed information being on precise budgeting for items of clothing was collected.[37] We can see these endeavours as attempts to 'mine down' into the characteristics of

---

[33] Agar (2003).   [34] Gray and Corlett (1950, 151).

[35] Though it is interesting to note that the differentiation between census and sample survey was one which was contested at this period. Madge (1967) disparages descriptive surveys as forms of census. The Royal Commission on Population in 1946 used (very large) sample measures but saw these as adjunct to census perspectives.

[36] Desrosieres (1998) makes the interesting point that the definition of the 'unemployed' has been fundamental to the development of quantitative social science expertise since the nineteenth century.

[37] See Ross (1948). This survey provided information for inflation rates until the 1950s when the Family Expenditure Survey was set up.

specified groups so that their features could be made visible. In this respect, what was to become a later justification for the sample survey, that it offered a reliable account of the 'national social structure' was absent.

We can see this similar impulse in the formation of the Government Social Survey in 1941. Most of the surveys conducted by this unit were designed to generate information internal to the government departments, to the extent that Claus Moser saw it as a major weakness that they could not usually be used for sociological analysis.[38] Table 8.1 lists the topics which the GSS researched during the later 1940s as they established their reputation as the most reputable survey organization in Britain. We see from Table 8.1 that only a few of these surveys were based on national samples, and that many were focused on particular population subsections – a means of delineating demand for particular services and the very meaning of social groups themselves. Sometimes very specific groups were sampled, such as '13–18-year-old boys in mining areas'. More commonly they abstracted social groups by sampling across geographical areas, notably through the frequent samples of housewives, women, children, or specified occupational groups. The attempt to draw a national sample of all adults was found in only a third of cases, and even here there was uncertainty about whether households or adults were being sampled.

We can note – contra Osborne and Rose – only relatively subdued interest in gauging public attitudes, in the few inquires into opinion towards colonial policy, and National Insurance legislation. We can also note that there were not, by and large, wide-ranging questions addressing issues of social and economic equity, as might be expected by those who see surveys as intrinsically linked to the 'political arithmetic' tradition. Concerns with poverty were absent, and there were no interests in education, other than the survey conducted for David Glass, which became the first study of social mobility.[39] This may reflect the concern of the GSS to avoid controversial topics which might offend powerful government ministers and lead to its closure.[40] We can see that the main interest was on economic and military mobilization, and on consumption (which in these days of rationing and austerity was also deemed pertinent to wider questions of mobilization).[41] Medical statistics continued to depend predominantly on hospital and other medical records, rather than on samples.[42] The sample survey, in fact, embodied the germs of a new technology which was deemed to provide information on the mobilization of national resources in a centrally planned and administered system.[43]

---

[38] See Moser(1949, 235).   [39] Glass (1954).

[40] 'Until the mid fifties (the GSS) was in perpetual danger of being closed down for offending powerful politicians' (Miller 1983, 51).

[41] Even apparently welfare-related surveys, such as that on sickness which had been conducted since 1943, had obvious relevance for military as well as welfare considerations.

[42] See also on the sickness surveys, Cotton and Heron (1948, 16).

[43] The argument that welfare was important to the genesis of the sample survey is evident in Abrams (1951). He defines poverty research as central to the emergence of surveys and then regards market researchers and public opinion poll researchers as 'borrowers'. However, Abrams's

Table 8.1 Government Social Survey (GSS) inquiries, 1946–9

Area	Survey focus	Sample composition
Health (8)	Survey of sickness	Adults 16+
	Pneumoconiosis	Certified as sufferers
	Road safety (2)	Adults 14+
	Extent of deafness	Civilians 16+
	Blood transfusion	Donors; civilians 16–64
	Nutrition of housewives	Housewives in four boroughs
	Nutrition of schoolboys	Schoolboys
Employment (8)	Recruitment to civil service	Tech/prof/clerical workers, parents,
	Recruitment to mining	children
	Recruiting women to industry	Boys 13–18 in mining areas
	Men and mining	Civilian women 16–60
	Lighting in offices	Men 16–60 (apart from miners)
	Agricultural labour recruitment	Office workers
	Lancashire cotton towns	Male civilians, farmers
	Recruitment of hospital nursing staff	Households in Great Britain (GB) Nurses
Defence related (4)	Demand for 'Defence' medals	Civilians 17+
	Demand for 'Campaign stars'	Ex-servicemen and women
	Re-enlistment to the Royal Air Force (RAF)	Ex-airmen; recruits
	Recruitment to the Territorial Army (TA)	Male and female civilians, ex-service men and women
Consumption related (10)	Demand for carpets	Working class households
	Shopping hours	Civilians 18+, holidaymakers, landladies
	Demand for holidays (2)	Civilians 15+
	Demand for fuel (2)	Housewives
	Attitude to meters	Housewives
	National savings	All civilians
	Expenditure on clothing	Households in GB
	Consumer expenditure series	Households in GB
Trade (1)	Attitudes to exports	Civilians 16+
Planning (5)	Attitudes to development of Willesden	Residents of Willesden
	Attitudes to house space	Residents of interwar houses
	House heating	Households in GB
	Crockery stocks	Households in GB
	Household waiting lists	Applicants on waiting lists
Children (3)	Children's out-of-school interests	Mothers of children 5–15, children 12–15
	Children and the cinema	Schoolchildren over 10, mothers
	Education and employment	Adults 18+
Other (3)	Attitudes to colonial affairs	Civilians 16+
	Attitudes to National Insurance scheme	Civilians, shopkeepers

Source: Gray and Corlett (1950, appendix).

Table 8.1 also reveals inconsistency over whether sampling was of households, adult civilians, children, mothers, or housewives. There was no unanimity at this stage that the national random sample of individuals should be the 'natural' sampling frame. The tension between individuals and households is pertinent, and is worth reflecting on by reflecting on the 'education and employment' survey which formed the basis for David Glass's landmark social mobility study. Glass's research team found it difficult to decide on how to operationalize measures of social mobility. Do you focus on the trajectories of individual men, women, or households? They vacillated. Data from respondents of both sexes were used to establish that there was considerable agreement about which occupations ranked highest, which were used to construct occupational classes, between which mobility could be measured. Here, they used the occupations of men as proxies for the position of households, and subsequent parts of the book then focused on the male data alone. On top of this, the emphasis on using occupation to measure social position posed the question of how women's standing was to be measured, given that they often were not employed, so could not easily be 'classed'. The result was that they were classified according to the occupation of their father or husband. Finally, and with no explanation whatsoever, the key chapter VII, which reported findings on social mobility, only looked at the male sample. The large amount of data on women was simply left 'on the table'. Willy-nilly, and despite the ostensible intentions of Glass and his team which had at their disposal large amounts of data on women, they came to prioritize men. Their resolution, which rendered the social position of women both as invisible and as dependent for their position on their male kin, needs to be seen as actively produced during the course of their work.[44] Whereas the mapping tradition focused on sexed households, the survey was based on individuals, and thus found the means of abstracting (male) individuals from wider household relations.

This was symptomatic of a wider uncertainty. When it was deemed necessary to gain information on households and individuals, the GSS experimented by trying to interview all household members one after the other: 'this method proved to have serious disadvantages since it is extremely difficult to interview separately at one visit all the individuals in a given household without another member of the household being present at the interview. The answers of the first person interviewed were very liable to influence those of the others.'[45] As a result of these difficulties, the GSS decided only to interview one adult per household, who would then provide aggregate information on the other household members.

---

account should not be treated as impartial. In seeking to establish the respectability of the sample survey he realized that it would look more effective to associate it with the poverty research tradition.

[44] 'It is remarkable that the information on women's mobility collected by Glass should have remained almost entirely unexploited for over thirty years, although accessible in coded form' (Goldthorpe 1987, 278).

[45] Gray and Corlett (1950, 169).

Through this means, household measures became articulated only through the responses of specific individuals. This was now a different procedure to that of earlier social investigators which sought to define household position by assessing all its component individuals. Statistically, it became possible to use weighting procedures to ensure that households with more individuals did not end up being under-represented in the sample as a whole. However, what was lost was the kind of analysis of household dynamics which was possible when more than one household member was interviewed, and which – as we have seen – Elizabeth Bott was to make famous in her social network analysis. The production of the 'individual respondent' – now an utterly routine and uncontentious feature of social research – involved the active marginalization of the household.

8.3 TECHNOLOGIES OF THE DEMORALIZED NATION

The crucial incubator of the sample survey was the Royal Statistical Society (RSS). This acted as the key intellectual hothouse in developing sampling theory and popularizing sampling methods during the key decade of the 1940s. It was able to do this because of its unique strengths and capacities to link both academics and practitioners around a shared commitment to statistical research methods. Its concerns ranged over demography and vital statistics; design and analysis of census and sampling; industrial experimentation (including quality control), econometrics; descriptive economics; medical statistics; and biological and agricultural research. Absent from its interests, we might note, is market research and studies of welfare.

The RSS was the largest learned body of its kind. With an illustrious history dating back to the Statistical Society of London in 1834, its membership rose dramatically after the Second World War, from 1,037 in 1934 to 1,978 by 1950. They felt strong and confident enough to attempt to professionalize on the medical model by petitioning parliament to allow them to regulate entry to any job with a statistical element through ensuring that only those who had passed RSS tests were suitably qualified. Ultimately defeated by the opposition of the Royal Economic Society, who also claimed statistical expertise, they nonetheless proved much more adept than the economists in developing wide-ranging links to practitioner concerns. Having begun the practice of organizing sections in 1928, by the 1940s they had formed 'industrial applications' sections in Birmingham, Sheffield, the North-East, London, and Teesside, which discussed issues such as quality control, market research, standardization, computing, control charts applied to sales data, methods of forecasting accidents, and 'control of coke testing by the shatter test'. Its membership included seventeen corporate entities, representing a remarkable range of interests, from trade organizations (British Road Federation), companies (Rowntree, Vauxhall, Standard Telephones, GEC), trade unions (the Amalgamated Engineering Union), professional groups (the Institute of Municipal Treasurers and Accountants, the University of

London Library, the Council for Monetary and Economic Research, Town and Country Planning), civic and political organizations (Royal Commission on Population, Luton Civic Society, the Fabian Society, Czech ministry), to newspapers (*The Economist*).

Recognizing the importance of the RSS – which is hardly mentioned in the histories by Abrams and Moser – alerts us to the way that sampling methods were not primarily derived from the tradition of social and welfare surveys, even allowing for Bowley's reputation. Rather, it was from the economic and military example that the key precedents were developed which came to preoccupy the RSS. One important source of thinking was from quality control where a sample of the finished artefacts could be used to make more general inferences about the quality of all products.[46] Agricultural research was especially important, and indeed the first continuous (repeated) survey was the National Farm Survey which began in 1941.[47] It was in the study of potato yields that Fisher first developed analyses of variance which could be used to detect when differences between units were significant rather than the result of sampling error. This estimation of the extent of sampling error allowed Clapham to devise the first practical methods for using stage sampling in agricultural research. Hubback's pioneering research on rice crop yields in India between 1923 and 1925 showed how it was possible to sample small fields at some distance from each other to avoid problems of collinearity.[48] This Indian work influenced comparable British research on agricultural productivity. Similar concerns were evident during data collected on wartime bombing. In order to assess the effectiveness of bombing campaigns, air crew were expected to take photographs of the areas which they had bombed, and the derivation of acceptable inferences from these photographs depended on the application of sampling theory.

These precedents allowed members of the RSS, in close association with the GSS, to develop methods of sampling which avoided the problematic quota sampling of the market researchers. This involved formulating principles of sample stratification, whereby a sample could be gathered from local units which were wide-ranging enough to allow the results to be aggregated up to provide a national frame of reference. Given that it was not feasible to sample in every single area of the nation, methods had to be devised to allow 'second stage' sampling units to be defined within each of these primary units to sample in only a small number of locations. This was achieved by firstly defining a series of 'first order' sampling units, in the form of regions or districts, with a proportional number of interviews given their population size, and then, the use of statistics on local areas to ensure that representative areas were chosen within these regions. One of the advantages enjoyed by psephologists from the 1960s was that parliamentary constituencies could easily be used as sampling units since these

---

[46] See the (brief) discussion in Weeks (1947, 96).

[47] See the discussion in Kempthorne (1946).

[48] Miller (1983, 20) traces early American sampling to the Department of Agricutlure Crop Reporting Service's forecasts of crop production using a sample of correspondents. On Fisher, see JRSS (1948, 342).

had roughly equivalent populations and their relative typicality could be assessed through examining their election results and demographic characteristics.[49] But the key point here is that the creation of effective national samples required considerable work and the samples themselves helped to create the concept of a flat, bounded, homogeneous national space which did not exist before the sample survey itself. The idea of the modern nation, which could be subject to rational planning, was itself dependent on the mobilization of sampling methodology.

The importance of this point is no better revealed than in the remarkable reception given by the RSS at its annual meeting of 1946 to a paper by the Indian statistician P. C. Mahalanobis who, according to the president of the RSS, had 'had the opportunity to apply statistical methods, the scientific technique of sampling, and the design of experiments on a scale so vast as to seem to someone like himself, inhabiting a small overcrowded island, almost astronomical'.[50] India served as the quintessential modern imagined nation, one which – unlike island Britain – appeared to have no natural geographical boundaries, and which was seen to be riven with cultural divisions. The idea of constructing the Indian nation through the deployment of survey measures was thus seen as being of great interest, especially in the context of decolonization and an emerging global geopolitics organized around nation states. Founded in 1931, the Indian Statistical Institute had rapidly become a large survey organization, which easily exceeded any comparable British equivalent. By 1945 it was employing the equivalent of 750 workers on survey-related work, with around half conducting surveys in the field, and the other half analysing the data on Hollerith machines. Mahalanobis's address focused almost entirely on how to gain adequate samples (both regional and national) in such a disparate and far-flung environment. It was indeed the Indian National Sample Survey, which Mahalanobis set up in 1950 'with the active support of Prime Minister Nehru', that was to prove the model for the British general-purpose surveys.[51]

This Indian example was telling in a further way. Moral, gentlemanly, social science depended on the trustworthy observer: there was no shortcutting the need for the educated social worker, clergyman, school inspector, or social researcher, who could by virtue of their position be trusted to record accurate information. When sample surveys began, this practice continued. Thus, in the Ministry of Labour's 1923 sample survey of the unemployed, 'it was deemed essential that all men claimants should be interviewed by the manager himself, and all women claimants by the senior woman officer'.[52] One of the innovations of the opinion polls was the idea that relatively unskilled interviewers could be used – but as I have shown, one result of this procedure was the suspicion directed towards them. The problem was that at several stages in the process, even the most well-meaning survey researcher could make mistakes – in understanding the respondent's replies, in writing down the responses correctly, and in entering

[49] Thus, parliamentary constituencies formed the sampling units for the influential Butler and Stokes Election Surveys from 1963 which I discuss later.

[50] Greenwood (1946, 325).   [51] Bulmer et al. (1986, 81).   [52] Jones(1949, 80).

the information into the Hollerith calculating machines. Compared to the moral observer, who by virtue of his or her authority could be expected to arrive at an authoritative judgement, lots could go wrong. The quality of the interviewer was a particular worry. Claus Moser put the point emphatically: 'however refined the sampling design, however well the investigation has been planned, ultimately the value of a survey depends on the accuracy of the information obtained by the average interviewer. At present, little is known about the best means of selecting and training interviewers'.[53] This was a further objection to the market researchers, who used quota surveys, which made it very difficult to assess interviewer bias.[54] The random sample, by contrast, constrained the interviewer to pick a given individual and hence could allow bias to be assessed more accurately.

The Indian example as discussed by Mahalanobis was a powerful one because it fed into the racist prejudices of the British statisticians that Indian investigators would be especially prone to be unreliable.[55] Major Elphinstone picked up the theme: 'Even those who care for good work are apt to be worn down by the continuous amount of energy required.... Heat engenders fixed opinions and unreasoned prejudices'.[56] Mahalanobis's commentators were thus fascinated by how the Indian Statistical Survey dealt with the problem of human error in the collection and analysis of the data. They heard that in their studies of crop yields, two different surveyors were sent to measure crops, so allowing the ISS to compare their relative reports, and statistically assess the extent of any discrepancy between them. As Mahalanobis went on to relate: 'in socio-economic studies special efforts have been made to study the personal equation or bias of the investigating staff'.[57] Analyses of the variance obtained between the different fieldwork interviewers allowed a systematic means of assessing their reliability. Mahalanobis also talked about the way that errors in the data processing and analysis stage could be spotted as punched cards were entered into Hollerith machines. This involved verifying the punch cards by running them again, but substituting a small number of false dummies within the sample, so that the extent to which a particular worker correctly identified the resulting errors could be used to assess whether they were doing their job effectively.

---

[53] See the discussion following Gray and Corlett (1950, 201). See further Moser's paper (1951, 28) where he notes that 'there are weak links in the methods, and if the confidence in surveys is to be maintained, more attention will have to be paid to strengthening them. One of the weakest links is the personal interview. Most of the inquiries...use field interviewers, yet very little is known about the errors, both systematic and otherwise, which may be introduced by them.'

[54] See Louis Moss in the discussion of Gray and Corlett (1950, 202), and Yates (ibid., 204), who urged the GSS to 'say something about the results they obtained on the experimental comparison between interviewers which they had promised to make'.

[55] We might also note that one of the RSS's leading methodologists of sampling, Yates, had spent many years as researcher in Africa. Yates's pioneering account of sampling issues in which he laid out principles of stratification, 'A review of recent statistical developments in sampling and sample surveys', was published in 1946 and he was a keen contributor to the debate following Mahalanobis's paper.

[56] Greenwood (1946, 374). His racism was not lost on D. M. Sen, who insisted that 'recording mistakes is not a regional phenomenon...they are common whenever large scale surveys are undertaken. It would be totally wrong to try to correlate recording mistakes with "intellectual competence"'.

[57] Greenwood (1946, 346).

We see in these debates the recognition that one of the great potentials of sample survey analysis was the possibility of controlling for interviewer-induced bias through the analysis of the responses themselves. Thus, rather than having to rely on trusted observers, it was possible to use adequately skilled interviewers and subsequently check whether these individuals were prone to generate disproportionate kinds of bias through an analysis of the results themselves. This was a momentous discovery. Whereas previous inspection of collaborative worker output involved putting in place surveillance and monitoring measures as supplements to the work process itself (for instance, using supervisors to report on the efficiency of different workers), the sample survey allowed such surveillance to be built into the very nature of the work product – the survey responses – itself. In this respect, the sample survey contained the technology for fundamentally new ways of organizing work, and was the incubator for the kinds of digital monitoring which is now utterly routine in environments such as call centres, supermarket checkouts, and so forth.

8.4 THE EMERGENCE OF THE SOCIAL SCIENTIFIC NATIONAL SURVEY, 1950–70

I have argued against the view that there is a straightforward 'political arithmetic tradition' from which the modern sample survey traces a lineage from older poverty inquiries and projects of social observation. I have also argued against Osborne and Rose's view that the wider history of the survey can be read from an angle based on the experience of opinion polls. Rather, it was the experience of war, and concerns with productivity, mobilization, production, and destruction which were the forging ground in which the sample survey method was pioneered, and it was especially here that key innovations in design of stratified samples were made. It was the wartime experience and its immediate aftermath, including that of decolonization and the concern with defining nations, which was central. During the post-war period, the capacity to conduct sample surveys itself became a key feature of the modern state. In the British case, the Family Expenditure Survey began in 1957, which became a central device for generating indicators such as the inflation rate, followed by the General Household Survey in 1971. Sampling methods were first incorporated into the census in 1961, and in 1966 a one in ten sample was used to conduct the census in its entirety. We might further note that the failure of the Scottish and (especially) Welsh to develop a national survey conducting capacity was a fundamental feature of their lack of statehood.[58] The Northern Irish were even more marginalized in this respect.

In understanding the appeal of surveys for the modern national project, a key issue was education, or more generally, the 'developmental individual'. Surveys

---

[58] Famously, a separate Scottish social mobility study was carried out in contrast to that conducted by Halsey on England and Wales in 1972 (see Payne 1987). On distinctively Scottish research, see Kent (1981, 177–8).

played a key role in the educational reform projects of the 1950s and (especially) 1960s. From the mid-1960s the number of surveys conducted jumps dramatically.[59] In 1969, thirty-one different sample surveys are archived by the Economic and Social Data Service, compared to just three listed for 1960.

Survey methods were used to trace individuals over time so that their changes could be analysed and appropriated into an understanding of the 'developmental individual'.[60] Many early surveys took a panel form, in which the same individuals were re-interviewed on a regular basis. These date back to the earliest forms of audience research in the 1930s, when the BBC commissioned panels to review their attitudes to radio programmes. Mass-Observation also deployed a panel design into their use of directives. These panel studies were then elaborated in the form of the 1946 cohort study and the 1958 National Child Development Study (NCDS). A panel design was used in the first General Election surveys from 1963 onwards. The NCDS was the clearest example of how this kind of panel design could be used to further the interests of the 'psy-sciences' in understanding individual development. Thus, in the 1964 wave of the NCDS (when the respondents were 5 years old), six kinds of assessment were used, including a reading test, social adjustment guide, copying design test, 'drawing a man test', and arithmetic test, and these were then followed up with intensive responses by teachers and parents.

The strength of these kinds of panel design at this period indicates the fundamental role of research methods in addressing issues of education, psychology, and personal development. The NCDS originally emerged out of the extensive testing apparatus linked to the 1944 Education Act, in which tests conducted on 11-year-olds were used to differentiate the successful (who went to grammar schools) from the failures (who went to secondary modern schools or occasionally to technical schools). This apparatus was the most important legacy of the eugenics movement of the early twentieth century, with its concern to distinguish the most intellectually able from the common herd, so that they could be nurtured and supported to lead the nation.[61] This requirement to develop appropriate 'testing' led to the formation of the National Foundation for Educational Research in 1946, the prime national body with a responsibility for developing and refining intelligence tests which were supposed to measure 'pure' ability, abstracted from social context. Building on the views of socialist eugenicists such as Karl Pearson, such tests were assumed to be a device for distinguishing the really intelligent from those from privileged backgrounds.

The cultural power of intelligence testing ran deep. Its most marked manifestation was in the formation of MENSA in 1946, a voluntary association which only allowed those who were in the top 2 per cent of those who took IQ tests to join. This is a good example of how the self-definition of a particular social group, the 'very intelligent', depended on the mobilization of a distinctive social science

---

[59] The following paragraphs are based on an examination of survey sources held at the ESDS archive.

[60] See Rose (1999*a*) for the wider context.   [61] MacKenzie (1981, especially p. 43).

technology, and it is not coincidental that the ethos of MENSA was concerned to differentiate the idea of 'pure' intelligence from that of social background (hence refusing to conflate intelligence with the display of highbrow culture, for instance). Its founders thus 'had the idea of forming a society for bright people, the only qualification for membership of which was a high IQ. The original aims were, as they are today, to create a society that is non-political and free from all racial or religious distinctions'.[62] This mobilization of intelligence tests allowed children to be separated according to cognitive measures, and seemed to allow no scope for social factors to be made visible in the process of educational sifting. And it was this which proved to be the catalyst to those educational reformers who were convinced that it was working-class children who disproportionately lost out in the selective system.

We can see here how the survey's interest in the 'developmental individual' brought with it a new interest in change. The intelligence test can be seen as a residue of a gentlemanly formation in which one's destiny was stamped on you at birth. The survey, by contrast, allowed change over time to be measured through the analysis of responses obtained at different points in time. It thus offered the machinery for observing change. And, simultaneously, it produced measures of the structure within which change could be seen to take place. Thus, in order to be able to assess whether there were social disadvantages in access to different secondary schools, it was necessary to mobilize appropriate information on the social background of pupils. Such information did not readily exist in the 1950s. It has become such a familiar, even banal, point that the middle classes tend to be disproportionately successful in selective education that it is easy to forget that it was only on the basis of sample survey evidence (recording information on the occupations of the parents and respondents) that such conclusions could be drawn, and that this was entirely obscure to contemporaries of the 1940s and 1950s who believed the technocratic view that pure intelligence, as measured by IQ tests, could be separated from social position and hence that no social injustice was being done. This explains why survey analysis was championed almost from the outset of the intelligence-testing regime, as necessary for demonstrating its meritocratic credentials. They were thus used in the *Report to the Royal Commission on Population* (1946) and by the leading statistician Cyril Burt in 1946.[63] Floud, Martin, and Halsey's local surveys of education and social mobility proved vitally important in showing how a sociological perspective could break from a psychologistic one through demonstrating the importance of social background in influencing educational attainment.[64]

This explains why, during the 1950s, the politics of the 'developmental individual' proved the key terrain on which sample surveys were generated, with their effective critique of the cognitive psychologism of the intelligence test. Regular reading surveys held in 1948, 1952, 1956, 1961, and 1964 took place in a small number of local authority areas. The aim of these was to gain

---

[62] Details from MENSA web site.   [63] See the discussion in Moser (1958, 33f).
[64] Floud et al. (1956).

aggregate national data on the overall reading skills of 11- and 15-year-olds, results from which were then used to assess whether overall standards were rising. These surveys hence allowed the deployment of national indicators which could be utilized as 'measures of the nation', and more particularly, whether the nation's educational standards were improving. It is worth underlining how utterly novel this ability was to divine national indicators in this way, and to emphasize their reliance on sample survey evidence.

By the 1960s this deployment of survey evidence became the centrepiece of government educational reform, in the commissions established to consider higher education (the Robbins Report, which was published in 1962), secondary education (the Crowther Report, published in 1965), and on primary education (the Plowden Report, 1967).[65] Halsey's account of his role in the Plowden Report is telling.

> being an enthusiast for the potential capacity of social science to raise the level of political debate and, in the mood of the 1960s, ambivalent if not hostile to the role of the establishment as a benign brake on the engine of progress towards democratic socialism in Britain.[66]

It is not incidental that the first volume of Plowden's policy recommendations was outflanked in size by the giant second volume, with its fourteen research reports. The survey component included a questionnaire sent out to teachers, a 1964 national survey of 3,092 parents (with a remarkable 95 per cent response rate) along with a local survey-based study of Manchester to explore the relationship between neighbourhood characteristics and school performance. These survey sources dwarfed the more conventional use of administrative data, such as that derived from medical officers of health on school children. The national survey deliberately sought out mothers as respondents, but the class position of households was established by using the occupation of men. The survey itself thus assumed the conventional household as its form. It is worth also remembering that Plowden suggested that national surveys of education should be undertaken every ten years, so instituting research itself as a fundamental part of educational provision.

It was not just in the area of primary schooling that surveys proved vital. Higher education was an important field of study in part because of the energizing efforts of A. H. Halsey. The Robbins Report of 1963, which encouraged the building of new universities to allow the increasing numbers of young people born during the post-war baby boom, also contained a huge statistical appendix, including a sample survey conducted under the aegis of Claus Moser, which involved a '1 in 5' sample of all university academics in 1962 (with 3,098 responses). *Universities Quarterly* breathlessly reported that 'Appendix Three was sold out in Blackwells on the first morning.... What have the Hollerith cards foretold? The appendix runs to more than 250 pages and contains more than 250 statistical tables.... An unprecedented assemblage of fact'.[67] Halsey's subsequent

[65] See Acland (1980).   [66] A. H. Halsey (1987, 3).
[67] Watt (1963–4, 129).

role is fundamental. Whereas previous survey evidence had mainly been left confined to governmental concerns, he took the step of conducting supplementary research on the basis of the Robbins sample and using it to push forward academic concerns about the changing nature of higher education, at considerable remove from the immediate policy context.[68] In this respect, his work was vitally important in demonstrating that academics too could use surveys.

Education was a key domain in showing how surveys allowed the simultaneous definition of 'developmental individuals' (the sampled cases) and social groups (the measures between which development and mobility could be defined). Other areas where this kind of dual formation was in evidence was in mobility (as with the Labour mobility survey (1953–63) which had a national sample of 10,000), and in income and savings. There continued to be an interest in using surveys to delineate 'hard to reach' groups, for instance in examining the incomes of selective occupational groups, especially as a means of assessing whether significant additional income (or income from self-employment) was being earned (i.e. over and above that which employers were aware of and which could hence be analysed using employer-based documentary sources). Surveys of this kind were conducted on doctors (as part of the Pilkington Commission, 1957–60) and on university teachers (as part of a University Grants Commission (UGC) and in a Department of Education inquiry in 1964. Perhaps the most important of these was the use of survey methods to define and demarcate racial and ethnic minorities. W. W. Daniel's PEP survey of racial discrimination allowed clear evidence demonstrating the disadvantages of ethnic minorities, which proved important in providing the evidence base for the 1968 Race Relations Act which extended and tightened the provision of the 1965 Act.[69]

There were, however, few survey-based studies of work and employment.[70] Where this was studied, it tended to be linked to political concerns, as with the survey used by Fulton in its inquiry into the civil service, or was associated with education and training. There were also surprisingly few survey-based studies into health, with the exception of the important 'Patients and their Doctors' study of 1964. Although the GSS had conducted surveys on sickness during the 1940s, this was discontinued in the 1950s, and in 1957 Moser had to observe wryly that 'we know far more about mortality (from death certificate information) than about morbidity'.[71] During the 1960s the Institute for Social Studies in Medical Care was formed, an offshoot from the Institute of Community Studies, which came to conduct some medical research and to have close relationships with the Department of Health. However, this remained relatively marginal to the work of practising doctors as most of this research focused on the 'soft' patient–doctor interface rather than in medical interventions themselves.

---

[68] See Halsey and Trow (1971), which is discussed in Chapter 4.

[69] Michael Banton (private communication).

[70] With the exceptions of local studies such as Goldthorpe and Lockwood's of Luton and Brown's of Tyneside shipbuilders.

[71] Moser (1958, 34).

In the area of consumption, we can see a notable shift from the 1940s. Alongside the National Food Surveys, there was a large-scale privatization of consumption surveys, notably into market research companies, but also into the activities of the Consumers' Association which in 1969 began the survey-based inquiries into products which continue to this day in the publication *Which?* The *Reader's Digest* was also involved in consumer research. Public surveys show no interest now in consumption which is deemed to be a matter of private concern.

What we see in these surveys from the 1960s is the juxtaposition of three different survey rationales: accounts of the nation, nearly always led by government; accounts of the developmental individual, focused on education, training, and development; and concerns to delineate specific social groups, where surveys delineated the characteristics of particular sub-populations (e.g. the handicapped and impaired, students, young people, and so forth). Moral concerns were now much less visible, with people's attitudes being defined as their private tastes, as manifest on consumption surveys. Very few of these surveys see a strong academic social science presence, leaving aside the special case of education. The survey then, at this point, is predominantly a tool of government, not academic research. This reflects the fact that surveys continued to be labour-intensive and only in the later 1960s with the development of mainframe computers could survey data be transported to remote locations.

We do, however, see a route by which academic social scientists did assert their distinctive authority, which was to become marked during the late 1960s and early 1970s.[72] This was in the arena of politics, based in psephology, but taking a wider-ranging set of interests around the social structure, social mobility, and class relations. Birch's study of Glossop, as well as the studies of Greenwich and Hertford undertaken by Glass's team, all used systematic local samples during the 1950s. In the 1960s, national sample surveys were conducted on these themes, all of them strongly influenced by American models. Berkeley-educated W. G. Runciman's survey of 1962, written up in *Relative Deprivation and Social Justice* (1966), was funded by American sources. This was the first ever to be led by a British academic social scientist and funded by non-government sources. This strong American framing was also evident in other surveys focusing on political mobilization, notably the British election studies from 1963, and Almond and Verba's comparative study of political attitudes conducted in 1959/60 and published as *Civic Culture* in 1963. This incorporation of American methods was taken a step further in Butler and Stokes's *Political Change in Britain*. This study drew upon the panel election studies which had begun in 1963 to offer the first survey-based account of political alignments. In a manner which has close parallels to Halsey's deployment of survey research within educational research, they used the concept of class – as derived from survey measures – as fundamental to their demonstration of the value of survey analysis itself. Much of their focus is on showing how survey measures can provide definite proof of the assumption

---

[72] See the discussion in Miller (1983), especially chapter 8.

that class is central to political identification. Through this process, measures of class which can only be generated through survey processes become means of establishing the respectability of the survey itself.

This motif, in which survey measures were used to make visible subterranean features of the social landscape was seen in Peter Townsend's path-breaking work which demonstrated the power of sample surveys to a wide academic and policy audience. His innovation was the idea of re-analysis of survey data, with his reworking of the Family Expenditure Survey. This re-energized debates about poverty in *The Poor and the Poorest*, published in 1965.[73] He followed this with dedicated survey analysis of his own. Conducted between 1966 and 1969, and published in 1972. This was the same period that Goldthorpe and Halsey collaborated on the Nuffield Mobility Study, which was to prove a benchmark in the study of mobility and social class. This was to prove a vital model in showing how the national sample survey could be used to mobilize an account of the national class structure, and in particular how the cross-sectional survey could be used to develop a conception of change. Halsey's plan was to study whether social mobility had changed compared to Glass's survey carried out in 1949. Goldthorpe was also interested in assessing how social mobility compared to that which Blau and Duncan had examined in the United States, in their famous study *The American Occupational Structure*. Like earlier generations of social researchers, they were thus committed to the idea of the replication study as a means of assessing change, in which the results from two separate studies could be compared. Yet it became clear in the design stages that replication would not be possible. The Hall-Jones occupational categories used by Glass to measure class were too imprecise to allow occupations from the Nuffield survey to be consistently coded to them. Halsey and Goldthorpe, therefore, had to find an alternative means of inferring change, which they did through the comparison of cohorts within the Nuffield survey alone, where they followed the demographic model developed by Glass.[74] Yet, in order to have enough cases to allow the comparison of cohorts, they controversially decided to sample only men, a decision which was to have repercussions during the 1970s when a powerful feminist critique emphasized the limitations of this strategy.[75] Once again, we can see how the deployment of survey methods involved the removal of women from view. Regardless, the result was vitally important in allowing a new conception of change to be embedded in the survey, whereby it was not necessary to compare separate studies, but in which change could be inferred through the internal analysis of one data source. To be sure, this process of inference was always problematic, since it was not

---

[73] Abel-Smith and Townsend (1965).

[74] See Halsey's review of Glass's work (1954, 171), which revealingly records its demographic origins: 'by dividing the sample into cohorts of birth, it was possible to trace changes over time in the relation between fathers and sons, the social origins of brides and grooms, and the experience of successive waves of children through the expanding educational system'.

[75] This debate rumbled on into the 1980s, with Goldthorpe (1983) mounting a doomed, though highly vocal, counter-insurgency strategy in his paper. See Marshall et al. (1988) for an overview of the debate.

possible to isolate age from cohort effects, but what mattered here was the way that the survey could become an engine for defining change.

It is important to emphasize, in view of the canonical status that the Nuffield Mobility Study went on to command, that it was almost never funded. The Sociology Committee of the Social Science Research Council turned it down. The London School of Economics (LSE) sociologists did not approve of the loss of their status which was entailed in the project being led from Oxford. Margaret Stacey argued that support should instead be put into local community studies. In the end, the support of the statisticians allowed funding to go ahead. But it was a close-run thing.

In the early 1970s the Government Statistical Service remained by far the most important vehicle for social research in the United Kingdom, with 350 professional statisticians and 5,500 auxilliary staff, with a total complement of 1,853 at administrative grade or higher: a remarkable concentration of research capacity which no university social science department could hope to compete with.[76] At the same time, links had now been forged with academic social science departments who were committed to survey analysis: at Essex (through Townsend), and also at Nuffield College Oxford, founded in 1937, which by the late 1960s had a distinctive cluster of survey-based researchers, notably the political scientist David Butler, A. H. Halsey, and the statistician David Cox. This marked a striking new current, in which academic social scientists muscled in on sample survey research, which had by this time existed for well over thirty years, claiming it for their own concerns, in the name of a 'political arithmetic tradition' devoted to delineating the changing national social structure.

The remarkable take up of survey analysis is nowhere more apparent than in the work of Goldthorpe and Lockwood. Having emphasized the limits of questionnaire research in elaborating the need for their Affluent Worker study in the early 1960s, they ended up championing the survey method by the end of the decade, with Goldthorpe embarking on the survey-based studies of social mobility for which he was to become internationally famous.[77] Whereas in the early 1960s, the Institute of Community Studies had been trailblazers in their use of local, large-scale qualitative studies, just ten years later, their work was seen as idiosyncratic, unrepresentative, and unscientific.[78] In a few short years, the sample survey had emerged as a powerful, even though contested, form of social science research. It did this through a new mobilization of the conception of the social structure allied to concerns over change which fused governmental interests with the burgeoning social sciences. Rather than taking up the difficult task of comparing separate studies which was already appearing problematic, Goldthorpe and Lockwood developed the technology for detecting change within their own modus operandi. Using a panel design, repeated interviews could be conducted on the same individuals and/or family members. It thus became

---

[76] See Moser (1973).   [77] Goldthorpe (1987).
[78] See notably, Jennifer Platt's withering attack (1971).

possible to produce accounts of the 'changing' individual directly through comparisons of observations on the same person. Even for those surveys which were cross-sectional, conducted at one moment in time, it was possible to explore change by separating out cohorts within the sample. This method was first used by David Glass in 1948, and was central to his endeavour to examine whether there were any trends in the patterning of social mobility over time. More fundamentally still, by collecting data on family of origin within sample surveys, it became possible, for the first time, to assess how far people had been 'socially mobile'. It is for this reason that the deployment of the sample survey was an essential feature of those arguing for comprehensive, rather than selective education, as it allowed them to marshal evidence showing that those from working-class backgrounds were relatively disadvantaged compared to those from the middle classes. Finally, the creation of annual repeat surveys, notably the Family Expenditure Survey (from 1957), the General Household Survey (from 1962), and the New Earnings Survey (from 1971), with their deliberate concern to use standardized measures between surveys allowed 'accurate' assessments of change over time to be made. This ability to track changes allowed sample surveys to be mobilized in order to measure changing inflation rates, crime rates, poverty rates and the like, becoming fundamental to the proliferation of 'change'.

By the early 1970s, the survey mobilized social democratic concerns with poverty and inequality, a focus on change and modernity, the expertise of a new breed of social scientists, and the resources of the Office of Population Censuses and Surveys (OPCS) in a powerful constellation. This axis institutionalized in leading social science centres, notably at the LSE, Essex University, and Nuffield College Oxford. It demonstrated the capacity of a new social science infrastructure which could mobilize interview methods to develop accounts of the modern nation which were both sociological and administrative.

8.5 CONCLUSIONS

In this chapter, I have shown how the sample survey makes possible the delineation of a flat, homogeneous, bounded nation, composed of changing individuals and social groups. Rather than social relations being inherently located in households and localities, subject to visual observation by the educated and trustworthy observer, the sample survey brings with it new possibilities for imagining the nation. It provides mechanisms for bypassing the gentlemanly observer through allowing statistical methods for assessing (and hence correcting) for interviewer bias. It allows change to be detected not by the careful inspection of different historical sources, but through the scrutiny of the survey source alone, both in the form of the panel study and through the cross-sectional survey.

Yet, no sooner had the survey become such a central device, that its importance began to be called into question. The return of a Labour government in 1974 publicly committed to addressing issues of equity, led to a permanent Royal

Commission on the Distribution of Wealth and Income, in which survey sources were used to regularly monitor changing inequalities. As Bulmer records, social scientists made themselves indispensable to its deliberations. Yet, a postscript to his account strikes an altogether more sombre tone. 'This chapter was completed in March 1979. In May 1979 a new Conservative government was elected'. James Prior, Secretary of State for Employment, decided that because the government's regular statistics were now providing better data, there was no need for the Commission. There were two other examples of major survey-based inquiries which reported after the election of a Conservative government, which now sought to downplay their findings: the Black Report on health inequalities, and Townsend's new poverty inquiry.

The key issue here was time. Although the survey allowed change and time to be addressed in new ways, it was itself a Fordist device, which took time to plan, administer, and analyse. But the time it took to conduct surveys made it difficult to fit with government decision-making. During the 1960s, Royal Commissions were prepared to wait for their findings, since they were deemed potentially momentous. As survey research matured, and as their findings became more mundane, it seemed less compelling to wait so long. The heroic moment of the 1960s passed. Academic social scientists could increasingly analyse data according to their own, more elongated, time scale, whilst government became more catholic and eclectic in its choice of research methods.

Part III

Popular Identities and Social Change

9

1948 to 1962: The Remaking of Social Class Identities

Class relations during the nineteenth and early twentieth century were premised on dual relationships of service and skill. Within households, domestic service involved the routine appropriation of physical, emotional, and sexual labour, usually from women.[1] These tensions overlapped with those in industry, where technique and skill were recognized to be under the jurisdiction of autonomous, usually male, work groups. Even though craft controls were largely eliminated during the nineteenth century, labour-intensive production was transferred to new industrial sectors.[2] Complex forms of cultural hierarchy were organized out of these relationships. The largely invisible, private, servicing activities of women were the necessary underbelly on which an active public realm of genteel culture could rest. Self-consciously intellectual cultures also reacted against the constraints which were deemed to define, and ultimately to pollute, manual life. Gentlemanly, highbrow cultural pursuits thus became the preserve of the middle and upper classes, supported by a hidden world of service.[3] Although the interests of labour were widely recognized and seen as legitimate, they were deemed to have limited powers. As Ross McKibbin and Jon Lawrence have shown,[4] political alignments during the first part of the twentieth century depended on celebrating a national public interest seen as greater than – and in opposition to – a more narrowly sectional labour interest. Through this mechanism, the world of manual labour was allowed a certain visibility and legitimacy, whilst at the same time it was also circumscribed and isolated.

I have shown in Chapters 2 and 3 how this cultural settlement was disrupted by the emergence of technical identities and capacities associated with new scientific occupations and the deployment of technical skills. Technical identities challenged the cultural division between manual skills on the one hand and intellectual highbrow culture on the other, by borrowing from idioms of both skilled handicraft and professional expertise. What I trace in this chapter is how

---

[1] See Todd (2008) and Steedman (2005).

[2] Important accounts of these work cultures are given in More (1980) and McIvor (2001). See the overview in Savage and Miles (1994).

[3] See Light (2008) for a pertinent case study.   [4] McKibbin (1998) and Lawrence (1998).

this cultural realignment had consequences both for working-class and middle-class identities which persist to this day. The appropriation of technique to an academic and managerial identity had the indirect effect of severing its association with working-class culture, which could only be identified in deficit terms. By contrast, middle-class identities could be reinforced and enhanced through their embrace of these currents, and their explicitly classed dimensions concealed and universalized.

I begin by examining the arguments made about working-class identities in the 1960s in two influential studies by Richard Brown on Tyneside shipbuilders and John Goldthorpe and David Lockwood on affluent workers in Luton. These studies focused on very different occupational groups, located in different parts of England, and were taken to exemplify the traditional proletarian culture on the one hand, and new privatized, instrumental, affluent workers on the other. Actually, I argue, the field notes suggest that the differences were muted, but this was obscured through the concern of the sociologists to focus on conceptual differences between power and money models of social identities. These studies also reveal how these workers' class identities differentiated themselves from the visible public elites of the past, rather than from the emerging cadre of technical and industrial managers. For this reason, their sense of class was premised on old, rather than emerging, social relations and was to prove unable to recharge itself effectively in the decades to come.

By contrast, I show how middle-class identities were – at least on the face of it – able to move away from the snobbish, gentlemanly motif which was evident in the 1930s towards a more inclusive and apparently democratic model through appealing to technique, skill, and expertise as if these were socially neutral resources. Through this means the cultural meanings of class were remade in ways which allowed the middle classes to represent themselves as 'natural' rather than as a sectional class group. We are still living with this model today.

9.1 MEANINGS OF MANUAL LABOUR

In the later 1960s, a young industrial sociologist from Durham, Richard Brown, former colleague of John Goldthorpe at Leicester, commenced a sophisticated study of shipbuilders at Wallsend, in the north-east of England. His study explored the working practices and values of the workers sympathetically, using the latest sociological methods. A systematic one in ten sample of the varied skilled trades was conducted and a structured questionnaire applied to 266 workers. Detailed ethnographic observation was also conducted, with a particular interest in the repartee and interaction amongst the work groups.

The shipbuilders defined themselves as a group apart. 'I don't think you Cockneys understand us. You think we're Pakistanis, or talking Yiddish, or something.' They evoked a world apart, in which the manual skill, strength, and dexterity of the male tradesman was central to their sense of self and their beliefs about how social interaction should take place.

> Its dog eat dog on piece. If you're in the toilet it costs money. These habits stay even though we're off piece now. Some trades have their habits like reading the paper in the toilet. We read ours before or after work. . . . A man needs an incentive; no more until the work is done . . . the outside blacksmith must be a statesman. He relies on others. If the welder won't do it, you have to shove him on. You don't want to upset him so you carry his stuff. The burners you beg, plead with them. Have a crack with them to make them laugh to get the work done. Keep in with them.[5]

This is effectively the world of the preindustrial artisan, translated into the ship-yards of modern Britain.[6] Workers retained control of their skills and methods, and were responsible for managing their own working relationships. Strong bonding to one's work group entailed the existence of powerful cultural boundaries with neighbouring work groups. The men were aware of the way that this was a localized world, incorporating this into a sense of their own inferiority. The evocation of these feelings using terms from preindustrial social relations – statesmen, peasants, and serfs – is revealing.

> You have to split the country into two groups. The southern half is better than the northern half. We are but no more than peasants in this part of the country and I think we are complacent about it. We are called the hardy people of the north and what they really mean is the hardy idiots of the north. We are more at the serfdom level.[7]

The workers in Luton who were studied by Goldthorpe and Lockwood a few years earlier were located in this southern half. Most of them had migrated to the town, many from Wales and the North-East. Few of them presented a localized account of their identities along the lines of these Wallsend shipbuilders, or of Jackson's Huddersfield working class.[8] The role of migration in shaping the values of the modern assembly-line workers was not studied by Goldthorpe and his colleagues, who instead sought out the differences between 'old' and 'new' workers, comparing the cultural values associated with modern industrial workers living on suburban housing estates with traditional proletarians from mining and shipbuilding communities.[9] They emphasized the strength of instrumental, rather than soli-daristic, values, which they saw as due to their money-based vision of the social order. Rather than talking directly about class in terms of power or prestige, it was money which seemed to be at the forefront of the Luton workers' perceptions. Such emphases are indeed readily apparent in the interview transcripts.

---

[5] SN 5514, Box 1.

[6] More generally on the craft cultures of shipyard production into the twentieth century, see Roberts (1993), who also provides an interesting case study of the North-East shipyard culture.

[7] SN 5514, BU02. [8] See Chapter 1.

[9] The debate was initiated by David Lockwood in his famous paper 'Sources of variation in working class images of society'. An important collection of case studies is that collected by Martin Bulmer; see the more recent discussion in Devine et al. (2004).

People with money can do what they like – money talks. Many people have got money – not through honest work either.

Main difference is money: if you've got money, live in a nice house, in a nice area, and a car and all the rest of it.

Money is nearly 90% of everything.[10]

Yet these references to money were not necessarily so different from the accounts of the Tyneside shipbuilders. They evoked an awareness of the separation of social classes and the fundamental differences between them which identified money with power.

[M]oney is the only difference between them (classes). If you're working class it is because you have only a certain amount of money. Those who have more must be in a different class. You can't keep up.... Take Oxford and Cambridge, it takes money to get in there. You can only get this if your parents can let you go (The rich class are) society and Mayfair Johnnies, people who've inherited money. Take my old guv'nor, he paid the headmaster of the school to coach him and pushed him into Christ's Hospital. Only money done that. It goes right through like that ... its not ability, that's how it works.

(The upper class is) rich tycoons. I suppose that's how we base our classes, on wealth and if we put a good accent on our speech ... from the top they give a lead of corruption.... I suppose they want to hang on for grim death to what they have inherited.... We are crying out for new towns and the upper should be forced to give up some of their grouse shoots and parks for them.[11]

This was very similar to the Wallsend shipbuilders, when asked about 'the main thing which makes one class different from another', no less than 60 per cent identified money as the main difference, well ahead of the 20 per cent who talked about education-related factors. Money was the marker of power: 'Finance: cash (is the) only difference: Onassis and Princess Alexandra had money and breeding'.[12] Or in the words of another worker, '"money means class"', says Sir John Hunter'. This focus on money was important since it allowed workers to refuse any moralization of their lower position. They were not culturally inferior or morally disreputable – they just happened to have less money.

It is striking that although Runciman emphasized the restricted reference groups of the working class in his survey analysis during the 1960s, both the Luton and Wallsend samples were almost unanimous in identifying a rich, upper class elite as central to their understanding of class.[13] Only 5 per cent of Luton respondents and 20 per cent of Wallsend respondents did not refer to an upper class of some description,[14] and there was far more certainty about its existence than there was about that of the working or middle classes, the existence of which significant

---

[10] Quotes from SN 4871 Luton Interviews 39, 75, 3.   [11] SN 4871 Luton, Interviews 190, 137.
[12] SN 5514, Ss14.   [13] Runciman (1966).
[14] The Luton workers were probed more intensively in these questions compared to the Wallsend workers who were responding to more structured questions.

minorities denied. Indeed, 55 per cent of the Luton workers, and 40 per cent of Wallsend workers talked about the 'upper class' before mentioning any other class.

This upper class was seen predominantly as an aristocratic, landed, class ('lords, ladies, the gentry, sirs...Generals and all that crowd'[15]). Sometimes, industrialists were also placed in this upper class. In Wallsend Lord Armstrong and Sir John Hunter were mentioned. But it could also take in celebrity: 'snobby, lords, the Beatles, anyone with money or breeding'.[16] Talking about the upper class in this way was a means of differentiating a small visible elite from the 'average' person. Thus, in Luton, the very rich could be seen as 'big combines. Macmillan and the property men like Chow. People that manipulate the financial state of the country', and the working class by contrast 'get a wage every week'.[17] The upper class is public, visible, whereas most people are relatively private; it is a class which does not have to work, whereas most people do; it is a class where money is abundant, whereas most people have to watch carefully; it is a class whose position is based on inheritance, whereas most people have to 'make their own way'. This very strong and clear identification of an upper class which combines having lots of money, with high status, public visibility, power, and social connections qualifies Goldthorpe et al.'s claim for the Luton workers that 'few saw society as being divided into two confronting classes on the basis of the possession or non-possession of power and authority'.[18] Although most respondents did not differentiate middle from working class, or white collar from blue collar, on the basis of workplace relationships, their views could be seen as eminently compatible with one rendering of a Marxist differentiation between a small bourgeois class and a large working class, if the former is taken to include landowners. This sense was sometimes linked to clear statements about the inequity of these arrangements, as in this case from Luton.

> [S]ome people thieve it; some of those rich people, why are they rich? Because they hold thousands of acres of land that don't belong to them, thieved years ago and handed down'. The duke of Bedfordshire, what right does he have to half of Bedfordshire? Hundreds of years ago they fought – 'let's have a fight here'...if people couldn't pay taxes, that land was taken from the people, that's how these big estates come about.[19]

The interesting point here is that this frame of reference makes the managerial and technical middle classes largely invisible and outside the purview of the Luton workers. This was partly because many workers did not have a strong occupationally based view of class, in which particular occupations were definitively associated with certain classes. It was the visible, public world of the

---

[15] SN 4871, Luton Interview 81.   [16] SN 5514, P08.   [17] SN 4871, Luton Interview 178.
[18] Goldthorpe and Lockwood (1969, 146). It does, by contrast, support the arguments of Brown and Cousins in their own interpretation of their data, as well as Platt's observations about the way that money and power could be linked together in the Luton study.
[19] SN 4871, Luton Interview 34.

aristocratic or plutocratic upper class which they identified against. A good example of the difficulties of defining class in terms of occupations in the minds of these manual workers was from a Luton worker who was asked

What sorts of people do you think are in the upper class?

I suppose directors – people who've had a good education, and get a good job which they know nothing about.…

Lower class?

Well, we'll say a manager – well union officials, they've got a good job [I think a somewhat surprised look must have crossed my face at this point]

When pressed about the main factor which determined someone's class position, the respondent was puzzled and finally replied

It's the way he acts socially – not so much the money – you can find a rich man.… [he stopped abruptly, apparently fatigued by his Herculean efforts] [20]

We see here the respondent's difficulty in deciding which occupations fit into certain classes, leading in this case the interviewer to lose patience with him. [21] Examination of the Luton interview schedules also shows that it was not uncommon to identify highly visible, gentlemanly, professionals, such as lawyers or doctors, as middle class. By contrast, white-collar and newer technical workers were less visible. An exchange on this point reveals both how tenuous the worker's occupationally based view of class was, and how the technical and industrial managerial class did not figure extensively in it.

Well, there are different classes

What are they?

Well, you've got people who're financially in a safe and secure position – business and professional people. I mean they do tend to form classes of their own, don't they.

Are there other classes?

You've got people with the money and people without – they form their own classes.

What do you call these people?

The upper class and the lower class – I think the middle class is nearly extinct (wife – I think we're all middle class unless we're very rich or very poor). Umm (wife – well, what do you call us then?) Working class – what do you say? (wife – well, we're all middle class now)

---

[20] SN 4871, Luton Interview 80.

[21] John Goldthorpe has indicated in personal communication how he felt the questions on class failed because they did not tap beliefs which were pertinent to people's daily lives. He found, from experience, that asking them which occupations belonged to which classes seemed contrived. It is not incidental that he later abandoned a concern to root cultural values in class position, and instead preferred a structural approach to class in which the expert sociologist decided the nature of the class structure.

What about this middle class?

(Wife – I think there's a poor, rich and middle class....) but take the so called working class people earning good money in factories, they're really working class people, even though they may call themselves middle class.[22]

It was common to regard managing directors as part of an upper, or at least middle, class, and similarly to recognize managers as a distinctive occupational group. However, in Luton these were rarely seen directly in class terms, in part because class was often associated with personal characteristics such as being ordinary, natural, and authentic. Therefore managers were not necessarily middle class if they behaved like normal people, and since many were promoted from the shop floor, this was quite possible.

Here there is a contrast with the Wallsend shipbuilding workers, who were significantly more likely to identify managers as part of the upper, or alternatively middle, class. They shared with their Luton colleagues a sense that the aristocracy was an important constituent of the upper class. Thirty-three out of 115 identified the upper class in terms of being aristocratic, titled, landed, or by reference to some kind of ascriptive characteristics (such as having been to private school). By contrast, forty-six identified the upper class as being industrialists, directors, managers, or tycoons. In some cases, class divisions were clearly anchored in the yard hierarchy: one shipbuilder saw three classes, with the working class being all those who work for Swan Hunter, the middle classes being other factory workers, and the upper class being all the Swan Hunter directors.[23] Yet this tendency to identify senior management with upper rather than middle class also indicates how the class referents of the Wallsend workers tended not to focus on the white-collar class.

What mattered in both cases was in differentiating between ordinary, natural workers, and a public, visible elite class normally based on status markers which defined them as extraordinary. Ordinariness was a means of refusing both a stigmatized, pathologized identity ('we are ordinary: we think we are ordinary. We are. We are not the lowest'[24]) at the same time as it refuses a privileged position:

[T]he likes of myself and friends I've got and the majority of people on this estate. People who've had to work for a living all their lives and never had it handed to them like a silver platter.[25]

We can see some characteristic versions of this kind of thinking in Wallsend where E27 characteristically distinguishes high class 'lords and ladies, people with money' from middle-class 'business men' and the working-class 'average person'. For F 14, the distinctions ran between the upper-class 'aristocracy', the middle 'educated working class', and the working class (proper) who were 'ordinary people without much ambition'. The working class was not associated with particular kinds of employment relations or places of residence, but was seen as normal, authentic people. By differentiating it from a public, upper-class elite,

---

[22] SN 4871, Interview 56.   [23] SN 5514, Interview 167.   [24] SN 4871, 137.
[25] SN 4871, Luton Interview 31.

respondents could see themselves as ordinary people, largely devoid of social distinction.

Goldthorpe et al. were correct in pointing to the general lack of obvious status awareness amongst the Luton workers. On the whole, respondents made little of distinctions between white-collar and manual worker, or between skilled and unskilled workers. Here there was a significant contrast with Wallsend where these differences were more in evidence. Yet in both places, it was rare for workers to look down on any group beneath them. Some respondents were happy to identify themselves as both working class and middle class. Claims to either working-or middle-class position allowed respondents to identify themselves as 'normal individuals'. Even amongst those respondents who identified a distinction between the middle and the working class, what still mattered was their concern to be 'ordinary individuals', people able to live their own lives without any given privilege but making the choice to live life their own way.

> it all depends on the individual, whether they make a go of it – some do, some don't.
>
> we prefer to be individuals...we don't like the middle class who jump up – and we can't mix with the upper class and there's a certain amount of people like us
>
> Taking them as individuals there is not much difference between any human beings.... (*Why are there different classes*) – 'you've got me on this one. There shouldn't be, we are all human beings. We are supposed to be the same, but are we? Personally I think I'm as good as the man with thousands in his pocket (but), it's only nature, isn't it.
>
> I don't think about class really, there's no one above me, when I go anywhere I am as good as they are...everyone's the same in my book.[26]

Similar themes can be found at Swan Hunter. One worker distinguished 'ordinary working men, that are underpaid', from the 'snobbery class' who 'make money and think they're better than anyone else', and the 'gentry' 'born to money, never had any worries, but not snobs'.

This is not a sociological approach to class, concerned to differentiate people into groups according to occupational criteria. Rather, we can see these views as articulating a strong naturalistic and individualistic ethic.[27] Ultimately, people are individuals, and leaving aside the special case of the upper class, everyone is in the same boat. 'Natural' divisions of sex and ethnicity are seen as primordial, bestowing modes of deportment that are given and unchangeable by society. This is a basic, elemental individualism, with little conception of the individual as a social product, but rather an insistent declaration on the individual as 'natural' sovereign of their own lives. Within this conception, the class structure exists in a shadowy way, not as a social system differentiating occupational groups, but as the stage on which the individual necessarily acts. As Goldthorpe et al. themselves noted, the class structure 'was represented as a basic *datum* of social existence...

---

[26] SN 4871, Luton Interviews 1, 44, 49, 77.   [27] See Strathern (1990).

which individuals had in the main to accept and adapt to'.[28] Respondents often thought it important to have classes so that individual's 'natural' desire to get ahead can lead to appropriate rewards.

> You've got to have somebody who is that little bit better – if everyone is on the same basis, how can I put it...say you've got a man with £1000 and a man with £5...you've got to have something to go for, to have a figurehead to get up with, if we were on the same level there would be no reasons for trying to get on.[29]

We can see here how the idea of the upper class serves as the reference point to the 'ordinary individual'. By being a visible class, in the public eye of media and 'society' it defines everyone else as private, as responsible for their own lives. As a rich class who do not have to worry for money, it is differentiated from everyone else who are bound up with the grafting world of making a living. By being a powerful class it recognizes the relative powerlessness of everyone else. However, the reference to the upper class does more than this, since it partly unsettles the individualistic ethic itself. By recognizing that those in the upper class are not 'normal individuals', it raises the worrying prospect that people are not in fact so primordially 'given' as people might like to think. It is this tension that helps explain the 'everywhere but nowhere' references to class. The idea of class is needed to sustain individualistic identities, but because it also disrupts it, it then is pushed back into the wings.

In this formulation, the 'social' should not be seen to impinge on the 'natural'. This explains why a minority of the respondents were happy to defer to the upper class as born to rule because they saw their position as natural: it was in their 'blood'. It is also this which explains the remarkably numerous references to class divisions arising from relationships between 'lords and serfs'. Whereas few respondents related class to the social relations of industrial capitalism, numerous respondents in Luton were able to give a potted history of slavery and feudalism as an explanation of how class originated.

> [I]n this country it stems from so far back. From the lords and barons, they graded them out so long ago they've never got over it.

> There's always been the serfs, the hobnobs and the rulers. Then again it started through education and heredity...originally it started with landowners and started like that. The workers were never allowed to expand and they were just kept down. The Tolpuddle martyrs spoke up and they were deported.

> It's from way back – when some bod' owned a bit of land and it's come down. Way back, no doubt we were serfs, which no doubt we still are. For example, look at the Duke of Bedford – what's he? It's only what his dad left him...those at the top fight to keep us down.[30]

The reason for these historical references is due to the desire to 'naturalize' class as an exogenous force over which respondents have little real say. In part this

---

[28] Goldthorpe et al. (1968*a*, 154).   [29] SN 4871, Luton Interview 52.
[30] SN 4871, Luton Interviews 114, 115, 193.

appeal to nature construes the technical as also an asocial domain, not itself part of the class system. The same process also explains the centrality of money, which could be seen as an externalized, 'objective' feature of social life, which people need in order to get by, but which is 'untainted' by personal or subjective factors. Precisely because money is impersonal, it is possible for people to be differentiated on the basis of how much money they have without this being deemed to undermine their individual, human qualities. To define groups in terms of their cultural taste, or lifestyle would contaminate the human with the social, raising issues about whether there are morally better ways to live. Invoking money allows you to recognize social difference without overtly talking about different kinds of people. Here is one especially striking example:

> [A]s far as I'm concerned everybody's got one head, one body, two arms and two legs. There's no difference between me and Lord Clare; he's got the money and I haven't. He may have a bit more brains, must have I suppose, but we're still equal in other parts. Even a roadsweeper's equal to me; I earn twice as much as he does but it doesn't make much difference to me, he's my equal.[31]

We see in these reflections the complexity and internal tensions of a view of the world which was premised around the centrality of the primordial individual, who is not a social cipher, and who is expected to differ because of their 'nature'. This was a situation in which scientific and technical practices and skills did not carry the kind of hierarchical implications that snobbishness possessed. Indeed, by effacing the social and the natural through their role as intermediaries between these two realms, the technical offered a certain utopian potential. The evidence from the Affluent Worker study reveals, therefore, an awareness of class that did not have the technicians, managers, or white-collar workers in its sights. It remained fixed on the public, visible, and aristocratic elite, by contrast with which the workers could identify their ordinariness and normality.

The Wallsend interviews demonstrate the power of a cultural world view steeped in the tradition of manual skilled labour, which differentiated between the everyday world of male production teams and the visible and public world of the elite. This was a world, however, which the shipbuilders themselves recognized was being eclipsed. They knew that the shipyards were dying. When asked their views about 'the best job for boys these days', to a man they saw no future in the shipyards. Very few thought that a boy should seek work there. 'If a man is not going into higher education, I wouldn't let them start in the shipyard: they get 100% more outside'.[32] Yet, although the shipyards were finished, few wanted their boys to go into white-collar, clerical, or professional work. Those who did mention such occupations often chose examples close to their own construction experience, notably as draughtsmen or architects. Very few mentioned that boys should go to university and gain academic qualifications, for these were seen as belonging to a different cultural world.

---

[31] SN 4871, Luton Interview 33.   [32] Wallsend Interview fl17.

The hopes of the shipbuilding workers were focused on new technical fields, notably those associated with electronic and computer technology. No less than 40 per cent named electrical-related work as attractive for their boys to work in. Many also talked about the appeal of engineering, computer-related work, research, and scientific employment. One man thought the best prospects were in 'economics and space travel'. Several were enthusiasts for research. Another optimistically pointed to 'electricians, technicians, TV engineers, the jobs of the future'.[33] These men embraced a technological future in which the manual skills of the skilled tradesmen could be translated into new areas of technological advance, so allowing the migration of skilled manual work cultures into new environments – in precisely the way that had been characteristic of industrial development in the previous two centuries.[34] These were forms of social mobility which did not involve becoming a snob or acting unnaturally.

In reality, this transplantation of the culture of skilled trade into the deployment of new technological skills never took place. Those young working-class boys of Tyneside (other than the minority who did well at school) had poor prospects. Electronic and computer skills became appropriated to credentialized modes of office-based working. Apprenticeship collapsed as the dominant mode of training: whereas in the early 1970s there were more apprentices than university graduates, by the end of that decade apprenticeship had largely disappeared and the acquisition of formal credentials had become of central importance. This was a shift of huge cultural, social, and technical significance: whereas previous generations of middle and upper classes had shunned technology as dirty and associated with the uncouth world of trade, the transformations of the previous decades had made the technical fully respectable. Through this realignment of technique with academia and intellectuality, the claims of male manual workers to have distinctive cultural resources of their own were undermined. On this platform the subsequent stigmatization and marginalization of the white working class which became increasingly apparent in the later years of the twentieth century rested.[35]

9.2 TECHNICAL IDENTITIES AND THE EFFACEMENT OF CLASS

In Chapter 3 I showed how technocratic identities mutated out of the concerns of middle-class intellectuals to avoid snobbery through claiming managerial privileges. They were able to evoke an appeal to science and technology which spanned both skilled manual work cultures and the activities of gentlemanly science. What happens in ensuing decades, however, is that these technocratic identities

---

[33] SN 5514, P08.

[34] For discussion of this handicraft character of British industrial development, see the discussion in Savage and Miles (1994).

[35] See the discussion in Savage (2000) and Skeggs (2004).

lose their affiliation to skilled manual work, become increasingly credentialist in orientation, and also conceal their covertly privileged nature through invoking achievement-oriented terms. This is a very subtle but important shift, in which the literate middle classes no longer see classes in ascriptive terms in which one is simply born (or not) into the right kind of middle-class family, but rather see classes as navigated by strategically mobile individuals. Let me trace through how we can see the middle classes shifting in their identities as part of this process.

In 1948 Mass-Observation was scarcely ten years old, but it was already in steep decline. Its heady days of the later 1930s, when it developed an unusual surrealist ethnographic approach to everyday life, had already given way in the war years to a more established interest in studying popular opinion for the benefit of government.[36] After the war it struggled to find a new role for itself. Its main hope lay in marketing research, where it increasingly came up against the power of the new opinion polling companies who saw its lack of representativeness as fatal to its credibility. The post-war directives sent out to Mass-Observers indicate the uncertain ambitions of Mass-Observation in this period, with requests for focused marketing information often appearing in the same directives as broad-ranging inquiries about everyday life. So it was in September 1948, when the Mass-Observers were asked a series of almost sociological questions about their views about class, followed by questions about whether it was indecent for couples to make love in public, and then their views about Christian Dior's New Look which, with its longer dress lengths was sweeping the fashion world. The three faces of Mass-Observation were thus simultaneously on display; its interest in academic social sciences; its surrealist interest in quizzing the boundaries of public decency; and its attempts at market research. The Mass-Observers themselves seemed to take this mixture in their stride: nearly all those who replied attempted to answer all three questions, although with varying degrees of enthusiasm and interest. And indeed there was remarkable unanimity: pretty much everyone was appalled when couples made love in public (though quite a few wondered what exactly this coy phrase actually meant: kissing, holding hands, intercourse, or just looking fondly at each other?), whilst the New Look commanded widespread enthusiasm, especially from women, though there was the occasional grump that it was anti-patriotic because it required more cloth than shorter skirts and hence would lead to clothes shortages.

And so it was too with the questions on class. We need to note that the framing of the directive (see the appendix) contrasted the middle and working classes, and encouraged the respondents to think less in terms of the emerging technical identities which I have discussed in Chapters 2 and 3, and more in terms of comparing themselves with workers.

> I object intensely to the term 'working class' judging by the way productivity in certain industries has fallen it is a misnomer. I consider the professional classes usually do more work than the so-called working classes.

[36] Jeffrey (1999), Hubble (2006), and Kushner (2004).

I went to public school, have never been short of the necessaries of life, and do not regard myself as a member of the working class.

Although definitely not class conscious, I usually refer to any form of manual worker or uneducated person to a class apart from myself, which I generally term the working class.[37]

This opposition was generally thought of as representing the difference between brain work and manual work. The idea that the middle classes worked with their brains, and hence were more intellectual, cultivated, and superior to the working class runs very deep for many of the Mass-Observers. Yet at the same time, only a minority identified themselves confidently and readily as belonging to a class,[38] and these hesitancies underscore the moral power and rightness of the professional middle class as somehow 'above class'. In talking about class, rather than about national well-being, ideas of technical virtuosity rarely surfaced, and much more inchoate accounts were rendered. This refusal actually testified to the fact that they actually had a clear sense of themselves in the social hierarchy.

I hate class distinctions and do not think any definite lines can be drawn between social classes, but if there has to be a division, I consider myself to belong to the upper middle class.

This kind of account shaded into the view which in one breath denied the relevance of class before, in the next breath, claiming a clear social identity.

I would like to think of myself as not belonging to any particular social class....If one recognises the professional middle class as an entity, I was born into it. None of my forbears has had the initiative to become anything other than a soldier, doctor, lawyer or clergyman.[39]

This is a very revealing formulation. The hesitancy in describing class comes from seeing the professional middle class as 'above' class, as a category, which in some ways overrides class distinctions. The reason for this lies in the way that the professional middle classes identified themselves as a 'cultured' class, with this culture being seen as elevating them above the mundane and practical business of class.[40] This is the culture of class which refuses to name itself, whose references are oblique and opaque.

Purely financially I come under working class, but keep company with anybody, mainly upper middle class. My mentality is (pardon me) intellectually above 'class'. So I can't class myself.[41]

To openly identify yourself as a member of the professional middle class would, in a sense, be to indicate a degree of vulgarity that might in fact put a question

---

[37] M-O: 4–1587, 35–2002, 41–4389.

[38] My analysis offers a rather different account from that given by Marwick (1996, 41–2), who quotes testimony from four housewives from this directive to emphasize the strength and clarity of the middle-class self-image. However, his four cases are not representative of the broader sample.

[39] M-O: 2–195, 9–458.   [40] See McKibbin (1998, chapter 3).

[41] M-O: 11–1814.

mark around one's membership of that class. So it is, that many of the more eloquent Mass-Observers seem to register hesitancy about class in the very same breath as stating an apparently clear and unequivocal social identity.

> I strongly resent the emphasis that is placed on differences of class and all the snob-bery and inverted snobbery that is associated with it, but however reluctantly I must admit that I do consider myself as belonging to a particular class, though I don't stress it and certainly don't consider my class superior to any other.... I have a university degree and I have certain standards of security which I think the middle class hold out as an ideal, even if they don't attain them, standards such as owning a house, with an amount of space in it which is more than the working class would consider reasonable, such as having sufficient savings to provide for emergencies, to enable one to change jobs, to remove across the country, to educate one's children on a higher standard than the working class would consider neces-sary...work with the brains rather than with the hands.[42]

This woman, the wife of a university lecturer, at one moment resists the idea that she is better than anyone else, before going on to precisely identify her superior standards: an interesting way in which one disavows social superiority through the very process of reaffirming it. It is also this which explains why so few of the sample saw income or occupation as being the defining feature of class: for if this were so, they would be judging themselves by crude, material, or monetary criteria, rather than by the cultural standards that they held so dear. The further implication was that the high-status gentlemen were a class apart. As one man put it with disarming honesty:

> I maintain two very distinct standards – a wide tolerance for the mobile[43] – and a very different standard for those who are, or should be, my equals. In fact a 'gentleman' does not display his emotions in public, any more than he appears drunk in public.[44]

The professional middle class here are almost a caste apart, and even those who rise into its ranks cannot be treated as bona fide members. In this respect it is the mirror view to that of the manual workers whose values we have examined above, who also identify themselves in reaction to a public elite associated with visible status markers. But we also see in this account how claims to membership of this group rested on a striking abnegation of agency on behalf of the middle class itself. In the quote above, this is hinted at by the pride in not displaying emotions, in only displaying etiquette as a kind of collective code announcing latent membership of the group as a whole. Membership of this class is seen as ascrip-tive, as something which you are born into, and which one cannot claim as an individual reward. One is middle class not through one's own efforts, aptitudes, and skills, but through claiming membership of a social group through social ties of family, education, friendship, and the like over which one has no direct control. Hence the insistence that middle-class status was handed down by

---

[42] M-O (E): 13–368.   [43] That is, the upwardly socially mobile.   [44] M-O (E): 23–055.

one's parents and extended family more generally. One engineering draughtsman argued that he was middle class because of his family environment.

> My parents were able to give me a public school education and being the son of a naval officer had always to be an example to him.[45]

> I try to eliminate all class distinctions from my social life...however I suppose I have been brought up with a middle class outlook as....For the most part of ten years my father has been a regular army officer.[46]

As one young woman, an art student, explored the role of her family in identifying with class.

> Actually, class is not a subject I give much thought to....However when the subject *has* come up, mammy always said we were professional class...of course I think of some people as 'common' but these always seem to be awful anyway....It's difficult to say *why* I think I belong to this class, but presumably it is because daddy is a mining engineer and all my recent ancestors on both sides of the family were either doctors, or mining engineers, excepting mammy's father who was a vetinary surgeon and amateur steeplechaser.[47]

Another housewife talked about her upper-middle-class identity in the following terms

> Because my forbears have been brought up Christian gentlemen for many generations....Because one of my grandfathers was a church of England parson, and the other the headmaster of a private school, both were at Cambridge, and because my father was scholar at Charterhouse and Trinity College Cambridge, and a wrangler.[48]

Every one of these criteria celebrate conformity to certain norms and standards and announce that the upper-middle-class identity is dependent on doing things 'correctly', 'conventionally', and in an 'accepted' manner. The widespread identification of an appropriate education for middle-class status is also revealing. It might be thought that this invokes some claims to individual achievement, but in fact what nearly always matters is the type of education one has, not whether a high level of distinction was achieved in qualifications (for the only exception, see 7–2003 above). Not a single Mass-Observer mentioned the class of degree they had, or the number of examinations they had passed: what mattered was the kind of school they went to, and having a university education of any kind was a badge of a middle-class, and usually professional middle-class, identity. Those observers who talked more fully about education saw themselves not as agents, as people who did especially well, but as the recipients of the benefits education could bestow. A student said he was upper middle class since 'when I conclude my studies, I will be fitted for a job which will put me in this category'.[49]

Identifying oneself as middle class hence involved not making claims about one's individual distinctiveness – your skills, talents, achievements – but was

---

[45] M-O (E): 40–4507.   [46] M-O (E): 40–4519.   [47] M-O (E): 15–4343.
[48] M-O (E):7–2003.   [49] M-O (E): 40–4597.

Table 9.1 Class identities of Mass-Observer sample, September 1948

	% who readily identify with class	% claiming to be upper middle class	% claiming to be middle class	% claiming to be working class	% claiming to be no, or other, class
Male	33%	22%	70%	9%	21%
Female	16%	13%	76%	10%	14%

ultimately about showing how you belonged to a social group through birth, through having appropriate manners, and other social ties. Numerous respondents talked about the distinctive culture which they had, which was often seen as particular kinds of habits, forms of speech, modes of address, and dress, which ultimately proclaimed people to be bearers of a class identity.

> The way I dress, by my interests, by my tone of voice, manner of address, subjects of conversation.[50]

This is very different from those few people who did espouse a working-class identity. Consider these examples:

> As a worker with hand and brain who has carved his own way from the handicap of being left, an orphan at 10 years of age, served an apprenticeship at the printing craft and climbed the ladder after an absorbing life of 'fight'.[51]

> In my own opinion, anyone who works for a weekly wage irrespective of remuneration belongs to the working class, and even although my own wage would qualify me as middle class financially, I am a tradesman and therefore consider myself working class.[52]

> I work for a living – it seems to me that anyone doing a job of work for his living is working class and anyone who has the means of living without having to work is very lucky.[53]

What we see here is that claiming working-class identity is a means of individualizing one's identity, marking one's difference from these ascriptive markers. This is especially clear with the first case, a process engraver, who claims a record of individual achievement as part of his working-class identity. Yet the same motif is present, in more limited ways, in the third case where being working class is a means of emphasizing that you have to work for your living and are hence necessarily constructed as an agent who cannot get by on unearned income. The second quote indicates individuality of judgement, where a working-class identity is a means of showing that he is able to think for himself and come to his own idea about where he should be 'placed'. The overlaps with the Wallsend and Luton workers is apparent here, in allying the 'ordinary individual' as a working-class agent, set apart culturally from the public middle class.

[50] M-O (E): 23–836.   [51] M-O (E): 21–4658.   [52] M-O (E): 26–4564.
[53] M-O (E): 30–4509.

We can see how middle-class identities were both powerful yet also inarticulate: they depended on being implicit and taken for granted. This is a set of values which was premised on the cultural superiority of those born into professional middle-class households. These values are precisely those which we traced in Chapters 2 and 3, as associated with the older moral and gentlemanly formations which were to be disrupted by the very being of the social sciences which emerged so powerfully from the 1950s. It is therefore pertinent that studies of the middle classes in the 1960s begin to reveal some new idioms of middle-class identity emerging, though only hesitantly.

9.3 MIDDLE-CLASS IDENTITIES IN THE 1960s

As part of their preparation for the Affluent Worker study, Goldthorpe and Lockwood conducted 150 interviews with 'lower-middle-class' respondents, mainly teachers, grocers, electricians, and bank workers, in Cambridge in 1961.[54] Here, just thirteen years after the Mass-Observation directive we have discussed above, we can detect some new modes of talking about class. There was now much more willingness to talk about and reflect upon class. Indeed, especially amongst the bank workers, there was usually a clear and crisp recognition of the existence of hierarchical class divisions, possibly the product of the very strong boundaries between staff and clerical grades which were found in banks at this time.

We can still occasionally detect the existence of 'cultural' modes of thinking about class, which insisted that manners and style were central and which made reference to old genteel models. One respondent noted, on old-fashioned lines that,

> with new babies, a course of study and day to day work, I am snowed under. I found it most distasteful – I just do not – and never have done – classify individuals on occupations. My grouping is how I think they would sort themselves out if shipwrecked together – provided that suitable introductions were made and assuming the clerk to be male.... I've steeped myself in arts and crafts, I tend to, I tend to think (as most people do) that that is all important because to me it is; I like to think I have a similar outlook to...not so much the medieval craftsmen, but to our ideal of what he thought. I just like the making, producing, designing things, etc.[55]

Here we see the persistence of literary and historical motifs in talking about social class. This respondent tellingly opposes the linking of class to occupations, and distances himself from a crude sociological determinism. We see the Robinson Crusoe experiment as well as arts and crafts being used to articulate notions of class. However, there is also an ability to talk about class in a more distant manner, one which suggests that class is 'all in the eye of the beholder'.

---

[54] These interviews were never used in any of their published work.

[55] SN 4871, Cambridge Interview 3; see also Interview 5 which evokes the Eliza Doolittle character with the importance of 'character'.

Class now is relativized and externalized, seen as something which is not innate but as a contested mode of classification.

Some respondents also preferred to talk about class in the language of 'breeding' familiar from the 1940s, evoking innate cultural traits, and the inability to acquire middle-class status later in life.

> Breeding if you like, no doubt about it, it is breeding. My mother didn't have very much, but she was middle class, you could tell it, it's just something you either have or you haven't. A lot of people try to ape it, they'll either acquire an accent, and the coffee parties and the piano lessons and the ballet, and the private schools and the children don't pass the 11+ 'oh dear, oh dear we must look for a private school'...
> I don't think you can change your breeding, you can improve your position – I think there are lots of people today trying to make out they're middle class, and in many ways they live in a world of artificiality – you can be a beggar but you can still have your breeding.[56]

Similarly, the Colonel Blimp image was evoked, though in a way that increasingly marked out the respondent as eccentric, even strange. The researchers put a special marker on the transcript of one 'old gentleman', a bank accountant, who keenly stepped up to the stereotype of the 'upper-class twit'.

> I'm a great believer in classes, in class distinctions, because I think they make life colourful. The English system has always been excellent...ours has always been comparatively fluid. When I was young – in the teens of the century there were a lot of the aristocracy who were marrying chorus girls. I'm all for that, it brought new blood....I'm a right wing conservative, I come from East Anglian farming stock and I say to the reds that there is nothing to prevent a man who has guts to raise himself....It has tended to be birth, good breeding and education, that's what it has been and still is....I don't like how on wireless or television you get so called singers making noises out of tune and in an American accent and his fortune is made. There are features of American civilisation I deplore, we're adapting American culture. This is appalling and is riding hand in hand with material progress.[57]

Such accounts however jostle alongside those who evoke more technical terms, in which moral judgements are seen to follow from scientific judgements. Various interviewees defined the lower class as the 'educationally subnormal', as 'mentally deficient', people who 'live in poverty'.[58] Several respondents talked about the importance of the social environment for assessing class.[59] Others talked about the 'class structure', the 'class system' or the way that class was defined by the 'education system'.[60] The idea that there was an 'Establishment', as popularized by Anthony Sampson and Henry Fairlie, came in for much discussion.[61] In the words of a bank manager:

---

[56] SN4871, Cambridge Interview 27.   [57] SN 4871, Cambridge Interview 59.
[58] SN 4871, Cambridge Interviews 12, 13, 14.
[59] For example, SN 4871, Cambridge Interview 35.
[60] SN 4871, Cambridge Interviews 50, 52, 40.
[61] For example, SN 4871, Cambridge Interview 22.

> There's the establishment and all that sort of thing....It's a very vague thing. It's the upper class, a small class, which governs the country to a large extent, by politics or finance. There's a lot of nepotism about it....I think it's largely bound up with people with titles, mostly, I suppose. And the House of Lords still has terrific influence.
>
> What I deplore about them, the establishment generally is their smugness and complacency in this present age – the cry of 'you've never had it so good', when a year later we've never had it so bad, the lack of foresight and planning, the hotchpotch of our architecture – the sympathy I have for people like Arnold Wesker, great playwright that he is, who's flogging a dead horse – although he wrote his trilogy for the working class and about the working class, and if he thinks they're going to pour out in large numbers to see it he's more sanguine than I am.[62]

Alongside references to the professional middle class is the occasional idea, absent amongst the 1948 Mass-Observers, that one could be trained to be a professional. 'Most people who are trained for professions are able to express themselves well, the training improves their command of words.'[63] An especially common refrain here is the idea that education is not an innate product of social background, and can be a vehicle which creates and sustains social mobility, and notably when nurtured in schools. The motif of intelligence and education, seen as conducive of efficiency and national planning, now serve as linchpin for many of these respondents: 'what education you've got leads to occupation. The ordinary secondary school person who's gone through B & C forms is the bottom group', as one scientific assistant put it.[64] Twenty-four respondents, and especially those who were working as school teachers, emphasized education as central to class, yet in a meritocratic fashion which saw the type of school attended as less important than the acquisition of skill and knowledge. Education is now allied to the possibility of mobility.

> [E]ducation helps considerably, a boy in a poor family who gets to grammar school soon feels out of touch with his surroundings, tries to mix with people from better homes, etc.
>
> I would have thought that if a person had character, had the opportunity to gain education to qualify for a job, he could easily move from the working class into the middle class.
>
> Education has a lot to do with it, it's inclined to create distinctions; I've noticed this myself. I went to grammar school and had to leave through illness: in grammar school you're taught to appreciate different things – Shakespeare and classical music – while in secondary modern these things are not taught so much, and these things do create a barrier in later life. One person will want to go to a concert at the Festival Hall, another to Elvis on TV.[65]

It is for this reason that intelligence was also seen as a powerful and independent force for good.

---

[62] SN 4871, Cambridge Interviews 54, 22.   [63] SN 4871, Cambridge Interview 18.
[64] Cambridge Interview 6.   [65] SN 4871, Cambridge Interviews 3, 5, 6.

In some cases, this ethic blended into a strong appeal to a rational, planned, social structure, linked to a critique of old-fashioned, gentlemanly government. Education is now seen as an independent force for good, able to intervene to create a more just and better planned nation. One secondary modern art teacher put it in the following terms:

> Frankly I'm disgusted with certain aspects of English life that could do with a jolly good rinse – looking forward to being included in the European scheme, we've got to make drastic changes; in some ways we are very complacent. I don't think the present government would help us, we're going to need a very brave and drastic socialist government to do it, and we're going to have to sacrifice a lot of our rather dusty traditions. There's too much pomp and circumstance in British life at this top class level – I always remember that when I was in the forces and came back to England, I was very pleased to get back, I like the English people, I think we're a very stable and consistent people but we've got to abandon some of our ideas. Town planning, we've got to make drastic changes, abandon our pseudo-Tudor homes and have them built on a national scheme, still comfortable, but not just individuals going berserk with rock gardens and so forth. There should be national committees set up with the best talents to deal with town planning. The government ought to be prepared to compensate for a lot of demolition....To sum this all up, I think the answer lies in education. We've got a very mercenary and unenlightened education policy throughout the country; the first step is to spend more on education, the first move by these committees should be a drastic educational policy, heavily subsidised by the government...by no means least there should be an equally large committee set up to work on the recreation and development of the arts and so on.[66]

We can identify here a mobilization of planning and technique in defining a modern role for the educated middle class, and one which by contrast was content to put the less well educated into working-class jobs. For one secondary school teacher, 'A boy in the D stream here one would expect to become a labourer, he'll become a dustman, etc. It is not until you get to your A's that you'll get your apprenticeship'.[67] We can see here clear echoes of the technocratic identities of the post-war Mass-Observers, with a determination not to view the middle classes as a backward, traditional formation, reliant on status handed down from the past, but as a force for change, modernity, and advancement. The forces of history are now pitted against the elite figure of the discredited Establishment, and through this move the forces of progress and modernity become allied with an emerging middle class awareness-worthy, skilled, and intelligent people.

9.4 CONCLUSIONS: CLASS IDENTITIES IN POST-WAR BRITAIN

In this chapter I have explored how the decoupling of technique from skilled male identities and its appropriation within an academic frame was associated

---

[66] SN 4871, Cambridge Interview 14; see also Cambridge Interview 19 for critical remarks about the 'upper crust' and an advocacy of the 'solid middle class'.

[67] SN 4871, Cambridge Interview 1.

with the development of new kinds of middle-class identities. This follows on from my discussion in Chapters 2 and 3 which traced the rise of new technocratic identities among key sections of the middle class who sought a way of differentiating themselves from 'vulgar' workers on the one hand and the 'genteel' aristocracy on the other.

In the early twenty-first-century class there seems no place for snobbery and cultural elitisim. It is rare for people to overtly claim status privilege or state that they are better than others. Some have identified this as marking the end of class society, with the rise of individualized and reflexive identities. I have argued in this chapter for a different perspective; one which sees the contemporary refusal to admit class hierarchy as the working out of longer-term processes which were set in train during the 1950s and 1960s. During these decades two processes worked together which eroded the long-term cultural stand-off between working and middle class that had existed during the twentieth century. Firstly, I have used the accounts of very different groups of male manual workers, from Tyneside and from Buckinghamshire, to show that the deeply held class framings of these workers were organized around a major contrast between the public and private, the social and natural, which differentiated an ascriptive upper class from an ordinary popular class. These workers therefore, did not see white collar workers, technicians, or even managers in terms of class, and therefore did not see class relations precisely where sociologists and socialists saw them – at the point of production in the large capitalist factory. More tellingly still, these workers valued practical skill and applied technical capacity. The result was that with de-industrialization and end of apprenticeship, key badges of respectability and independence were lost to them.

The trajectory for the middle classes ran in the opposite direction. From a scorn towards practical skill and an insistence on cultural hierarchy evident in the 1930s, there was an increasing embrace of merit, technique, and skill as the markers of managerial and leadership capacity. Initially it was often recognized that this bore a distinctive middle-class imprint, but during the 1960s there was an increasing preparedness to use a language of merit, educational qualification, and skill in ways which quite effaced overt and visible classifications. By this time, significant sections of the middle class were more confident and assertive in their deployment of a technocratic language of expertise, planning, and class. This is the germ of a process, now hegemonic, which constructs the educated middle classes as the quintessential autonomous and reflexive individuals of contemporary capitalism, as those who no longer need to position themselves as superior to either the working class or the gentry, but as those who command the key terms of contemporary normalcy, hence masking their own privileges and powers.[68]

---

[68] The argument developed in this chapter is an extension of that which I made in *Class Analysis and Social Transformation* and which is also elaborated in *Culture, Class, Distinction* (especially in chapter 10). Skeggs' (2004) is also an important statement on these issues.

Unpacking these relations is complex. We don't learn much just by inspecting questionnaire responses over time. It is the changing *form* of people's accounts, drawn from archived sources, which is a more pertinent indicator than simply whether people identify themselves as middle or working class. In terms of content, there is little change: most people define themselves as middle class, though generally ambiguously and ambivalently in both periods. Mass-observers rarely announced a clear and unambiguous class identity and wanted to define their identities in altogether more coded ways. However, this apparent constancy of content looks very different when we examine the form of accounts of class. The meanings of class identity rest on their latent, ambivalent, and opaque character, the way they reveal as well as conceal. Thus we can see that those social theorists who define individualization as marking a break from class misconceive the key processes at stake. Instead, I have argued for an interpretation of change in which there is no simple 'break' with the past, but rather a deepening of old identities through the same process by which they are reworked.

Conclusion

2009: The Politics of Method

I have, in this book, analysed the battery of techniques and methods that could be used to expose the social tissue during the post-war decades, and the technical identities associated with them. These mined down into everyday life using sampling, interviews, and surveys to reveal unknown aspects of social life. Avoiding the grand functionalist theorizing of American sociology, the focus was on eliciting accounts from which sociologists could unravel how people's ordinary situations shaped their lives, actions, thoughts, and endeavours. This was an intimate, critical, and usually compassionate sociology. At the same time, these repertoires became resources which could be used to define the modern rational nation and to sell products. I have argued that they were involved in a subtle reworking of who is able to speak about the present, and with what relationship to prior historical knowledge. The interview and the survey provide a vehicle for analysing trends, allowing history to be arrayed by manipulating aspects of a singular data source, hence wrenching the present out of a necessarily separated, and therefore fraught relationship with past sources. Through this means, the analysis of 'now-time' could be seized away from the embrace of the differentially constituted past. As part of this process, I have shown how the social sciences systematically conceal their own tracks through their deployment of ethical issues as a kind of screen which distinguishes past from present.

We need to see this shift not as simply a matter of scientific progress or the advance of knowledge, but also as related to the remaking of cultural hierarchies, and the redrawing of class, gender, and national boundaries, crystallized through a mode of knowing the modern rational nation in the image of a social scientific methodology which mobilized sociological aggregates. I have therefore resisted a purely technical account of methodological advance and sought to render the social sciences in a messy, competitive context, whereby the roles of different kinds of intellectuals, technical experts, and social groups are at stake. At the same time, because a range of social agents were implicated in these projects – most notably as 'respondents' – their own voices mattered. There were limits to how far they could be enrolled into social science projects. This allows me to avoid a purely constructivist account which focuses on the 'making up' of subjects as if they could be constructed freely.[1]

---

[1] I thus part company from Latour 's emphasis in *Reassembling the Social* (2005) that a focus on networks, technologies, and contingencies involves displacing such categories.

A crucial feature of these battles concerned the mobilization of the ordinary and everyday as the constellation of the popular. Rather than the elucidation of the morally problematic, deemed to deviate from unquestioned cultural norms, the focus lay on scrutinizing and defining the routine itself, in the name of a social science concerned to intervene in the social fabric. During the middle years of the twentieth century, social scientists intervened in the elucidation of everyday accounts in novel and effective ways, through seeking accounts of people's social roles and relationships. Viewing their endeavours, fifty or so years later, I have tried to avoid the temptation to criticize them – their sexism, class prejudices, and so forth – from the unassailable vantage point of the present. I have sought to wrest these interventions out of teleological histories of the discipline, and instead return them to their original historical context, placing them alongside other cultural and political currents from which they emerged. I have stressed the productivity of these interventions and intimated that these technologies have come to inform key organizational and social practices today.[2] Such an approach allows us to render their true originality, even greatness, in terms of marking a break with powerful currents of gentlemanly social science, with its preoccupation with mapping and moralizing. The project of a critical social science, more strongly evident in Britain than in many other nations, notably the United States, has been an enduring legacy which we need to defend.

In this conclusion, I reiterate my themes and pull out some contemporary ramifications for the social sciences. Firstly, returning for the final time to Mass-Observation, I demonstrate the ubiquity of social science narrative, showing how it is now routinely invoked in the statements of literate middle classes. I ponder what this implies for the boundaries between the humanities and social sciences, claiming that the retirement of literary and historical expertise as means of understanding the present leads to an unfortunate stand-off between past- and future-centred modes of knowledge. Secondly, taking the story up to date, I consider the challenge of informationalism, the way that the proliferation of digital data sources allows new levers to position the social, in ways which question the jurisdiction of the social sciences themselves and form an appropriate set of reflections on which to conclude this book.

CONTEMPORARY POPULAR NARRATIVES

We move forward in time to 1990, the last year of Thatcher's premiership, the year after the fall of the Berlin Wall, and, according to the sociological commentators, part of a new globalized and postmodern era. The contemporary panel of

---

[2] This argument is akin to that of Boltanski and Chiapello (2003), who also seek to show that currents of 1960s liberatory politics have become incorporated into contemporary managerial practices, as well as that of Thrift (2003).

Mass-Observers were asked to write about social inequality. Here are three extended examples, which convey a clear flavour of their use of narrative:

> I am close on 59 now and I feel that no matter what I have achieved I might well have done better had I not been dogged by a complex about my working class background, a very basic education, and a perceptible Midlands accent....(The) son of a small trader....I was ill at ease....when invited to the home of a girlfriend who lived in a wealthy quarter of Wolverhampton. I was there for lunch, and while I was quietly confident my table manners would stand scrutiny, I was disconcerted to find a linen table napkin rolled in an ivory ring on my side plate. It was my first encounter with a napkin and while I knew it should be laid on the lap and not tucked into the shirt collar I could not think what to do with it when the meal was finished. It worried me greatly and finally I laid it nonchalantly on my plate in a crumpled heap....
>
> Classes? Money makes people what they are – those with a lot, those with little and those in between with neither too much nor too little.[3]

> 2) first preliminary jottings on this topic have revealed what a difficult subject it is; so many blurred edges, so many emotive connections....So I just propose writing in essay form, using your suggestions as guide points.
>
> I'll start by looking at my own life, past and present, and comment on any social divisions that spring to mind. Even in my own (extended family) I 'feel' there are divisions, caused by achievements in some cases, money and/or education in others.
>
> My working life has been much more ordinary, and mostly I've just been 'a housewife' – married to a draughtsman as lacking in ambition as I am, I seem to have positioned myself on a very low rung of the social ladder.
>
> What class do I think I belong to? It would be a hard job trying to define my position according to my family background – my relations include such different characters. The one brother, in particular, who is on several boards of directors....That's at one end of the scale, – at the other, our own youngest son, unemployed and with a yen for a somewhat bohemian lifestyle....All a bit of a mixture. Forget my family and judge me by my friends and associates, but it is still confusing – several classes represented....what about my education? Now here is a puzzling fact – I was the only one of a family of five to receive private education....In fact my brothers and sisters have without doubt made more social progress than I have. I think the definition I like best is to link my social status with the area in which I live. This is the area my husband and I have chosen and in which we feel most comfortable and secure....this is the level of society that suits us and I suggest that to some extent one does choose the stratum of society to which you are most suited.
>
> ...the one thing which annoys me is terms like 'social class A B C1'.[4]

> 3) When I am thinking about stereotyping I want to get out the way of the last paragraph of your checklist....I am so terrified of stereotyping – and of being considered racist – that I am adamant there is not such thing as a national characteristic.

[3] M-O (H): B1654.   [4] M-O (H): A2168.

In London class and race were the divisions and there wasn't really a great breaking down of either, only minor ones. Class has always been significant to me: born the child of a white-collar worker in London dockland, a working class Tory of the bluest type, a royalist, a snob. That was my father, though I loved him and he had many attractive qualities.

I rose, through education, to being middle class in my profession and in my leisure pursuits – that is the way I define class.

To sum up, I believe that British society is class ridden, with money being the basis for this. In Britain money buys a better education, leading to better job prospects and power in whatever sphere.[5]

In 1990, extensive narratives about social divisions were now provided (these three examples above being taken from much longer letters). One woman wrote a reply stretching over fifty-two pages, with around 20,000 words.[6] Compared to the gobbets produced by the 1948 Mass-Observers, there is much more to say. In 1990, class proves to be a powerful hook for hanging stories on, rather similar to the way that novelists and early social scientists had also imagined in their post-war inquiries. Sociological accounts, as it were, are now part of routine life itself. Accordingly, the correspondents seem to recognize that what is interesting is not the actual statements so much as the way they can be folded into a more revealing narrative. The art of writing self-accounts in the form of narratives had been separated out from that of providing more factual information.

We secondly see the appeal of the autobiographical account, sometimes stretching to ten pages or more. The power of this kind of personal mobility story is evident in numerous forms, for instance in the leakage between media social representations and popular accounts.[7] Such life narratives are designed to exemplify the singularity of the correspondents' life, rather than the way that they might exemplify typical patterns. There is a striking shift here from earlier interviews where respondents were more likely to talk about themselves as exemplifying certain common social group properties in terms of having common educational or family experiences. To this extent, class narratives have become individualized.

A third difference can also be discerned. The 1990 correspondents draw upon a series of public repertoires around class: the 'essay form' is invoked, market research categories are mentioned. There is recognition of the politics of stereotyping (one should not do it!) and an awareness of the power of classification itself. These concerns are nearly entirely absent from the earlier period. Whereas the meaning of class for the gentlemanly generation lies in its unstated quality, in the way one has no control over it and it defines the nature of social life, it is now the explicit narratives and positionings which take place in the name of class that matter. Talking about class is a means of connecting personal narratives with public repertoires, in a rather similar way to that in which the melodrama of class mobility had been evoked by the first generation of interview researchers in the

---

[5] M-O (H): B1533.   [6] M-O (H): A1530.
[7] See further Skeggs and Wood on 'reality TV' or Abercrombie and Longhurst (1998) on the significance of performative audiences, and Bennett et al. (2009, chapter 12).

early 1960s. In this respect, the Mass-Observers deploy technical and social scientific accounts, already evident in 1948, and certainly in the 1960s narratives of Cambridge respondents. Yet this repertoire has matured and expanded, as correspondents recognize that social scientific ideas are part of their world. One Mass-Observer included an English school essay on the class system in his response.[8] Another used her reply to stage a critique of the Communist Party's thinking about class, ruminating that, 'it's no wonder I got a third class honours in 1978 from the polytechnic of North London. If you ask me I was lucky to get a third for I did not see any real reason to lick the boots of our Marxified/phenomenological bosses'. Others referred explicitly to their experience as market researchers, or the way that their education allowed them access to respond to the question, often through a subtle attempt to use this to resist classification themselves.

> I'm not sure how, or even if I could be classified. I have a university degree (albeit via the OU[9]), I work for the local authority in a management capacity, I like classical music and the arts, support the National Trust, and similar projects and like dining out and entertaining at home. These things could make me middle class but I live in a council flat and have many working class aspirations such as a need for instant gratification.... Perhaps the dichotomy explains why I'm such a mess.

> This is a MO[10] of enormous scope. Because it emanates from a university, one imagines one is expected to produce something akin to a dissertation on social and class matters, with appropriate research context.

> ...as I have a degree in sociology, I suppose I should have a clear picture of what the terms middle class and working class mean, yet even among academic sociologists one finds, if not large differences of opinion, at least differences of definition.... One lecturer, of the functionalist school, warned us that we should not confuse economic class with social status.

> One of my daughters once said I was a fascist when she caught me drawing in the sand with the end of my walking stick. This embarrassed me greatly because a man greatly likes to be counted liberal by his children, especially when they've been to Essex University.[11]

At times, this concern to demonstrate scholarly knowledge involved deploying relevant references. One man, a psychologist, sent in a reference to his own research. Other Mass-Observers referred to the feminist Mary Daly, the economist J. K. Galbraith, the historian Arthur Marwick, and the social researcher Jonathan Bradshaw. To be sure, these were minority responses. It is noteworthy, however, that literary references of the kind which littered earlier Mass-Observation directives were rare, though one elderly man looks back to George Orwell.[12] The most potent term, discussed by no fewer than fourteen of the Mass-Observers was that of 'the Establishment', which had first been defined in the later 1950s and which was still felt to exist thirty years later. This old, elite status

---

[8] M-O (H): B2436.   [9] Open University.   [10] Mass-Observation directive.
[11] M-O (H): A18, A2005, D1989, B2238.   [12] M-O (H): 1440.

group was still a foil which all Mass-Observers could freely identify against. This ability to engage in 'class talk' is itself now a means of making a statement that one is 'knowing' about the subtext associated with class, and is aware of the politics of classification.

Fourthly, Mass-Observers in the 1990s deploy an individualized framing of their identities, in which no kind of social relationship is deemed to be primordial and somehow outside the purview of classificatory processes. In the 1940s and 1950s, family relationships were identified as natural, defining people's fate and fortune. I have shown how sex differences were seen as immutable. By 1990, however, families were often constructed as comprising members from different classes. Correspondents were much more likely to trace their movement between different class fractions within the family, so that the correspondents could emphasize their 'liminal' or 'ambivalent' class positions vis-à-vis other family members. This again strikes chords with other recent research where the same kinds of hybrid family histories were often emphasized.[13] This, again, appears to be a means of allowing the correspondents to refuse a unitary class position, hence making a statement to those who 'classify'. Here, we see how class is hence inscribed as part of an individual identity, albeit one which is fluid. Compared to the earlier Mass-Observers, the accounts in 1990 are much fuller, more confident, and placed more in terms of the individual's experiences – of not knowing how to use a napkin, being a housewife, rising to a middle-class job. Class is presented as a matter of agency, rather than as something handed down, something which anchors an individual's biography in a larger frame. Hence, we can see how the kinds of individualized identities that have been emphasized by recent social theorists such as Beck and Giddens require benchmarks of class as a means of measuring change.[14]

Fifthly, the 1990 correspondents link their discussions of class to those of specific places. As we saw in Chapter 1, it was unusual to mention a particular named place in the 1950s, and where exceptions exist they mainly comprise references to regions as a whole. By the 1990s, references to place are related to claims of class identity. One writer even explicitly states that their class identity is related to their choice of residential location. Here we see the power of the enchanted landscape, as elaborated in Chapter 1. This attention to place appears to be linked to a sense of the fluidity of identity and the ability of people to make some kind of choice. Other examples of this reference to place are easy to find.

> I was born in a (very) working class area and to a working class family and – by virtue of marriage and native intelligence – have been translated into the middle class. The end result is a hybrid; I feel comfortable with neither group and in fact often find I dislike both working class and middle class manifestations equally.[15]

What we see in all these points is a careful concern to position oneself amidst a situation of multiple classifications, in which people wish to state their

---

[13] Savage et al. (2001).
[14] Beck (1992) and Giddens (1991). See the discussion in Savage (2000), and Atkinson (2007).
[15] M-O (H): B1224.

ordinariness, their mobility, and their individuality as a means of resisting being easily positioned by any one classificatory mechanism. These are social relationships saturated by positioning devices.

These shifts exemplify the wrestling of older modes of knowing the social associated with the arts and humanities into new modes of popular narration, one in which the social sciences are significant agents. This was not bound to happen, but followed a wide-ranging jurisdiction battle over who can speak for the social, and a transformation as to what is to count as social knowledge. Whereas in earlier periods, expertise in literature, history, geography, and the arts more generally was concerned with the present as much as the past, and was a means of delineating the nature and meaning of social life itself, in the post-war years the social sciences came to claim control over the social, circumscribing the role of literature and the humanities so that they could not speak so centrally to these concerns. Until the 1950s, I have argued, gentlemanly modes of social research depended on construing the nature of the social through the use of categories which assumed an innate cultural hierarchy, where observers were in positions of unassailable moral and intellectual authority, and where observation and the inspection of urban environments and documents were the prime mode of accessing knowledge. This form of social science could work closely in association with literary and historical scholarship which mobilized everyday accounts as a means of eliciting social and personal relationships. Indeed, at this point, it was literature which defined the popular. In 1953, Erich Auerbach had praised realist literature for its 'serious treatment of everyday reality, the rise of more extensive and socially inferior groups to the position of subject matter'.[16]

Yet only a few years afterwards, in the 1960s, the *Times Literary Supplement* (TLS) in a special issue on 'The British Imagination' bemoaned the inability of novelists to unravel social change, and more particularly their failure to relate personal issues to public events. It noted the peculiarly narrow outlook of novelists.

> the truth is that most English novelists are educated in a way that precludes any wide range of practical experience.... many of them never do a day's work in their lives (except in wartime) which brings them into close touch with people of a class outside their own.[17]

Recognizing the collapse of the modernist project, it reflected on the closure of literary journals and the lack of contemporary equivalents of Wells's *New Age* and Leavis's *Scrutiny*. 'Literary scholarship, needless to say, exists, but by comparison it does not have this seminal quality, this interesting and learned aptness for the critic.'[18] All this was in striking contrast to the cudgels which C. Wright Mills was taking up, at the same time, for sociology, in terms of its capacity to link personal troubles and public issues, in his book *The Sociological Imagination*.

Fifty years later, we see not the end of narrative, but its radical deployment and popularization. It was the social scientists who took leading themes of the literary

---

[16] Quoted in Lucas (2004, 552).   [17] See TLS, 9 September 1960, vii.
[18] See TLS, 9 September 1960, xi.

imagination, notably the melodrama of class mobility, and enshrined it in influential devices. What we see in this period is an emerging sociology taking over the mantle of the ordinary as its concern, and being able to mobilize this through the deployment of the novel devices of interview and survey, with their ability to define averages and aggregates. We might see this, in Moretti's terms, as the takeover of the 'filler'. Pointing to the way that the novel emerged as a device for stuffing routine, non-memorable events, into narrative form, and thus coding up bourgeois society, we can see in this social science a concern to render these 'fillers' in the form of narrative and questionnaire for a scientific purpose.

As I have endeavoured to emphasize in this book, the breaks are not neat or simple. Down to the 1970s, it remained possible for literary and humanities scholars to insist on their capacity to unravel social and political affairs. Throughout the 1960s and into the 1970s, Raymond Williams elaborated a form of social analysis and cultural studies based on his literary expertise. The development of oral history methods, championed by Paul Thompson, allowed historians access to interview-based narrative methods, and the emergence of History Workshop during the 1970s, which was largely sceptical of the pretensions of the academic social sciences, insisted on the capacity of history to engage contemporary affairs through its embrace of socialist politics.[19] But, these later currents only become visible when associated with a clearly demarcated, usually left-wing, politics: they could not appear objective in the manner of the social sciences.

I have therefore argued that the production of popular, ordinary, narratives is related to the enhanced role of technical identities, which I have traced back to the 1940s and which came to be increasingly prominent into the 1950s. I have argued that these were actually very significant in affecting middle-class identities, in removing the resources of technique and skill from the domain of manual workers, and in remaking the nature of academic expertise and skill. Rather than portraying the youth cultures of the 1960s as central to social change, they might better be understood as deploying the kinds of resources which had originated in the previous decade. This shift, I have argued, requires that we modify influential accounts of cultural expertise, notably those of Pierre Bourdieu, at least in the post-war English context. Although I am indebted to Bourdieu's field analysis, his insistence on the tensions between literary and cultured intellectuals on the one hand and wealthy industrialists on the other, obscures the way that the technically oriented middle classes became a key force in post-war England, in ways which entailed a somewhat different aesthetic orientation which did not necessarily celebrate the Kantian aesthetic of the distance from the necessary.[20]

---

[19] Perhaps the last great moment of this current was the History Workshop held at Oxford in 1979 which saw Edward Thompson, Richard Johnson, Stuart Hall, and other leading socialists jousting over the merits of structuralist Marxism. I attended this conference as a final year undergraduate and it has left an enduring mark.

[20] The contemporary implications of this argument are pursued at length in Bennett et al. (2009).

THE CHALLENGE OF INFORMATIONALISM

During the very same years that the social sciences discovered the potential for interviewing, sampling, and surveying, new methods of computerized data analysis were being developed in mathematics and the natural sciences. During the 1950s and 1960s, there was relatively little intersection between these two worlds. Although interviews were tape-recorded from the mid-1960s, they were not digitalized until the later 1990s. The early use of sample surveys was reliant on Hollerith machines, and mechanical rather than electronic forms of analysis remained the norm well into the 1960s.[21] Early computers were mainly used within government to analyse administrative data, rather than sample surveys.[22] From the 1960s, the potential of using mainframe computers became apparent. When Goldthorpe and Lockwood were donated an end-of-range mainframe in the mid-1960s to analyse the 229 Affluent Worker questionnaires, they only used it to check the results from the Hollerith machines. Even so, they were later told that they used computers more than any other Cambridge researchers apart from the crystallographers.[23] The government social survey increasingly used computerized means to analyse its census and survey data, and the formation of the Social Science Data Bank at Essex in 1965 allowed data to be stored and sent to other researchers. Probably the first sustained piece of secondary data analysis, Abel-Smith and Townsend's *The Poor and the Poorest* took four years to compare two surveys; the authors had to visit the Ministry of Labour's offices, and rely extensively on its research support, to access and analyse the Ministry's surveys in 1953 and 1960.[24] It was not until the later 1970s that the potential of transmitting data files electronically, so that researchers could analyse different data sets without leaving their offices, precipitated a growing interest in 'secondary data analysis'.[25] By the later 1960s, experiments in networking computers were under way, by banks, in the post office, and through regional computing centres.[26] Yet, even into the 1970s, universities had to collaborate in regional networks to allow them access to mainframe computers, and the early issues of the *Times Higher Education Supplement* in 1971 are as likely to announce the acquisition of a new collaborative mainframe as the creation of a new university department. Only in the later 1960s was statistical software developed, notably through the emergence of SPSS which allowed the ready manipulation and analysis of survey data, though even here the early batch versions were time consuming.[27]

---

[21] One of my childhood memories, from the later 1960s, was that of my aunt, who was a psychiatric social worker, using knitting needles to sort the record cards of a sample of patients on which she was conducting research.

[22] See Agar (2003).   [23] John Goldthorpe (personal communication).

[24] See Abel-Smith and Townsend (1965, 6–7).

[25] On the important Surrey School of secondary data analysis, see Dale et al. (1988).

[26] See Calder (1967, 542).

[27] See Uprichard et al. (2008).

The developments I have traced here in the crucial post-war decades, therefore, took place at some remove from developments in computer technology. Yet by the early 1970s the potential of computers to allow a 'quantitative revolution' became ever more apparent, with economics in particular turning to the routine use of mainframe computers. It was, however, in the natural and information sciences that computerized analysis became normalized and increasingly integral to research practice, though there continued to be resistance by scientists down to the 1980s.[28] With the introduction of the microcomputer from the 1980s, and notably the development of networked computer systems, informational processes proliferated and increasingly colonized routine administrative processes.

During the 1980s and 1990s, the social science research repertoire continued to operate at significant distance from these computerized systems. Although the data collected through interviews and surveys was increasingly stored and transmitted digitally, they were not generated through digital processes themselves till the deployment of computer-aided interviewing and the use of digital recorders in the early twenty-first century. The increasing importance of digitalized transactional and administrative data, collected routinely as a by-product of organizational and commercial processes, lay largely outside the purview of the social sciences. In a rather similar manner to the way that in the mid-twentieth century, gentlemanly social sciences had scorned the grubby world of the opinion pollster, the science establishment viewed the proliferation of digital data as slightly vulgar and nothing to do with them. It is only recently that the significance of digital data for exposing the limited resources of the social sciences for conducting contemporary social research is becoming apparent.[29]

Five issues are posed by the emergence of transactional and administrative digital data. Firstly, whereas interview-based social science methods elicit individual accounts and make these the centrepiece of social research, sometimes enshrined in theoretical framings such as rational choice theory which specifically justify such a methodologically individualistic focus, new data sources champion a networked account of social process. Transactional and administrative data records switches, as two or more parties do business together. Such data thereby allows a return to older models of associations, a kind of social analysis which is focused on ties and relationships. Although this has affinities with the associational sociology of Latour's contemporary actor–network theory, it might also be seen to recover the kind of field analysis which was evident in the sociometry of Kurt Lewin, the Tavistock Institute, and sociological research of the 1950s. These data sources hence allow post-individualist, non-humanist accounts of the social, where it is the play of transactions which can be studied in all their fluidity and dynamism.

Secondly, whereas conventional social science sources prioritize time, new data sources are spatial systems. I have traced how both interviews and surveys

---

[28] On the hostility of mathematicians to computer-generated proofs and the insistence that sentient human mathematicians needed to be able to demonstrate proofs, see MacKenzie (2008).

[29] See more generally, Savage and Burrows (2007).

elicit the possibility of detecting change not by comparing disparate sources, but through internal inspection of a unitary data or linked data set. It allows the prospect of recovering trends through internal analysis. I have also shown how these procedures involved the eclipse of landscaped and territorial approaches to the social, due to the way that they depend on abstracting sampled individuals from their environment, increasingly by using the national boundary as the unit in which societies were deemed to operate. This focus on the temporal dimensions of surveys has been strengthened in recent years through the British Household Panel Study and even more recently the UK Longitudinal Study, which interviews the same panel on an annual basis. By contrast, new data sources elicit networks and connections stretching across locations, hence producing new kinds of synthetic, mobile spatialities. By contrast, they have a different perspective on time, concerned not with the delineation of long-term trends, but rather the identification of factors which shape 'unknown futures'.[30] Such a perspective offers a shifting platform on which to view change as risk factors are modified. Digital data is not routinely archived and because it is not focused on the individual, it has no unifying unit which can allow for comparison over time.[31] It thus elicits a flat, pliable landscape.

Thirdly, whereas social science methods were dependent on sampling, and hence the generation of social knowledge on the basis of data derived from only a few people, new data sources work on the basis of entire systems of records. Through these means, there is a return to a problematic of 'whole populations', in which it is not enough to allow aggregate properties of the social world, but through which everyone and every transaction can be scanned, monitored, and subject to analysis and intervention. Every individual who uses a Tesco Clubcard has a unique 'DNA' profile which records their spending patterns, and those who analyse such data insist on its value in allowing a granular knowledge which surpasses aggregated social groups. This concern with whole populations also elicits a descriptive mode of analysis which clusters and classifies to produce social maps which are also moralized and normative. A good example of these is the extensive geo-demographic profiles which are widely used within marketing. It is instructive to note the similarities between the 'lifestyle' maps which are produced by these systems with the maps generated by Booth and Rowntree 100 years earlier.

Fourthly, survey and interview methods demand intervention from the expert social scientist. I have in this book shown that the idea that an academic can actually generate empirical data is one which was largely new in the post-war years, and eclipsed their older gentlemanly role. Nonetheless, the idea that experts had to intervene in the social world to gather appropriate data which would otherwise be absent and would limit social science was absolutely central to the emergence of critical social science. However, new digital sources create social

---

[30] See Amoore (2009).

[31] The detailed account of transactions collected as part of the Tesco loyalty card system, for instance, is not preserved for more than two years.

data as a by-product. One does not have to conduct special research on Amazon customers to identify which other books customers are likely to buy, through a questionnaire or interview. Such data is routinely gathered through normal transactional processes and allows customers to be bombarded with information about what people like themselves have bought.

Fifthly, these data sources also allow the public to be enrolled into data generation processes in active ways, with Web 2.0 technologies being especially important here. We once again need to remind ourselves that rather than being new, this is a return to the tradition of Mass-Observation and the various field research activities of the mid-twentieth century, all of which emphasized how the public could research themselves through projects of writing and observing. This current persisted well into the 1960s, perhaps most notably in the Consumers' Association journal *Which?*, which that relied on letters from the public to judge the quality of products. By contrast, the new repertoires of the post-war years sought to construct respondents in more passive forms so that their accounts could be rendered comparable and equivalent to each other.

These reflections lead us to note that digital data sources are in many respects not new, but actually mark the renewal of older forms of social research, concerned with mapping whole populations using (amongst other things) administrative data. Perhaps, then, I can conclude my book with a suggestion that a particular window on the social which was opened in the middle years of the twentieth century is now being closed, or at least stands as only one, by no means dominant, vantage point over the landscaped social. This does not mean that the social sciences will themselves simply collapse: rather, we might anticipate that just as literature lost the pulse of ordinary life in the post-war decades, so the social sciences might also, as the ordinary, mundane, and routine filler becomes mobilized by ever more powerful processes of digital collection and manipulation. Perhaps the social sciences can survive by recovering their earlier role (associated with Spencer and Hobhouse) as synthesizers and generalizers.

The merits of these digital data sources are the subject of much critical reflection.[32] From the perspective of many social scientists, these new data sources are wanting in numerous ways. They usually lack detailed information on people's social characteristics. It is difficult to use them to engage in causal analysis so that the effects of specific social factors can be readily delineated. In the words of Scott Lash, they do not permit the kind of critical analysis that social scientists typically want to engage in since it is not possible to go behind the surface data to question their terms or values.[33] These points are true, but only if one stays within the paradigmatic assumptions of the social sciences themselves, which I have shown are themselves mutable and contested. One of the aims of my historical analysis in this book is to insist on the need to historically ground methodological repertoires, in which we do not see any automatic or natural reasons why one method is better than another at capturing 'the social', but instead try to be alive

---

[32] See Savage and Burrows (2007), as well as the responses by Crompton (2008) and Webber(2009).
[33] Lash (2002).

to the contested devices and jurisdictions which might define it. The outcome of this contestation is not preordained. Survey data continues to command huge power in defining measures of national society and in delineating long-term processes and trends. Epidemiological and developmental research relies critically on long-term panel studies of this kind, and this is unlikely to change. Furthermore, social scientists themselves are now well represented within the corridors of power, and will lobby effectively and cogently to protect their jurisdiction.

The second half of the twentieth century was the golden age of the academic social sciences. It is the argument of this book that if we are to sustain and nurture the most positive aspects of this tradition – its preparedness to take nothing for granted, its refusal of conventional normative framings, and its determination to respect the everyday and the ordinary – we need to broaden our repertoire and recognize the changing stakes involved in the circuits of 'knowing capitalism'. We cannot simply carry on interviewing or sampling people as if the world is unchanged by fifty years of extensive social research and the emergence of new forms of organization and administration.[34] What we can do instead is a different kind of recovery, one which is alive to the critical elements of post-war 'demoralized' sociology and its subsequent role in defining the modern imagined nation.

The very success of the post-war social sciences has itself helped to generate a proliferation of classificatory devices which now change the very meaning of social identities and relationships. If there is a future for the social sciences, it consists in forming intellectual and technical alliances with ways of knowing – from the humanities, sciences, and informational systems – with which they are currently only weakly affiliated. Whether they have the inclination, aptitudes, or resources to do this remains to be seen.

---

[34] See Savage and Burrows (2007).

APPENDIX

Manuscript sources consulted

Qualidata Archive

SN 4852: Family and Social Network: Roles, Norms and External Relationships in Ordinary Urban Families, 1930–53 (Bott)

This research was among the first to attempt to study families, in their natural habitat – the home. It was concerned with two main areas of family organization: relationships to kin, friends, and neighbours; and the way in which husband and wife carry out their respective roles. Elizabeth Bott's *Family and Social Network* became a foundational social science text both for the sociology of the family, and in social network analysis. All records were consulted, including household notes and miscellaneous correspondence (Box 1). The study is discussed in greater detail in my paper 'Elizabeth Bott and the formation of modern British sociology'.

<http://www.esds.ac.uk/findingData/snDescription.asp?sn = 4852>

SN 4870: Brian Jackson collection (1962–83)

I have consulted a small collection of Jackson's material, namely Box C1 ('The working class'), C2 ('Working class community'), and C3/C4 ('The working class'). Other parts of his collection have been scanned. Some of the records I have used here were source material, or related correspondence, for his book *Working Class Community*, a study of social life and interaction in his hometown of Huddersfield. This book never enjoyed the success of his earlier study *Education and the Working Class* (whose records I have not consulted) and was indeed dismissed by one critic as 'romantic dilettantism'.

<http://www.esds.ac.uk/findingData/snDescription.asp?sn = 4870>

SN 4871: Affluent Worker in the Class Structure, 1961–2 (Goldthorpe and Lockwood)

The Affluent Worker project was undertaken during 1961–2 to test empirically the thesis of working class 'embourgeoisement'. Married male workers from three Luton factories were interviewed at work and then, once again, with their wives at home. Additionally, a sample of white-collar workers from the same factory was interviewed at home. This material formed the basis for one of the most influential sociological publications of the 1960s, *The Affluent Worker in the Class Structure*. Aside from the book, there were also two long reports based upon the project. Reviews of its arguments include Devine *Affluent Workers Revisited*, Heath, 'Class and political partisanship', Kavanagh, 'Ideology, sociology and the strategy of the British Labour Party', as well as my own 'Class identities in the 1960s'. In this, 227 household interviews examined, with a specific focus on questions on class identity and interviewer notes, stored in Boxes 7–12. I also examined thirty-eight pilot interviews with white-collar workers in Cambridge (Boxes 15 and 19).

<http://www.esds.ac.uk/findingData/snDescription.asp?sn = 4871>

SN 4863: Lifestyles and Patterns of Mobility in Hertfordshire Commuter Villages, 1964–5 (Pahl)

This data set includes research material collected from the 'Survey of the Wife in the Family, 1964–65', carried out as part of the activities of the University of Cambridge

Extra-Mural Studies Department. The collection includes thirty brief interview notes and three completed questionnaires, stored in box (Pahl, Box 15, Files 1–3).
<http://www.data-archive.ac.uk/findingData/snDescription.asp?sn = 4863>

SN 4864: Managers and Their Wives: A Study Of Career and Family Relationships in the Middle Classes, 1965–7 (Pahl)

Began as a project on the careers of male 'spiralist' managers, arising from course taught by Pahl at Cambridge, and was extended to include the views of their wives as a means of exploring how male mobility affected marital relations. This includes 172 questionnaire responses to male managers and their wives, with miscellaneous correspondence and papers. (Pahl, Box 15, Files 4–15). The study was written up as Pahl and Pahl, *Managers and Their Wives*.
<http://www.esds.ac.uk/findingData/snDescription.asp?sn = 4864>

SN 4877: Three Hertfordshire Villages Survey (Pahl)

The first social study of the influx of middle-class managerial and professional commuters to Hertfordshire villages, and the impact of this selective migration on rural communities. I examined the questionnaires and miscellaneous papers, contained in Box Pahl: 13. For publications arising, see Pahl 'Class and community', 'Education and social class', 'The two class village', and *Urbs in Rure*
<http://www.data-archive.ac.uk/findingData/snDescription.asp?sn = 4877>

SN 5514: Orientation to Work and Industrial Behaviour of Shipbuilding Workers on Tyneside, 1968–1970 (Richard Brown)

This was one of Richard Brown's – who was to become one of the most influential sociologists of work and employment – earliest studies. Engaging with the *Affluent Worker Study*, it examined the occupational roles and cultures of shipbuilding workers. It considered the technology and organization of production in a 'craft' industry, and the 'orientation to work' of workers coming from traditional working-class communities. The methodology included intensive observation in the work situation, interviews with a sample of shipbuilding workers and with other informants. I examined 193 interviews with shipbuilders and examined detailed notes on attitudes to place, belonging, and social class, and ethnographic notes and miscellaneous papers. No book monograph was ever produced, but some of the findings appeared in Brown and Brannen 'Social relations and social perspectives amongst shipbuilding workers' and Cousins and Brown 'Patterns of paradox: shipbuilding workers' images of society'.
<http://www.esds.ac.uk/findingData/publicationListForSN.asp?sn = 5514>

Mass-Observation Directives

Directives were sent out to a panel of Mass-Observers who would then write in with their comments and reflections. In general, it is entirely up to the correspondents how long and detailed their replies are, and what particular form they should take, though the early directives in 1939 are more structured, with correspondents often replying on a pro forma. The footnotes indicate the specific directive used (identified by the letter below). In A, these are full names which are anonymized here by using only the first letter of the name. From B onwards, a code number is used.

(A) 1939 Directive on social class and attitudes to place

107 Directive letters (men), sixty-seven letters (women)

(B) 1946 Directive on reading books at home, November 1946

1. Describe in detail the whereabouts of the books in your house.
2. List the books.
3. Attitude to paperback.
4. Attitudes to Americans and Russians.

Sampled women, Boxes H–P, and men

(C) 1948 Directive on morals and manners, May

1. What are your feelings about the manners, morals, and customs of the younger generation today (i.e. those born after 1918). How do you think they compare with those of the older generation?

2. Which three people alive today are doing the greatest good to the greatest number, and which three people are doing the greatest harm to the greatest number?

3 (a) What are your feelings about obscenity?

3 (b) What words do you consider obscene?

4 (a) What are the main things that embarrass you?

4 (b) Are there any questions which we have asked you in the past that have caused you embarrassment?

Twelve men and six women

(D) 1948 Directive on inconveniences, October–November

1. List six main inconveniences of modern living.
2. Has attitude to of any of the following things changed since the Second World War?
   (a) money
   (b) clothes
   (c) security
   (d) people in different social classes from yourself
   (e) sex
   (f) politics
3. Give your menu for all meals.
4. Do you consider that your present occupation allows you sufficient outlet for personal initiative or not?
   (a) If not, in what ways do you feel yourself to be restricted?
   (b) What sort of changes would increase your personal satisfaction in your work?

Fifty-three women and men, Boxes A–C

(E) 1948 on social class

1. Do you think of yourself as belonging to any particular social class? If so, which class?
2. Why would you say you belong to this class?
3. Give a list of ten jobs you consider typical middle class and ten jobs you consider typical working class.

(F) 1949, Directive on grumbles

1. List six main grumbles of modern life.
2. Do your immediate family do things as a group?
3. List the following radio personalities in order of liking: (a) Charlie Chester, (b) Richard Murdoch and Kenneth Horne, (c) Joy Nichols and Jimmy Edwards,

(d) Wilfred Pickles, (e) Ted Ray, (f) Jack Train, (j) Stewart Macpherson, (k) Bebe Ben Lyon and Vic Oliver – or name someone you like.
  4. Do you listen to crooners?

Thirteen directives sampled

(G) January 1949

  1. What value do you attach to the continued existence of the middle classes? Please discuss in as much detail as possible.
  2. What are the things you most like and dislike in yourself?

Sampled women B (sixty-one in total), men T, V (twenty in total)

(H) Spring 1990: On social identities

  1. Are there some major divisions in your own environment – class, race, gender, religion, 'culture', etc – that invite comment and are typical of contemporary society?
  2. What does it mean to be 'middle class'?
  3. What does it mean to be 'working class'?
  4. Do terms 'upper middle class' and 'lower middle class' correspond to anything in your experience? Please give examples.
  5. Can you give local instances of snobbishness?

(J) Autumn 1995

  1. Please start with your city, town, or village. It would be helpful if you explained your relationship with the place you describe.
  2. How long have you lived there? Where else have you lived? Please provide a rough list with dates if you can.
  3. If you are not living in the place of your birth, why did you move there? Have you moved a lot?
  4. Are you happy with where you live? Do you feel you belong? Do you expect to stay there for long?
  5. Describe your surroundings.
  6. What kind of image do you think your hometown has? What words would you use to describe it? Please distinguish between your own neighbourhood and the image of the whole town or city.
  7. Do you think the way other people think about your hometown is the same as the way you think about it? What kind of an image does it have, do you think, in newspapers and on TV or radio? Has there been much of a change over time? How do you think these images come about?

Sampled twenty-four women, A, B

Geoffrey Gorer Archive (University of Sussex)

Material consulted includes

  • post-war studies of culture and national character
  • published and unpublished writings, from 1955 to 1975

Paul Thompson's life history interviews with classic social scientists

Not in the public domain. I am grateful to Paul Thompson for showing the transcripts to me and allowing me to quote from them. Interviews with the following have been consulted in detail:

Frank Bechhofer
Colin Bell
Lenore Davidoff
David Lockwood
David Marsden
Ray Pahl
Margaret Stacey
Peter Townsend
W. M. Williams
Michael Young

Interviews with social scientists

I have conducted my own interviews or discussions with several sociologists, whom I thank for their enthusiasm and interest. These include the following:

Elizabeth Bott (telephone interview, Autumn 2002).
John Goldthorpe (interview, November 2008).
Email exchanges and discussion with Ronnie Frankenberg, Jennifer Platt, and Ray Pahl.

Bibliography

(a) Journals consulted (specific articles cited are indicated under (d) below)

British Journal of Sociology, 1950–69.
Encounter, 1954–69.
Human Relations, 1947–69.
Journal of the Royal Statistical Society, 1940–60.
New Society, 1962–70.
New Statesman, 1965–8.
Proceedings of the British Academy, 1945–69.
Sociological Review, 1945–69.
Times Literary Supplement, occasional.
The Yearbook of the Universities of the Commonwealth, 1949–50, London, Bell and Sons.
Twentieth Century, 1945–60.

(b) Government reports

Clapham Report (1946), 'To consider whether additional provision was necessary for research into social and economic questions', Parliamentary Paper.
Fulton Committee (1968), *The Report of the Committee on the Civil Service*, Cmnd 3638.
Plowden Report (1967), *Children and their Primary Schools, Report of the Central Advisory Council for Education, England*, London, HMSO.
Redcliffe-Maud Report (1969), *Royal Commission on Local Government in England, 1966–69*, Cmnd 4040.
Robbins Report (1963), *Higher Education, Report of Committee Appointed by the Prime Minister under the Chairmanship of Lord Robbins 1961–1963*, Cmnd 2154.

(c) Research monographs 1940–70

Abel-Smith, B., and Townsend, P. (1965), *The Poor and the Poorest: A New Analysis of the Ministry of Labour's Family Expenditure Surveys of 1953–54 and 1960*, London, Bell.
Abrams, M. (1951), *Social Surveys and Social Action*, London, Heinemann.
—— and Rose, R. (1960), *Must Labour Lose?*, Harmondsworth, Penguin.
Almond, G.A., and Verba, S. (1963), *The Civic Culture: Political Attitudes and Democracy in Five Nations*, Princeton, NJ, Princeton University Press.
Banton, M. (1960), *White and Coloured: The Behaviour of British People Towards Coloured Immigrants*, Piscataway, NJ, Rutgers University Press.
Bell, C. (1968), *Middle Class Families: Social and Geographical Mobility*, London, Routledge.
Birch, A.H. (ed) (1959), *Small Town Politics: A Study of Political Life in Glossop*, Oxford, Oxford University Press.
Blau, P., and Duncan, O.D. (1967), *The American Occupational Structure*, New York, Wiley.
Bonham, J. (1954), *The Middle Class Vote*, London, Faber.
Bott, E. (1971), *Family and Social Network*, 2nd edition, London, Tavistock.

Brennan, T., Cooney, E.W., and Pollins, H. (1954), *Social Change in South West Wales*, London, Watts & Co.

Bulmer, M. (ed) (1975), *Working Class Images of Society*, London, Routledge.

Butler, D. (1952), *The British General Election of 1951*, Basingstoke, Macmillan.

——and Stokes, D. (1969), *Political Change in Britain: Forces Shaping Electoral Choice*, Basingstoke, Macmillan.

Cousins, F., and Brown, R. (1975), 'Patterns of paradox: shipbuilding workers images of society', in M. Bulmer (ed), pp. 55–82.

Davies, E., and Rees, A. (1960), *Welsh Rural Communities*, Aberystwyth, University of Wales Press.

Davis, S.C.H. (1952), *Car Driving as an Art*, London, Illife and Sons.

Dennis, N., Henriques, F., and Slaughter, C. (1956), *Coal Is Our Life: An Analysis of a Yorkshire Mining Community*, London, Eyre & Spottiswoode.

Elias, N., and Scotson, J. (1965), *The Established and the Outsiders*, London, Frank Cass.

Eliot, T.S. (1949), *Notes on the Definition of Culture*, London, Harcourt.

Emmett, I. (1964), *A North Wales Parish*, London, Routledge.

Firth, R. (1956), *Families and their Relatives: Kinship in a Middle Class Sector of London*, London, Routledge.

Floud, J.E., Halsey, A.H., and Martin, F.M. (1956), *Social Class and Educational Opportunity*, London, Heinemann.

Frankenberg, R. (1957), *Village on the Border*, London, Cohen & West.

——(1966), *Communities in Britain*, London, Penguin.

Frieden, B. (1963), *The Feminine Mystique* New York, W.W. Norton.

Glass, D.V. (ed) (1954), *Social Mobility in Britain*, London, Routledge & Kegan Paul.

Goldthorpe, J.H., Lockwood, D., Bechhofer, F., and Platt, J. (1968*a*), *The Affluent Worker: Industrial Attitudes and Behaviour*, Cambridge, Cambridge University Press.

————————(1968*b*), *The Affluent Worker: Political Attitudes and Behaviour*, Cambridge, Cambridge University Press.

————————(1969), *The Affluent Worker in the Class Structure*, Cambridge, Cambridge University Press.

Gorer, G. (1948), *The American People: A Study in National Character*, New York, Norton.

—— (1955), *Exploring English Character*, London, Cresset Press.

Halsey, A.H. (1996), *No Discouragement: An Autobiography*, London, Macmillan.

——and Trow, M. (1971), *British Academics*, Cambridge, MA, Harvard University Press.

Hargreaves, D. (1967), *Social Relations in a Secondary School*, London, Routledge.

Hyman, H.H. (1955), *Survey Design and Analysis*, New York, Free Press.

Jackson, B. (1968), *Working Class Community*, London, Routledge.

——and Marsden, D. (1965), *Education and the Working Class*, Harmondsworth, Penguin.

Jacques, E. (1951), *The Changing Culture of the Factory: A Study of Authority and Participation in an Industrial Setting*, London, Tavistock.

Jones, D. Caradog. (1949), *Social Surveys*, London, Hutchinson.

Kerr, M. (1957), *The People of Ship Street*, London, Routledge.

Lacey, C. (1970), *Hightown Grammar: The School as Social System*, Manchester, Manchester University Press.

Lockwood, D. (1957), *The Blackcoated Worker*, London, Allen & Unwin.

Lynd, H., and Lynd, S. (1929), *Middletown: A Study in American Culture*, New York, Harcourt, Brace.

———(1937), *Middletown in Transition: A Study in Cultural Conflicts*, New York, Harcourt, Brace.

Madge, C. (1967), *The Origins of Scientific Sociology*, New York, Free Press.

Mann, M. (1973), *Consciousness and Action Amongst the Western Working Class*, London, Macmillan.

Marshall, T. (1951), *Citizenship and Social Class and Other Essays*, Oxford University Press.

Moser, C. (1958), *Survey Methods in Social Investigation*, London, Heinemann.

Pahl, R. (1965), *Urbs in Rure*, London, LSE, Geographical Papers.

———(1970*a*), *Whose City? And Other Essays on Sociology and Planning*, London, Longman.

———(1970*b*), *Patterns of Urban Life*, London, Longmans.

Perkin, H. (1970), *New Universities in the United Kingdom*, OECD.

Platt, J. (1971), *Social Research in Bethnal Green: An Evaluation of the Work of the Institute of Community Studies*, London, Macmillan.

Rees, A. (1951), *Life in a Welsh Countryside*, Cardiff, University of Wales Press.

Robb, J.H. (1954*a*), *Working Class Anti-Semite: A Psychological Study in a London Borough*, London, Tavistock.

Rosser, C., and Harris, C. (1960), *The Family and Social Change*, London, Routledge.

Rowntree, B.S. (1941), *Poverty and Progress: A Second Social Survey of York*, London, Longmans.

———(2000), *Poverty: A Study of Town Life*, Bristol, Policy Press (1st edition 1901).

———and Lavers, G. (1951), *Poverty and the Welfare State: A Third Social Survey of York Dealing only with Economic Questions*, London, Longmans.

Runciman, W.G. (1966), *Relative Deprivation and Social Justice: A Study of Attitudes to Social Inequality in Twentieth Century England*, London, Routledge.

Sampson, A. (1962), *The Anatomy of Britain*, London, Hodder & Stoughton.

Smith, H.L. (1930–5), *New Survey of London Life and Labour*, 9 volumes, London, Kings.

Snow, C.P. (1969), *The Two Cultures and a Second Look*, Cambridge, Cambridge University Press.

Spender, S. (1963), *The Struggle of the Modern*, Berkeley, CA, University of California Press.

Stacey, M. (1960), *Tradition and Change*, Oxford, Oxford University Press.

———(1969), *Methods of Social Research*, Oxford, Pergamon.

———Batstone, E., Bell, C., and Murcott, A. (1975), *Power, Persistence and Change: A Second Study of Banbury*, London, Routledge.

Taylor, A.J.P. (1961), *The Origins of the Second World War*, Harmondsworth, Penguin.

Trevor-Roper, H. (1947), *The Last Days of Hitler*, London, Macmillan.

Trevor-Roper, H. (1953), *The Gentry, 1540–1640*, Cambridge, Cambridge University Press.

Vezey-Fitzgerald, B. (n.d., *c*.1950), *The British Countryside in Pictures*, London, Oldham.

Webb, S., and Webb, B. (1932), *Methods of Social Study*, Cambridge, Cambridge University Press.

Williams, R. (1958), *Culture and Society*, London and New York, Columbia University Press.

———(1960), *Border Country*, London, Chatto & Windus.

———(1961), *The Long Revolution*, London and New York, Columbia University Press.

Williams, W.M. (1956), *Sociology of an English Village: Gosforth*, London, Routledge.

Wootton, B. (1959), *Social Science and Social Pathology*, London, Allen & Unwin.

Young, M.D., and Willmott, P. (1957), *Family and Kinship in East London*, London, Routledge.

(d) Novels, memoirs, and journal papers from 1940 to 1970 (including reference to the edition cited here if different from the original)

Abel-Smith, B. (1961), 'Research Report No. 4: Department of Social Administration, London School of Economics and Political Science', *Sociological Review*, 10(3), 329–42.

Anderson, P. (1964), 'Origins of the Present Crisis', *New Left Review*, I(23).

Annan, N. (1960–1), 'Peck Orders Among Universities', *Universities Quarterly*, 351–9.

Arnold, G. (1955), 'Collectivism Reconsidered', *British Journal of Sociology*, 6(1), 1–15.

Ballard, J.G. (2008), *Miracles of Life*, London, Harper Perennials.

Barnes, J. (1954), 'Class and Committees in a Norwegian Island Parish', *Human Relations*, 7, 39–58.

Bastide, R. (1952), 'The Field, Methods, and Problems of the Basic Personality School', *British Journal of Sociology*, 3(1), 1–13.

Beveridge, W. (1946), 'Science and the Social Sciences', *Universities Quarterly*, 1(3), 235–42.

Bott, E. (1954), 'The Concept of Class as a Reference Group', *Human Relations*, 7(3), 259–85.

Briggs, A. (1962), 'University Social Studies: The Sussex Idea', *New Statesman*, 3, 20–2.

Brown, R.K. (1974), 'Attitudes, expectations and social perspectives of shipbuilding apprentices', in Timothy Leggatt (ed), *Sociological Theory and Survey Research. Institutional Change and Social Policy in Great Britain*, London, Sage, pp. 109–51.

Brown, R. and Brannen, P. (1970), 'Social Relations and Social Perspectives amongst Shipbuilding Workers – A Preliminary Statement, Parts 1 and 2', *Sociology*, 4(1), 71–84, and 4(2), 197–211.

——Cousins, J., and Samphire, M. (1973), 'Leisure in work: The occupational culture of shipbuilding workers', in Michael Smith, Stanley Parker, and Cyril Smith (eds), *Leisure and Society in Britain*, London, Allen Lane, pp. 97–110.

Calder, N. (1967*a*), 'Computers on Tap', *New Statesman*, 21 April, 542.

Calder, N. (1967*b*), 'The Scientific Third Dimension', *New Statesman*, 8 September.

Castle, W.M., and Gittus, E. (1957), 'The Distribution of Social Defects in Liverpool', *Sociological Review*, 5, 43–64.

Chambers, R. (1958), 'Family and Social Network' (book review), *British Journal of Sociology*, 9(2), 186–7.

Cole, G.D.H. (1947), 'The Teaching of Social Studies in British Universities', *Universities Quarterly*, 2(1), 260–9.

Cotton, H., and Heron, D. (1948), 'The Collection of Morbidity Data from Hospitals', *Journal of the Royal Statistical Society*, 111(1), 14–43.

Cousins, J., and Brown, R. (1975), 'Patterns of paradox: Shipbuilding workers' images of society', in M. Bulmer (ed), *Working-Class Images of Society*, London, Routledge & Kegan Paul, pp. 55–82.

Curle, A. (1947), 'Transitional Communities and Social Re-connection: A Follow up Study of Civil Resettlement of British Prisoners of War', *Human Relations*, 1, 43–52.

——and Trist, E. (1947), 'Transitional Communities and Social Re-connection: A Follow up Study of Civil Resettlement of British Prisoners of War', pt 2, *Human Relations*, 258–84.

Ellis, A.E. (1958), *The Rack*, London, Heinemann (Penguin 1961).

Evans Pritchard, E. (1967), 'Social Anthropology and the Universities in Great Britain', *Universities Quarterly*, March, 167–81.

Eysenck, H.J. (1951), 'Primary Social Attitudes as Related to Social Class and Political Party', *British Journal of Sociology*, 2(3), 198–209.

Festinger, L., Cartwright, D., Barber, K., Flieschel, J., Gottsdanker, J., Keysen, A., and Leavitt, G. (1948), 'A Study of Rumour: Its Origin and Spread', *Human Relations*, 1(4), 464–87.

Finer, S. (1954), 'A Profile of Science Fiction', *Sociological Review*, 2, 239–56.

Florence, P.S. (1950), 'Patterns in Recent Social Research', *British Journal of Sociology*, 1(3), 221–39.

Fowles, J. (2003), *The Journals, vol. 1*, London, Vintage.

Glass, D.V. (1950), 'The Application of Social Research', *British Journal of Sociology*, 1(1), 17–30.

Goldthorpe, J.H. (1970), 'L'Image des classes chezles travailleurs manuel aisés', *Revue Francaise de Sociologie*, 11, 3.

——and Lockwood, D. (1963), 'Affluence and the British Class Structure', *Sociological Review*, 11, 2.

Gray, P.J., and Corlett, T. (1950), 'Sampling for the Social Survey', *Journal of the Royal Statistical Society*, 113(2), 150–206.

Greenwood, M. (1946), 'Proceedings of a Meeting of the Royal Statistical Society held on July 16th, 1946', *Journal of the Royal Statistical Society*, 109(4), 325–78.

Gross, J. (1962), 'Culture and the Card Index', *New Society*, (11 October), 32.

Halsey, A.H. (1954), 'Social Mobility in Britain – a Review', *Sociological Review*, 2, 169–77.

Harvey, A. (1967), 'A Million Poor Children', *New Statesman*, 14 July.

Hill, J.M.M., and Trist, E.L. (1953), 'A Consideration of Industrial Accidents as a Means of Withdrawal from the Work Situation', *Human Relations*, 6(4), 357–80.

Hobsbawm, E.J. (2002), *Interesting Times*, London, Allen Lane.

Jobling, R.C. (1969), 'Some Sociological Aspects of University Development in England', *Sociological Review*, 17(1), 11–26.

Kelvin, R.P. (1963), 'What Sort of People – II', *New Society*, 33, 11–13.

Kempthorne, O. (1946), 'The Use of a Punched-Card System for the Analysis of Survey Data, with Special Reference to the Analysis of the National Farm Survey', *Journal of the Royal Statistical Society*, 109(3), 284–95.

Larkin, P. (1999), *Selected Letters of Phillip Larkin, 1940–1985* (edited by Anthony Thwaite) London, Faber.

Lewin, K. (1947), 'Frontiers in Group Dynamics: Concept, Method and Reality in Social Science; Social Equilibria and Social Change', *Human Relations*, 1, 1.

Little, K. (1960), 'Research Report No. 2: Department of Social Anthropology, University of Edinburgh', *Sociological Review*, 8(2), 255–66.

Lockwood, D. (1966), 'Sources of Variation in Working Class Images of Society', *Sociological Review*, 14, 249–67.

Logan, R.F., and Goldberg, E.M. (1953), 'Turning Eighteen in a London Suburb', *British Journal of Sociology*, 4(4), 323–46.

Marshall, T. (1953), 'Conference of the British Sociological Association, 1953', *British Journal of Sociology*, 4, 201–9.

——(1960), 'Review', *British Journal of Sociology*, 11(1), 82–6.

Martin, D. (1954), 'Some subjective elements of class', in D.V. Glass (ed), *Social Mobility in Britain*, London, Routledge.

McLachlan, N. (1962), 'Why No Social Research Council', *New Society*, 4 (25 October), 14–15.

Menzies, I. (1950), 'Factors Affecting Family Breakdown in Urban Communities', *Human Relations*, 3(4), 363–74.

Miller, K. (ed) (1968), *Writing in England Today: The Last Fifteen Years*, Harmondsworth, Penguin.

Morris, C.R. (1960–1), 'Claims, Ancient and Modern', *Universities Quarterly*, 15(5).

Moser, C. (1949), 'The Use of Sampling in Great Britain', *Journal of the American Statistical Association*, 44(246), 231–59.

——(1951), 'Interviewer Bias', *Revue de l'Institut International de Statistique/Review of the International Statistical Institute*, 19(1), 28–40.

——(1973), 'Staffing in the Government Statistical Service', *Journal of the Royal Statistical Society*, Series A (General), 136(1), 75–88.

Orwell, G. (2001*a*), 'The lion and the unicorn', in G. Orwell (ed), *Orwell's England*, London, Penguin.

——(2001*b*), 'Your questions answered', in G. Orwell (ed), *Orwell's England*, London, Penguin, pp. 217–18.

Pahl, R.E. (1968), 'Newcomers in town and country', in L.M. Munby (ed), *East Anglian Studies*, Cambridge, Heffer.

Perkin, H. (1972), 'University Planning in the 1960s', *Higher Education*, February, 111–20.

Platt, J. (1971), 'Variations in Answers to Different Questions on Perceptions of Class', *Sociological Review*, 19, 409–41.

Powys, J.C. (1932), *A Glastonbury Romance*, London, The Bodley Head.

Priestley, J.B. (1929), *The Good Companions*, London, Heinemann.

——(1934), *English Journey*, London, Penguin (1977 edition).

Rice, A.E., Hill, J.M.M., and Trist, E.L. (1950), 'The Representation of Labour Turnover as a Social Process', *Human Relations*, 3(4), 349–72.

Richardson, L.E. (1947), 'Social Science in the Gap between the Royal Society and the British Academy', *Nature*, 159(4034), 269.

Robb, J.H. (1954*b*), 'Clinical Studies in Marriage and the Family: A Symposium on Methods', *British Journal of Medical Psychology*, XXVI, parts 3 and 4, 215–21.

Ross, K.H. (1948), 'Working Class Clothing Consumption 1937–38', *Journal of the Royal Statistical Society*, 111(2), 145–60.

Scott, W.H. and Mays, J.B. (1960), 'Research Report No. 1: Department of Social Science, the University of Liverpool', *Sociological Review*, 8(1), 109–17.

Shils, E. (1955), 'The Intellectuals', *Encounter*.

——and Young Michael, (1953), 'The Meaning of the Coronation', *Sociological Review*, 1(2), 63–81.

Simey, T. (1953), 'The Analysis of Social Problems', *Sociological Review*, NS 1 (1), 71–86.

Simon, Lord (1947), 'The Social Sciences: a Symposium', *Universities Quarterly*, 2(1).

Sprott, W.J.H. (1952), 'Principia Sociologica', *British Journal of Sociology*, 3(3), 203–21.

Stone, F.S. (1947–8), 'Research in the Social Sciences', *Universities Quarterly*, 2(1), 270–80.

Trist, E.L., and Bamforth, K.W. (1951), 'Some Social and Psychological Consequences of the Longwall Method of Coal Mining', *Human Relations*, 4(1), 3–38.

Tynan, K. (1994), *Kenneth Tynan Letters*, London, Weidenfeld & Nicolson.

Watt, I. (1963–4), 'The Seminar', *Universities Quarterly*, 161, 369–89.

Waugh, E. (1955), 'Review of Mitford', *Encounter*, 5(5).

Weeks, H.T. (1947), 'Statistics and the Statistician in Industry', *Journal of the Royal Statistical Society*, 110(2), 95–107.

Willmott, P., and Young, M. (1961), 'Research Report No. 3: Institute of Community Studies, London', *Sociological Review*, 9(2), 203–13.

Wilson, A.T.M. (1948), 'Some Reflections and Suggestions on the Treatment of Marital Problems', *Human Relations*, 233–52.

Wilson, C. (2004), *Dreaming to Some Purpose*, London, Arrow.

Wilson, R. (1960), 'Un-conformity in the Affluent Society', *Sociological Review*, 8(1), 119–28.

Wyndham, J. (2008*a*), *The Day of the Triffids*, London, Penguin (1st edition 1951).
—— (2008*b*), *The Midwich Cuckoos*, London, Penguin (1st edition 1957).

(e) Other secondary sources

Abbott, A. (1988), *The System of Professions*, Chicago, University of Chicago Press.
—— (2001), *Time Matters*, Chicago, University of Chicago Press.
Abercrombie, N., and Longhurst, B.J. (1998), *Audiences: A Sociological Theory of Performance and Imagination*, London, Sage.
Abrams, P. (1968), *The Origins of British Sociology, 1830–1914*, Chicago, University of Chicago Press.
Acland, H. (1980), 'Research as stage management: The case of the Plowden Committee', in M. Bulmer (ed), *Social Research and Royal Commissions*, 34–57.
Addison, P. (1975), *The Road to 1945: British Politics and the Second World War*, London, Cape.
Agar, J. (2003), *The Government Machine*, Boston, MA, MIT Press.
Amin, A., and Thrift, N. (2002), *Cities: Reimagining the Urban*, Cambridge, Polity Press.
Amoore, L. (2009), 'Lines of Sight, on the Visualisation of Unknown Futures', *Citizenship Studies*, 13, 27–30.
Anderson, B. (1982), *Imagined Communities*, London, Verso.
Annan, N. (1991), *Our Age: The Generation That Made Post-War Britain*, London, Fontana.
—— (1999), *The Dons: Mentors, Eccentrics and Geniuses*, London, Harper Collins.
Appadurai, A. (1996), *Modernity at Large*, Minneapolis, MN, University of Minnesota Press.
Atkinson, W. (2007), 'Beck, Individualization and the Death of a Class: a Critique', *British Journal of Sociology*, 58(3), 349–66.
Barker, P. (ed) (2006), *Arts in Society*, Nottingham, Five Leaves.
Bauman, Z. (1998*a*), *Work, Consumerism and the New Poor*, Milton Keynes, Open University Press.
—— (1998*b*), *Globalisation: The Human Consequence*, Oxford, Blackwell.
Bechhofer, F. (2004), 'Qualitative Data and the Affluent Worker: A Missed Opportunity?' in P. Thompson and L. Corti (eds), 'Special Issue – Celebrating Classic Sociology: Pioneers of Contemporary British Qualitative Research', *Social Research Methodology*, 7(1), 45–50.
Beck, U. (1992), *Risk Society*, London, Sage.
—— (2002*a*), *What Is Globalization?* Cambridge, Polity Press.
—— (2002*b*), 'The Cosmopolitan Society and Its Enemies', *Theory, Culture and Society*, 19, 17–44.
Bell, C., and Newby, H. (1977), *Doing Sociological Research*, London, Allen & Unwin.
Bellah, R., Madsen, R., Sullivan, W.M., Swidler, A., and Tipton, S. (1985), *Habits of the Heart: Individualism and Commitment in American Life*, Berkeley, CA, University of California Press.
Benjamin, W. (2003), 'On the concept of history', in *Walter Benjamin: Selected Writings, vol. 4*, Cambridge, MA, Harvard University Press.
Bennett, T. (2007), 'Making Culture, Changing Society: The Perspective of Culture Studies', *Cultural Studies*, 21(4–5), 610–29.
—— and Frow, J. (eds) (2008), *Handbook of Cultural Analysis*, London, Sage.
—— Savage, M., Silva, E.B., Warde, A., Gayo-Cal, M., and Wright, D. (2009), *Culture, Class, Distinction*, London, Routledge.
Bertaux, D., and Bertaux-Wiame, I. (1981), 'Life stories in the baker's trade', in D. Bertaux (ed), *Biography and Society*, London, Sage.
—— and Thompson, P. (1997), *Pathways to Social Class*, Oxford, Clarendon Press.

Billig, M. (1995), *Banal Nationalism*, London, Sage.

Black, L. (2003), *The Political Culture of the Left in Affluent Britain, 1951–1964*, Basingstoke, Macmillan.

——and Pemberton, H. (eds) (2004), *An Affluent Society: Britain's Post-war 'Golden Age' Revisited*, Aldershot, Ashgate.

Blokland, T. (2003), *Urban Bonds*, Cambridge, Polity Press.

——and Savage, M. (eds) (2008), *Networked Urbanism: Social Capital on the Ground*, Aldershot, Ashgate.

Boltanski, L., and Chiapello, E. (2003), *New Spirits of Capitalism*, London, Verso.

Booker, C. (1970), *The Neo-philiacs: Revolution in English Life in the Fifties and Sixties*, Boston, MA, Gambit Inc.

Bott-Spillius, E. (1988), *Melanie Klein Today*, London, Routledge.

—— (2005), 'Anthropology and Psychoanalysis: A Personal Concordance', *Sociological Review*, 53(4), 658–71.

Bottero, W. (2004), *Stratification: Social Division and Inequality*, London, Routledge.

Bourdieu, P. (1985), *Distinction*, London, Routledge.

——(2001), *Pascalian Meditations*, Cambridge, Polity Press.

——(2002), *Social Structures of the Economy*, Cambridge, Polity Press.

Bradley, H. (1999), *Gender and Power in the Workplace*, London, Palgrave.

Bulmer, M. (1979), *Censuses, Surveys and Privacy*, London, Macmillan.

——(ed) (1988), *Social Research and Royal Commissions*, London, Allen & Unwin.

——Banting, K.G., Blume, S., Carley, M., and Weiss, C. (1986), *Social Science and Social Policy*, London, Allen & Unwin.

——Bales, K., Kish, K. (eds) (1992), *The Social Survey in Historical Perspective*, Cambridge, Cambridge University Press.

Burawoy, M., Blum, J., George, S., Gille, Z., Gowan, T., Haney, L., Klawiter, M., Lopez, S., O'Riann, S., and Thayer, M. (2000), *Global Ethnography: Forces, Connections and Imaginations in a Postmodern World*, Berkeley, CA, University of California Press.

Burk, K. (2000), *Troublemaker: The Life and History of A.J.P. Taylor*, New Haven, CT, Yale University Press.

Butler, T., and Robson, G. (2003), *London Calling: The Middle Classes and the Remaking of Inner London*, Oxford, Berg.

Cain, P., and Hopkins, T. (2001), *British Imperialism, 1688–2000*, 2nd edition, London, Longmans.

Calder, A. (1992), *The People's War, 1939–1945*, London, Pimlico.

Callon, M. (ed) (1998), *The Laws of the Markets*, Oxford, Blackwell.

Carey, J. (1992), *The Intellectuals and the Masses: Pride and Prejudice Among the Literary Intelligentsia, 1880–1939*, London, Faber.

Castells, M. (1996), *The Rise of the Network Society*. Oxford: Blackwell.

——(1998), *End of the Millennium*, Oxford, Blackwell.

Charlesworth, S. (2000), *A Phenomenology of Working Class Experience*, Cambridge, Cambridge University Press.

Clark, J., Modgil, C., and Modgil, S. (eds) (1990), *John H Goldthorpe: Consensus and Controversy*, Brighton, Falmer.

Clarke, J. Critcher, C., and Johnston, R. (eds) (1979), *Working Class Culture*, London, Hutchinson.

Clapson, M. (1998), *Invincible New Suburbs, Brave New Towns: Social Change and Urban Dispersal in Post-War England*, Manchester, Manchester University Press.

Cohen, A.P. (1985), *The Symbolic Construction of Community*, London, Tavistock.

—— (ed) (1988), *Belonging: Identity and Social Organization in British Rural Communities*, Manchester, Manchester University Press.

—— (2005), 'Village on the Border, Anthropology at the Crossroads – The Significance of a Classic British Ethnography', *Sociological Review*, 53(4), 603–20.

Collini, S. (1979), *Liberalism and Sociology: L.T. Hobhouse and Political Argument in England, 1880–1914*, Cambridge, Cambridge University Press.

—— (1999), *English Pasts: Essays in Culture and History*, Oxford, Oxford University Press.

—— (2006), *Absent Minds*, Oxford, Clarendon Press.

Connor, S. (2004), 'Modernity and myth', in L. Marcus and P. Nicholls (eds), *The Cambridge History of Twentieth Century English Literature*, pp. 251–68.

Corti, L. (2004), 'Archiving qualitative data', in M. Lewis-Beck et al. (eds), *The Sage Encyclopaedia of Social Science Research Methods, Vol. 1*, London, Sage.

Cosgrove, D. (1998), *Social Formation and Symbolic Landscape*, Madison, WI, University of Wisconsin Press.

—— Roscoe, B., and Rycroft, S. (1996), 'Landscape and Identity at Ladybower Reservoir and Rutland Water', *Transactions of the Institute of British Geographers*, 21, 534–51.

Coxon, A., and Jones, P.D.M. (1986), *Images of Social Stratification: Occupational Structures and Class*, London, Sage.

Crompton, R. (1998), *Class and Stratification*, 2nd edition, Cambridge, Polity Press.

—— (2008), 'Forty Years of Sociology: Some Comments', *Sociology*, 42(6), 1281–27.

Cronin, J.E. (1984), *Labour and Society in Britain, 1918–1979*, New York, Schocken Books.

Crow, G. (2008), 'Recent Rural Community Studies', *International Journal of Social Research Methodology*, 11(2), 131–9.

—— and Allan, G. (1994), *Community Life an Introduction to Local Social Relations*, Hemel Hempsted, Harvester Wheatsheaf.

Cunnison, S. (1982), 'The Manchester factory studies, the social context, bureaucratic organisation, sexual divisions and their influence on patterns of accommodation between workers and management', in R. Frankenberg (ed), pp. 94–139.

Dahrendorf, R. (1995), *LSE: A History of the London School of Economics and Political Science*, Oxford, Oxford University Press.

Dale, A., Arber, S., and Proctor, M. (1988), *Doing Secondary Analysis*, London, Unwin Hyman.

Deleuze, G., and Guattari, F. (1987), *A Thousand Plateaux: Capitalism and Schizophrenia*, Minneapolis, MN, University of Minnesota Press.

Dennis, N., and Halsey, A.H. (1988), *English Ethical Socialism: Thomas More to R.H. Tawney*, Oxford, Clarendon Press.

Desrosieres, A. (1998), *The Politics of Large Numbers: A History of Statistical Reasoning*, Cambridge, Harvard University Press.

Devine, F. (1992), *Affluent Workers Revisited*, Edinburgh, Edinburgh University Press.

—— (2003), 'Talking about class in Britain', in F. Devine and M. Walters (eds), *Social Inequalities in Comparative Perspective*, Oxford, Blackwell, pp. 191–213.

—— Savage, M., Crompton, R., and Scott, J. (eds) (2004), *Class, Cultures and Lifestyles*, Basingstoke, Palgrave.

Dirks, N. (2003), *Castes of Mind*, Princeton, NJ, Princeton University Press.

Donzelot, J. (1980), *The Policing of Families*, London, Hutchinson.

Edgerton, D. (2006), *Warfare State: Britain, 1920–1970*, Cambridge, Cambridge University Press.

Edwards, J. (2000), *Born and Bred*, Oxford, Clarendon Press.

Emmett, I., and Morgan, D.H.J. (1982), 'Max Gluckman and the Manchester shop floor ethnographies', in R. Frankenberg (ed), pp. 140–65.

ESRC. (2006), *Demographic Review of the UK Social Sciences*, Swindon, ESRC.

Fielding, N. (2004), 'Getting the most from archived qualitative data: epistemological, practical and professional obstacles', in P. Thompson and L. Corti (eds), pp. 97–104.

Floud, R., and Johnson, P. (2004), *The Cambridge Economic History of Modern Britain, vol. 3, Structural Change and Growth, 1939–2000*, Cambridge, Cambridge University Press.

Flynn, T. (2003), 'Foucault's mapping of history', in G. Gutting (ed), *The Cambridge Companion to Foucault*, Cambridge, Cambridge University Press, pp. 29–48.

Foucault, M. (1971), *The Order of Things*, London, Tavistock.

——(1977), *Discipline and Punish: The Birth of the Prison*, London, Allen Lane.

——(1979), *The History of Sexuality, vol. 1*, London, Allen Lane.

Frankenberg, R. (ed) (1982*a*), *Custom and Conflict in British Society*, Manchester, Manchester University Press.

——(1982*b*), 'A social anthropology for Britain?', in R. Frankenberg (ed), 1–35.

Furbank, P.N. (1986), *Unholy Pleasure: The Idea of Social Class*, Oxford, Oxford University Press.

Fyfe, G. (2000), *Art, Power and Modernity: English Art Institutions 1750–1950*, London, Leicester University Press.

Garfield, S. (2004), *Our Hidden Lives: The Everyday Diaries of a Forgotten Britain, 1945–1948*, London, Ebury.

Gayo-Cal, M. (2006), 'Leisure and Participation in Britain', *Cultural Trends*, 15(2/3), 175–92.

——Savage, M., and Warde, A. (2006), 'A cultural map of the United Kingdom, 2003', *Cultural Trends*, 15(2/3), 213–39.

Gerlach, N., and Hamilton, S. (2003), 'A History of Social Science Fiction', *Science Fiction Studies*, 161–73.

Giddens, A. (1971), *Capitalism and Modern Social Theory*, Cambridge, Cambridge University Press.

——(1991), *The Consequences of Modernity*, Cambridge, Polity Press.

Gilloch, G. (1997), *Myth and Metropolis: Walter Benjamin and the City*, Oxford, Polity Press.

Glaser, B., and Strauss, A. (1968), *The Discovery of Grounded Theory: Strategies for Qualitative Research*, London, Weidenfeld & Nicolson.

Gluckman, M. (1971), preface to Bott, *Family and Social Network* 2nd edition, London, Tavistock.

Goldmann, L. (2002), *Science, Reform and Politics in Victorian Britain: The Social Science Association 1857–1886*, Cambridge, Cambridge University Press.

Goldthorpe, J.H. (1983), 'Women and Class Analysis: A Defence of the Conventional View', *Sociology*.

——(1987), *Social Mobility and the Class Structure in Modern Britain*, Oxford, Clarendon Press, (1st edition 1980).

——(1991), 'The Uses of History in Sociology: Reflections on Some Current Tendencies', *British Journal of Sociology*, 42(2), 211–31.

——(2007), *On Sociology*, Chicago, IL, University of Chicago Press.

Green, S. (2005), *Notes from the Balkans*, Princeton, NJ, Princeton University Press.

Griffiths, J.L. (2003), *NFER: The First Fifty Years, 1946–1996*, Slough, National Foundation for Educational Research.

Hacking, I. (2006), 'Making Up People', *London Review of Books*, 17 August.

Halford, S., Savage, M., and Witz, A. (1997), *Gender, Career and Organization*, Basingstoke, Macmillan.

Hall, S. (1972), 'The Social Eye of *Picture Post*', *Working Papers in Cultural Studies*, 2.

Halsey, A.H. (1987), 'Plowden: History and Prospect', *Oxford Review of Education*, 13(1).

—— (1992), *The Decline of Donnish Dominion*, Oxford, Clarendon Press.

—— (2004), *A History of Sociology in Britain*, Oxford, Clarendon Press.

—— and Webb, J. (eds) (2000), *Twentieth Century British Social Trends*, Basingstoke, Macmillan.

Hammersley, M. (1997), 'Qualitative Data Archiving: Some Reflections on its Prospects and Problems', *Sociology*, 31(1), 131–42.

—— (2004), 'Towards a Usable Past for Qualitative Research', in P. Thompson and L. Corti (eds), pp. 19–28.

Han, B. (2001), *Foucault's Critical Project*, Stanford, CA, Stanford University Press.

Harrison, B. (2009), *Seeking a Role: The United Kingdom 1951–1970*, Oxford, Clarendon Press.

Heimann, J. (2003), *The Most Offending Soul Alive: Tom Harrrison and his Remarkable Life*, London, Aurum.

Hennessy, P. (2006), *Having It So Good: Britain in the Fifties*, London, Allen Lane.

Hennock, E.P. (1976), 'Poverty and Social Theory: The Experience of the Eighteen Eighties', *Social History*, 67–91.

Higgs, E. (2004), *The Information State in England*, Basingstoke, Macmillan.

Hilton, M. (2008), *Consumerism in Twentieth Century Britain*, Cambridge, Cambridge University Press.

Hoggart, R. (1957), *The Uses of Literacy*, Harmondsworth, Penguin.

Hubble, N. (2006), *Mass Observation and Everyday Life: Theory, Culture, History*, Basingstoke, Palgrave Macmillan.

Ignatieff, M. (1998), *Isaiah Berlin: A Life*, London, Chatto & Windus.

Igo, S. (2007), *The Averaged American: Surveys, Citizens and the Making of a Mass Public*, Cambridge, MA, Harvard University Press.

Inglehart, R. (1990), *Culture Shift in Advanced Industrial Societies*, Princeton, NJ, Princeton University Press.

—— (1997), *Modernization and Post-Modernization: Cultural, Economic and Political Change in 43 countries*, Princeton, NJ, Princeton University Press.

Ingold, T. (2000), *The Perception of the Environment: Essays on Livelihood, Dwelling and Skill*, London, Routledge.

Jager, M. (1986), 'Class definition and the aesthetics of gentrification: Victoriana in Melbourne', in P. Williams and N. Smith (eds), *Gentrification of the City*, London, Allen & Unwin, pp. 78–91.

James, O. (2007), *Affluenza*, London, Vermilion.

Jeffrey, T. (1999), 'Mass-Observation: a short history', *Mass-Observation Archive Occasional Paper*, No. 10, University of Sussex Library.

Johnson, T. (1972), *Professions and Power*, Basingstoke, Macmillan.

Jolly, M. (2001), 'Historical Entries: Mass-Observation Diarists, 1937–2001', *New Formations*, 44(Autumn), 110–27.

Joyce, P. (1990), *Visions of the People*, Cambridge, Cambridge University Press.

—— (2003), *The Rule of Freedom: Liberalism and the Modern City*, London, Verso.

—— *Technostate*, mimeo, forthcoming.

Judt, T. (2005), *Post-war: A History of Europe Since 1945*, London, Pimlico.

Kent, R. (1981), *A History of British Empirical Sociology*, Aldershot, Gower.

Knox, H., Savage, M., and Harvey, P. (2006), 'Social Networks and the Study of Relations: Networks as Method, Metaphor and Form', *Economy and Society* 35(1), 113–40.

Koven, S. (2004), *Slumming: Sexual and Social Politics in Victorian London*, Princeton, NJ, Princeton University Press.

Kumar, K. (2003), *The Making of English National Identity*, Cambridge, Cambridge University Press.

Kushner, T. (2004), *We Europeans? Mass-Observation, 'Race' and British Identity in the Twentieth Century*, Avebury, Ashgate.

Kynaston, D. (2007), *Austerity Britain*, London, Bloomsbury.

Lash, S. (2002), *Critique of Information*, London, Sage.

Latour, B. (1988), *The Pasteurisation of France*, Cambridge, MA, Harvard University Press.

——(2005), *Reassembling the Social: An Introduction to Actor Network Theory*, Oxford, Oxford University Press.

——and Woolgar, S. (1979–86), *Laboratory Life: The Construction of Scientific Facts*, Princeton, NJ, Princeton University Press.

Law, J. (1994), *Organising Modernity*, Oxford, Blackwell.

——(2004), *After Method*, London, Taylor & Francis.

——(2009), 'Seeing Like a Survey', *Cultural Sociology*, 3(2), 239–56.

Lawler, S. (2000), *Mothering the Self*, London, Routledge.

Lawrence, J. (1998), *Speaking for the People: Party, Language and Popular Politics in England, 1867–1914*, Cambridge, Cambridge University Press.

Lee, R. (2008), 'David Riesman and the Sociology of the Interview', *The Sociological Quarterly*, 49, 285–307.

Le Roux, B., Rouanet, H., Savage, M., and Warde, A. (2008), 'Class and Cultural Division in the UK', *Sociology*, 42(6), 1049–71.

Lewis, J. (2006), *The Life and Times of Allen Lane*, London, Penguin.

Li, Y., Pickles, A., and Savage, M. (2005), 'Social Capital and Social Trust in Britain', *European Sociological Review*, 21(2), 109–23.

——Savage, M., and Warde, A. (2008), 'Social Mobility and Social Capital in Contemporary Britain', *British Journal of Sociology*, 59(3), 391–411.

Light, A. (2008), *Mrs Woolf and the Servants*, London, Penguin.

Longhurst, B., Bagnall, G., and Savage, M. (2007), 'Place, elective belonging and the diffused audience', in J. Gray, C. Sandvoss, and C. Lee Harrington (eds), *Fandom: Identities and Communities in a Mediatised World*, New York, New York University Press.

Lucas, J. (2004), 'The sixties: Realism and experiment', in L. Marcus and P. Nicholls (eds), *Twentieth Century English Literature*, pp. 545–62.

Macdonald, S., Edwards, J.E., and Savage, M. (2005), 'Introduction', *The Sociological Review*, 53(4), 587–602.

MacFarlane, A. (1980), *The Origins of Modern English Individualism*, Oxford, Blackwell.

MacKenzie, D. (1981), *Statistics in Britain, 1965–1930*, Edinburgh, Edinburgh University Press.

——(2008), *An Engine Not a Camera: How Technology Shapes Financial Markets*, Boston, MA, MIT Press.

Mackenzie, W.J.M. (1982), 'Knights of the textbooks', in R. Frankenberg (ed), *Customs and Conflict in British Society: Essays in Honour of Max Gluckmann*, Manchester, Manchester University Press.

Majima, S. (2008), 'Affluence and the Dynamics of Spending in Britain, c. 1961–2004', *Contemporary British History*, 22(4), 573–98.

——and Savage, M. (2007), 'Have There Been Culture Shifts in Britain?', *Cultural Sociology*, 1(3), 293–315.

——and Warde, A. (2008), 'Elite consumption in Britain, 1961–2001', in M. Savage and K. Williams (eds), *Remembering Elites*, Sociological Review Monograph, Oxford, Blackwell.

Mandler, P. (2009), 'One World, Many Cultures: Margaret Mead and the Limits to Cold War Anthropology', *History Workshop Journal* 68, 122–48.

Marcus, L. (2001), 'Introduction: The Project of Mass-Observation', *New Formations*, 44(Autumn), 5–20.

Marsh, C. (1982), *The Survey Method: The Contribution of Surveys to Sociological Explanation*, London, Allen & Unwin.

Marshall, G. (1983), 'Some Remarks on the Study of Working Class Consciousness', *Politics and Society*, 12, 263–301.

——(1990), *In Praise of Sociology*, London, Allen & Unwin.

——Rose, D., Newby H., and Vogler, C. (1988), *Social Class in Modern Britain*, London, Hutchinson.

Martin, J. (2003), 'What Is Field Theory?', *American Journal of Sociology*, 109(1), 1–49.

Marwick, A. (1996), *Social Change in Britain Since 1945*, Harmondsworth, Penguin.

Mason, J. (1998), *Qualitiative Researching*, London, Sage.

Massey, D. (2005), *For Space*, London, Sage.

Matless, D. (1998), *Landscape and Englishness*, London, Reaktion.

McIvor, A. (2001), *A History of Work in Britain, 1880–1950*, Basingstoke, Palgrave Macmillan.

McKibbin, R. (1998), *Classes and Cultures: England, 1918–1951*, Oxford, Clarendon Press.

Miller, P., and Rose, N. (1995), 'Production, Identity and Democracy', *Theory and Society*, 24(3), 427–67.

Miller, W. (1983), *The Survey Methods in the Social and Political Sciences: Achievements, Failures, Prospects*, London, Pinter.

Mische, A., and White, H. (1999), 'Between Conversation and Situation: Public Switching Dynamics across Network Domains', *Social Research*, 65(3), 695–724.

Mitchell, T. (2002), *The Rule of Experts: Egypt, Techno-politics, Modernity*, Berkeley, CA, University of California Press.

Mol, A., and Law, J. (1994), 'Regions, Networks and Fluids: Anaemia and Social Topology', *Social Studies of Science*, 24, 641–71.

Moore, N. (2006), 'The Context of Context: Broadening Perspectives in the Reuse of Qualitative Data', *Methodological Innovations Online*, 1(2), December, <http://erdt.plymouth.ac.uk/mionline/public_html/viewarticle.php?id=27>.

——(2007), '(Re)using Qualitative Data?', *Sociological Research Online*, 12(3), <http://www.socresonline.org.uk/12/3/1.html>.

More, C. (1980), *Skill and the English Working Class 1870–1914*, London, Taylor & Francis.

Moretti, F. (1999), *Atlas of the European Novel 1800–1900*, London, Verso.

——(2006), *The Novel, vol. 2, Forms and Themes*, Princeton, NJ, Princeton University Press.

Morgan, K.O. (2007), *Michael Foot: A Life*, London, Harper Press.

Moss, L. (1991), *The Government Social Survey: A History*, London, HMSO.

Nalson, B. (1982), 'The quiet revolution in traditional society' in R. Frankenberg (ed), pp. 70–94.

Newby, H. (1980), *Green and Pleasant Land: Social Change in Rural England*, London, Penguin.

Nisbet, R. (1953), *The Quest for Community*, London, Oxford University Press.

Offer, A. (2005), *The Challenge of Affluence*, Oxford, Clarendon Press.

Osborne, T. and Rose, N. (1999), 'Do the Social Sciences Create Phenomena? The Example of Opinion Poll Research', *British Journal of Sociology*, 50(3), 367–96.

——— (2004), 'Spatial Phenometechnics: Making Space with Charles Booth and Patrick Geddes', *Environment and Planning D: Society and Space*, 22, 209–28.

——— and Savage, M. (2008), 'Editors Introduction: Reinscribing British Sociology: Some Critical Reflections', *Sociological Review*, 56(4), 519–34.

Pahl, R. (2008), 'Have personal communities replaced geographical communities?', Elia Campbell Lecture, London.

Parrinder, P. (2004), 'Early twentieth century science and knowledge', in L. Marcus and P. Nicholls (eds), *The Cambridge History of Twentieth Century English Literature*, Cambridge, Cambridge University Press.

Payne, G. (1987), *Mobility and Change in Modern Society*, Basingstoke, Macmillan.

Platt, J. (1984), 'The Affluent Worker revisited', in C. Bell and H. Roberts (eds), *Social Researching*, London, Routledge & Kegan Paul, pp. 178–98.

——— (2003), *A Sociological History of the British Sociological Association*, London, Taylor & Francis.

Podolny, J. (2005), *Status Signals: A Sociological Interpretation of Market Competition*, Princeton, NJ, Princeton University Press.

Poovey, M. (1998), *A History of the Modern Fact: Problems of Knowledge in the Science of Wealth and Society*, Chicago, University of Chicago Press.

Prakash, G. (1990), *Another Reason: Science and the Imagination of Modern India*, Princeton, NJ, Princeton University Press.

Pullan, B., and Abendstern, M. (2004), *A History of the University of Manchester 1973–1990*, Manchester, Manchester University Press.

Reay, D. (1998), 'Rethinking Social Class: Qualitative Perspectives on Class and Gender', *Sociology*, 32, 259–75.

Redcliffe-Maud, Lord and Wood, B. (1974), *English Local Government Reformed*, London, Oxford University Press.

Robbins, B. (2006), 'A portrait of the artist as a social climber: upward mobility in the novel', in F. Moretti (ed), pp. 409–35.

Roberts, I. (1993), *Craft, Class and Control: The Sociology of a Shipbuilding Community*, Edinburgh, Edinburgh University Press.

Robertson, R. (1995), 'Glocalisation: time–space and homogeneity–heterogeneity', in M. Featherstone, S. Lash, and R. Robertson (eds), *Global Modernities*, London, Sage, pp. 25–44.

Rose, D. (ed) (2000), *Researching Social and Economic Change: The Uses of Household Panel Studies*, London, Routledge.

Rose, J. (2001), *The Intellectual Life of the British Working Classes*, New Haven, CT, Yale University Press.

Rose, N. (1999*a*), *Governing the Soul*, London, Routledge.

——— (1999*b*), *Powers of Freedom*, Cambridge, Cambridge University Press.

——— (2004), 'Governing the social', in N. Gane (ed), *The Future of Social Theory*, London, Continuum, pp. 167–85.

Russell, D. (2004), *Looking North: Northern England and the National Imagination*, Manchester, Manchester University Press.

Sandbrook, D. (2004), *Never Had It So Good: A History of Britain from Suez to the Beatles*, London, Little Brown.

——— (2006), *White Heat: A History of Britain in the Swinging Sixties*, London, Little Brown.

Saunders, P. (1990), *A Nation of Home-Owners*, London, Unwin Hyman.

Savage, M. (1988), *The Dynamics of Working Class Politics: The Labour Movement in Preston 1880–1940*, Cambridge, Cambridge University Press.

——(1999), 'Sociology, class and male manual work cultures', in J. Mcilroy, N. Fishman, and A. Campbell (eds), *British Trade Unions and Industrial Politics: The High Tide of Trade Unionism, 1964–1979*, Aldershot, Ashgate, pp. 23–42.

——(2000), *Class Analysis and Social Transformation*, Buckingham, Open University Press.

——(2005a), Revisiting Classic Qualitative Studies', *Historical Social Research/Historische Sozialforschung*, 30(1), 118–39.

——(2005b), 'Working Class Identities in the 1960s: Revisiting the Affluent Worker Study', *Sociology*, 39(5), 929–46.

——(2007), 'Changing Social Class Identities in Post-war Britain: Perspectives from Mass-observation', *Sociological Research Online*, 12(3), May 29.

—— (2008a), 'Culture, class and classification', in T. Bennett and J. Frow (eds), *The Sage Handbook of Cultural Analysis*, London, Sage, pp. 467–87.

——(2008b), 'Histories, Belongings, Communities', *International Journal of Social Research Methodology*, 11(2), 151–62.

——(2008c), 'Elizabeth Bott and the Formation of Modern British Sociology', *Sociological Review*, 56(4), 579–605.

——(2008d), 'Affluence and Social Change in the Making of Technocratic Middle Class Identities: Britain, 1939–1955', *Contemporary British History*, 22(4), 457–76.

——(2009a), 'Sociology and Descriptive Assemblage', *European Journal of Social Theory*.

——(2009b), 'Against Epochalism: An Analysis of Conceptions of Change in British Sociology', *Cultural Sociology*, 3(2), 239–56.

——(2010), 'The Lost Urban Sociology of Pierre Bourdieu and its Deleuzian Prospects', in G. Bridges and S. Waters (eds), *The Companion to the city*, London, Routledge.

——and Burrows, R. (2007), 'The Coming Crisis of Empirical Sociology', *Sociology*, 41(5), 885–99.

——and Majima, S. (2008), 'Affluence and Social Change', Editorial Introduction to Special Issue of *Contemporary British History*, 22(4), 445–56.

——and Miles, A. (1994), *The Remaking of the English Working Class*, London, Routledge.

——and Williams, K. (2008a), 'Elites: remembered by capitalism but forgotten by social sciences', in M. Savage and K. Williams (eds), *Remembering Elites*, Sociological Review Monograph, Oxford, Blackwell, pp. 1–24.

——and Williams, K. (eds) (2008b), *Remembering Elites*, Sociological Review Monograph, Oxford, Blackwell.

——Barlow, J., Dickens, P., and Fielding, A.J. (1992), *Property, Bureaucracy and Culture: Middle Class Formation in Contemporary Britain*, London, Routledge.

——Bagnall, G., and Longhurst, B.J. (2001), ' "Ordinary, Ambivalent and Defensive": Class Identities in the Northwest of England', *Sociology*, 35, 875–92.

——Bagnall, G., and Longhurst, B.J. (2005), *Globalisation and Belonging*, London, Sage.

—— Warde, A., and Devine, F. (2005), 'Capitals, Assets, and Resources: Some Critical Issues', *British Journal of Sociology*, 56(1), 31–48.

Scott, J.C. (1998), *Seeing Like a State: How Certain Schemes to Improve the Human Condition have Failed*, New Haven, CT, Yale University Press.

Scott, J. (1991), *Social Network Analysis: A Handbook*, London, Sage.

Sharpe, L.J. (1980), 'Research and the Redcliffe-Maud Commission', in M. Bulmer (ed), *Social Research and Royal Commissions*, pp. 18–33.

Sheridan, D. (2001), 'Charles Madge and the Mass Observation Archive: A Personal Note', *New Formation*, 44(Autumn), 21–5.

Shils, E. (1975), *Center and Periphery: Essays in Macrosociology*, Chicago, IL, University of Chicago Press.

Silva, E.B. (2006), 'Sociologies of Social Space and Elective Affinities: Researching Cultural Capital', *Sociology*, 40(6), 1171–89.

Skeggs, B. (1997), *Formations of Class and Gender*, London, Sage.

——(2004), *Class, Self, Culture*, London, Routledge.

Skidelsky, R. (2003), *John Maynard Keynes 1883–1946: Economist, Philosopher, Statesman*, London, Macmillan.

Smart, C. (1984), *The Ties that Bind: Law, Marriage, and the Reproduction of Patriarchal Relations*, London, Routledge.

Smith, D. (2008), *Raymond Williams: A Warriors's Tale*, Library of Wales, Aberteifi, Parthian.

Stacey, M., and Thompson, P. (2008), 'Tradition and Change in an English Town', *International Journal of Social Research Methodology*, 11(2), 97–102.

Stanley, L. (1995*a*), *Sex Surveyed 1949–1994: From Mass-Observation's 'Little Kinsey' to the National Surveys and the Hite Reports*, London, Taylor & Francis.

——(1995*b*), 'Women have Servants and Men Never Eat: Issues in Reading Gender, Using the Case Study of Mass-Observation', *Women's History Review*, 4(1), 85–101.

——(2008), 'It Has Always Been Known and We Have Always Been "Other": Knowing Capitalism and the "Coming Crisis" of Sociology Confront the Concentration System and Mass-Observation', *Sociological Review*, 56(4), 535–51.

Strathern, M. (1981), *Kinship at the Core: An Anthropology of Elmdon in North-West Essex, in the Nineteen Sixties*, Cambridge, Cambridge University Press.

——(1990), *After Nature*, Oxford, Clarendon Press.

Steedman, C. (1986), *Landscape for a Good Woman*, London, Virago.

——(2005), *Master and Servant: Love and Labour in the English Industrial Age*, Cambridge, Cambridge University Press.

Stevenson, R. (2004), *The Oxford Literary History, vol. 12, 1960–2000: The Last of England?* Oxford, Oxford University Press.

Summerfield, P. (1985), 'Mass-Observation: Social Research or Social Movement?', *Journal of Contemporary History*, 20, 429–52.

——(1988), *Women Workers in the Second World War: Production and Patriarchy in Conflict*, London, Routledge.

Sutherland, J. (2007), *The Boy who Loved Books: A Memoir*, Edinburgh, John Murray.

Szreter, S. (1996), *Fertility, Class and Gender in Britain, 1860–1914*, Cambridge, Cambridge University Press.

Terkel, S. (1997), *Working: People Talk About What They Do All Day and How They Feel About What They Do*, New York, New Press.

Thrift, N. (2003), *Knowing Capitalism*, London, Sage.

Thompson, E.P. (1965), 'The Peculiarities of the British', *Socialist Register*, 311–62.

——and Yeo, E. (1972), *The Unknown Mayhew*, Harmondsworth, Penguin.

Thompson, P., and Corti, L. (2004), Special Issue – Celebrating Classic Sociology: Pioneers of Contemporary British Qualitative Research', *Social Research Methodology*, 7(1), 1–108.

Todd, S. (2008), 'Affluence, Class and Crown Street: Reinvestigating the Post-war Working Class', *Contemporary British History*, 22(4), 501–18.

——(2009), 'Domestic Service and Class Relations in Britain, 1900–1950', Issue 203, 181–204.

Uprichard, E., Byrne, D., and Burrows, R. (2008), 'SPSS as an "Inscription Device": From Causality to Description', *Sociological Review*, 56(4), 606–22.

Urry, J. (2000*a*), *Sociology Beyond Societies*, London, Routledge.

——(2000*b*), Editor's Introduction: 'Sociology Facing the Millennium', *British Journal of Sociology*, 51(1), 1–3.

Wagner, P., Weiss, C.H., Wittrock, B., and Wollmann, H. (1991), *Social Sciences and Modern States: National Experiences and Theoretical Crossroads*, Cambridge, Cambridge University Press.

Wahrman, D. (1995), *Imagining the Middle Class: The Political Representation of Class in Britain c.1780–1840*, Cambridge, Cambridge University Press.

Walkerdine, V., Lucey, H., and Melody, J. (2001), *Growing Up Girl*, Basingstoke, Palgrave.

Walkowitz, J. (1992), *City of Dreadful Delight: Narratives of Sexual Danger in Late Victorian London*, Chicago, IL, University of Chicago Press.

Ward, S. (ed) (2001), *British Culture and the Decline of Empire*, Manchester, Manchester University Press.

Warde, A., and Bennett, T. (2008), 'A culture in common: The cultural consumption of the UK managerial elite', in K. Williams and M. Savage (eds), *Rethinking Elites*, Sociological Review Monograph, Oxford, Blackwell.

——Wright, D., and Gayo-Cal, M. (2007), 'Understanding Cultural Omnivorousness or the Myth of the Cultural Omnivore', *Cultural Sociology*, 1(2), 143–64.

Webber, R. (2009), 'Response to "The Coming Crisis of Empirical Sociology": An Outline of the Research Potential of Administrative and Transactional Data', *Sociology*, 43(1), 169–78.

Weight, R. (2002), *Patriots: National Identity in Britain, 1940–2000*, London, Pan.

Weininger, E. (2004), 'Foundations of Pierre Bourdieu's class analysis', in E.O. Wright (ed), *Approaches to Class Analysis*, Cambridge, Cambridge University Press, pp. 82–118.

Welshman, J. (2009), 'Where Lesser Angels Might have Feared to Tread: The Social Science Research Council and Transmitted Deprivation', *Contemporary British History*, 23(2), 199–219.

White, H. (2000), *Identity and Control*, Cambridge, MA, Harvard University Press.

Williams, K., Froud, J., Leaver, A., and Tampubolon, G. (2008), 'Everything for sale: How non-executive directors make a difference', in M. Savage and K. Williams (eds), *Remembering Elites*, Sociological Review Monograph, Oxford, Blackwell.

Williams, W.M., and Thompson, P. (2008), 'From Continuing Tradition to Continuous Change', *International Journal of Social Research Methodology*, 11(2), 97–102.

Wolfe, A. (1999), *One Nation, After All: What Americans Really Think About God, Country, Family, Racism, Welfare, Immigration, Homosexuality, Work, The Right, The Left and Each Other*, London, Penguin.

Wright, P. (1985), *On Living in an Old Country*, London, Verso.

Yeo, E. (1996), *The Contest for Social Science: Relations and Representations of Gender and Class*, London, Rivers Oram.

Zweiniger-Bargielowska, I. (2001), *Austerity in Britain: Rationing, Controls, and Consumption 1939–1955*, Oxford, Clarendon Press.

Name Index

Although one of my aims in this book is to query a clear distinction between researcher and researched, for the benefit of readers I have placed the names of those who are primarily the subjects of my analysis with their full names (e.g. Churchill, Winston), or their full initials when these are well known (e.g. Wells, H.G). The names of those who I am mainly using as academic sources are identified with one initial only.

Place Index

References to Britain or the UK are not included.

Subject Index

For the specific studies analysed in this book, refer to either the relevant authors (in the name index) or the places studied concerned (see Appendix 1 for details).